THE COLLECTED WORKS OF RALPH WALDO EMERSON

Joseph Slater, General Editor
Douglas Emory Wilson, Textual Editor

Editorial Board

The Collected Works of Ralph Waldo Emerson

VOLUME II
ESSAYS: FIRST SERIES

Introduction and Notes by Joseph Slater

*Text Established by Alfred R. Ferguson
and Jean Ferguson Carr*

The Belknap Press of Harvard University Press
Cambridge, Massachusetts, and London, England
1979

Library of Congress Cataloging in Publication Data

Emerson, Ralph Waldo, 1803–1882.
Essays, first series.
(The collected works of Ralph Waldo Emerson; v. 2)
Includes bibliographical references and index.
I. Ferguson, Alfred Riggs.   II.   Carr, Jean
Ferguson.

PS1600.F71 vol. 2   [PS1608.A2]   814'.3s [814'.3] 79–13724
ISBN 0–674–13980–1

CENTER FOR
SCHOLARLY EDITIONS
AN APPROVED EDITION
MODERN LANGUAGE
ASSOCIATION OF AMERICA

Editorial expenses for the preparation of this volume have been
supported by grants from the National Endowment for the Humanities and administered through the Center for Editions of
American Authors of the Modern Language Association.

ALFRED RIGGS FERGUSON

1915–1974

The death of Alfred Riggs Ferguson on May 5, 1974, a few months after he had turned a first draft of this volume over to the Harvard University Press, left his friends and associates in stunned sorrow. A life of total commitment to scholarship had come to an end when it seemed to be at the height of its powers.

It was Fergie who, back in 1960, initiated with his three editorial associates the monumental *Journals and Miscellaneous Notebooks of Ralph Waldo Emerson,* and it was Fergie who later summoned a group of fellow Emersonians to undertake a new edition of *The Collected Works of Ralph Waldo Emerson,* the first volume of which appeared under his general editorship in 1971. As his collaborator on that volume, I learned to appreciate the warmth, the integrity, and the humane understanding he brought to the vital task of critically establishing the text of a major work of literature.

Fortunately, Alfred Ferguson left his papers with a wife and daughter who had worked closely with him from the start and with the collaborator who had shared this volume with him, so that the continuation of the edition is virtually assured. In taking over this responsibility, the reorganized Editorial Board hopes that it may inherit the wisdom and commitment of its first leader.

Robert E. Spiller

881126

PREFACE

After the death in 1974 of Alfred R. Ferguson, who had been the textual editor of this volume, his work was taken up and, where necessary, revised and completed by his daughter, Jean Ferguson Carr. The establishment of the text, the writing of the Textual Introduction and the Textual Apparatus, and the compilation of the Parallel Passages were thus a collaboration between them. The Historical Introduction and the Informational Notes were written by Joseph Slater. However, all three editors worked closely together, and their edition represents a greater degree of collaboration than is perhaps apparent.

Many institutions and individuals have helped bring this volume to completion. The National Endowment for the Humanities, through the Center for Editions of American Authors and later through the Committee on Scholarly Editions, provided support for planning the whole edition as well as aid for this volume. Ohio State University and Colgate University granted research leaves to Professors Ferguson and Slater; Carnegie-Mellon University gave secretarial and technical assistance to Professor Carr. William H. Bond, Carolyn Jakeman, Marte Shaw, and the staff of the Houghton Library of Harvard University were generous, as always, with learned and courteous help and with permissions to quote and reproduce. The Ralph Waldo Emerson Memorial Association gave both financial support and permission to use Emerson materials. The Concord Free Public Library kindly permitted the use of a portrait in its possession.

Among those who helped most in the tracing of allusions and

of quotations were John E. Rexine and Robert L. Murray of Colgate's Classics Department and Douglas Emory Wilson, who succeeded Alfred Ferguson as textual editor of *The Collected Works of Ralph Waldo Emerson*. Aid in the preparation of the text and the Textual Apparatus was given by Nicole Plumstead, Joseph P. Sperry, and Genevieve W. Tucker, and by Stephen L. Carr, who also helped prepare the index. Katherine M. Loring, Nancy A. Metz, and James Paul worked on Parallel Passages and made sight collations; Sandra Katz, Suzan Rakaczky, and Nancy Sastri assisted in proofreading. Natalie Frohock and Ann Louise McLaughlin of Harvard University Press edited copy with stern and learned eyes. William L. Howarth, for CEAA, William M. Gibson, for CSE, Wallace E. Williams, editor of Emerson's lectures, and Douglas Emory Wilson read the entire volume and gave thorough and valuable criticism and advice. Margaret W. Ferguson prepared a first draft of the Textual Introduction from her father's notes. Mary Anne H. Ferguson helped in countless ways to complete this volume, both before and after her husband's untimely death.

CONTENTS

ILLUSTRATIONS

(following page xxviii)

Historical Introduction

Statement of Editorial Principles

Textual Introduction

ABBREVIATIONS

Acct. Book | Unpublished account books of James Munroe, 1841–1845. Houghton bMS AM 1280.M5653Z.

BAL | Jacob Blanck. *Bibliography of American Literature.* New Haven, Yale University Press, 1959. III, 16–70.

CEC | *The Correspondence of Emerson and Carlyle.* Edited by Joseph Slater. New York, Columbia University Press, 1964.

CW I | *The Collected Works of Ralph Waldo Emerson.* Introductions and Notes by Robert E. Spiller. Text Established by Alfred R. Ferguson. Vol. I. Cambridge, The Belknap Press of Harvard University Press, 1971.

EL | *The Early Lectures of Ralph Waldo Emerson, 1833–1842.* Edited by Stephen E. Whicher, Robert E. Spiller, and Wallace E. Williams. 3 vols. Cambridge, The Belknap Press of Harvard University Press, 1959–1972.

Houghton | The Houghton Library, Harvard University.

J | *Journals of Ralph Waldo Emerson.* Edited by Edward Waldo Emerson and Waldo Emerson Forbes. 10 vols. Boston and New York, Houghton Mifflin Company, 1909–1914.

JMN | *The Journals and Miscellaneous Notebooks of Ralph Waldo Emerson.* Edited by William H. Gilman, Alfred R. Ferguson, Merrell R. Davis, George Clark, Merton M. Sealts, Harrison Hayford, Ralph H. Orth, A. W. Plumstead, Linda Allardt, J. E. Parsons, and Susan S. Smith. 14 vols. to date. Cambridge, The Belknap Press of Harvard University Press, 1960– .

L | *The Letters of Ralph Waldo Emerson.* Edited by Ralph L. Rusk. 6 vols. New York, Columbia University Press, 1939.

Ledger | Unpublished account books of Emerson. Houghton bMS 1280 H 112 a–j.

PP | Parallel Passages.

R | *Emerson's Complete Works.* Edited by J. E. Cabot. Riverside Edition. 12 vols. Boston, Houghton, Mifflin and Company, 1883–1893.

Rusk | Ralph L. Rusk. *The Life of Ralph Waldo Emerson.* New York, Charles Scribner's Sons, 1949.

Sterling | *A Correspondence between John Sterling and Ralph Waldo Emerson.* Edited by Edward Waldo Emerson. Boston and New York, Houghton, Mifflin and Company, 1897.

W | *The Complete Works of Ralph Waldo Emerson.* Edited by Edward Waldo Emerson. Centenary Edition. 12 vols. Boston and New York, Houghton, Mifflin and Company, 1903–1904.

Ward | *Letters from Ralph Waldo Emerson to a Friend, 1838–1853.* Edited by Charles Eliot Norton. Boston and New York, Houghton, Mifflin and Company, 1899.

Webster | *An American Dictionary of the English Language.* Edited by Noah Webster. 2 vols. Boston, 1828.

Worcester | *A Comprehensive Pronouncing and Explanatory Dictionary of the English Language.* Edited by Joseph E. Worcester. Boston, 1838.

Historical Introduction

On Saturday morning, March 20, 1841, the *Boston Daily Advertiser* carried this announcement: "EMERSON'S ESSAYS. Essays by Ralph Waldo Emerson, 300 pp., 16 mos. Contents — Essay 1, History; 2, Self Reliance; 3, Compensation; 4, Spiritual Laws; 5, Love; 6, Friendship; 7, Prudence; 8, Heroism; 9, The Over Soul; 10, Circles; 11, Intellect; 12, Art. This day published by JAS. MUNROE & CO. 134, Washington Street." Four other booksellers advertised that the book was available at their shops, among them Joseph Dowe of Court Street, who included in his notice a quoted sentence: "Life is a series of surprises." To Emerson, reading his *Advertiser* in Concord that Saturday, Dowe's quotation from "Circles" might for a moment have seemed a teasing comment on the book's tardiness. This volume of essays had been long in the making and long promised.

Six years before, in 1835, a young widower, a preacher without pulpit, living with his mother in Concord in the Old Manse which his grandfather had built, he had chided himself: "When will you mend Montaigne? . . . Where are your Essays? . . . Have you not thoughts & illustrations that are your own . . . the law of Compensation . . . the sublimity of Self-reliance?" (*JMN*, V, 40) . But his life grew busy and complex. At the request of his fellow-townsmen he wrote that summer a historical address to celebrate the two-hundredth anniversary of the founding of Concord. He remarried. He bought a large house which seemed to fill immediately with relatives, friends, and servants. He was shattered by the death of his beloved brother Charles.

His first child, Waldo, was born. To supplement the modest income he received from his first wife's estate he became once again a public speaker, not from a pulpit but from the platforms of lecture halls and meetinghouses in the cities and villages of Massachusetts. When his first book appeared, in 1836, it was not a volume of essays but the single long essay *Nature,* and he described it as "a little book . . . only a naming of topics . . . an entering wedge . . . for something more worthy and significant" (*CEC,* p. 149).

In the spring of 1837 he wrote his brother William a letter full of family affairs. Their mother, he thought, should not join William in Staten Island but should stay a bit longer in Concord now that it was "just beginning to be pleasant to the eye & passable to the feet." Their brother Bulkeley, mentally retarded and disordered, had been released after a year from the asylum in Charlestown and seemed "quite well & affectionate." The little boy, Waldo, was coughing and wheezing; but otherwise all was well in Concord: "Our little worldkin is very quiet & nothing is new therein. I found so much audience for my opinions & speculations this winter as to feel much courage to vent all that I find in my manuscripts. And mean this summer to write & think very freely & heedfully & if I can I shall collect & print" (*L,* II, 59–60).

When he wrote William again in September, he was obliged to report a less fruitful summer than he had anticipated: "We have had a great deal of company lately and I get no time to do my work which is book & lectures. If I can once get alone, I shall work hard" (*L,* II, 96). The months which had produced *An Oration Delivered before the Phi Beta Kappa Society, at Cambridge, August 31, 1837* could hardly have seemed idle ones, even to a scion of New England Puritanism, but apparently the unwritten book remained a nagging presence in Emerson's mind.

The lectures which he considered part of his "work" were serious work indeed. Extensive study in the libraries of Boston and Cambridge as well as in his own books, note-taking — in short, research — lay behind them; and, because they were not extemporized or even spoken from outlines but *read,* they were as carefully written as if their destination had been a printing press in

Cambridge rather than a lectern in Boston or Salem. Most of them were parts of what he advertised as "courses" and delivered to subscription audiences on Wednesday evenings for six, ten, or twelve weeks, with each lecture something like a chapter in what might well have been a book. The lectures which "company" had kept him from completing during the summer of 1837 became his fourth such course and were read the following winter, as the first three had been, to large congregations in the auditorium of the Masonic Temple on Tremont Street in Boston. He had thought of calling the course "Ethics," but decided on "Human Culture" as an ampler cloak for the "extreme & fantastic" things he had to say. "I religiously read lectures every winter," he wrote to his friend Carlyle, "& at other times whenever summoned" (*CEC*, p. 168). He was a prolific writer of published but unprinted books.

In the spring of 1838 there came two invitations to lecture, one from Harvard and one from Dartmouth, which Emerson found irresistible. Writing the lectures consumed a large part of the following summer. He reported the events, drily enough, to Carlyle on August 6: "I have written & read a kind of Sermon to the senior class of our Cambridge Theological School a fortnight ago; and an address to the Literary Societies of Dartmouth College; for though I hate American pleniloquence, I cannot easily say *No* to young men who bid me speak also. And both these are now in press. The first, I hear is very offensive. I will now try to hold my tongue until next winter" (*CEC*, p. 191). Carlyle's reply was encouraging, but surely also embarrassing: the new pamphlets would be greedily awaited by readers of *Nature,* more than one of whom had asked, "Has that Emerson of yours written nothing else?" (*CEC*, p. 195).

Ironically, one reason why Emerson had published so little, especially in England, was that he had been entangled since 1835 in the American publication of Carlyle's books. In 1836 he had written a preface for the first edition of what Carlyle later called the "New-England Book," *Sartor Resartus.* In 1837, to gain Carlyle dollars as well as readers in an age of book piracy, he had contracted for, financed, advertised, promoted, and reviewed a

Boston edition of *The French Revolution*. A few days after delivering the Dartmouth College address, he sent Carlyle a bill of exchange for £50, the first fruits of the American *French Revolution;* in the same letter he announced that an even more complex and laborious benefaction, a complete edition of Carlyle's *Critical and Miscellaneous Essays,* was half finished. Two hundred and fifty sets of the first two volumes had already been sold in Boston, and the author's copies were on their way across the Atlantic. They were followed next summer by volumes III and IV and later by a second edition; then came *Chartism* and *Heroes and Hero-Worship*. Emerson had become, through accident and good nature, an overly successful and busy literary agent.

His own work and way of working seemed to him, in the spring of 1838, most unpromising: "Here I sit & read & write with very little system & as far as regards composition with the most fragmentary result: paragraphs incompressible each sentence an infinitely repellent particle" (*CEC*, p. 185) . Nevertheless, stimulated no doubt by the quality of his Divinity School address and its effect on the orthodox, he turned to the writing of his fifth course of winter lectures: "Human Life in Ten Lectures," as he lightheartedly described it to Margaret Fuller, "or the Soul of man neatly done up in ten pinboxes exactly ten" (*L*, II, 179) . He wrote under pressure, sometimes finishing dangerously close to platform time. On Christmas Day he apologized to William for an ink-blotted letter: "I have almost no time to write as I lecture upon *Love* tomorrow night 40 pp. is the rule & I now count but 21 finished" (*L*, II, 177) . Even so, the ten lectures "prospered very well," he told Carlyle, despite or perhaps because of the polemical mud that had been thrown at him during the autumn, and if he had not been silenced by an attack of bronchitis he would have added two more (*CEC*, p. 217) . Four days after the end of the course, his second child was born, "a blessed babe, named Ellen" (*CEC*, p. 217) in memory of his first wife. "Fair fall the name & every beautiful vision it recalls," he wrote, "on this new dreamer of the Dream of Human Life" (*L*, II, 189) .

Undaunted, after the Divinity School address, by the angry blasts from pulpits and newspapers which seemed to endanger the lectures of the coming season, Emerson had written in his journal: "Steady, steady. . . . Society has no bribe for me, neither in politics, nor church, nor college, nor city. My resources are far from exhausted. If they will not hear me lecture, I shall have leisure for my book which wants me" (*JMN*, VII, 60). After the success of "Human Life," in the spring of 1839, his book still called him, and there seemed to be leisure for it. "I have been writing a little and arranging old papers more," he told Bronson Alcott in April, "and by and by, I hope to get a shapely book of Genesis" (*L*, II, 194). By the first of June he was writing what he was bold enough to describe as an essay: its subject he called "Offsets" (*L*, II, 201), by which, presumably, he meant "Compensations" (*CW*, I, 62 and *W*, XI, 423). But in 1839, as always, the summer months brought company — clergymen from Calcutta, learned young ladies from Boston, who stayed for a few days or a few weeks — and work went slowly. He set up a self-defensive summer schedule: he rose at six, had coffee brought to him in his study, and saw no one, family or visitors, till noon. Under this regime he felt confident and jaunty enough to tell Margaret Fuller, who was working on a life of Goethe, "I shall have a book full of Essays ready by autumn, and your Biography will not be half written" (*L*, II, 203).

On the Fourth of July, in a letter to Carlyle, he was more guarded: "I am getting on with some studies of mine prosperously for me, have got three essays nearly done, and who knows but in the autumn I shall have a book?" (*CEC*, p. 243). Writing to Carlyle made him, as usual in those years, aware of money matters. A month before, he had had to borrow $200 for printer's bills; in two weeks he would have to pay $462 for paper for volumes III and IV of the *Critical and Miscellaneous Essays,* and that meant borrowing again. His stocks were not doing well. His tax bill was excessive, and he feared a road tax too. Bulkeley was back in the Charlestown hospital, where his support was more expensive than ever. "I see plainly," he wrote to William at the end of the summer, "I shall have no choice about lecturing again next winter; I must do it" (*L*, II, 218).

His new course was entitled "The Present Age." It occupied,

in preparation and delivery, much of the fall of 1839 and most of the winter, and took him to the Masonic Temple every Wednesday evening for ten weeks and thereafter to New York and Providence. The tone of his comments on it was resentful: "my old trade," "my foolish lectures," "this fever fit of Lecturing," "this vagrancy of mine," "a dereliction." It had forced him, he kept saying, to put off his book until next summer; he ought not to have undertaken it. "I ought to have written," he told Carlyle, "in silence & serenity." And yet he knew himself well enough to realize that lecturing was more than a trade and a dereliction. "I work better," he confessed, "under this base necessity and then I have a certain delight (base also?) in speaking to a multitude" (*CEC*, p. 255). But next summer would be the summer of the essays. He might even write two volumes.

Actually he took up his work again in the spring of 1840. Writing to his mother from Providence late in March, he referred to the lectures he had read there, "Love" and "Politics" among them, as "essays" (*L*, II, 266), and early in April he assured his correspondents — and himself — that he had been hard at work every morning. "I read no books," he told Margaret Fuller. "I am become a scrivener" (*L*, II, 283). By the middle of the month he had almost finished the "chapter" which he called either "Doctrine of the Soul" or "The Oversoul." On the morning of June 11 he "transcribed" the essay on love, though he was not wholly satisfied with it (*JMN*, VII, 368). On June 22 he was far enough along with his "Chapter on Friendship" to propose sending it to Samuel Ward for "commentary" (Ward, pp. 21–22). Sometime in June he entered in his journal three tabular arrangements of "chapter" titles, one of which, except for its thirteenth "Chapter on Nature," was to become the book's table of contents (*JMN*, VII, 498). Even the June flowers spoke to him of his plans and promises: "The asters & eupatoriums are maturing their leaves & buds, the gerardia is getting ready its profuse flowers warning me that my book should be ended before their capsules are filled with seed" (*JMN*, VII, 375–376).

The book was not ended by seedtime. On October 30, Emerson sent Carlyle an accountant's statement of their business relations, a copy of the second number of *The Dial*, and a merry account of New England's reformist and communitarian madness. Of himself he said, "I am ashamed to tell you, though it seems most due, anything of my own studies they seem so desultory idle & unproductive. I still hope to print a book of Essays this winter, but it cannot be very large. I write myself into letters, the last few months, to three or four dear & beautiful persons my country-men & women here. I lit my candle at both ends, but will now be colder & scholastic. I mean to write no lectures this winter" (*CEC*, p. 284). Many occasions had conspired against the Essays, but less the lure of Brook Farm than the demands of *The Dial*, and less *The Dial* than the "beautiful persons" associated with it. Shortly before Christmas of the preceding year, Emerson had written to his aunt about "a certain wonderful Journal which is to be born next spring or summer of which Margaret Fuller is to be Editor & Geo Ripley Geo Bancroft & twenty more, whereof I am least, to be contributors" (*L*, II, 245). What he became was not the least of contributors but, against his will, almost coeditor. He resisted and protested. "My own book is necessarily primary with me," he wrote Margaret Fuller in March 1840, "and the Journal, if it exist, I only wish to aid" (*L*, II, 271). Nevertheless, manuscripts, queries about editorial policy, and requests for contributions came constantly to Concord, and Emerson for the most part did what he was asked to do.

Almost as frequently came the editor herself. Margaret Fuller was no newcomer to Emerson's house — her first visit had been made in the summer of 1836 and had lasted for three weeks — or to his intellectual life, but *The Dial* fostered a new kind of intimacy. Brilliant and learned she had always been; now she was charming, teasing, and flirtatious, and Emerson not only referred to her as "my wise woman" but wrote of "her sultry Southern nature" and "her enchantments" (Sterling, p. 79). With her often came Caroline Sturgis, a younger and prettier transcendentalist, and sometimes the New Orleans beauty Anna Barker, who was soon to marry Emerson's young friend Samuel Ward. Concord was an altered village during that first *Dial* summer, humming with confidences, crushes, and long sentimental conversations and letters about true friendship. Emerson was by no means a detached observer. When, in mid-August, Margaret Fuller and Caroline Sturgis taxed him with "inhospitality of soul" and an unwillingness to be their friend in "the full & sacred sense," he confessed to coldness and prudence, but added, in the idiom of that summer, "If I count & weigh, I love also. I cannot tell you how warm & glad the naming of your names makes my solitude. You give me more joy than I could trust my tongue to tell you" (*L*, II, 325). He and Caroline agreed that they were "brother & sister by divine invisible parentage." He addressed her as "dear sister" and "dear child"; she began a letter to him — one of the letters he called her "golden epistles" — with this ardent sentence: "And you, my dearest brother, shall be my saint & purify me, for this is the joy of friendship" (*L*, II, 326, 327, 332; Caroline Sturgis to Emerson, September 11, 1840, Houghton Library).

Emerson knew what was happening to his essays: "in these extraordinary enlargements of my little heart," he wrote, "I am in danger of becoming a mere writer of letters" (*L*, II, 332). He gently caricatured an indolence which in another mood he was to scorn: "The old gentleman in the study wastes, it must be owned, good time: dips a pen in ink, affects to write a little from upper dictation, but presently falls to copying old musty papers, — then to reading a little in Plato, a little in the Vedas, then picks his pea vines a little, or waters his melons, or thins his carrots; walks a little, talks a little, and the marvellous Day has fled forevermore" (*L*, II, 319–320). When he looked back from October, the summer seemed idle but happy, and the letters he had written were romances. Perhaps he knew, too, that the essay "Friendship" could not have been completed without the enlargement, the tension, the introspection, and the self-defense of the summer. He had sketched it out for Margaret Fuller in January; he had thought it finished in June, and again in July when he sent it to Ward. But surely its strange complexities are a response to the August complaints of Margaret and Caroline, and the strange letter embedded in it seems a distillation of the letters he was still writing to them in October.

His publication goal was now New Year's Day, which meant

that he dared write and read no new course of lectures. In September he told Elizabeth Hoar, "My chapter on 'Circles' begins to prosper and when it is October I shall write like a Latin Father" (*L*, II, 331). Early in October he was, presumably, working on "Heroism"; at any rate, he reread Ockley's *History of the Saracens,* from which the motto of that essay was drawn (*L*, II, 344). Late in October he was vexed that his "chapter" on self-reliance was unfinished (*JMN*, VII, 521). But shortly before Christmas he could write his brother, "My book creeps along uncertain whether it shall be one volume or two. If one, it is ready now" (*L*, II, 372). He had contracted with James Munroe and Company, who had published *Nature* and the Phi Beta Kappa and Divinity School addresses, to print 1500 copies, at his own expense, with 30 percent of any profit as Munroe's commission. By the end of December he had decided that what was ready was one volume rather than two, and on New Year's Day he wrote: "I begin the year by sending my little book of Essays to the press. What remains to be done to its imperfect chapters I will seek to do justly" (*JMN*, VII, 411).

Clearly, much remained to be done. Perhaps the most important task he had left himself was finishing the thirteenth essay, "Nature," which he had conceived as a complement to "Art." He did not have time for it. When, after less than a fortnight, the proofsheets began to arrive in Concord, he found that there were many imperfections in essays he had considered finished. For weeks he was busy "parsing & spelling & punctuating, & repairing rotten metaphors, & bringing tropes safe into port, & inspecting suspicious places in . . . logic" (*L*, II, 378). But he was not wholly dissatisfied with what he was rereading. Remembering the pines which had waved over his thoughts and daydreams, he asked himself, "Shall I not then call my little book Forest Essays?" (*JMN*, VII, 417). By the 5th of February he had inspected and repaired one hundred and twenty pages, halfway through "Spiritual Laws" (*L*, II, 378). By the 25th he had proof for almost everything before "Circles" (*L*, II, 383). He prefixed to "Prudence" a humorously self-deprecatory paragraph, newly composed, and when the proofs of "Intellect" came he added two sentences at the beginning and seven at the end. He retouched the final paragraph of "Art" with half a dozen phrases he had written in February. By the middle of March he held a copy of the book itself in his hand, a trim volume of 303 pages, bound in sober brown and entitled simply *Essays*. On March 19 he sent copies to forty-six relatives and friends — among them his aunt Mary Moody Emerson, Margaret Fuller, Caroline Sturgis, Alcott, Lowell, Thoreau, Wordsworth, Carlyle, Sterling, and Harriet Martineau — and to two reviews (*JMN*, VII, 413–414, 420, 546).

The first American reaction to the book was partisan and predictable. Mary Moody Emerson spoke for orthodoxy when she characterized it as a "strange medly of atheism and false independence" and a disgrace (Rusk, pp. 283–284). George P. Bradford, a transcendentalist and a schoolmaster, who had been a classmate of Emerson's at Harvard College and at the Divinity School, wrote that he had "owed to it many illuminated hours and many glowing & happy feelings; it has made the spheral music clearer & sweeter to me" (Bradford to Emerson, March 31, 1841, Houghton Library). The first two reviews, both published promptly in April, represented the same polarity of opinion. *The New York Review*, which considered Bostonian transcendentalism "a *lusus naturae,* feeble, and we trust short lived," called *Essays* "a godless book," but concluded with a judgment more balanced and charitable than that of Aunt Mary: "In a style which on every page delights us by its simplicity and grace, and offends us by an affected quaintness, showing brilliant fancy and curious scholarship, he has uttered many brave truths, many gross and perilous errors, hints in which the meditative and wise man may find ambrosial food, but which will prove poison to the simple and undiscerning" (VIII, 509–512). Orestes Brownson, in his *Boston Quarterly Review,* though he characterized himself as "cold, stoical, and untranscendental," wrote as glowingly as George Bradford. *Essays* had warmed him, he said, not just to admiration but to "reverence." It was "a profound and significant word" which would "take hold of the heart of the age, perhaps of the ages . . . he who reads it will find, that he is no longer what he was. A new and a higher life has been quickened in him, and he can never again feel, that he is merely a child of time and space, but that he is transcendental and immortal" (VI, 258).

The first British readers responded with bravos and loud applause. Carlyle received his copy of the book on May 6 and spent all of the next day reading it. "My friend, I *thank* you for this volume of yours," he wrote. "*Euge!* say I, from afar . . . it is once more the voice of a *man*. Ah me, I felt as if in the wide world there were still but this one voice that responded intelligently to my own . . . as if this alone were true and alive. . . . Persist, persist; you have much to say and to do. . . . You are a new era, my man, in your new huge country" (*CEC*, pp. 295–296). John Sterling thought it "The only book of any pith and significance that has dawned here lately . . . far ahead in compass and brilliancy of almost everything England has of late years (generations) produced" (Sterling, p. 37). Richard Milnes was so delighted with the book that he determined to write a review for *Fraser's Magazine* (Charles Sumner to Emerson, August 23, 1841, Houghton Library). The art historian Alexis-François Rio, unable to borrow Milnes's borrowed copy, persuaded Jane Carlyle to lend him hers. He intended to "read it *four* times," he said (*CEC*, p. 302). Harriet Martineau, who had been an invalid, confined to a sofa for two years, found it "a visitation of health . . . like a breeze, like a handful of wild flowers" "My prophecy," she wrote Emerson, "would be that this book will live 1000 years" (August 8, 1841, Houghton Library).

By the end of June an English edition of 750 copies was being printed, for which Carlyle had written an introduction and was to read proof. In November he reported: "The book of Essays . . . makes what one may call a kind of appropriate 'sensation' here. Reviews of it are many, in all notes of the gamut; — of small value mostly. . . . The worst enemy admits that there are piercing radiances of perverse insight in it; the highest friends, some few, go to a very high point indeed. . . . Still better . . . I learn that 'the sale of the Essays goes very steadily forward,' . . . So Emerson henceforth has a real Public in Old England as well as New" (*CEC*, p. 312).

To all of this Emerson responded with courtesy and gratitude but without much satisfaction. Even before the book was published it had seemed to him merely a raft — "only boards & logs tied together" (*CEC,* p. 291). Later it was "a poor little arid book," the work of a cramped hand (*CEC,* p. 303). By October 1841 the preparation and delivery of next winter's course of lectures seemed an artistic as well as a financial necessity. "I fancy, I need more than another to *speak,*" he wrote to Carlyle, "with such a formidable tendency to the lapidary style. I build my house of boulders" (*CEC,* p. 308). And to William, "I shall one day write something better than these poor cramp arid 'Essays' which I almost hate the sight of" (*L,* II, 444). He did admit to Sterling that the thoughts in the book had been "honest in their first rising & honestly reported." But, like other true things, he now felt, they had been spoiled by "interference, or what we miscall art" (Emerson to Sterling, March 31, 1841, Houghton Library).

To some extent this dissatisfaction was not unlike that which is produced by the backward glance of any growing artist and which results, for good or ill, in the changing and polishing, the cutting and adding, of all "new and revised" editions. But it seems in Emerson to have been also the result of a painful conflict between theory and practice, between the doctrines of *Essays* and the way the book came into being. The voice that speaks in these pages is that of "an experimenter . . . an endless seeker with no Past at [his] back," an enemy of imitation and interference, a scorner of those who quote from saints and sages. It reveres innovation and originality, the here and the now, impulsiveness, acquiescence, and abandonment. It trusts only the flashes which come from within — instinctive, involuntary, and spontaneous. The book itself is the product of choice and design. It is, as Harriet Martineau immediately saw, a millennial if not an immortal masterwork. It is also a collage, a chrestomathy, a mosaic of Byzantine intricacy.

During the many months of the book's gestation, Emerson rarely said simply that he was writing. Rather he was "writing a little and arranging old papers more," making "a fair copy of

some of the reveries of the past winters," "redacting a chapter
. . . out of many papers of various date," "collating or compil-
ing," spinning "some single cord out of my thousand and one
strands of every color & texture that lie ravelled around me in
old snarls" (*L*, II, 194, 244, 282; Emerson to Caroline Sturgis,
December 21, 1841, Harvard College Library; *CEC*, p. 267).
What he meant was that he was changing a lecture into an essay
or leafing through his indexed journals for sentences and paragraphs that could be fitted together to make a new chapter of his
book. Ever since boyhood he had copied into those journals
what seemed most valuable in the day's reading and had recorded
there the flashes which came to him from within. But what had
once been spontaneity and newness now seemed to him, as he arranged it into essays, to be "dead thoughts." And the art of
arrangement — the forging of shape and coherence, introductions
and transitions, grammar and logic — seemed cold, mechanical
work in which he could take no satisfaction. "There is no magic
in it," he wrote; "I do not wish to see it again" (*JMN*, VII, 405).

And indeed the author's reaction is not entirely incomprehensible. The very first sentence of his book — "There is one mind
common to all individual men" — had been written five years before it appeared in print (*JMN*, V, 222). The second sentence
— "Every man is an inlet to the same and to all of the same" —
had been published in *The Dial* in January 1841 (II, 374). An
eloquent passage in "Compensation" was fifteen years old (*JMN*,
II, 340–341). Parts of "History" and "Self-Reliance" had been
read in lectures as early as 1833. With the exception of "Circles,"
all of the essays had been used, substantially or entirely, on the
lecture platform. Ninety-five percent of "History" was drawn
from the pages of the journals, fitted together, and sometimes
revised. Even "Circles," the latest of the essays, which was not
even begun until September 1840, is more than half made up of
passages written in the journal as early as 1835. Only a thorough
collation of parallel passages in journals, lectures, and essays —
which this edition facilitates — can show fully how Emerson spun
a single cord out of his thousand and one raveled strands. But an
examination of the first ten paragraphs of this most spontaneous,

least journal-derived of the essays will illustrate the spinner's craft.

"Circles" begins with two arresting sentences — on the circle as eye, horizon, and "highest emblem in the cipher of the world" — which had not appeared before in journals or done duty in lectures. For his third sentence, however, Emerson turned back to a journal page of 1835 (*JMN,* V, 57) and paraphrased a sentence which he thought had been written by St. Augustine. The clause "around every circle another can be drawn" he revised from an entry in his journal of 1839, where it had served as an illustration of the idea of "Progress" (*JMN,* VII, 283). But most of the first paragraph, and all of the second, he would have considered new.

The opening of paragraph three is a variation on the theme of fluidity and volatility which he had dealt with first in 1836, entered in his journal (V, 182), and used in the final paragraph of *Nature.* The third sentence and the sentence on Greek sculpture were part of his journal entry of June 1, 1840 (VII, 364). For the opening of paragraph four he turned back a few pages in that journal to copy four and a half sentences he had written on May 25 (VII, 354), and then for his three final sentences he transcribed what had immediately followed the Greek sculpture passage. Paragraph five is entirely new. Paragraph six is entirely secondhand: its first ten sentences were copied from the lecture "The Head," which he had first read in Boston in December 1837 (*EL,* II, 254–255); its last three came from the journal entry of May 25, 1840. Paragraph seven is new. Paragraph eight had been entered in the journal on October 25, 1840 (VII, 524). Paragraph nine has new opening and concluding sentences; the rest had been composed on May 6, 1840, after some reflections on a conversation with Bronson Alcott (VII, 347). Paragraph ten, except for its last two sentences, came from the journal of November 1839, where the words "today," "tomorrow," and "yesterday" had the immediacy of a diary (VII, 293); the semi-final exclamation and the startling antithesis "I am God in nature; I am a weed by the wall" were part of a sequence of paragraphs on circular transcendence which had been written on May 31, 1840 (VII, 362).

And "Circles" is, genetically, a somewhat uncharacteristic chapter of *Essays!* Most of it was written later than the other chapters. More of it than of the others was written consciously as a part of a work with a title, a subject, and a shape. Less of it had been used and reused on lecture platforms. For all of these reasons, probably, it was the essay Emerson altered least when he was preparing the new edition of 1847. Nevertheless, if "Circles" were the only essay that could be traced to its sources, it would represent accurately enough the ways in which the artist gave shape and texture to the materials he had gathered.

It is representative, also, of his handling of other men's words and thoughts. To be sure, most of the poetry and scripture he quoted or alluded to — *Paradise Lost* and *Night Thoughts* and an epistle of Samuel Daniel, Acts and Corinthians and Peter — he assumed to be part of the common memory and so not in need of identification. But he treated less familiar quotations in the same way. Oliver Cromwell, he wrote, had said, "A man never rises so high as when he knows not whither he is going." A memorable statement. But when and where, asks even a specialist in seventeenth-century English history, did Cromwell say that? Was the common reader of 1841 any more likely to know that Emerson's source was a footnote by Bishop Warburton in Clarendon's *History of the Rebellion and Civil War?* And was there not scholarly irresponsibility in writing, "St. Augustine described the nature of God as a circle whose . . ." when the sentence had been gleaned from a seventeenth-century divine, John Norris, who did not attribute it to Augustine or anybody else? Was there even, perhaps, something like dishonesty in quoting a sentence from Coleridge — "Nothing great was ever achieved without enthusiasm" — and not mentioning his name or using quotation marks? No. No dishonesty. No irresponsibility. The proprieties of scholarship had no place in a meditation like "Circles," and Emerson, for all his vast and various learning, was no more a scholar than Shakespeare was. The apothegms and anecdotes he copied into what he would have enjoyed calling his memory bank were interleaved there with his own, inspired his own, and became his own. Usually in his essays he named his saints and sages; sometimes he got them wrong; sometimes he mistook them for himself. Augustine or Bernard or John Norris, Cromwell or Clarendon or Warburton, Coleridge or Emerson — it did not matter much. They were there for luster and illumination, not for proof.

In "Circles" only a handful of the pieces Emerson fitted together were the found objects of his reading. Mainly, there and in the other essays, he worked with what he had himself made — or had found in meditation and introspection. Both kinds of pieces were scattered through the pages of his journals as if they had been jotted down by an anthologist, and Emerson's shaping and ingenious eye sought them back and forth in time, after paragraph ten as much as before, from May to November of 1840, then to February of 1839, then August 1837, and then to the fertile spring of 1840 again.

He drew on his lectures too, of course, and on his letters, even on his memory of letters he had not kept copies of. "Do you," he wrote to Margaret Fuller in the summer of 1840, "happen to possess . . . an old one from me dated 12 Oct 1838. I have quoted a sentence out of it into my journal which makes me think I may find a word there to fill up a bad hole in a paragraph" (*L*, II, 314). There were many such holes, within and between paragraphs, more of them in "Circles" than in the other essays, which he was obliged to fill with newly written sentences and paragraphs. But so uniform is the quality of the prose, so well does old blend with new, journal entry with quotation with filler, that the reader's eye cannot differentiate. "Nothing great was ever achieved without enthusiasm. The way of life is wonderful: it is by abandonment": the Coleridge sentence was copied into a journal of 1835; the second was written, it would seem, in the winter of 1840–41. "The universe is fluid and volatile" is a late revision of a journal sentence of 1836 (V, 182); "We grizzle every day. I see no need of it" is the beginning of a journal entry of July 1840 (VII, 380); *"so to be* is the sole inlet of *so to know"* is part of a paragraph written to fill a bad hole between paragraphs.

The journals are mostly fragments and flashes, unconnected sentences and paragraphs, parts of nothing except the mind that

Ralph Waldo Emerson,
about 1843.

Lidian and Edward Emerson,
about 1849.

Abel Adams
from his friend
R.W.E.
14 March, 1841.

ESSAYS.

Half-title page of the first edition of *Essays: First Series,* inscribed by Emerson to his close friend and financial adviser Abel Adams.

The reference of all production at last to an Aboriginal Power, explains the traits common to all works of the highest art, that they are universally intelligible ; that they restore to us the simplest states of mind ; and are religious.   Since what skill is therein shown is the reappearance of the original soul, a jet of pure light ; it should produce a similar impression to that made by natural objects.   In happy hours, nature appears to us one with art ; art perfected, — the work of genius.   And the individual in whom simple tastes and susceptibility to all the great human influences/ overpower/ the accidents of a local and special culture, is the best critic of art.   Though we travel the world over to find the beautiful, we must carry it with us, or we find it not.   The best of beauty is a finer charm than skill in surfaces, in outlines, or rules of art can ever teach, namely, a radiation from the work of art, of human character, — a wonderful expression through stone or canvas/ or musical sound of the deepest and simplest attributes of our nature, and therefore most intelligible at last to those souls which have these attributes.   In the sculptures of the Greeks, in the masonry of the Romans, and in the pictures of the Tuscan and Venetian masters, the highest charm is the universal language they speak. A confession of moral nature, of purity, love, and hope, breathes from them all.   That which we carry to them, the same we bring back more fairly illustrated in the memory.   The traveller who visits the Vatican, and passes from chamber to chamber through galleries of statues, vases, sarcophagi, and candelabra, through all

A page of the Abel Adams copy of *Essays: First Series,* showing errors in punctuation, grammar, and spelling marked by Emerson for correction.

Oct 16 The babe stands alone today for the first time.

In History, our imagination makes fools of us, plays us false. Why all this deference to Sidney & Hampden to Pym & Vane? Suppose they were virtuous, did they wear out virtue? As great a stake depends, as mighty motives move your private act today, as touched their public & renowned steps. See p. 173

Knowledge alters every thing & makes every thing fit for use. The vocabulary of two omniscient men would embrace words & images now excluded from all polite conversation. The wise will use the language which once he reject= ed. Wisdom is free. See p. 181

Culture inspects our dreams also. The pictures of the night will always bear some proportion to the visions of the day.

I looked over the few books in the young cler- gyman's study yesterday till I shivered with cold Priestley; Noyes; Rosenmuller; Joseph Allen & other Sunday School books; Schleusner; Norton; & the Satur- day Night of Taylor; The dirty comfort of the farmer could easily seem preferable to the elegant poverty of the young clergyman.

A page of Emerson's journal written in October 1837 (*JMN*, V, 398). The second paragraph was used in "Self-Reliance," the first two sentences of the third were used in "The Poet," and the second sentence of the fourth ap- peared in "Spiritual Laws."

wrote them. On a page dated October 16, 1837, for example, there appear, in almost unbroken succession, a paragraph that found its way into "Self-Reliance," two sentences that were used in "The Poet," and one sentence that became part of "Spiritual Laws" (*JMN*, V, 398). On a page of the journal of November 1839, Emerson wrote, "Trust thyself. Every heart vibrates to that iron string." Then he left a space, as if he had been staring at the bare trees outside his study, and set down a definition: *"Tantalus* means the impossibility of drinking the waters of thought which are always gleaming & waving within sight of the soul." That definition he eventually combined with another passage on the symbolic truths of mythology written the following June, and he used the two to make a paragraph of "History" (VII, 297, 385). What happened in the spinning together of such strands was often the alteration, extension, sometimes even the discovery of meaning through combination. On its journal page "Trust thyself . . ." stands alone; in *Essays* it is part of "Self-Reliance" and is immediately followed by a second injunction: "Accept the place the divine Providence has found for you; the society of your contemporaries, the connexion of events." In this new context it has become broader, richer, more subtle.

It was only through selection and interweaving that the brilliant strands of the journals attained wholeness, only through the craft of organization that the essays became complex artistic structures. Once, at least, Emerson seemed not only aware of what he was doing but pleased. When he finally sent the manuscript of "Friendship" to Ward he said he had got it at last "into some shape, not yet symmetrical but approximate to that." He had "written nothing with more pleasure" (Ward, pp. 25, 22). Surely he felt a similar pleasure when he plucked the paragraph beginning "And thus, O circular philosopher" from a journal page dealing with self-reliance (VII, 521), put it into the mouth of a reader, and made it the climactic point of "Circles." Even stronger is the sense of excitement at the end of "History," the least "original" of the essays, when the speaker suddenly reverses himself in a "new" paragraph that begins, "Is there something overweening in this claim? Then I reject all I have written" and turns to listen to "the rats in the wall . . . the fungus under foot, the lichen on the log." What had been a learned meditation has changed into a dramatic monologue.

These were what Emerson, in his darker moods, called the "tinkering arts." He was, he thought, coldly exhibiting the dead thoughts of other months and years and "inventing transitions like solder to weld irreconcileable metals" (*L*, II, 378). In such work, he sometimes felt, his genius deserted him (*JMN*, VII, 404-405). But his moods did not know each other. He himself wrote in "Intellect" the best answer to his own complaints: "In the intellect constructive, which we popularly designate by the word Genius, we observe the same balance of two elements, as in intellect receptive. The constructive intellect produces thoughts, sentences, poems, plans, designs, systems. . . . To genius must always go two gifts, the thought and the publication. The first is revelation, always a miracle. . . . But to make it available, it needs a vehicle or art by which it is conveyed to men. . . . The thought of genius is spontaneous; but the power of picture or expression, in the most enriched and flowing nature, implies a mixture of will, a certain control over the spontaneous states . . . a strenuous exercise of choice." It was the genius of publication, of design and system, of control and will which was at work when Emerson thought that the magic had departed. Without it he would have been a collector and polisher of precious stones and bright bits of stained glass; with it he made diadems and rose windows.

He also misjudged his book when he called it a miscellany or a raft. His vision had been clearer when he told Alcott in 1839 that he hoped for a "shapely" work. His conscious concern about shape and symmetry is evident in the alternative arrangements of "chapters" in his journal entry of June 1840 and in his dismay that he had not completed "Nature" in time to use it as a balance to "Art." But no evidence other than the table of contents itself is necessary to demonstrate the book's complex symmetry. Twelve essays arranged in six pairs, three of which — "Love" and "Friendship," "Prudence" and "Heroism," "Intellect" and "Art" — are identifiable just from their titles; twelve essays arranged in three quatrains, in an A-B-A order, general-particular-general: the table alone looks like a rhyme scheme. Within the book all the pairings become explicit. History is the record of the one mind which is common to all men; self-reliance is the knowledge that what is true for you is true for all men and that to worship the past is to conspire against the sanity of the soul. Recording "facts that indicate the path of the law of Compensation" is announced as the task of both "Compensation" and "Spiritual Laws," but Emerson expects to draw only "the smallest arc of this circle." In the first paragraph of "Circles" he writes of this first and highest of symbols: "One moral we have already deduced in considering the circular or compensatory character of every human action. Another analogy we shall now trace; that every action admits of being outdone." Throughout the book there are such anticipations and references, tying essay to essay, couplet to couplet, quatrain to quatrain, and end to beginning — as "History" is echoed in the final paragraph of "Art": "Beauty will not come at the call of a legislature, nor will it repeat in England or America, its history in Greece. It will come, as always, unannounced, and spring up between the feet of brave and earnest men. It is in vain that we look for genius to reiterate its miracles in the old arts."

More important than such intricate interrelationship of parts is the wholeness of *Essays*. Few books have been oftener dissected and partially exhibited than this one; few chapters have suffered more from the loss of context than these essays. Even "Self-Reliance" is not an autonomous work; it needs "History" and "Intellect." "Friendship" without "Love" is as cold-blooded as Melville thought it was. "Compensation" is one of two chapters which try to draw an arc. And nothing in the book can be safely read without this warning which comes only thirty pages from the end: "lest I should mislead any when I have my own head, and obey my whims, let me remind the reader that I am only an experimenter. Do not set the least value on what I do, or the least discredit on what I do not, as if I pretended to settle anything as true or false. I unsettle all things. No facts are to me sacred; none are profane; I simply experiment, an endless seeker, with no

Past at my back." Politely, perversely, Emerson called his elaborate construction a raft, and among the vessels which he said it was not he listed a clipper ship. Yet what he had built was much more like that masterpiece of design.

He mocked his style as "lapidary," acknowledging his ability to carve maxims and epigrams, regretting the writer's cramp that came between him and the ordinary speech of ordinary men. In this judgment there was some truth: his essays needed — and were in the future to get — more of the ease and openness which his letters and his lectures had. But he was not so bookish as he feared. "Are they *my* poor?" and "alms to sots" could have been snarled by the hard lips of a farmer at any town meeting. "If we walk in the woods, we must feed musquitoes: if we go a fishing, we must expect a wet coat," might have been spoken over cake and cider at the Concord Social Circle.

More important, his prose was poetic in ways which "lapidary" does not suggest. The sentences which set hearts as various as Whitman's and Nietzsche's to vibrating were not just graven jewels; they were also instruments of drama and music. The seldom, or perhaps never, quoted clause "for, *so to be* is the sole inlet of *so to know*" not only states in thirteen syllables the essence of Emerson's epistemology but sings a climactic pattern of alliteration and assonance, varies the tempo of its monosyllables by italics, and sets its single, central metaphor in its only disyllable. Time is gently destroyed by one euphonious simile: "we refer all things to time, as we habitually refer the immensely sundered stars to one concave sphere." Not just sentences but sequences of sentences are shaped into intricate crescendi, as in this aria where length, complexity, and concreteness grow to a climax in the repetitions and inversions of the final clause: "Crime and punishment grow out of one stem. Punishment is a fruit that unsuspected ripens within the flower of the pleasure which concealed it. Cause and effect, means and ends, seed and fruit, cannot be severed; for the effect already blooms in the cause, the end preëxists in the means, the fruit in the seed." Baroque intricacy is balanced by a local and natural imagery, the forest imagery of forest essays: "Commit a crime, and it seems as if a coat of snow fell on the ground, such as reveals in the woods the track of every partridge and fox and squirrel and mole. You cannot recall the spoken word, you cannot wipe out the foot-track, you cannot draw up the ladder, so as to leave no inlet or clew." It is a prose that moves pliantly, subtly, in the dancing of ideas: "The things we now esteem fixed, shall, one by one, detach themselves, like ripe fruit, from our experience, and fall. The wind shall blow them none knows whither. The landscape, the figures, Boston, London, are facts as fugitive as any institution past, or any whiff of mist or smoke, and so is society, and so is the world."

Almost a century and a half have passed since *Essays* was published and Orestes Brownson and Harriet Martineau declared it to be a book for the age, the ages, the millennium. Now, even more than then, its ideas seem profound and significant and the words and patterns in which they dance seem timelessly beautiful. Perhaps the predictions of those first admirers were not so extravagant as they must have seemed to Emerson.

Statement of Editorial Principles

The intention of this edition is to provide for the first time definitive texts of those works of Emerson which were originally published in his lifetime and under his supervision. The canon and order follow the physical arrangement which Emerson himself suggested in 1869 when he sent his first six volumes of prose to the printer as text for the first American edition of his collected prose. To this group have been added as volumes seven, eight, and nine respectively, *Society and Solitude, Letters and Social Aims,* and the *Poems,* in the positions assigned to them in all collected editions since they were first included in the Little Classic edition of 1876. One volume of the prose pieces published by Emerson but not collected in any permanent position by him replaces the three posthumous volumes of prose included in the Riverside and Centenary editions. The other material included in those posthumous volumes will be published in the separate edition of Emerson's later lectures, newly edited from the manuscripts used by James Elliot Cabot and Edward Emerson.

Adapting the theories of Sir Walter Greg to the particular problems of nineteenth-century American printed texts, the present edition is critical and unmodernized. It neither provides a reprint of any single earlier edition, nor limits itself to the authority of earlier editions.

The central editorial principles of this edition are that the copy-text is that text closest to the author's initial coherent intention and that determining his subsequent intention depends on the use of evidence from other relevant forms of the text according to conservative editorial procedures. The rationale of copy-text assumes that in printed works each resetting is likely to introduce additional non-authorial corruption into the text, both in substantives and in accidentals. The earliest feasible form, therefore, is normally chosen as copy-text. In cases where the manuscript or printer's proof has not survived, this edition chooses the first printed form as copy-text, except that magazine or newspaper publication of only part of an essay is not so used. When earlier forms, such as the printer's copy for *Representative Men,* have been chosen, the choice has been made on the argument that they better preserve Emerson's intention than the first published forms.

Each emendation of copy-text is carefully justified on the basis of error, as in obvious misprints, or on the basis of authorial intervention. In the case of variant accidentals there is generally no evidence on which to base emendation, and copy-text is usually followed, even though this means, in the case of printed copy-text, following much house styling. For substantive emendation clearer evidence is usually available, and this must be adduced to support the claims of authorial intervention and to exclude subsequent substantive variants which have no authority.

In practical terms there are three principal classes of evidence for emendation of copy-text: the author's handwritten corrections and revisions in extant texts; external authorial instructions concerning the text; and subsequent variants which correct, modify, add, or delete.* The first and second classes apply to both substantives and accidentals. The third applies primarily to substantive emendation, and even so must be justified as authorial: known similar revision, context, kind of revision, and the like must be weighed as probabilities against non-authorial emendation (sophistication) or printer's error. All emendation, however, involves editorial judgment and responsibility; and these

---

* Volume I of *The Collected Works of Ralph Waldo Emerson* printed the fullest version of the text by rejecting most of Emerson's revisions which shortened the original and accepting only those which expanded or clarified it. Because the textual problems of subsequent volumes differ, all revisions identifiable as Emerson's will ordinarily be accepted.

classes of evidence for emendation do not preclude the rare and judicious emendation of obvious and gross error or misprint overlooked by the author and by printers, proofreaders, and editors in all relevant forms — on the assumption that the author did not intend such error, but with the proviso that the errors constitute impossibilities and not mere inelegancies or irregularities. In emendation, pre-copy-text forms and parallel passages from journals and lectures, as well as Emerson's established usage and preference, may cautiously be adduced as supporting evidence without diminishing the primary editorial responsibility.

In order to preserve a clear page, free of all subsidiary information except Emerson's own footnotes, the record of emendations and relevant variant readings is appended at the end of each volume in the textual apparatus. The list of Emendations in Copy-Text reports all changes made in copy-text, whether in accidentals or substantives, except for certain types of emendation made silently and explained in the prefatory remarks. A list of Rejected Substantives records those variants (including, in some cases, variants in spelling and word-division) which are not accepted into the present edition; or a Historical Collation, which may be used in place of the Rejected Substantives list in those volumes where it is more effective in presenting the data, includes both substantive emendations and rejected substantive variants. Textual notes are introduced into those lists to justify editorial choices which require special explanation. Variants in the Riverside and Centenary editions are included in these lists even though those texts are not authoritative. Variants in British editions which are not authoritative are not normally included, although some are cited when they are of historical interest or when it is thought that they may throw some light on prepublication states of the text. Lists of line-end hyphenations (in the copy-text and in the present edition) are also included in the textual apparatus. Revisions in the manuscript are recorded in those volumes where this is appropriate. Finally, the list of Parallel Passages from Emerson's other writings, although included primarily for other reasons, may also provide evidence for the solution of textual problems.

Statement of Editorial Principles

The Textual Introduction includes a history of the text, a bibliographic description of the work insofar as it bears on the establishment of copy-text, an explanation of any special editorial problems and practices relating to the particular volume, and the identification and location of those copies of the book actually used in the collation.

Textual Introduction

This book provides for the first time an established text of Emerson's first collection of essays. Although the volume here printed was originally titled simply *Essays,* we have adopted Emerson's own later usage and refer to it as *Essays: First Series* (or, in abbreviation, *Essays I*), the title he gave its 1847 revision to distinguish it from *Essays: Second Series,* published in 1844.

A thorough search of leading manuscript archives, especially the large collection of Emerson material in the Houghton Library at Harvard University, has revealed no surviving manuscript or proof sheets of *Essays I*.[1] Although the book derives largely from lectures given in several previous years, Emerson revised, reworked, and combined that material with passages gleaned from other lectures and from his journals. The lecture and journal manuscripts are, therefore, not considered here as "pre-copy-text forms," since they do not present finished literary versions of any of the sections of *Essays I,* a collection conceived and published as a unified book.

As explained in the Statement of Editorial Principles, the text of this volume attempts to reflect as closely as possible Emerson's

1. Emerson rarely saved manuscripts of his published works, although manuscripts of letters, journals, lectures, and sermons survive in abundance. The manuscript of *Representative Men* in the Buffalo Public Library is a significant exception. Drafts of separate essays exist, and the Berg Collection of the New York Public Library has one manuscript leaf of *Essays II.* See also Kenneth Cameron's serialized article on his manuscript findings, "Some Collections of Emerson Manuscripts," *Emerson Society Quarterly* (1956), II, 3, 1–3; IV, 5, 20–21; (1957), I, 6, 21–23, 26–27; (1958), IV, 13, 36–41.

original formulation and his subsequent corrections and revisions. He invested Transcendentalism with a pragmatic Yankee concern for the idea incarnated not only in words, but in print, and his interest in revising and proofreading almost every detail of his printed books makes him a somewhat special case for a modern editor. Early editions of his works contain few typographical errors, and the bulk of substantive variants (changes in words or syntax) for a single volume of his early works is very high compared to books by other writers of his time. Because later editions had to be reset to accommodate many substantive revisions, the number of changes in accidentals (spelling, punctuation, capitalization, and hyphenation) is also very high. But variants in accidentals cannot be attributed solely to Emerson's printers, for Emerson concerned himself with such details as his eccentric spellings and personal punctuation habits. We know from written instructions, for example, that he wanted single quotation marks used for one purpose, double for another.[2] It is extremely difficult, therefore, for an editor to determine which of such variants were introduced by typesetters and which by Emerson.

In an effort to preserve as closely as possible the author's own accidentals, we have chosen as copy-text the first printed version: the 1841 edition. The 1847 American edition contains substantial revisions by Emerson, but does not constitute a rewriting of any of the essays; we have therefore rejected that edition as a possible copy-text, although we have accepted as emendations in copy-text almost all of its substantive alterations and corrections, and those changes in accidentals which appear to be the author's. To determine Emerson's intentions further, we have used his handwritten corrections and notes for revision in two copies of the first edition (the Abel Adams and Ruth Emerson copies[3])

2. In a letter to John Chapman, March 26, 1845, Emerson wrote: "There is a general correction I should like also to make in your edition in regard to the use of quotation marks. My practice is, when I make a *bona fide* quotation from any person, to mark it with double commas, but when the quotation is only rhetorical, or in the form, I use single commas"; "Emerson to Chapman: Four Letters about Publishing," ed. Charles W. Mignon, *ESQ* (1973), IV, 19, 228.

3. Houghton, *AC85.Em345.841e (F) and (B), respectively.

and his notes and instructions for changes in his journals and in letters to his various printers. No emendations have been silently made.

The 1841 version has been collated by machine and sight against the subsequent impressions and editions supervised by Emerson, as well as against editions included for their importance in establishing Emerson's reputation (two posthumous editions, two English authorized editions, and English piracies). Multiple copies of all major editions have also been collated (by machine where possible) to establish errors and variants within each impression and to identify the different printings of any one edition.[4]

This edition benefits from the cumulative restudy of Emerson's surviving manuscript materials, which provide a context within which his published works can be more fully understood and more accurately edited. Three modern contributions to Emer-

4. For a complete listing of the editions that appear in the apparatus, see the Table of Collated Editions, p. 265 below. We have collated fourteen copies of the 1841 edition (*BAL* 5189); five copies of the first impression of the 1847 revision and twelve copies of later impressions from the stereotyped plates of that edition (*BAL* 5213); two copies of the 1865 Blue and Gold edition (*BAL* 5370); two copies of the *Prose Works*, Volume I, in separate impressions (*BAL* 5375); thirteen copies of different impressions of the 1876 Little Classic edition (the earliest and latest collated, intervening impressions checked) (*BAL* 5384); two copies of the Riverside edition (*BAL* 5414); and one copy of the Centenary edition (*BAL* 5463). We checked various other posthumous editions as well. Of English editions, three copies of the 1841 Fraser (*BAL* 5338) and one of the 1853 Chapman (*BAL* 5365) have been collated, and six copies of various editions, including piracies, have been checked. A complete list of copies collated and checked is on file at Colgate University Library and at the Houghton Library, Harvard University.

Machine collations of all later impressions made from the type of the first 1841 impression, and of impressions of subsequent authorized editions resulting from new typesettings, were each done three times by Alfred R. Ferguson and his assistants, Otto van Os, Nicole Plumstead, Joseph P. Sperry, and Genevieve W. Tucker. Sight collations of the English editions (including piracies) and of later American editions against the 1841 edition were made in each case by several group readings and subsequent independent readings performed by the readers named above, as well as by Jean Ferguson Carr, Joseph Slater, and (1841 against 1847 only) Douglas Emory Wilson.

xl

son scholarship have been especially helpful: Rusk's edition of the letters, supplemented by *The Correspondence of Emerson and Carlyle* and by the four volumes of letters which Eleanor Tilton will soon publish and which she has generously made available to Emerson scholars; the edition of the journals undertaken by Gilman, Ferguson, Orth, and others; and the printing from manuscript of the early lectures, edited by Whicher, Spiller, and Williams. Emerson's habit of using his journals, his lectures, and even occasionally his letters as a "savings bank" from which to draw over and over again ideas, paragraphs, and sentences makes these newly and carefully edited manuscripts crucial companions for the printed works. Especially in the absence of manuscript for these essays, the journals and lectures enable us to establish Emerson's normal usage patterns, to distinguish between Emersonian errors and printer's errors, and to judge when accidentals may derive from a misreading of Emerson's handwriting.[5] The manuscript of *Representative Men* (the holograph used as printer's copy in 1849) now being prepared as Volume IV of this edition has also contributed further knowledge on these points. The journals, works, and lectures have been carefully compared by their editors to provide tables of parallel passages which assist the reader in following Emerson's multiple uses of an idea or statement. Such a collection of parallel passages is especially important for this first set of collected essays, in which Emerson drew so thoroughly on previous material from the journals and lectures.

In his journal for 1869 Emerson showed how much he saw revision as part of his definition of *"good writing"*: "All writing should be selection in order to drop every dead word. Why do you not save out of your speech on thinking only the vital things. . . . If a man would learn to read his own manuscript severely, —

5. An example of a misreading caused probably by the difficulty of reading Emerson's handwriting is the error "Hankal" for "Haukal" in "Heroism" (see the Informational and Emendations notes for 150.11). For questionable spellings, Emerson's usage has been compared with Worcester's *Dictionary* (1838), which he used until 1878, and also with the *OED* and Webster's *American Dictionary* (1828).

becoming really a third person, and search only for what interested him, he would blot to purpose, — and how every page would gain" (*J*, X, 302–303). Emerson was speaking from experience, describing what he had practiced since his first published essay. He was a painstaking editor, continuing to polish and revise his writings long after the point at which many authors regard them as complete. His belief in writing as a continuous process, a matter of vision and revision, is especially evident in this second volume of his published works. In a letter to Margaret Fuller, written when he was seeing the first edition of *Essays I* through the press, he revealed characteristic perfectionism as well as frustration with the time and effort involved: "Of making one book there is no end, & since my proofs begin to come, I am but as a hen with one chicken" (January 12, 1841, *L*, II, 376). The textual history of *Essays I* indicates that the attempt to improve the original text through a patient exercise of the "tinkering arts" of revision (Emerson to William Emerson, February 5, 1841, *L*, II, 378) continued almost until his death.

By the time *Essays I* was published, Emerson's experience with his earlier essays and with the American editions of Carlyle's *Sartor Resartus* and *Critical and Miscellaneous Essays* had thoroughly acquainted him with the process of bookmaking. His letters to Carlyle and to his own printers during this period show how knowledgeable he was about various aspects of publishing. As was common for nineteenth-century authors, Emerson retained ownership of the standing type and periodically issued orders to his printer, Freeman and Bolles (for James Munroe and Co.), to print and bind the number of copies he thought necessary to fulfill the demand for the work.[6] "I print them at my own risk," he wrote to Evert Duyckinck, "& Munroe & Co have 30 per cent as their commission" (October 14, 1845, *L*, III, 308).

6. Emerson discusses his handling of Carlyle's publishing accounts, warns Carlyle of piracies of his books, and urges him to check Emerson's figures (*CEC*, pp. 262, 267–269, 282–285, 292–293). James Munroe's account books record Emerson's supervision of Carlyle's American publications (see Acct. Bk. #6 and #7). They also carry detailed records of Emerson's own books, of copies at hand and copies ordered bound.

Essays I was not set in stereotype until Emerson was satisfied that sales justified a second edition; in fact, he maintained ownership of the stereotype plates throughout his life and required written requests from the publishers to issue new printings of his works. In 1841, although 1500 copies of *Essays I* had been printed, by October 1 only 896 copies had been bound. The edition continued to sell slowly but well and was sold out by 1845.[7]

The major alteration involved the revised edition, called *Essays: First Series,* published in 1847 by James Munroe. In the summer of that year, under pressure from the publishers to reprint *Essays I* and angered because his work was already appearing in pirated versions in England, Emerson undertook extensive revision of the book. This was part of a general effort during 1846–1849 to polish earlier work before turning to new material. The appearance of *Essays: Second Series* (1844) and *Poems* (1846) had established Emerson as a notable writer, though relatively small sales show that he was not yet popular. He had begun to receive invitations to lecture in England, and Margaret Fuller had written him about the growing enthusiasm of French readers for *Essays I* and *II.*[8] In the spring of 1846 he had written his English publisher, John Chapman: "Munroe & Co have pressed me to reprint the first & second series of Essays in two uniform volumes. But I do not find even that easy, for I wish, if I can, to keep the first series in one volume, & the second needs a

7. Metcalf and Co.'s bill of August 11, 1847, for stereotyping the revised *Essays I* for Munroe and Co. is tipped into Emerson's Ledger 11, where he also records the payment of $233.77 on February 11, 1848 (p. [5]). In Ledger 5, Emerson wrote: "The plates of ⟨my⟩ 'Emerson's Essays First Series,' in the hands of J. Munroe & Co., are my property" (p. [24]). In a memo of October 24, 1859, about his arrangements with Ticknor and Fields, who were replacing Phillips, Sampson, and Company as his publishers, Emerson explained that he owned the stereotyped plates of his first six books, but wished to deposit them with a printer and issue periodic written orders for more copies: "and no copies shall be taken from the plates without such written order from me" (loose sheet inserted in Ledger 11).

8. Carlyle wrote on October 31, 1843, that, "to the horror of poor Nickisson (Bookseller Fraser's successor), a certain scoundrel interloper here has reprinted *Emerson's Essays* on greyish paper to be sold at two shillings" (*CEC,* p. 349). See also Rusk, pp. 285, 324, 327.

considerable addition to go as its companion."[9]   A desire to make the two volumes uniform in length may have caused the condensation of material in the 1847 revision.   But Emerson's general tendency in revising was, as Paul Lauter has demonstrated, toward a more concentrated prose style involving a tightening of syntax and the omission of multiple illustrations of his points. The revisions which remove tautology, smooth grammatical and stylistic awkwardness, and eliminate structural devices of repetition may, as Lauter suggests, represent a deliberate movement away from the "spoken" style developed in Emerson's pulpit and platform experience, toward a tighter written style.[10]

Between the first publication of *Essays I* in 1841 and its revision in 1847, Emerson's early exuberance and optimism had been somewhat muted by the death in 1842 of his son Waldo, and by his observation and subsequent rejection in 1841 of the Brook Farm experience.   The revision reflects in part his growing awareness of man's limitations.   He eliminated many strong or absolute adjectives and adverbs (never, all, continually, great, eternal, perfect) ; he sometimes replaced the first person with the third person   (see 47.32, 102.21).   The revision excludes or softens such phrases as "the snout of this sensualism" (107.3), the assertion that "the mush of concession . . . turns the stomach, it blots the daylight" (122.35), and the description of pride in a friend's virtues as "wild, delicate, throbbing property" (115.29), which may have come to seem intemperate or excessive.   Even in new passages that are longer than the ones they replace (as in 13.18), the tone tends to be quieter and more reserved than in the first version.

Despite his concern for revising particular passages, Emerson was eager to move on to new material, as he wrote in a letter to his brother William on September 24, 1847: "And now in these weeks having been detained tediously by reprinting & correcting & motting my old First Series, *Essays,* I came to the preparation of lectures for England" (*L*, III, 417).   He revised the first four essays heavily, especially the troublesome "History."   The later

9. Emerson to Chapman, May 15, 1846, in the Berg Collection.

10. Paul Lauter, "Emerson's Revisions of *Essays (First Series),*" *American Literature,* 33 (May 1961), 143–158; see especially p. 144.

essays, which, with the exception of "Circles," were taken more directly from their lecture counterparts, have considerably fewer and less drastic revisions than do the first four. Whether Emerson tired of his labors or whether the later essays seemed satisfactory, the number of revisions decreased steadily throughout the volume from essay to essay.

The 1847 edition of 1500 copies was the first to be set in stereotype; it was the seminal copy for all later authorial editions and continued to be reprinted almost every two years until 1878, long after it had theoretically been superseded by "new and revised" editions. Although the title pages of later impressions vary as to publisher and date, there were no changes in the original plates of the text until 1861, when the impression by Ticknor and Fields, Emerson's new publishers, finally corrected a small error that the author had noted in 1847: the misprint of "stringing" for "stinging" in "Prudence" (133.30).

Three further editions of *Essays I* were supervised by Emerson, although none of them received the extensive substantive revision of the 1847 edition. In May 1864 Emerson wrote to Ticknor and Fields confirming plans for a third edition, which was to appear, with *Essays II,* in a single volume. He wrote to Fields that he agreed to an edition "of 3000 copies in 'blue & gold' " and promised to send a list of corrections: "I have been looking over the books with a view to correction, & will send you presently a short list of *errata*" (May 13, 1864, *L,* V, 376–377). This Blue and Gold edition was copyrighted in 1865 and announced for publication on April 6 of that year; it included not only the *Essays* but also a separate volume containing a new edition of the *Poems* (see letters of May 19, 1864, and November 11, 1868, *L,* V, 377, and VI, 39).[11] Emerson probably never saw proof for the 1865

11. On April 14, 1864, Emerson wrote that he "gave an order for transfer of the plates of these books from Houghton & Co. to Welch, Bigelow & Co." (Ledger 7, p. [168]). Rusk notes that "Ticknor and Fields announced in the *Boston Daily Advertiser,* April 6, 1865, that their 'Blue and Gold' edition of the Essays, containing both series in one volume, was published on that day" (*L,* V, 376n.). The record of the Blue and Gold electrotyping by Welch, Bigelow & Co. and the progress of subsequent editions appear in the Ticknor and Fields Cost Books (Houghton bMS AM 1185.6, 3–9).

edition, which contains typographers' errors as well as many variants in accidentals. The printer ignored Emerson's idiosyncratic practices, revised and simplified his punctuation, and standardized his preferred spellings of words like "Shakspeare," "leger," and "skeptic." This edition corrected the errata for the 1847 edition that Emerson had noted in his *Index Major 1847* (Houghton 106, pp. 94–95).

The fourth American edition of the *Essays* was made for the first authorized "new and revised" collection of Emerson's complete prose works in a two-volume edition. On July 26, 1869, Emerson noted: "This morning sent my six prose volumes, revised and corrected, to Fields and Company for their new edition in two volumes" (*J*, X, 295; see also letter of July 26, 1869, *L*, VI, 78). It is unlikely, considering Emerson's age and state of health, that he supervised the printing with the same painstaking care he had devoted to it over twenty years earlier. But apparently he did make minor corrections in the proof, for on August 18 he sent the publishers a note including "one or two *Errata* for the printer of the New Edition" (*L*, VI, 83). This edition was printed from electrotype by Welch, Bigelow, and Company on September 28 and appeared after the middle of October in a printing of 2000 sets, though all observed copies of the original impression are dated 1870. The edition, like that of 1847, was reprinted at need in subsequent years.[12] The *Prose Works* edition of *Essays I* contains few substantive revisions, but many errors, most of which were corrected by the editors of the 1876 and Riverside editions. It rejects in several instances printer's changes introduced in the 1865 edition, although it follows that edition's practice of standardizing some of Emerson's idiosyncratic spellings.

The final American edition to appear in Emerson's lifetime was the Little Classic of 1876, also called, on its title pages, a "new and revised edition." This theoretically complete edition of

12. On October 26, 1869, Emerson noted that he had received payment for copyright on "1700 copies of Emerson's Prose Works Complete in 2 volumes at 50 cents each set" (Ledger 8, loose sheet). Publishers' cost books show reprintings at an average rate of one a year for a number of years thereafter.

Emerson's works — nine single volumes in a small and attractive format — was probably prepared mainly by Emerson's daughter Ellen, who had, with James Elliot Cabot, assisted her father in putting together *Letters and Social Aims*.[13] Emerson participated in some of the proofing of the edition, for, in a letter to Titus Coan on May 21, 1876, he remarked that it was hard for an old man to write letters, especially when he was "correcting proof every other day which the printers send him of a new edition of all his old books."[14] Reimpressions of the edition with minor plate corrections were made for a run of 150 copies in March 1877 and one of 280 in July 1879. The plates of this edition were also used for an edition of the works in five volumes, printed in 1880 and for several years thereafter. The Little Classic edition of *Essays I* contains only a few substantive revisions: it corrected some errors introduced in the 1865 and 1870 texts and returned to some of Emerson's preferred spellings, such as "Shakspeare" for the 1865–1870 "Shakespeare." It also introduced several proof errors, corrected in the Riverside edition.

The textual apparatus of this book also includes citations from two posthumous editions of Emerson's works: the Riverside edition (1883–1893), edited by James Elliot Cabot, and the Centenary edition (1903–1904), edited by Edward Waldo Emerson. Both of these "purified" the text of many changes made since the 1847 revision. In several cases the editors used versions from the 1841 edition, though they generally followed the 1847 text for *Essays I*. Both editors replaced Emerson's heavy punctuation and antiquated spelling with more modern versions (a revision begun by the editors or printers of the Blue and Gold edition). Both announced in their introductions that, apart from some changes in punctuation and the correction of some "obvious mistakes,"

13. Ellen's letters of the period are full of detailed references to her collaboration with Cabot in helping her father revise his books; see Rusk, pp. 485–487, 495. In a letter to Ellen written about 1875, Emerson acknowledged: "you write all my letters — (not to mention all my lectures)" (*L,* VI, 288).

14. Quoted by William White, "Thirty-three Unpublished Letters of Ralph Waldo Emerson," *American Literature,* 33 (May 1961), 175.

they were printing Emerson's "collected Essays as he left them" (see *R,* I, iii; *W,* I, vi) . E. W. Emerson also undertook an extensive and useful annotation of the works, which enabled him to correct some historical and geographical inaccuracies. Occasionally his corrections were themselves in error, as in the case of Emerson's spelling, "Genelas," which E. W. Emerson erroneously emended to "Venelas" (see the Rejected Substantives note for 20.2 below) .

English editions of *Essays I* abounded in the nineteenth century — both in approved editions done under the careful guidance of Carlyle and in piracies. In gratitude for Emerson's efforts in the American publication of his works, Carlyle arranged for and supervised an 1841 English edition (printed from the American 1841 edition in London by Fraser & Co.), and wrote a preface. He also proofread the volume, which Emerson saw only after it appeared.[15] Sight collation of this authorized edition reveals only thirteen substantive variants, some of which are almost surely printer's changes, such as words dropped, word-order reversed, and grammar corrected. It also includes some changes that Emerson marked for correction in the Abel Adams copy, which suggests that he had sent Carlyle or Fraser a list of these. Numerous piracies followed this edition in England, prompting Emerson's friends to arrange for an authorized reissue of *Essays I* by the London publisher John Chapman.[16] The reissue was intended to meet the growing interest in and demand for Emerson's works created in part by the 1844 publication of *Essays II,* the 1846 publication of *Poems,* and an 1846 reprint of Emerson's lecture "Man

15. Carlyle wrote to Emerson on June 25, 1841: *"Emerson's Essays,* the Book so-called, is to be reprinted here; nay, I think, is even now at press. . . . T. Carlyle writing a Preface, — which accordingly he did . . . last night and the foregoing days. Robson [the printer] will stand by the text to the very utmost; and I also am to read the Proof-sheets. The edition is of 750; which Fraser thinks he will sell" (*CEC,* p. 302) .

16. See note 8 above. The pirate was W. Tweedie, who probably also printed a second pirated edition in 1852 and a third in 1854. William Smith's Standard Library series printed *Essays I* in a cheap paper edition in 1844. Chapman offered his services as publisher to Emerson the summer (1844) before he published *Essays II* (L, III, 265n.) .

the Reformer" (Rusk, p. 326) . Emerson wrote to Chapman from Manchester on November 15, 1847: "I have no material corrections to make, & as my new American Edition is almost as good as I could make it, if the printer will only adhere to that text, I shall be contented without seeing the proofs. Neither have I at this moment any preface to set before it. . . . At present, I have only one erratum to offer: — On p. 205, of the new American Edition [*for* stringing *read* stinging]" (*L*, III, 439–440) . Chapman may have followed Emerson's instructions to print from the 1847 American edition, and his publishing firm did place advertisements for such an edition, which Jacob Blanck notes as "possibly an importation. . . . Presumably the text of the Boston edition (Oct. 1847) ."[17] Neither Blanck nor the editors of the *Collected Works*, however, have located a copy of such an edition, and it seems possible that Chapman simply reissued the 1841 English edition; for a copy in the Boston Athenæum that carries the name of James Fraser (as publisher) and the date 1841 on the title page has "Emerson's Essays First Series . . . John Chapman London" on the spine, and a twenty-four-page catalogue of books published by Chapman (dated October 1, 1847) tipped in the back. This copy carries all the substantive variants of the 1841 English edition.

The appearance in 1853, however, of a cheap paper edition published by Chapman, with the claim to be "reprinted" from the "English edition," suggests that Chapman may have published a revised edition some time between 1847 and 1853. This 1853 edition is the earliest English one so far located that shows the influence of the American 1847 revision; it does not retain the substantive variants introduced in the 1841 English edition except for those that also appear in the 1847 American edition. It solves the problem of editorial choice by persistently conflating readings from the first edition with the 1847 revisions, and thus becomes the longest, though not the most readable, edition of *Essays I*. We have accepted no emendations from this edition, since Emerson almost certainly had no part in its proofreading.

17. The edition was advertised in *The Athenæum,* November 20, 1847 (*BAL,* p. 66) .

This brief summary of the textual history of *Essays: First Series* reveals how integral, though at times frustrating, the act of revision was to Emerson's writing process. The man who in *Nature* portrayed himself as a "transparent eye-ball," a "part or particle of God," capable of viewing the universe in unmediated vision, acknowledged in a letter to Margaret Fuller that the process of correcting his own essays had brought a knowledge governed by an inevitably mediated perspective: "I have nothing left me but that most miserable *self knowledge* which consists in the study of *proof-sheets* where one beholds his wit as in a cramp distorting lookingglass" (February 9, 1841, *L*, II, 381).

HISTORY

There is no great and no small
To the Soul that maketh all:
And where it cometh, all things are;
And it cometh everywhere.

I am owner of the sphere,
Of the seven stars and the solar year,
Of Cæsar's hand, and Plato's brain,
Of Lord Christ's heart, and Shakspeare's strain.

ESSAY I

HISTORY

There is one mind common to all individual men. Every man is an inlet to the same and to all of the same. He that is once admitted to the right of reason is made a freeman of the whole estate. What Plato has thought, he may think; what a saint has felt, he may feel; what at any time has befallen any man, he can understand. Who hath access to this universal mind, is a party to all that is or can be done, for this is the only and sovereign agent.

Of the works of this mind history is the record. Its genius is illustrated by the entire series of days. Man is explicable by nothing less than all his history. Without hurry, without rest, the human spirit goes forth from the beginning to embody every faculty, every thought, every emotion, which belongs to it in appropriate events. But the thought is always prior to the fact; all the facts of history preëxist in the mind as laws. Each law in turn is made by circumstances predominant, and the limits of nature give power to but one at a time. A man is the whole encyclopædia of facts. The creation of a thousand forests is in one acorn, and Egypt, Greece, Rome, Gaul, Britain, America, lie folded already in the first man. Epoch after epoch, camp, kingdom, empire, republic, democracy, are the application of his manifold spirit to the manifold world.

This human mind wrote history and this must read it. The Sphinx must solve her own riddle. If the whole of history is in one man, it is all to be explained from individual experience. There is a relation between the hours of our life and the centuries of time. As the air I breathe is drawn from the great repositories of nature, as the light on my book is yielded by a star a hundred millions of miles distant, as the poise of my body depends on the equilibrium of centrifugal and centripetal forces, so the hours should be instructed by the ages, and the ages explained by the hours. Of the universal mind each individual man is one more incarnation. All its properties consist in him. Each new fact in his private experience flashes a light on what great bodies of men have done, and the crises of his life refer to national crises. Every revolution was first a thought in one man's mind, and when the same thought occurs to another man, it is the key to that era. Every reform was once a private opinion, and when it shall be a private opinion again, it will solve the problem of the age. The fact narrated must correspond to something in me to be credible or intelligible. We as we read must become Greeks, Romans, Turks, priest and king, martyr and executioner, must fasten these images to some reality in our secret experience, or we shall learn nothing rightly. What befell Asdrubal or Cæsar Borgia, is as much an illustration of the mind's powers and depravations as what has befallen us. Each new law and political movement has meaning for you. Stand before each of its tablets and say, 'Under this mask did my Proteus nature hide itself.' This remedies the defect of our too great nearness to ourselves. This throws our actions into perspective: and as crabs, goats, scorpions, the balance and the waterpot, lose their meanness when hung as signs in the zodiack, so I can see my own vices without heat in the distant persons of Solomon, Alcibiades, and Catiline.

It is the universal nature which gives worth to particular men and things. Human life as containing this is mysterious and inviolable, and we hedge it round with penalties and laws. All laws derive hence their ultimate reason; all express more or less distinctly some command of this supreme illimitable essence. Property also holds of the soul, covers great spiritual facts, and instinctively we at first hold to it with swords and laws, and wide and complex combinations. The obscure consciousness of this fact is the light of all our day, the claim of claims; the plea for education, for justice, for charity, the foundation of friendship and love, and of the heroism and grandeur which belong to acts of self-reliance. It is remarkable that involuntarily we always read as superior beings. Universal history, the poets, the romancers, do not in their stateliest pictures — in the sacerdotal, the imperial palaces, in the triumphs of will, or of genius — anywhere lose our ear, anywhere make us feel that we intrude, that this is for better men; but rather is it true that in their grandest strokes we feel most at home. All that Shakspeare says of the king, yonder slip of a boy that reads in the corner, feels to be true of himself. We sympathize in the great moments of history, in the great discoveries, the great resistances, the great prosperities of men; — because there law was enacted, the sea was searched, the land was found, or the blow was struck *for us*, as we ourselves in that place would have done or applauded.

We have the same interest in condition and character. We honor the rich because they have externally the freedom, power and grace which we feel to be proper to man, proper to us. So all that is said of the wise man by stoic or oriental or modern essayist, describes to each reader his own idea, describes his unattained but attainable self. All literature writes the character of the wise man. Books, monuments, pictures, conversation, are portraits in which he finds the lineaments he is forming. The silent and the eloquent praise him, and accost him, and he is stimulated wherever he moves as by personal allusions. A true aspirant, therefore, never needs look for allusions personal and laudatory in discourse. He hears the commendation, not of himself, but more sweet, of that character he seeks, in every word that is said concerning character, yea, further, in every fact and circumstance, — in the running river, and the rustling corn. Praise is looked, homage tendered, love flows from mute nature, from the mountains and the lights of the firmament.

These hints, dropped as it were from sleep and night, let us use in broad day. The student is to read history actively and not passively; to esteem his own life the text, and books the commentary. Thus compelled, the muse of history will utter oracles, as never to those who do not respect themselves. I have no expectation that any man will read history aright, who thinks that what was done in a remote age, by men whose names have resounded far, has any deeper sense than what he is doing to-day.

The world exists for the education of each man. There is no

age or state of society or mode of action in history, to which there is not somewhat corresponding in his life. Every thing tends in a wonderful manner to abbreviate itself and yield its own virtue to him. He should see that he can live all history in his own person. He must sit solidly at home, and not suffer himself to be bullied by kings or empires, but know that he is greater than all the geography and all the government of the world; he must transfer the point of view from which history is commonly read, from Rome and Athens and London to himself, and not deny his conviction that he is the Court, and if England or Egypt have any thing to say to him, he will try the case; if not, let them forever be silent. He must attain and maintain that lofty sight where facts yield their secret sense, and poetry and annals are alike. The instinct of the mind, the purpose of nature betrays itself in the use we make of the signal narrations of history. Time dissipates to shining ether the solid angularity of facts. No anchor, no cable, no fences avail to keep a fact a fact. Babylon, Troy, Tyre, Palestine, and even early Rome, have passed or are passing into fiction. The Garden of Eden, the Sun standing still in Gibeon, is poetry thenceforward to all nations. Who cares what the fact was, when we have made a constellation of it to hang in heaven an immortal sign? London and Paris and New York must go the same way. "What is History," said Napoleon, "but a fable agreed upon?" This life of ours is stuck round with Egypt, Greece, Gaul, England, War, Colonization, Church, Court, and Commerce, as with so many flowers and wild ornaments grave and gay. I will not make more account of them. I believe in Eternity. I can find Greece, Asia, Italy, Spain, and the Islands, — the genius and creative principle of each and of all eras in my own mind.

We are always coming up with the emphatic facts of history in our private experience, and verifying them here. All history becomes subjective; in other words, there is properly no History; only Biography. Every mind must know the whole lesson for itself — must go over the whole ground. What it does not see, what it does not live, it will not know. What the former age has epitomized into a formula or rule for manipular convenience, it will lose all the good of verifying for itself, by means of the wall of that rule. Somewhere, sometime, it will demand and find compensation for that loss by doing the work itself. Ferguson discovered many things in astronomy which had long been known. The better for him.

History must be this or it is nothing. Every law which the state enacts, indicates a fact in human nature; that is all. We must in ourselves see the necessary reason of every fact, — see how it could and must be. So stand before every public and private work; before an oration of Burke, before a victory of Napoleon, before a martyrdom of Sir Thomas More, of Sidney, of Marmaduke Robinson, before a French Reign of Terror, and a Salem hanging of witches, before a fanatic Revival, and the Animal Magnetism in Paris, or in Providence. We assume that we under like influence should be alike affected, and should achieve the like; and we aim to master intellectually the steps, and reach the same height or the same degradation that our fellow, our proxy has done.

All inquiry into antiquity, — all curiosity respecting the pyramids, the excavated cities, Stonehenge, the Ohio Circles, Mexico, Memphis, — is the desire to do away this wild, savage and preposterous There or Then, and introduce in its place the Here and the Now. Belzoni digs and measures in the mummy-pits and pyramids of Thebes, until he can see the end of the difference between the monstrous work and himself. When he has satisfied himself, in general and in detail, that it was made by such a person as he, so armed and so motived, and to ends to which he himself should also have worked, the problem is solved; his thought lives along the whole line of temples and sphinxes and catacombs, passes through them all with satisfaction, and they live again to the mind, or are *now*.

A Gothic cathedral affirms that it was done by us, and not done by us. Surely it was by man, but we find it not in our man. But we apply ourselves to the history of its production. We put ourselves into the place and state of the builder. We remember the forest dwellers, the first temples, the adherence to the first type, and the decoration of it as the wealth of the nation increased; the value which is given to wood by carving led to the carving over the whole mountain of stone of a cathedral. When we have gone

7

through this process, and added thereto the Catholic Church, its cross, its music, its processions, its Saints' days and image-worship, we have, as it were, been the man that made the minster; we have seen how it could and must be. We have the sufficient reason.

The difference between men is in their principle of association. Some men classify objects by color and size and other accidents of appearance; others by intrinsic likeness, or by the relation of cause and effect. The progress of the intellect is to the clearer vision of causes, which neglects surface differences. To the poet, to the philosopher, to the saint, all things are friendly and sacred, all events profitable, all days holy, all men divine. For the eye is fastened on the life, and slights the circumstance. Every chemical substance, every plant, every animal in its growth, teaches the unity of cause, the variety of appearance.

Upborne and surrounded as we are by this all-creating nature, soft and fluid as a cloud or the air, why should we be such hard pedants, and magnify a few forms? Why should we make account of time, or of magnitude, or of figure? The soul knows them not, and genius, obeying its law, knows how to play with them as a young child plays with greybeards and in churches. Genius studies the causal thought, and far back in the womb of things, sees the rays parting from one orb, that diverge ere they fall by infinite diameters. Genius watches the monad through all his masks as he performs the metempsychosis of nature. Genius detects through the fly, through the caterpillar, through the grub, through the egg, the constant individual; through countless individuals the fixed species; through many species the genus; through all genera the steadfast type; through all the kingdoms of organized life the eternal unity. Nature is a mutable cloud, which is always and never the same. She casts the same thought into troops of forms, as a poet makes twenty fables with one moral. Through the bruteness and toughness of matter, a subtle spirit bends all things to its own will. The adamant streams into soft but precise form before it, and, whilst I look at it, its outline and texture are changed again. Nothing is so fleeting as form; yet never does it quite deny itself. In man we still trace the remains or hints of all that we esteem badges of servitude in the lower races, yet in him they enhance his nobleness and grace; as Io, in Æschylus, transformed to a cow, offends the imagination, but how changed when as Isis in Egypt she meets Osiris-Jove, a beautiful woman, with nothing of the metamorphosis left but the lunar horns as the splendid ornament of her brows.

The identity of history is equally intrinsic, the diversity equally obvious. There is at the surface infinite variety of things; at the centre there is simplicity of cause. How many are the acts of one man in which we recognize the same character. Observe the sources of our information in respect to the Greek genius. We have the *civil history* of that people, as Herodotus, Thucydides, Xenophon, and Plutarch have given it — a very sufficient account of what manner of persons they were, and what they did. We have the same national mind expressed for us again in their *litera-ture*, in epic and lyric poems, drama, and philosophy; a very complete form. Then we have it once more in their *architecture*, a beauty as of temperance itself, limited to the straight line and the square, — a builded geometry. Then we have it once again in *sculpture*, the "tongue on the balance of expression," a multitude of forms in the utmost freedom of action, and never transgressing the ideal serenity; like votaries performing some religious dance before the gods, and, though in convulsive pain or mortal combat, never daring to break the figure and decorum of their dance. Thus, of the genius of one remarkable people, we have a fourfold representation: and to the senses what more unlike than an ode of Pindar, a marble Centaur, the Peristyle of the Parthenon, and the last actions of Phocion?

Every one must have observed faces and forms which, without any resembling feature, make a like impression on the beholder. A particular picture or copy of verses, if it do not awaken the same train of images, will yet superinduce the same sentiment as some wild mountain walk, although the resemblance is nowise obvious to the senses, but is occult and out of the reach of the understand-ing. Nature is an endless combination and repetition of a very few laws. She hums the old well known air through innumerable variations.

9

Essay I

Nature is full of a sublime family likeness throughout her works; and delights in startling us with resemblances in the most unexpected quarters. I have seen the head of an old sachem of the forest, which at once reminded the eye of a bald mountain summit, and the furrows of the brow suggested the strata of the rock. There are men whose manners have the same essential splendor as the simple and awful sculpture on the friezes of the Parthenon, and the remains of the earliest Greek art. And there are compositions of the same strain to be found in the books of all ages. What is Guido's Rospigliosi Aurora but a morning thought, as the horses in it are only a morning cloud. If any one will but take pains to observe the variety of actions to which he is equally inclined in certain moods of mind, and those to which he is averse, he will see how deep is the chain of affinity.

A painter told me that nobody could draw a tree without in some sort becoming a tree; or draw a child by studying the outlines of its form merely, — but, by watching for a time his motions and plays, the painter enters into his nature, and can then draw him at will in every attitude. So Roos "entered into the inmost nature of a sheep." I knew a draughtsman employed in a public survey, who found that he could not sketch the rocks until their geological structure was first explained to him. In a certain state of thought is the common origin of very diverse works. It is the spirit and not the fact that is identical. By a deeper apprehension, and not primarily by a painful acquisition of many manual skills, the artist attains the power of awakening other souls to a given activity.

It has been said that "common souls pay with what they do; nobler souls with that which they are." And why? Because a profound nature awakens in us by its actions and words, by its very looks and manners, the same power and beauty that a gallery of sculpture, or of pictures, addresses.

Civil and natural history, the history of art and of literature, must be explained from individual history, or must remain words. There is nothing but is related to us, nothing that does not interest us — kingdom, college, tree, horse, or iron shoe, the roots of all things are in man. Santa Croce and the Dome of St. Peter's are lame copies after a divine model. Strasburg Cathedral is a material counterpart of the soul of Erwin of Steinbach. The true poem is the poet's mind; the true ship is the ship-builder. In the man, could we lay him open, we should see the reason for the last flourish and tendril of his work, as every spine and tint in the sea-shell preëxist in the secreting organs of the fish. The whole of heraldry and of chivalry is in courtesy. A man of fine manners shall pronounce your name with all the ornament that titles of nobility could ever add.

The trivial experience of every day is always verifying some old prediction to us, and converting into things the words and signs which we had heard and seen without heed. A lady, with whom I was riding in the forest, said to me, that the woods always seemed to her *to wait*, as if the genii who inhabit them suspended their deeds until the wayfarer has passed onward: a thought which poetry has celebrated in the dance of the fairies which breaks off on the approach of human feet. The man who has seen the rising moon break out of the clouds at midnight, has been present like an archangel at the creation of light and of the world. I remember one summer day, in the fields, my companion pointed out to me a broad cloud, which might extend a quarter of a mile parallel to the horizon, quite accurately in the form of a cherub as painted over churches, — a round block in the centre which it was easy to animate with eyes and mouth, supported on either side by wide-stretched symmetrical wings. What appears once in the atmosphere may appear often, and it was undoubtedly the archetype of that familiar ornament. I have seen in the sky a chain of summer lightning which at once showed to me that the Greeks drew from nature when they painted the thunderbolt in the hand of Jove. I have seen a snow-drift along the sides of the stone wall which obviously gave the idea of the common architectural scroll to abut a tower.

By surrounding ourselves with the original circumstances, we invent anew the orders and the ornaments of architecture, as we see how each people merely decorated its primitive abodes. The Doric temple preserves the semblance of the wooden cabin in which the Dorian dwelt. The Chinese pagoda is plainly a Tartar

tent. The Indian and Egyptian temples still betray the mounds
and subterranean houses of their forefathers. "The custom of
making houses and tombs in the living rock," (says Heeren, in his
Researches on the Ethiopians) "determined very naturally the
principal character of the Nubian Egyptian architecture to the
colossal form which it assumed. In these caverns already prepared
by nature, the eye was accustomed to dwell on huge shapes and
masses, so that when art came to the assistance of nature, it could
not move on a small scale without degrading itself. What would
statues of the usual size, or neat porches and wings have been, associated with those gigantic halls before which only Colossi could
sit as watchmen, or lean on the pillars of the interior?"

The Gothic church plainly originated in a rude adaptation of
the forest trees with all their boughs to a festal or solemn arcade,
as the bands about the cleft pillars still indicate the green withes
that tied them. No one can walk in a road cut through pine
woods, without being struck with the architectural appearance
of the grove, especially in winter, when the bareness of all other
trees shows the low arch of the Saxons. In the woods in a winter
afternoon one will see as readily the origin of the stained glass
window with which the Gothic cathedrals are adorned, in the
colors of the western sky seen through the bare and crossing
branches of the forest. Nor can any lover of nature enter the old
piles of Oxford and the English cathedrals without feeling that the
forest overpowered the mind of the builder, and that his chisel,
his saw, and plane still reproduced its ferns, its spikes of flowers,
its locust, elm, oak, pine, fir, and spruce.

The Gothic cathedral is a blossoming in stone subdued by the
insatiable demand of harmony in man. The mountain of granite
blooms into an eternal flower with the lightness and delicate finish
as well as the aerial proportions and perspective of vegetable
beauty.

In like manner all public facts are to be individualized, all
private facts are to be generalized. Then at once History becomes
fluid and true, and Biography deep and sublime. As the Persian
imitated in the slender shafts and capitals of his architecture the
stem and flower of the lotus and palm, so the Persian Court in its
magnificent era never gave over the Nomadism of its barbarous

tribes, but travelled from Ecbatana, where the spring was spent, to Susa in summer, and to Babylon for the winter.

In the early history of Asia and Africa, Nomadism and Agriculture are the two antagonist facts. The geography of Asia and of Africa necessitated a nomadic life. But the nomads were the terror of all those whom the soil or the advantages of a market had induced to build towns. Agriculture therefore was a religious injunction because of the perils of the state from nomadism. And in these late and civil countries of England and America, these propensities still fight out the old battle in the nation and in the individual. The nomads of Africa were constrained to wander by the attacks of the gadfly, which drives the cattle mad, and so compels the tribe to emigrate in the rainy season and to drive off the cattle to the higher sandy regions. The nomads of Asia follow the pasturage from month to month. In America and Europe the nomadism is of trade and curiosity; a progress certainly from the gadfly of Astaboras to the Anglo and Italo-mania of Boston Bay. Sacred cities, to which a periodical religious pilgrimage was enjoined, or stringent laws and customs, tending to invigorate the national bond, were the check on the old rovers; and the cumulative values of long residence are the restraints on the itineracy of the present day. The antagonism of the two tendencies is not less active in individuals, as the love of adventure or the love of repose happens to predominate. A man of rude health and flowing spirits has the faculty of rapid domestication, lives in his wagon, and roams through all latitudes as easily as a Calmuc. At sea, or in the forest, or in the snow, he sleeps as warm, dines with as good appetite, and associates as happily, as beside his own chimneys. Or perhaps his facility is deeper seated, in the increased range of his faculties of observation, which yield him points of interest wherever fresh objects meet his eyes. The pastoral nations were needy and hungry to desperation; and this intellectual nomadism, in its excess, bankrupts the mind, through the dissipation of power on a miscellany of objects. The home-keeping wit, on the other hand, is that continence or content which finds all the elements of life in its own soil; and which has its own perils of monotony and deterioration, if not stimulated by foreign infusions.

Every thing the individual sees without him, corresponds to his states of mind, and every thing is in turn intelligible to him, as his onward thinking leads him into the truth to which that fact or series belongs.

The primeval world, — the Fore-World, as the Germans say, — I can dive to it in myself as well as grope for it with researching fingers in catacombs, libraries, and the broken reliefs and torsos of ruined villas.

What is the foundation of that interest all men feel in Greek history, letters, art and poetry, in all its periods, from the heroic or Homeric age, down to the domestic life of the Athenians and Spartans, four or five centuries later? What but this, that every man passes personally through a Grecian period. The Grecian state is the era of the bodily nature, the perfection of the senses, — of the spiritual nature unfolded in strict unity with the body. In it existed those human forms which supplied the sculptor with his models of Hercules, Phœbus, and Jove; not like the forms abounding in the streets of modern cities, wherein the face is a confused blur of features, but composed of incorrupt, sharply defined and symmetrical features, whose eye-sockets are so formed that it would be impossible for such eyes to squint, and take furtive glances on this side and on that, but they must turn the whole head. The manners of that period are plain and fierce. The reverence exhibited is for personal qualities, courage, address, self-command, justice, strength, swiftness, a loud voice, a broad chest. Luxury and elegance are not known. A sparse population and want make every man his own valet, cook, butcher, and soldier, and the habit of supplying his own needs educates the body to wonderful performances. Such are the Agamemnon and Diomed of Homer, and not far different is the picture Xenophon gives of himself and his compatriots in the Retreat of the Ten Thousand. "After the army had crossed the river Teleboas in Armenia, there fell much snow, and the troops lay miserably on the ground covered with it. But Xenophon arose naked, and taking an axe, began to split wood; whereupon others rose and did the like." Throughout his army exists a boundless liberty of speech. They quarrel for plunder, they wrangle with the generals on each new order, and Xenophon is as sharp-tongued as any, and sharper-tongued than most, and so gives as good as he gets. Who does not see that this is a gang of great boys with such a code of honor and such lax discipline as great boys have?

The costly charm of the ancient tragedy and indeed of all the old literature is, that the persons speak simply, — speak as persons who have great good sense without knowing it, before yet the reflective habit has become the predominant habit of the mind. Our admiration of the antique is not admiration of the old, but of the natural. The Greeks are not reflective, but perfect in their senses and in their health, with the finest physical organization in the world. Adults acted with the simplicity and grace of children. They made vases, tragedies, and statues such as healthy senses should — that is, in good taste. Such things have continued to be made in all ages, and are now, wherever a healthy physique exists; but, as a class, from their superior organization, they have surpassed all. They combine the energy of manhood with the engaging unconsciousness of childhood. The attraction of these manners is, that they belong to man, and are known to every man in virtue of his being once a child; besides that there are always individuals who retain these characteristics. A person of childlike genius and inborn energy is still a Greek, and revives our love of the muse of Hellas. I admire the love of nature in the Philoctetes. In reading those fine apostrophes to sleep, to the stars, rocks, mountains, and waves, I feel time passing away as an ebbing sea. I feel the eternity of man, the identity of his thought. The Greek had, it seems, the same fellow beings as I. The sun and moon, water and fire, met his heart precisely as they meet mine. Then the vaunted distinction between Greek and English, between Classic and Romantic schools seems superficial and pedantic. When a thought of Plato becomes a thought to me, — when a truth that fired the soul of Pindar fires mine, time is no more. When I feel that we two meet in a perception, that our two souls are tinged with the same hue, and do, as it were, run into one, why should I measure degrees of latitude, why should I count Egyptian years?

The student interprets the age of chivalry by his own age of chivalry, and the days of maritime adventure and circumnavigation by quite parallel miniature experiences of his own. To the sacred history of the world, he has the same key. When the voice of a prophet out of the deeps of antiquity merely echoes to him a sentiment of his infancy, a prayer of his youth, he then pierces to the truth through all the confusion of tradition and the caricature of institutions.

Rare, extravagant spirits come by us at intervals, who disclose to us new facts in nature. I see that men of God have, from time to time, walked among men and made their commission felt in the heart and soul of the commonest hearer. Hence, evidently, the tripod, the priest, the priestess inspired by the divine afflatus.

Jesus astonishes and overpowers sensual people. They cannot unite him to history or reconcile him with themselves. As they come to revere their intuitions and aspire to live holily, their own piety explains every fact, every word.

How easily these old worships of Moses, of Zoroaster, of Menu, of Socrates, domesticate themselves in the mind. I cannot find any antiquity in them. They are mine as much as theirs.

I have seen the first monks and anchorets without crossing seas or centuries. More than once some individual has appeared to me with such negligence of labor and such commanding contemplation, a haughty beneficiary, begging in the name of God, as made good to the nineteenth century Simeon the Stylite, the Thebais, and the first Capuchins.

The priestcraft of the East and West, of the Magian, Brahmin, Druid and Inca, is expounded in the individual's private life. The cramping influence of a hard formalist on a young child in repressing his spirits and courage, paralyzing the understanding, and that without producing indignation, but only fear and obedience, and even much sympathy with the tyranny, — is a familiar fact explained to the child when he becomes a man, only by seeing that the oppressor of his youth is himself a child tyrannized over by those names and words and forms, of whose influence he was merely the organ to the youth. The fact teaches him how Belus was worshipped, and how the pyramids were built, better than the discovery by Champollion of the names of all the workmen and the cost of every tile. He finds Assyria and the Mounds of Cholula at his door, and himself has laid the courses.

Again, in that protest which each considerate person makes against the superstition of his times, he repeats step for step the part of old reformers, and in the search after truth finds like them new perils to virtue. He learns again what moral vigor is needed to supply the girdle of a superstition. A great licentiousness treads on the heels of a reformation. How many times in the history of the world has the Luther of the day had to lament the decay of piety in his own household. "Doctor," said his wife to Martin Luther one day, "how is it that whilst subject to papacy, we prayed so often and with such fervor, whilst now we pray with the utmost coldness and very seldom?"

The advancing man discovers how deep a property he has in literature, — in all fable as well as in all history. He finds that the poet was no odd fellow who described strange and impossible situations, but that universal man wrote by his pen a confession true for one and true for all. His own secret biography he finds in lines wonderfully intelligible to him, dotted down before he was born. One after another he comes up in his private adventures with every fable of Æsop, of Homer, of Hafiz, of Ariosto, of Chaucer, of Scott, and verifies them with his own head and hands.

The beautiful fables of the Greeks, being proper creations of the Imagination and not of the Fancy, are universal verities. What a range of meanings and what perpetual pertinence has the story of Prometheus! Beside its primary value as the first chapter of the history of Europe, (the mythology thinly veiling authentic facts, the invention of the mechanic arts, and the migration of colonies,) it gives the history of religion with some closeness to the faith of later ages. Prometheus is the Jesus of the old mythology. He is the friend of man; stands between the unjust 'justice' of the Eternal Father, and the race of mortals; and readily suffers all things on their account. But where it departs from the Calvinistic Christianity, and exhibits him as the defier of Jove, it represents a state of mind which readily appears wherever the doctrine of Theism is taught in a crude, objective form, and which seems the self-defence of man against this untruth, namely, a discontent with the believed fact that a God exists, and a feeling that the obligation of reverence is onerous. It would steal, if it could, the fire of the Creator, and live apart from him, and independent of him. The Prometheus Vinctus is the romance of skepticism. Not less true to all time are the details of that stately apologue. Apollo kept the flocks of Admetus, said the poets. When the gods come among men, they are not known. Jesus was not; Socrates and Shakspeare were not. Antæus was suffocated by the gripe of Hercules, but every time he touched his mother earth, his strength was renewed. Man is the broken giant, and in all his weakness, both his body and his mind are invigorated by habits of conversation with nature. The power of music, the power of poetry to unfix, and as it were, clap wings to solid nature, interprets the riddle of Orpheus. The philosophical perception of identity through endless mutations of form, makes him know the Proteus. What else am I who laughed or wept yesterday, who slept last night like a corpse, and this morning stood and ran? And what see I on any side but the transmigrations of Proteus? I can symbolize my thought by using the name of any creature, of any fact, because every creature is man agent or patient. Tantalus is but a name for you and me. Tantalus means the impossibility of drinking the waters of thought which are always gleaming and waving within sight of the soul. The transmigration of souls is no fable. I would it were; but men and women are only half human. Every animal of the barn-yard, the field and the forest, of the earth and of the waters that are under the earth, has contrived to get a footing and to leave the print of its features and form in some one or other of these upright, heaven-facing speakers. Ah! brother, stop the ebb of thy soul — ebbing downward into the forms into whose habits thou hast now for many years slid. As near and proper to us is also that old fable of the Sphinx, who was said to sit in the roadside and put riddles to every passenger. If the man could not answer she swallowed him alive. If he could solve the riddle, the Sphinx was slain. What is our life but an endless flight of winged facts or events! In splendid variety these changes come, all putting questions to the human spirit. Those men who cannot answer by a superior wisdom these facts or questions of time, serve them. Facts encumber them, tyrannize over them, and make the men of routine, the men of *sense*, in whom a

18

literal obedience to facts has extinguished every spark of that light by which man is truly man. But if the man is true to his better instincts or sentiments, and refuses the dominion of facts, as one that comes of a higher race, remains fast by the soul and sees the principle, then the facts fall aptly and supple into their places; they know their master, and the meanest of them glorifies him.

See in Goethe's Helena the same desire that every word should be a thing. These figures, he would say, these Chirons, Griffins, Phorkyas, Helen, and Leda, are somewhat, and do exert a specific influence on the mind. So far then are they eternal entities, as real to-day as in the first Olympiad. Much revolving them, he writes out freely his humor, and gives them body to his own imagination. And although that poem be as vague and fantastic as a dream, yet is it much more attractive than the more regular dramatic pieces of the same author, for the reason that it operates a wonderful relief to the mind from the routine of customary images, — awakens the reader's invention and fancy by the wild freedom of the design, and by the unceasing succession of brisk shocks of surprise.

The universal nature, too strong for the petty nature of the bard, sits on his neck and writes through his hand; so that when he seems to vent a mere caprice and wild romance, the issue is an exact allegory. Hence Plato said that "poets utter great and wise things which they do not themselves understand." All the fictions of the Middle Age explain themselves as a masked or frolic expression of that which in grave earnest the mind of that period toiled to achieve. Magic, and all that is ascribed to it, is a deep presentiment of the powers of science. The shoes of swiftness, the sword of sharpness, the power of subduing the elements, of using the secret virtues of minerals, of understanding the voices of birds, are the obscure efforts of the mind in a right direction. The preternatural prowess of the hero, the gift of perpetual youth, and the like, are alike the endeavor of the human spirit "to bend the shows of things to the desires of the mind."

In Perceforest and Amadis de Gaul, a garland and a rose bloom on the head of her who is faithful, and fade on the brow of the inconstant. In the story of the Boy and the Mantle, even a mature reader may be surprised with a glow of virtuous pleasure at the triumph of the gentle Genelas; and indeed, all the postulates of elfin annals, — that the Fairies do not like to be named; that their gifts are capricious and not to be trusted; that who seeks a treasure must not speak; and the like, — I find true in Concord, however they might be in Cornwall or Bretagne.

Is it otherwise in the newest romance? I read the Bride of Lammermoor. Sir William Ashton is a mask for a vulgar temptation, Ravenswood Castle a fine name for proud poverty, and the foreign mission of state only a Bunyan disguise for honest industry. We may all shoot a wild bull that would toss the good and beautiful, by fighting down the unjust and sensual. Lucy Ashton is another name for fidelity, which is always beautiful and always liable to calamity in this world.

But along with the civil and metaphysical history of man, another history goes daily forward — that of the external world, — in which he is not less strictly implicated. He is the compend of time: he is also the correlative of nature. His power consists in the multitude of his affinities, in the fact that his life is intertwined with the whole chain of organic and inorganic being. In old Rome the public roads beginning at the Forum proceeded north, south, east, west, to the centre of every province of the empire, making each market-town of Persia, Spain and Britain, pervious to the soldiers of the capital: so out of the human heart go, as it were, highways to the heart of every object in nature, to reduce it under the dominion of man. A man is a bundle of relations, a knot of roots, whose flower and fruitage is the world. His faculties refer to natures out of him, and predict the world he is to inhabit, as the fins of the fish foreshow that water exists, or the wings of an eagle in the egg presuppose air. He cannot live without a world. Put Napoleon in an island prison, let his faculties find no men to act on, no Alps to climb, no stake to play for, and he would beat the air and appear stupid. Transport him to large countries, dense population, complex interests, and antagonist power, and you shall see that the man Napoleon, bounded, that is, by such a profile and outline, is not the virtual Napoleon. This is but Talbot's shadow;

History

"His substance is not here:
For what you see is but the smallest part,
And least proportion of humanity;
But were the whole frame here,
It is of such a spacious, lofty pitch,
Your roof were not sufficient to contain it."

Henry VI.

Columbus needs a planet to shape his course upon. Newton and Laplace need myriads of ages and thick-strown celestial areas. One may say a gravitating solar system is already prophesied in the nature of Newton's mind. Not less does the brain of Davy or of Gay-Lussac, from childhood exploring the affinities and repulsions of particles, anticipate the laws of organization. Does not the eye of the human embryo predict the light? the ear of Handel predict the witchcraft of harmonic sound? Do not the constructive fingers of Watt, Fulton, Whittemore, Arkwright predict the fusible, hard, and temperable texture of metals, the properties of stone, water and wood? Do not the lovely attributes of the maiden child predict the refinements and decorations of civil society? Here also we are reminded of the action of man on man. A mind might ponder its thought for ages, and not gain so much self-knowledge as the passion of love shall teach it in a day. Who knows himself before he has been thrilled with indignation at an outrage, or has heard an eloquent tongue, or has shared the throb of thousands in a national exultation or alarm? No man can antedate his experience, or guess what faculty or feeling a new object shall unlock, any more than he can draw to-day the face of a person whom he shall see to-morrow for the first time.

I will not now go behind the general statement to explore the reason of this correspondency. Let it suffice that in the light of these two facts, namely, that the mind is One, and that nature is its correlative, history is to be read and written.

Thus in all ways does the soul concentrate and reproduce its treasures for each pupil. He, too, shall pass through the whole cycle of experience. He shall collect into a focus the rays of

nature.   History no longer shall be a dull book.   It shall walk
incarnate in every just and wise man.   You shall not tell me by
languages and titles a catalogue of the volumes you have read.
You shall make me feel what periods you have lived.   A man
shall be the Temple of Fame.   He shall walk, as the poets have
described that goddess, in a robe painted all over with wonderful
events and experiences; — his own form and features by their
exalted intelligence shall be that variegated vest.   I shall find in
him the Foreworld; in his childhood the Age of Gold; the Apples
of Knowledge; the Argonautic Expedition; the calling of Abraham; the building of the Temple; the Advent of Christ; Dark
Ages; the Revival of Letters; the Reformation; the discovery of
new lands, the opening of new sciences, and new regions in man.
He shall be the priest of Pan, and bring with him into humble
cottages the blessing of the morning stars and all the recorded
benefits of heaven and earth.

Is there somewhat overweening in this claim?   Then I reject
all I have written, for what is the use of pretending to know what
we know not?   But it is the fault of our rhetoric that we cannot
strongly state one fact without seeming to belie some other.   I
hold our actual knowledge very cheap.   Hear the rats in the wall,
see the lizard on the fence, the fungus under foot, the lichen on
the log.   What do I know sympathetically, morally, of either of
these worlds of life?   As old as the Caucasian man, — perhaps
older, — these creatures have kept their counsel beside him, and
there is no record of any word or sign that has passed from one
to the other.   What connection do the books show between the
fifty or sixty chemical elements, and the historical eras?   Nay,
what does history yet record of the metaphysical annals of man?
What light does it shed on those mysteries which we hide under
the names Death and Immortality?   Yet every history should be
written in a wisdom which divined the range of our affinities and
looked at facts as symbols.   I am ashamed to see what a shallow
village tale our so-called History is.   How many times we must
say Rome, and Paris, and Constantinople.   What does Rome
know of rat and lizard?   What are Olympiads and Consulates to
these neighboring systems of being?   Nay, what food or experience

or succor have they for the Esquimaux seal-hunter, for the Kanàka in his canoe, for the fisherman, the stevedore, the porter?

Broader and deeper we must write our annals — from an ethical reformation, from an influx of the ever new, ever sanative conscience, — if we would truelier express our central and wide-related nature, instead of this old chronology of selfishness and pride to which we have too long lent our eyes. Already that day exists for us, shines in on us at unawares, but the path of science and of letters is not the way into nature. The idiot, the Indian, the child, and unschooled farmer's boy, stand nearer to the light by which nature is to be read, than the dissector or the antiquary.

SELF-RELIANCE

"Ne te quæsiveris extra."

"Man is his own star; and the soul that can
Render an honest and a perfect man,
Commands all light, all influence, all fate;
Nothing to him falls early or too late.
Our acts our angels are, or good or ill,
Our fatal shadows that walk by us still."

Epilogue to Beaumont and Fletcher's
Honest Man's Fortune.

Cast the bantling on the rocks,
Suckle him with the she-wolf's teat;
Wintered with the hawk and fox,
Power and speed be hands and feet.

ESSAY II

SELF-RELIANCE

I read the other day some verses written by an eminent painter which were original and not conventional. The soul always hears an admonition in such lines, let the subject be what it may. The sentiment they instil is of more value than any thought they may contain. To believe your own thought, to believe that what is true for you in your private heart, is true for all men, — that is genius. Speak your latent conviction and it shall be the universal sense; for the inmost in due time becomes the outmost, — and our first thought is rendered back to us by the trumpets of the Last Judgment. Familiar as the voice of the mind is to each, the highest merit we ascribe to Moses, Plato, and Milton, is that they set at naught books and traditions, and spoke not what men but what they thought. A man should learn to detect and watch that gleam of light which flashes across his mind from within, more than the lustre of the firmament of bards and sages. Yet he dismisses without notice his thought, because it is his. In every work of genius we recognize our own rejected thoughts: they come back to us with a certain alienated majesty. Great works of art have no more affecting lesson for us than this. They teach us to abide by our spontaneous impression with good-humored inflexibility then most when the whole cry of voices is on the other side. Else, to-morrow a stranger will say with masterly good sense precisely what we have thought and felt all the time, and we shall be forced to take with shame our own opinion from another.

There is a time in every man's education when he arrives at the conviction that envy is ignorance; that imitation is suicide; that he must take himself for better, for worse, as his portion; that though the wide universe is full of good, no kernel of nourishing corn can come to him but through his toil bestowed on that plot of ground which is given to him to till. The power which resides in him is new in nature, and none but he knows what that is which he can do, nor does he know until he has tried. Not for nothing one face, one character, one fact makes much impression on him, and another none. This sculpture in the memory is not without preëstablished harmony. The eye was placed where one ray should fall, that it might testify of that particular ray. We but half express ourselves, and are ashamed of that divine idea which each of us represents. It may be safely trusted as proportionate and of good issues, so it be faithfully imparted, but God will not have his work made manifest by cowards. A man is relieved and gay when he has put his heart into his work and done his best; but what he has said or done otherwise, shall give him no peace. It is a deliverance which does not deliver. In the attempt his genius deserts him; no muse befriends; no invention, no hope.

Trust thyself: every heart vibrates to that iron string. Accept the place the divine Providence has found for you; the society of your contemporaries, the connexion of events. Great men have always done so and confided themselves childlike to the genius of their age, betraying their perception that the absolutely trustworthy was seated at their heart, working through their hands, predominating in all their being. And we are now men, and must accept in the highest mind the same transcendent destiny; and not minors and invalids in a protected corner, not cowards fleeing before a revolution, but guides, redeemers, and benefactors, obeying the Almighty effort, and advancing on Chaos and the Dark.

What pretty oracles nature yields us on this text in the face and behavior of children, babes and even brutes. That divided and rebel mind, that distrust of a sentiment because our arithmetic has computed the strength and means opposed to our purpose, these have not. Their mind being whole, their eye is as yet unconquered, and when we look in their faces, we are disconcerted. Infancy conforms to nobody: all conform to it, so that one babe commonly makes four or five out of the adults who prattle and play to it. So God has armed youth and puberty and manhood no less with its own piquancy and charm, and made it enviable and gracious and its claims not to be put by, if it will stand by itself. Do not think the youth has no force because he cannot speak to you and me. Hark! in the next room his voice is sufficiently clear and emphatic. It seems he knows how to speak to his contemporaries. Bashful or bold, then, he will know how to make us seniors very unnecessary.

The nonchalance of boys who are sure of a dinner, and would disdain as much as a lord to do or say aught to conciliate one, is the healthy attitude of human nature. A boy is in the parlour what the pit is in the playhouse; independent, irresponsible, looking out from his corner on such people and facts as pass by, he tries and sentences them on their merits, in the swift summary way of boys, as good, bad, interesting, silly, eloquent, troublesome. He cumbers himself never about consequences, about interests: he gives an independent, genuine verdict. You must court him: he does not court you. But the man is, as it were, clapped into jail by his consciousness. As soon as he has once acted or spoken with eclat, he is a committed person, watched by the sympathy or the hatred of hundreds whose affections must now enter into his account. There is no Lethe for this. Ah, that he could pass again into his neutrality! Who can thus avoid all pledges, and having observed, observe again from the same unaffected, unbiassed, unbribable, unaffrighted innocence, must always be formidable. He would utter opinions on all passing affairs, which being seen to be not private but necessary, would sink like darts into the ear of men, and put them in fear.

These are the voices which we hear in solitude, but they grow faint and inaudible as we enter into the world. Society everywhere is in conspiracy against the manhood of every one of its members. Society is a joint-stock company in which the members agree for the better securing of his bread to each shareholder, to surrender the liberty and culture of the eater. The virtue in most request is conformity. Self-reliance is its aversion. It loves not realities and creators, but names and customs.

Whoso would be a man must be a nonconformist. He who would gather immortal palms must not be hindered by the name of goodness, but must explore if it be goodness. Nothing is at last sacred but the integrity of your own mind. Absolve you to yourself, and you shall have the suffrage of the world. I remember an answer which when quite young I was prompted to make to a valued adviser who was wont to importune me with the dear old doctrines of the church. On my saying, What have I to do with the sacredness of traditions, if I live wholly from within? my friend suggested — "But these impulses may be from below, not from above." I replied, "They do not seem to me to be such; but if I am the Devil's child, I will live then from the Devil." No law can be sacred to me but that of my nature. Good and bad are but names very readily transferable to that or this; the only right is what is after my constitution, the only wrong what is against it. A man is to carry himself in the presence of all opposition as if every thing were titular and ephemeral but he. I am ashamed to think how easily we capitulate to badges and names, to large societies and dead institutions. Every decent and well-spoken individual affects and sways me more than is right. I ought to go upright and vital, and speak the rude truth in all ways. If malice and vanity wear the coat of philanthropy, shall that pass? If an angry bigot assumes this bountiful cause of Abolition, and comes to me with his last news from Barbadoes, why should I not say to him, 'Go love thy infant; love thy wood-chopper: be good-natured and modest: have that grace; and never varnish your hard, uncharitable ambition with this incredible tenderness for black folk a thousand miles off. Thy love afar is spite at home.' Rough and graceless would be such greeting, but truth is handsomer than the affectation of love. Your goodness must have some edge to it — else it is none. The doctrine of hatred must be preached as the counteraction of the doctrine of love when that pules and whines. I shun father and mother and wife and brother, when my genius calls me. I would write on the lintels of the door-post, *Whim*. I hope it is somewhat better than whim at last, but we cannot spend the day in explanation. Expect me not to show cause why I seek or why I exclude company. Then, again, do not tell me, as a good man did to-day, of my obligation to put all poor men in good situations. Are they *my* poor? I tell thee, thou foolish philanthropist, that I grudge the dollar, the dime, the cent I give to such men as do not belong to me and to whom I do not belong. There is a class of persons to whom by all spiritual affinity I am bought and sold; for them I will go to prison, if need be; but your miscellaneous popular charities; the education at college of fools; the building of meeting-houses to the vain end to which many now stand; alms to sots; and the thousandfold Relief Societies; — though I confess with shame I sometimes succumb and give the dollar, it is a wicked dollar which by and by I shall have the manhood to withhold.

Virtues are in the popular estimate rather the exception than the rule. There is the man *and* his virtues. Men do what is called a good action, as some piece of courage or charity, much as they would pay a fine in expiation of daily non-appearance on parade. Their works are done as an apology or extenuation of their living in the world, — as invalids and the insane pay a high board. Their virtues are penances. I do not wish to expiate, but to live. My life is for itself and not for a spectacle. I much prefer that it should be of a lower strain, so it be genuine and equal, than that it should be glittering and unsteady. I wish it to be sound and sweet, and not to need diet and bleeding. I ask primary evidence that you are a man, and refuse this appeal from the man to his actions. I know that for myself it makes no difference whether I do or forbear those actions which are reckoned excellent. I cannot consent to pay for a privilege where I have intrinsic right. Few and mean as my gifts may be, I actually am, and do not need for my own assurance or the assurance of my fellows any secondary testimony.

What I must do, is all that concerns me, not what the people think. This rule, equally arduous in actual and in intellectual life, may serve for the whole distinction between greatness and meanness. It is the harder, because you will always find those who think they know what is your duty better than you know it. It is easy in the world to live after the world's opinion; it is easy in solitude to live after our own; but the great man is he who in the midst of the crowd keeps with perfect sweetness the independence of solitude.

The objection to conforming to usages that have become dead to you, is, that it scatters your force. It loses your time and blurs the impression of your character. If you maintain a dead church, contribute to a dead Bible-Society, vote with a great party either for the Government or against it, spread your table like base housekeepers, — under all these screens, I have difficulty to detect the precise man you are. And, of course, so much force is withdrawn from your proper life. But do your work, and I shall know you. Do your work, and you shall reinforce yourself. A man must consider what a blindman's-buff is this game of conformity. If I know your sect, I anticipate your argument. I hear a preacher announce for his text and topic the expediency of one of the institutions of his church. Do I not know beforehand that not possibly can he say a new and spontaneous word? Do I not know that with all this ostentation of examining the grounds of the institution, he will do no such thing? Do I not know that he is pledged to himself not to look but at one side, — the permitted side, not as a man, but as a parish minister? He is a retained attorney, and these airs of the bench are the emptiest affectation. Well, most men have bound their eyes with one or another handkerchief, and attached themselves to some one of these communities of opinion. This conformity makes them not false in a few particulars, authors of a few lies, but false in all particulars. Their every truth is not quite true. Their two is not the real two, their four not the real four: so that every word they say chagrins us, and we know not where to begin to set them right. Meantime nature is not slow to equip us in the prison-uniform of the party to which we adhere. We come to wear one cut of face and figure, and acquire by degrees the gentlest asinine expression. There is a mortifying experience in particular which does not fail to wreak itself also in the general history; I mean "the foolish face of praise," the forced smile which we put on in company where we do not feel at ease in answer to conversation which does not interest us. The muscles, not spontaneously moved, but moved by a low usurping wilfulness, grow tight about the outline of the face with the most disagreeable sensation.

For nonconformity the world whips you with its displeasure. And therefore a man must know how to estimate a sour face. The bystanders look askance on him in the public street or in the friend's parlor. If this aversation had its origin in contempt and resistance like his own, he might well go home with a sad countenance; but the sour faces of the multitude, like their sweet faces, have no deep cause, but are put on and off as the wind blows, and a newspaper directs. Yet is the discontent of the multitude more formidable than that of the senate and the college. It is easy enough for a firm man who knows the world to brook the rage of the cultivated classes. Their rage is decorous and prudent, for they are timid as being very vulnerable themselves. But when to their feminine rage the indignation of the people is added, when the ignorant and the poor are aroused, when the unintelligent brute force that lies at the bottom of society is made to growl and mow, it needs the habit of magnanimity and religion to treat it godlike as a trifle of no concernment.

The other terror that scares us from self-trust is our consistency; a reverence for our past act or word, because the eyes of others have no other data for computing our orbit than our past acts, and we are loath to disappoint them.

But why should you keep your head over your shoulder? Why drag about this corpse of your memory, lest you contradict somewhat you have stated in this or that public place? Suppose you should contradict yourself; what then? It seems to be a rule of wisdom never to rely on your memory alone, scarcely even in acts of pure memory, but to bring the past for judgment into the thousand-eyed present, and live ever in a new day. In your metaphysics you have denied personality to the Deity: yet when the devout motions of the soul come, yield to them heart and life, though they should clothe God with shape and color. Leave your theory as Joseph his coat in the hand of the harlot, and flee.

A foolish consistency is the hobgoblin of little minds, adored by little statesmen and philosophers and divines. With consistency a great soul has simply nothing to do. He may as well concern himself with his shadow on the wall. Speak what you think now in hard words, and to-morrow speak what to-morrow thinks in hard words again, though it contradict every thing you said to-day. — 'Ah, so you shall be sure to be misunderstood.' — Is it so bad then

33

to be misunderstood? Pythagoras was misunderstood, and Socrates, and Jesus, and Luther, and Copernicus, and Galileo, and Newton, and every pure and wise spirit that ever took flesh. To be great is to be misunderstood.

I suppose no man can violate his nature. All the sallies of his will are rounded in by the law of his being as the inequalities of Andes and Himmaleh are insignificant in the curve of the sphere. Nor does it matter how you gauge and try him. A character is like an acrostic or Alexandrian stanza; — read it forward, backward, or across, it still spells the same thing. In this pleasing contrite wood-life which God allows me, let me record day by day my honest thought without prospect or retrospect, and, I cannot doubt, it will be found symmetrical, though I mean it not, and see it not. My book should smell of pines and resound with the hum of insects. The swallow over my window should interweave that thread or straw he carries in his bill into my web also. We pass for what we are. Character teaches above our wills. Men imagine that they communicate their virtue or vice only by overt actions and do not see that virtue or vice emit a breath every moment.

There will be an agreement in whatever variety of actions, so they be each honest and natural in their hour. For of one will, the actions will be harmonious, however unlike they seem. These varieties are lost sight of at a little distance, at a little height of thought. One tendency unites them all. The voyage of the best ship is a zigzag line of a hundred tacks. See the line from a sufficient distance, and it straightens itself to the average tendency. Your genuine action will explain itself and will explain your other genuine actions. Your conformity explains nothing. Act singly, and what you have already done singly, will justify you now. Greatness appeals to the future. If I can be firm enough to-day to do right and scorn eyes, I must have done so much right before, as to defend me now. Be it how it will, do right now. Always scorn appearances, and you always may. The force of character is cumulative. All the foregone days of virtue work their health into this. What makes the majesty of the heroes of the senate and the field, which so fills the imagination? The consciousness of a train of great days and victories behind. They shed an united light on the advancing actor. He is attended as by a visible escort of angels. That is it which throws thunder into Chatham's voice, and dignity into Washington's port, and America into Adams's eye. Honor is venerable to us because it is no ephemeris. It is always ancient virtue. We worship it to-day, because it is not of to-day. We love it and pay it homage, because it is not a trap for our love and homage, but is self-dependent, self-derived, and therefore of an old immaculate pedigree, even if shown in a young person.

I hope in these days we have heard the last of conformity and consistency. Let the words be gazetted and ridiculous henceforward. Instead of the gong for dinner, let us hear a whistle from the Spartan fife. Let us never bow and apologize more. A great man is coming to eat at my house. I do not wish to please him: I wish that he should wish to please me. I will stand here for humanity, and though I would make it kind, I would make it true. Let us affront and reprimand the smooth mediocrity and squalid contentment of the times, and hurl in the face of custom, and trade, and office, the fact which is the upshot of all history, that there is a great responsible Thinker and Actor working wherever a man works; that a true man belongs to no other time or place, but is the centre of things. Where he is, there is nature. He measures you, and all men, and all events. Ordinarily every body in society reminds us of somewhat else or of some other person. Character, reality, reminds you of nothing else; it takes place of the whole creation. The man must be so much that he must make all circumstances indifferent. Every true man is a cause, a country, and an age; requires infinite spaces and numbers and time fully to accomplish his design; — and posterity seem to follow his steps as a train of clients. A man Cæsar is born, and for ages after, we have a Roman Empire. Christ is born, and millions of minds so grow and cleave to his genius, that he is confounded with virtue and the possible of man. An institution is the lengthened shadow of one man; as, Monachism, of the Hermit Antony; the Reformation, of Luther; Quakerism, of Fox; Methodism, of Wesley; Abolition, of Clarkson. Scipio, Milton called "the height of Rome;" and all history resolves itself very easily into the biography of a few stout and earnest persons.

Let a man then know his worth, and keep things under his feet. Let him not peep or steal, or skulk up and down with the air of a charity-boy, a bastard, or an interloper, in the world which exists for him. But the man in the street finding no worth in himself which corresponds to the force which built a tower or sculptured a marble god, feels poor when he looks on these. To him a palace, a statue, or a costly book have an alien and forbidding air, much like a gay equipage, and seem to say like that, 'Who are you, sir?' Yet they all are his, suitors for his notice, petitioners to his faculties that they will come out and take possession. The picture waits for my verdict: it is not to command me, but I am to settle its claims to praise. That popular fable of the sot who was picked up dead drunk in the street, carried to the duke's house, washed and dressed and laid in the duke's bed, and, on his waking, treated with all obsequious ceremony like the duke, and assured that he had been insane, owes its popularity to the fact, that it symbolizes so well the state of man, who is in the world a sort of sot, but now and then wakes up, exercises his reason, and finds himself a true prince.

Our reading is mendicant and sycophantic. In history, our imagination plays us false. Kingdom and lordship, power and estate are a gaudier vocabulary than private John and Edward in a small house and common day's work: but the things of life are the same to both: the sum total of both is the same. Why all this deference to Alfred, and Scanderbeg, and Gustavus? Suppose they were virtuous: did they wear out virtue? As great a stake depends on your private act to-day, as followed their public and renowned steps. When private men shall act with original views, the lustre will be transferred from the actions of kings to those of gentlemen.

The world has been instructed by its kings, who have so magnetized the eyes of nations. It has been taught by this colossal symbol the mutual reverence that is due from man to man. The joyful loyalty with which men have everywhere suffered the king, the noble, or the great proprietor to walk among them by a law of his own, make his own scale of men and things, and reverse theirs, pay for benefits not with money but with honor, and represent the Law in his person, was the hieroglyphic by which they obscurely signified their consciousness of their own right and comeliness, the right of every man.

The magnetism which all original action exerts is explained when we inquire the reason of self-trust. Who is the Trustee? What is the aboriginal Self on which a universal reliance may be grounded? What is the nature and power of that science-baffling star, without parallax, without calculable elements, which shoots a ray of beauty even into trivial and impure actions, if the least mark of independence appear? The inquiry leads us to that source, at once the essence of genius, of virtue, and of life, which we call Spontaneity or Instinct. We denote this primary wisdom as Intuition, whilst all later teachings are tuitions. In that deep force, the last fact behind which analysis cannot go, all things find their common origin. For the sense of being which in calm hours rises, we know not how, in the soul, is not diverse from things, from space, from light, from time, from man, but one with them, and proceeds obviously from the same source whence their life and being also proceed. We first share the life by which things exist, and afterwards see them as appearances in nature, and forget that we have shared their cause. Here is the fountain of action and of thought. Here are the lungs of that inspiration which giveth man wisdom, and which cannot be denied without impiety and atheism. We lie in the lap of immense intelligence, which makes us receivers of its truth and organs of its activity. When we discern justice, when we discern truth, we do nothing of ourselves, but allow a passage to its beams. If we ask whence this comes, if we seek to pry into the soul that causes, all philosophy is at fault. Its presence or its absence is all we can affirm. Every man discriminates between the voluntary acts of his mind, and his involuntary perceptions, and knows that to his involuntary perceptions a perfect faith is due. He may err in the expression of them, but he knows that these things are so, like day and night, not to be disputed. My wilful actions and acquisitions are but roving; — the idlest reverie, the faintest native emotion, command

37

my curiosity and respect. Thoughtless people contradict as readily the statement of perceptions as of opinions, or rather much more readily; for, they do not distinguish between perception and notion. They fancy that I choose to see this or that thing. But perception is not whimsical, but fatal. If I see a trait, my children will see it after me, and in course of time, all mankind, — although it may chance that no one has seen it before me. For my perception of it is as much a fact as the sun.

The relations of the soul to the divine spirit are so pure that it is profane to seek to interpose helps. It must be that when God speaketh, he should communicate not one thing, but all things; should fill the world with his voice; should scatter forth light, nature, time, souls, from the centre of the present thought; and new date and new create the whole. Whenever a mind is simple, and receives a divine wisdom, old things pass away, — means, teachers, texts, temples fall; it lives now and absorbs past and future into the present hour. All things are made sacred by relation to it, — one as much as another. All things are dissolved to their centre by their cause, and in the universal miracle petty and particular miracles disappear. If, therefore, a man claims to know and speak of God, and carries you backward to the phraseology of some old mouldered nation in another country, in another world, believe him not. Is the acorn better than the oak which is its fulness and completion? Is the parent better than the child into whom he has cast his ripened being? Whence then this worship of the past? The centuries are conspirators against the sanity and authority of the soul. Time and space are but physiological colors which the eye makes, but the soul is light; where it is, is day; where it was, is night; and history is an impertinence and an injury, if it be anything more than a cheerful apologue or parable of my being and becoming.

Man is timid and apologetic; he is no longer upright; he dares not say 'I think,' 'I am,' but quotes some saint or sage. He is ashamed before the blade of grass or the blowing rose. These roses under my window make no reference to former roses or to better ones; they are for what they are; they exist with God to-day. There is no time to them. There is simply the rose; it is perfect in every moment of its existence. Before a leaf-bud has burst, its whole life acts; in the full-blown flower, there is no more; in the leafless root, there is no less. Its nature is satisfied, and it satisfies nature, in all moments alike. But man postpones or remembers; he does not live in the present, but with reverted eye laments the past, or, heedless of the riches that surround him, stands on tiptoe to foresee the future. He cannot be happy and strong until he too lives with nature in the present, above time.

This should be plain enough. Yet see what strong intellects dare not yet hear God himself, unless he speak the phraseology of I know not what David, or Jeremiah, or Paul. We shall not always set so great a price on a few texts, on a few lives. We are like children who repeat by rote the sentences of grandames and tutors, and, as they grow older, of the men of talents and character they chance to see, — painfully recollecting the exact words they spoke; afterwards, when they come into the point of view which those had who uttered these sayings, they understand them, and are willing to let the words go; for, at any time, they can use words as good, when occasion comes. If we live truly, we shall see truly. It is as easy for the strong man to be strong, as it is for the weak to be weak. When we have new perception, we shall gladly disburden the memory of its hoarded treasures as old rubbish. When a man lives with God, his voice shall be as sweet as the murmur of the brook and the rustle of the corn.

And now at last the highest truth on this subject remains unsaid; probably, cannot be said; for all that we say is the far off remembering of the intuition. That thought, by what I can now nearest approach to say it, is this. When good is near you, when you have life in yourself, it is not by any known or accustomed way; you shall not discern the foot-prints of any other; you shall not see the face of man; you shall not hear any name; — the way, the thought, the good shall be wholly strange and new. It shall exclude example and experience. You take the way from man, not to man. All persons that ever existed are its forgotten ministers. Fear and hope are alike beneath it. There is somewhat low even in hope. In the hour of vision, there is nothing that can be called gratitude, nor properly joy. The soul raised over passion beholds identity and eternal causation, perceives the self-existence of Truth and Right, and calms itself with knowing that all things go well. Vast spaces of nature, the Atlantic Ocean, the South Sea, — long intervals of time, years, centuries, — are of no account. This which I think and feel underlay every former state of life and circumstances, as it does underlie my present, and what is called life, and what is called death.

Life only avails, not the having lived. Power ceases in the instant of repose; it resides in the moment of transition from a past to a new state, in the shooting of the gulf, in the darting to an aim. This one fact the world hates, that the soul *becomes;* for, that forever degrades the past, turns all riches to poverty, all reputation to a shame, confounds the saint with the rogue, shoves Jesus and Judas equally aside. Why then do we prate of self-reliance? Inasmuch as the soul is present, there will be power not confident but agent. To talk of reliance, is a poor external way of speaking. Speak rather of that which relies, because it works and is. Who has more obedience than I, masters me, though he should not raise his finger. Round him I must revolve by the gravitation of spirits. We fancy it rhetoric when we speak of eminent virtue. We do not yet see that virtue is Height, and that a man or a company of men plastic and permeable to principles, by the law of nature must overpower and ride all cities, nations, kings, rich men, poets, who are not.

This is the ultimate fact which we so quickly reach on this as on every topic, the resolution of all into the ever blessed ONE. Self-existence is the attribute of the Supreme Cause, and it constitutes the measure of good by the degree in which it enters into all lower forms. All things real are so by so much virtue as they contain. Commerce, husbandry, hunting, whaling, war, eloquence, personal weight, are somewhat, and engage my respect as examples of its presence and impure action. I see the same law working in nature for conservation and growth. Power is in nature the essential measure of right. Nature suffers nothing to remain in her kingdoms which cannot help itself. The genesis and maturation of a planet, its poise and orbit, the bended tree recovering itself from the strong wind, the vital resources of every animal and vegetable, are demonstrations of the self-sufficing, and therefore self-relying soul.

Thus all concentrates; let us not rove; let us sit at home with the cause. Let us stun and astonish the intruding rabble of men and books and institutions by a simple declaration of the divine fact. Bid the invaders take the shoes from off their feet, for God is here within. Let our simplicity judge them, and our docility to our own law demonstrate the poverty of nature and fortune beside our native riches.

But now we are a mob. Man does not stand in awe of man, nor is his genius admonished to stay at home, to put itself in communication with the internal ocean, but it goes abroad to beg a cup of water of the urns of other men. We must go alone. I like the silent church before the service begins, better than any preaching. How far off, how cool, how chaste the persons look, begirt each one with a precinct or sanctuary. So let us always sit. Why should we assume the faults of our friend, or wife, or father, or child, because they sit around our hearth, or are said to have the same blood? All men have my blood, and I have all men's. Not for that will I adopt their petulance or folly, even to the extent of being ashamed of it. But your isolation must not be mechanical, but spiritual, that is, must be elevation. At times the whole world seems to be in conspiracy to importune you with emphatic trifles. Friend, client, child, sickness, fear, want, charity, all knock at once at thy closet door and say, — 'Come out unto us.' But keep thy state; come not into their confusion. The power men possess to annoy me, I give them by a weak curiosity. No man can come near me but through my act. "What we love that we have, but by desire we bereave ourselves of the love."

If we cannot at once rise to the sanctities of obedience and faith, let us at least resist our temptations; let us enter into the state of war, and wake Thor and Woden, courage and constancy, in our Saxon breasts. This is to be done in our smooth times by speaking the truth. Check this lying hospitality and lying affection. Live no longer to the expectation of these deceived and deceiving people with whom we converse. Say to them, O father, O mother, O wife, O brother, O friend, I have lived with you after appearances hitherto. Henceforward I am the truth's. Be it known unto you that henceforward I obey no law less than the eternal law. I will have no covenants but proximities. I shall endeavor to nourish my parents, to support my family, to be the chaste husband of one wife, —, but these relations I must fill after a new and unprecedented way. I appeal from your customs. I must be myself. I cannot break myself any longer for you, or you. If you can love me for what I am, we shall be the happier. If you cannot, I will still seek to deserve that you should. I will not hide my tastes or aversions. I will so trust that what is deep is holy, that I will do strongly before the sun and moon whatever inly rejoices me, and the heart appoints. If you are noble, I will love you; if you are not, I will not hurt you and myself by hypocritical attentions. If you are true, but not in the same truth with me, cleave to your companions; I will seek my own. I do this not selfishly, but humbly and truly. It is alike your interest and mine and all men's, however long we have dwelt in lies, to live in truth. Does this sound harsh to-day? You will soon love what is dictated by your nature as well as mine, and if we follow the truth, it will bring us out safe at last. — But so you may give these friends pain. Yes, but I cannot sell my liberty and my power, to save their sensibility. Besides, all persons have their moments of reason when they look out into the region of absolute truth; then will they justify me and do the same thing.

The populace think that your rejection of popular standards is a rejection of all standard, and mere antinomianism; and the bold sensualist will use the name of philosophy to gild his crimes. But the law of consciousness abides. There are two confessionals, in one or the other of which we must be shriven. You may fulfil your round of duties by clearing yourself in the *direct*, or, in the *reflex* way. Consider whether you have satisfied your relations to father, mother, cousin, neighbor, town, cat, and dog; whether any of these can upbraid you. But I may also neglect this reflex standard, and absolve me to myself. I have my own stern claims and perfect circle. It denies the name of duty to many offices that are called duties. But if I can discharge its debts, it enables me to dispense with the popular code. If any one imagines that this law is lax, let him keep its commandment one day.

And truly it demands something godlike in him who has cast off the common motives of humanity, and has ventured to trust himself for a taskmaster. High be his heart, faithful his will, clear his sight, that he may in good earnest be doctrine, society, law to himself, that a simple purpose may be to him as strong as iron necessity is to others.

If any man consider the present aspects of what is called by distinction *society*, he will see the need of these ethics. The sinew and heart of man seem to be drawn out, and we are become timorous desponding whimperers. We are afraid of truth, afraid of fortune, afraid of death, and afraid of each other. Our age yields no great and perfect persons. We want men and women who shall renovate life and our social state, but we see that most natures are insolvent, cannot satisfy their own wants, have an ambition out of all proportion to their practical force, and do lean and beg day and night continually. Our housekeeping is mendicant, our arts, our occupations, our marriages, our religion we have not chosen, but society has chosen for us. We are parlor soldiers. We shun the rugged battle of fate, where strength is born.

If our young men miscarry in their first enterprizes, they lose all heart. If the young merchant fails, men say he is *ruined*. If the finest genius studies at one of our colleges, and is not installed in an office within one year afterwards in the cities or suburbs of Boston or New York, it seems to his friends and to himself that he is right in being disheartened and in complaining the rest of his life. A sturdy lad from New Hampshire or Vermont, who in turn tries all the professions, who *teams it, farms it, peddles*, keeps a school, preaches, edits a newspaper, goes to Congress, buys a township, and so forth, in successive years, and always, like a cat, falls on his feet, is worth a hundred of these city dolls. He walks abreast with his days, and feels no shame in not 'studying a profession,' for he does not postpone his life, but lives already. He has not one chance, but a hundred chances. Let a Stoic open the resources of man, and tell men they are not leaning willows, but can and must detach themselves; that with the exercise of self-trust, new powers shall appear; that a man is the word made flesh, born to shed healing to the nations, that he should be ashamed of our compassion, and that the moment he acts from himself, tossing the laws, the books, idolatries, and customs out of the window, we pity him no more but thank and revere him, — and that teacher shall restore the life of man to splendor, and make his name dear to all History.

It is easy to see that a greater self-reliance must work a revolution in all the offices and relations of men; in their religion; in their education; in their pursuits; their modes of living; their association; in their property; in their speculative views.

1. In what prayers do men allow themselves! That which they call a holy office, is not so much as brave and manly. Prayer looks abroad and asks for some foreign addition to come through some foreign virtue, and loses itself in endless mazes of natural and supernatural, and mediatorial and miraculous. Prayer that craves a particular commodity, — any thing less than all good, — is vicious. Prayer is the contemplation of the facts of life from the highest point of view. It is the soliloquy of a beholding and jubilant soul. It is the spirit of God pronouncing his works good. But prayer as a means to effect a private end, is meanness and theft. It supposes dualism and not unity in nature and consciousness. As soon as the man is at one with God, he will not beg. He will then see prayer in all action. The prayer of the farmer kneeling in his field to weed it, the prayer of the rower kneeling with the stroke of his oar, are true prayers heard throughout nature, though for cheap ends. Caratach, in Fletcher's Bonduca, when admonished to inquire the mind of the god Audate, replies, —

> "His hidden meaning lies in our endeavors,
> Our valors are our best gods."

Another sort of false prayers are our regrets. Discontent is the want of self-reliance: it is infirmity of will. Regret calamities, if you can thereby help the sufferer; if not, attend your own work, and already the evil begins to be repaired. Our sympathy is just as base. We come to them who weep foolishly, and sit down and cry for company, instead of imparting to them truth and health in rough electric shocks, putting them once more in communication

44

with their own reason. The secret of fortune is joy in our hands. Welcome evermore to gods and men is the self-helping man. For him all doors are flung wide: him all tongues greet, all honors crown, all eyes follow with desire. Our love goes out to him and embraces him, because he did not need it. We solicitously and apologetically caress and celebrate him, because he held on his way and scorned our disapprobation. The gods love him because men hated him. "To the persevering mortal," said Zoroaster, "the blessed Immortals are swift."

As men's prayers are a disease of the will, so are their creeds a disease of the intellect. They say with those foolish Israelites, 'Let not God speak to us, lest we die. Speak thou, speak any man with us, and we will obey.' Everywhere I am hindered of meeting God in my brother, because he has shut his own temple doors, and recites fables merely of his brother's, or his brother's brother's God. Every new mind is a new classification. If it prove a mind of uncommon activity and power, a Locke, a Lavoisier, a Hutton, a Bentham, a Fourier, it imposes its classification on other men, and lo! a new system. In proportion to the depth of the thought, and so to the number of the objects it touches and brings within reach of the pupil, is his complacency. But chiefly is this apparent in creeds and churches, which are also classifications of some powerful mind acting on the elemental thought of Duty, and man's relation to the Highest. Such is Calvinism, Quakerism, Swedenborgianism. The pupil takes the same delight in subordinating every thing to the new terminology, as a girl who has just learned botany in seeing a new earth and new seasons thereby. It will happen for a time, that the pupil will find his intellectual power has grown by the study of his master's mind. But in all unbalanced minds, the classification is idolized, passes for the end, and not for a speedily exhaustible means, so that the walls of the system blend to their eye in the remote horizon with the walls of the universe; the luminaries of heaven seem to them hung on the arch their master built. They cannot imagine how you aliens have any right to see, — how you can see; 'It must be somehow that you stole the light from us.' They do not yet perceive, that light, unsystematic, indomitable, will break into any cabin, even into theirs.   Let them chirp awhile and call it their own.   If they are honest and do well, presently their neat new pinfold will be too strait and low, will crack, will lean, will rot and vanish, and the immortal light, all young and joyful, million-orbed, million-colored, will beam over the universe as on the first morning.

2. It is for want of self-culture that the superstition of Travelling, whose idols are Italy, England, Egypt, retains its fascination for all educated Americans.   They who made England, Italy, or Greece venerable in the imagination, did so by sticking fast where they were, like an axis of the earth.   In manly hours, we feel that duty is our place.   The soul is no traveller: the wise man stays at home, and when his necessities, his duties, on any occasion call him from his house, or into foreign lands, he is at home still, and shall make men sensible by the expression of his countenance, that he goes the missionary of wisdom and virtue, and visits cities and men like a sovereign, and not like an interloper or a valet.

I have no churlish objection to the circumnavigation of the globe, for the purposes of art, of study, and benevolence, so that the man is first domesticated, or does not go abroad with the hope of finding somewhat greater than he knows.   He who travels to be amused, or to get somewhat which he does not carry, travels away from himself, and grows old even in youth among old things.   In Thebes, in Palmyra, his will and mind have become old and dilapidated as they.   He carries ruins to ruins.

Travelling is a fool's paradise.   Our first journeys discover to us the indifference of places.   At home I dream that at Naples, at Rome, I can be intoxicated with beauty, and lose my sadness.   I pack my trunk, embrace my friends, embark on the sea, and at last wake up in Naples, and there beside me is the stern Fact, the sad self, unrelenting, identical, that I fled from.   I seek the Vatican, and the palaces.   I affect to be intoxicated with sights and suggestions, but I am not intoxicated.   My giant goes with me wherever I go.

3. But the rage of travelling is a symptom of a deeper unsoundness affecting the whole intellectual action.   The intellect is vagabond, and our system of education fosters restlessness.   Our minds

travel when our bodies are forced to stay at home. We imitate; and what is imitation but the travelling of the mind? Our houses are built with foreign taste; our shelves are garnished with foreign ornaments; our opinions, our tastes, our faculties, lean, and follow the Past and the Distant. The soul created the arts wherever they have flourished. It was in his own mind that the artist sought his model. It was an application of his own thought to the thing to be done and the conditions to be observed. And why need we copy the Doric or the Gothic model? Beauty, convenience, grandeur of thought, and quaint expression are as near to us as to any, and if the American artist will study with hope and love the precise thing to be done by him, considering the climate, the soil, the length of the day, the wants of the people, the habit and form of the government, he will create a house in which all these will find themselves fitted, and taste and sentiment will be satisfied also.

Insist on yourself; never imitate. Your own gift you can present every moment with the cumulative force of a whole life's cultivation; but of the adopted talent of another, you have only an extemporaneous, half possession. That which each can do best, none but his Maker can teach him. No man yet knows what it is, nor can, till that person has exhibited it. Where is the master who could have taught Shakspeare? Where is the master who could have instructed Franklin, or Washington, or Bacon, or Newton? Every great man is a unique. The Scipionism of Scipio is precisely that part he could not borrow. Shakspeare will never be made by the study of Shakspeare. Do that which is assigned you, and you cannot hope too much or dare too much. There is at this moment for you an utterance brave and grand as that of the colossal chisel of Phidias, or trowel of the Egyptians, or the pen of Moses, or Dante, but different from all these. Not possibly will the soul all rich, all eloquent, with thousand-cloven tongue, deign to repeat itself; but if you can hear what these patriarchs say, surely you can reply to them in the same pitch of voice: for the ear and the tongue are two organs of one nature. Abide in the simple and noble regions of thy life, obey thy heart, and thou shalt reproduce the Foreworld again.

4. As our Religion, our Education, our Art look abroad, so

does our spirit of society. All men plume themselves on the improvement of society, and no man improves.

Society never advances. It recedes as fast on one side as it gains on the other. It undergoes continual changes: it is barbarous, it is civilized, it is christianized, it is rich, it is scientific; but this change is not amelioration. For every thing that is given, something is taken. Society acquires new arts and loses old instincts. What a contrast between the well-clad, reading, writing, thinking American, with a watch, a pencil, and a bill of exchange in his pocket, and the naked New Zealander, whose property is a club, a spear, a mat, and an undivided twentieth of a shed to sleep under. But compare the health of the two men, and you shall see that the white man has lost his aboriginal strength. If the traveller tell us truly, strike the savage with a broad axe, and in a day or two the flesh shall unite and heal as if you struck the blow into soft pitch, and the same blow shall send the white to his grave.

The civilized man has built a coach, but has lost the use of his feet. He is supported on crutches, but lacks so much support of muscle. He has a fine Geneva watch, but he fails of the skill to tell the hour by the sun. A Greenwich nautical almanac he has, and so being sure of the information when he wants it, the man in the street does not know a star in the sky. The solstice he does not observe; the equinox he knows as little; and the whole bright calendar of the year is without a dial in his mind. His note-books impair his memory; his libraries overload his wit; the insurance office increases the number of accidents; and it may be a question whether machinery does not encumber; whether we have not lost by refinement some energy, by a christianity entrenched in establishments and forms, some vigor of wild virtue. For every stoic was a stoic; but in Christendom where is the Christian?

There is no more deviation in the moral standard than in the standard of height or bulk. No greater men are now than ever were. A singular equality may be observed between the great men of the first and of the last ages; nor can all the science, art, religion and philosophy of the nineteenth century avail to educate greater men than Plutarch's heroes, three or four and twenty centuries ago. Not in time is the race progressive. Phocion, Socrates, Anaxagoras, Diogenes, are great men, but they leave no class. He who is really of their class will not be called by their name, but will be his own man, and, in his turn the founder of a sect. The arts and inventions of each period are only its costume, and do not invigorate men. The harm of the improved machinery may compensate its good. Hudson and Behring accomplished so much in their fishing-boats, as to astonish Parry and Franklin, whose equipment exhausted the resources of science and art. Galileo, with an opera-glass, discovered a more splendid series of celestial phenomena than any one since. Columbus found the New World in an undecked boat. It is curious to see the periodical disuse and perishing of means and machinery which were introduced with loud laudation, a few years or centuries before. The great genius returns to essential man. We reckoned the improvements of the art of war among the triumphs of science, and yet Napoleon conquered Europe by the Bivouac, which consisted of falling back on naked valor, and disencumbering it of all aids. The Emperor held it impossible to make a perfect army, says Las Cases, "without abolishing our arms, magazines, commissaries, and carriages, until in imitation of the Roman custom, the soldier should receive his supply of corn, grind it in his hand-mill, and bake his bread himself."

Society is a wave. The wave moves onward, but the water of which it is composed, does not. The same particle does not rise from the valley to the ridge. Its unity is only phenomenal. The persons who make up a nation to-day, next year die, and their experience with them.

And so the reliance on Property, including the reliance on governments which protect it, is the want of self-reliance. Men have looked away from themselves and at things so long, that they have come to esteem the religious, learned, and civil institutions, as guards of property, and they deprecate assaults on these, because they feel them to be assaults on property. They measure their esteem of each other, by what each has, and not by what each is. But a cultivated man becomes ashamed of his property, out of new respect for his nature. Especially he hates what he has, if he see that it is accidental, — came to him by inheritance, or gift, or crime; then he feels that it is not having; it does not belong to him, has no root in him, and merely lies there, because no revolution or no robber takes it away. But that which a man is, does always by necessity acquire, and what the man acquires is living property, which does not wait the beck of rulers, or mobs, or revolutions, or fire, or storm, or bankruptcies, but perpetually renews itself wherever the man breathes. "Thy lot or portion of life," said the Caliph Ali, "is seeking after thee; therefore be at rest from seeking after it." Our dependence on these foreign goods leads us to our slavish respect for numbers. The political parties meet in numerous conventions; the greater the concourse, and with each new uproar of announcement, The delegation from Essex! The Democrats from New Hampshire! The Whigs of Maine! the young patriot feels himself stronger than before by a new thousand of eyes and arms. In like manner the reformers summon conventions, and vote and resolve in multitude. Not so, O friends! will the God deign to enter and inhabit you, but by a method precisely the reverse. It is only as a man puts off all foreign support, and stands alone, that I see him to be strong and to prevail. He is weaker by every recruit to his banner. Is not a man better than a town? Ask nothing of men, and in the endless mutation, thou only firm column must presently appear the upholder of all that surrounds thee. He who knows that power is inborn, that he is weak because he has looked for good out of him and elsewhere, and so perceiving, throws himself unhesitatingly on his thought, instantly rights himself, stands in the erect position, commands his limbs, works miracles; just as a man who stands on his feet is stronger than a man who stands on his head.

So use all that is called Fortune. Most men gamble with her, and gain all, and lose all, as her wheel rolls. But do thou leave as unlawful these winnings, and deal with Cause and Effect, the chancellors of God. In the Will work and acquire, and thou hast chained the wheel of Chance, and shalt sit hereafter out of fear from her rotations. A political victory, a rise of rents, the recovery of your sick, or the return of your absent friend, or some other favorable event, raises your spirits, and you think good days are preparing for you. Do not believe it. Nothing can bring you peace but yourself. Nothing can bring you peace but the triumph of principles.

COMPENSATION

The wings of Time are black and white,
Pied with morning and with night.
Mountain tall and ocean deep
Trembling balance duly keep.
In changing moon, in tidal wave,
Glows the feud of Want and Have.
Gauge of more and less through space
Electric star and pencil plays.
The lonely Earth amid the balls
That hurry through the eternal halls,
A makeweight flying to the void,
Supplemental asteroid,
Or compensatory spark,
Shoots across the neutral Dark.

Man's the elm, and Wealth the vine;
Stanch and strong the tendrils twine:
Though the frail ringlets thee deceive,
None from its stock that vine can reave.
Fear not, then, thou child infirm,
There's no god dare wrong a worm.
Laurel crowns cleave to deserts,
And power to him who power exerts;
Hast not thy share? On winged feet,
Lo! it rushes thee to meet;
And all that Nature made thy own,
Floating in air or pent in stone,
Will rive the hills and swim the sea,
And, like thy shadow, follow thee.

ESSAY III

COMPENSATION

Ever since I was a boy, I have wished to write a discourse on Compensation: for, it seemed to me when very young, that, on this subject, Life was ahead of theology, and the people knew more than the preachers taught. The documents too, from which the doctrine is to be drawn, charmed my fancy by their endless variety, and lay always before me, even in sleep; for they are the tools in our hands, the bread in our basket, the transactions of the street, the farm, and the dwelling-house, greetings, relations, debts and credits, the influence of character, the nature and endowment of all men. It seemed to me also that in it might be shown men a ray of divinity, the present action of the Soul of this world, clean from all vestige of tradition, and so the heart of man might be bathed by an inundation of eternal love, conversing with that which he knows was always and always must be, because it really is now. It appeared, moreover, that if this doctrine could be stated in terms with any resemblance to those bright intuitions in which this truth is sometimes revealed to us, it would be a star in many dark hours and crooked passages in our journey that would not suffer us to lose our way.

I was lately confirmed in these desires by hearing a sermon at church. The preacher, a man esteemed for his orthodoxy, unfolded in the ordinary manner the doctrine of the Last Judgment. He assumed that judgment is not executed in this world; that the wicked are successful; that the good are miserable; and then urged from reason and from Scripture a compensation to be made to both parties in the next life. No offence appeared to be taken by the congregation at this doctrine. As far as I could observe, when the meeting broke up, they separated without remark on the sermon.

Yet what was the import of this teaching? What did the preacher mean by saying that the good are miserable in the present life? Was it that houses and lands, offices, wine, horses, dress, luxury, are had by unprincipled men, whilst the saints are poor and despised; and that a compensation is to be made to these last hereafter, by giving them the like gratifications another day, — bank-stock and doubloons, venison and champagne? This must be the compensation intended; for, what else? Is it that they are to have leave to pray and praise? to love and serve men? Why, that they can do now. The legitimate inference the disciple would draw was, — 'We are to have *such* a good time as the sinners have now;' — or, to push it to its extreme import, — 'You sin now; we shall sin by and by; we would sin now, if we could; not being successful, we expect our revenge tomorrow.'

The fallacy lay in the immense concession that the bad are successful; that justice is not done now. The blindness of the preacher consisted in deferring to the base estimate of the market of what constitutes a manly success, instead of confronting and convicting the world from the truth; announcing the Presence of the Soul; the omnipotence of the Will: and so establishing the standard of good and ill, of success and falsehood.

I find a similar base tone in the popular religious works of the day, and the same doctrines assumed by the literary men when occasionally they treat the related topics. I think that our popular theology has gained in decorum, and not in principle, over the superstitions it has displaced. But men are better than this theology. Their daily life gives it the lie. Every ingenuous and aspiring soul leaves the doctrine behind him in his own experience; and all men feel sometimes the falsehood which they cannot demonstrate. For men are wiser than they know. That which they hear in schools and pulpits without afterthought, if said in conversation, would probably be questioned in silence. If a man dogmatize in a mixed company on Providence and the divine laws, he is answered by a silence which conveys well enough to an observer the dissatisfaction of the hearer, but his incapacity to make his own statement.

I shall attempt in this and the following chapter to record some facts that indicate the path of the law of Compensation; happy beyond my expectation, if I shall truly draw the smallest arc of this circle.

Polarity, or action and reaction, we meet in every part of nature; in darkness and light; in heat and cold; in the ebb and flow of waters; in male and female; in the inspiration and expiration of plants and animals; in the equation of quantity and quality in the fluids of the animal body; in the systole and diastole of the heart; in the undulations of fluids, and of sound; in the centrifugal and centripetal gravity; in electricity, galvanism, and chemical affinity. Superinduce magnetism at one end of a needle; the opposite magnetism takes place at the other end. If the south attracts, the north repels. To empty here, you must condense there. An inevitable dualism bisects nature, so that each thing is a half, and suggests another thing to make it whole; as spirit, matter; man, woman; odd, even; subjective, objective; in, out; upper, under; motion, rest; yea, nay.

Whilst the world is thus dual, so is every one of its parts. The entire system of things gets represented in every particle. There is somewhat that resembles the ebb and flow of the sea, day and night, man and woman, in a single needle of the pine, in a kernel of corn, in each individual of every animal tribe. The reaction so grand in the elements, is repeated within these small boundaries. For example, in the animal kingdom, the physiologist has observed that no creatures are favorites, but a certain compensation balances every gift and every defect. A surplusage given to one part is paid out of a reduction from another part of the same creature. If the head and neck are enlarged, the trunk and extremities are cut short.

The theory of the mechanic forces is another example. What we gain in power is lost in time; and the converse. The periodic or compensating errors of the planets, is another instance. The influences of climate and soil in political history are another. The cold climate invigorates. The barren soil does not breed fevers, crocodiles, tigers, or scorpions.

The same dualism underlies the nature and condition of man. Every excess causes a defect; every defect an excess. Every sweet hath its sour; every evil its good. Every faculty which is a receiver of pleasure, has an equal penalty put on its abuse. It is to answer for its moderation with its life. For every grain of wit there is a grain of folly. For every thing you have missed, you have gained something else; and for every thing you gain, you lose something. If riches increase, they are increased that use them. If the gatherer gathers too much, nature takes out of the man what she puts into his chest; swells the estate, but kills the owner. Nature hates monopolies and exceptions. The waves of the sea do not more speedily seek a level from their loftiest tossing, than the varieties of condition tend to equalize themselves. There is always some levelling circumstance that puts down the overbearing, the strong, the rich, the fortunate, substantially on the same ground with all others. Is a man too strong and fierce for society, and by temper and position a bad citizen, — a morose ruffian with a dash of the pirate in him; — nature sends him a troop of pretty sons and daughters who are getting along in the dame's classes at the village school, and love and fear for them smooths his grim scowl to courtesy. Thus she contrives to intenerate the granite and felspar, takes the boar out and puts the lamb in, and keeps her balance true.

The farmer imagines power and place are fine things. But the President has paid dear for his White House. It has commonly cost him all his peace and the best of his manly attributes. To preserve for a short time so conspicuous an appearance before the world, he is content to eat dust before the real masters who stand erect behind the throne. Or, do men desire the more substantial and permanent grandeur of genius? Neither has this an immunity. He who by force of will or of thought is great, and overlooks thousands, has the charges of that eminence. With every influx of light, comes new danger. Has he light? he must bear witness to the light, and always outrun that sympathy which gives him such keen satisfaction, by his fidelity to new revelations of the incessant soul. He must hate father and mother, wife and child. Has he all that the world loves and admires and covets? — he must cast behind him their admiration, and afflict them by faithfulness to his truth, and become a byword and a hissing.

This Law writes the laws of cities and nations. It is in vain to build or plot or combine against it. Things refuse to be misman-aged long. *Res nolunt diu male administrari.* Though no checks to a new evil appear, the checks exist and will appear. If the government is cruel, the governor's life is not safe. If you tax too high, the revenue will yield nothing. If you make the criminal code sanguinary, juries will not convict. If the law is too mild, private vengeance comes in. If the government is a terrific de-mocracy, the pressure is resisted by an overcharge of energy in the citizen, and life glows with a fiercer flame. The true life and satisfactions of man seem to elude the utmost rigors or felicities of condition, and to establish themselves with great indifferency under all varieties of circumstances. Under all governments the influence of character remains the same, — in Turkey and in New England about alike. Under the primeval despots of Egypt, his-tory honestly confesses that man must have been as free as culture could make him.

These appearances indicate the fact that the universe is repre-sented in every one of its particles. Every thing in nature con-tains all the powers of nature. Every thing is made of one hidden stuff; as the naturalist sees one type under every metamorphosis, and regards a horse as a running man, a fish as a swimming man, a bird as a flying man, a tree as a rooted man. Each new form repeats not only the main character of the type, but part for part all the details, all the aims, furtherances, hindrances, energies, and whole system of every other. Every occupation, trade, art, trans-action, is a compend of the world, and a correlative of every other. Each one is an entire emblem of human life; of its good and ill, its trials, its enemies, its course and its end. And each one must somehow accommodate the whole man, and recite all his destiny.

The world globes itself in a drop of dew. The microscope can-not find the animalcule which is less perfect for being little. Eyes,

ears, taste, smell, motion, resistance, appetite, and organs of repro-
duction that take hold on eternity, — all find room to consist in
the small creature. So do we put our life into every act. The true
doctrine of omnipresence is, that God re-appears with all his parts
in every moss and cobweb. The value of the universe contrives
to throw itself into every point. If the good is there, so is the evil;
if the affinity, so the repulsion; if the force, so the limitation.

Thus is the universe alive. All things are moral. That soul
which within us is a sentiment, outside of us is a law. We feel its
inspiration; out there in history we can see its fatal strength. "It
is in the world and the world was made by it." Justice is not
postponed. A perfect equity adjusts its balance in all parts of life.
Οἱ κύβοι Διὸς ἀεὶ εὐπίπτουσι, — The dice of God are always loaded.
The world looks like a multiplication-table or a mathematical
equation, which, turn it how you will, balances itself. Take what
figure you will, its exact value, nor more nor less, still returns to
you. Every secret is told, every crime is punished, every virtue
rewarded, every wrong redressed, in silence and certainty. What
we call retribution, is the universal necessity by which the whole
appears wherever a part appears. If you see smoke, there must be
fire. If you see a hand or a limb, you know that the trunk to
which it belongs, is there behind.

Every act rewards itself, or, in other words, integrates itself, in
a twofold manner; first, in the thing, or, in real nature; and sec-
ondly, in the circumstance, or, in apparent nature. Men call the
circumstance the retribution. The causal retribution is in the
thing, and is seen by the soul. The retribution in the circumstance, is seen by the understanding; it is inseparable from the
thing, but is often spread over a long time, and so does not become
distinct until after many years. The specific stripes may follow
late after the offence, but they follow because they accompany it.
Crime and punishment grow out of one stem. Punishment is a
fruit that unsuspected ripens within the flower of the pleasure
which concealed it. Cause and effect, means and ends, seed and
fruit, cannot be severed; for the effect already blooms in the cause,
the end preëxists in the means, the fruit in the seed.

Whilst thus the world will be whole, and refuses to be disparted,

we seek to act partially, to sunder, to appropriate; for example, —
to gratify the senses, we sever the pleasure of the senses from the
needs of the character. The ingenuity of man has always been
dedicated to the solution of one problem, — how to detach the
sensual sweet, the sensual strong, the sensual bright, &c. from the
moral sweet, the moral deep, the moral fair; that is, again, to contrive to cut clean off this upper surface so thin as to leave it bot-
tomless; to get a *one end*, without an *other end*. The soul says,
Eat; the body would feast. The soul says, The man and woman
shall be one flesh and one soul; the body would join the flesh only.
The soul says, Have dominion over all things to the ends of virtue;
the body would have the power over things to its own ends.

The soul strives amain to live and work through all things. It
would be the only fact. All things shall be added unto it, —
power, pleasure, knowledge, beauty. The particular man aims to
be somebody; to set up for himself; to truck and higgle for a private good; and, in particulars, to ride, that he may ride; to dress,
that he may be dressed; to eat, that he may eat; and to govern
that he may be seen. Men seek to be great; they would have
offices, wealth, power and fame. They think that to be great is to
possess one side of nature — the sweet, without the other side —
the bitter.

This dividing and detaching is steadily counteracted. Up to
this day, it must be owned, no projector has had the smallest success. The parted water re-unites behind our hand. Pleasure is
taken out of pleasant things, profit out of profitable things, power
out of strong things, as soon as we seek to separate them from the
whole. We can no more halve things and get the sensual good,
by itself, than we can get an inside that shall have no outside, or
a light without a shadow. "Drive out nature with a fork, she
comes running back."

Life invests itself with inevitable conditions, which the unwise
seek to dodge, which one and another brags that he does not
know; that they do not touch him; — but the brag is on his lips,
the conditions are in his soul. If he escapes them in one part, they
attack him in another more vital part. If he has escaped them in
form, and in the appearance, it is because he has resisted his life,

and fled from himself, and the retribution is so much death. So
signal is the failure of all attempts to make this separation of the
good from the tax, that the experiment would not be tried, — since
to try it is to be mad, — but for the circumstance, that when the
disease began in the will, of rebellion and separation, the intellect is at once infected, so that the man ceases to see God whole
in each object, but is able to see the sensual allurement of an object, and not see the sensual hurt; he sees the mermaid's head, but
not the dragon's tail; and thinks he can cut off that which he
would have, from that which he would not have. "How secret
art thou who dwellest in the highest heavens in silence, O thou
only great God, sprinkling with an unwearied Providence certain
penal blindnesses upon such as have unbridled desires!"*

The human soul is true to these facts in the painting of fable,
of history, of law, of proverbs, of conversation. It finds a tongue
in literature unawares. Thus the Greeks called Jupiter, Supreme
Mind; but having traditionally ascribed to him many base actions,
they involuntarily made amends to Reason, by tying up the hands
of so bad a god. He is made as helpless as a king of England.
Prometheus knows one secret, which Jove must bargain for; Minerva, another. He cannot get his own thunders; Minerva keeps
the key of them.

> "Of all the gods I only know the keys
>   That ope the solid doors within whose vaults
>   His thunders sleep."

A plain confession of the in-working of the All, and of its moral
aim. The Indian mythology ends in the same ethics; and it would
seem impossible for any fable to be invented and get any currency which was not moral. Aurora forgot to ask youth for her
lover, and though Tithonus is immortal, he is old. Achilles is not
quite invulnerable; the sacred waters did not wash the heel by
which Thetis held him. Siegfried, in the Nibelungen, is not
quite immortal, for a leaf fell on his back whilst he was bathing in
the Dragon's blood, and that spot which it covered is mortal. And

---

* St. Augustine: Confessions, B. I.

so it must be. There is a crack in every thing God has made. It would seem, there is always this vindictive circumstance stealing in at unawares, even into the wild poesy in which the human fancy attempted to make bold holiday, and to shake itself free of the old laws, — this back-stroke, this kick of the gun, certifying that the law is fatal; that in Nature, nothing can be given, all things are sold.

This is that ancient doctrine of Nemesis, who keeps watch in the Universe, and lets no offence go unchastised. The Furies, they said, are attendants on Justice, and if the sun in heaven should transgress his path, they would punish him. The poets related that stone walls, and iron swords, and leathern thongs had an occult sympathy with the wrongs of their owners; that the belt which Ajax gave Hector dragged the Trojan hero over the field at the wheels of the car of Achilles, and the sword which Hector gave Ajax was that on whose point Ajax fell. They recorded that when the Thasians erected a statue to Theogenes, a victor in the games, one of his rivals went to it by night, and endeavored to throw it down by repeated blows, until at last he moved it from its pedestal and was crushed to death beneath its fall.

This voice of fable has in it somewhat divine. It came from thought above the will of the writer. That is the best part of each writer, which has nothing private in it; that which he does not know; that which flowed out of his constitution, and not from his too active invention; that which in the study of a single artist you might not easily find, but in the study of many, you would abstract as the spirit of them all. Phidias it is not, but the work of man in that early Hellenic world, that I would know. The name and circumstance of Phidias, however convenient for history, embarrass when we come to the highest criticism. We are to see that which man was tending to do in a given period, and was hindered, or, if you will, modified in doing, by the interfering volitions of Phidias, of Dante, of Shakspeare, the organ whereby man at the moment wrought.

Still more striking is the expression of this fact in the proverbs of all nations, which are always the literature of Reason, or the statements of an absolute truth, without qualification. Proverbs, like the sacred books of each nation, are the sanctuary of the Intuitions. That which the droning world, chained to appearances, will not allow the realist to say in his own words, it will suffer him to say in proverbs without contradiction. And this law of laws which the pulpit, the senate and the college deny, is hourly preached in all markets and workshops by flights of proverbs, whose teaching is as true and as omnipresent as that of birds and flies.

All things are double, one against another. — Tit for tat; an eye for an eye; a tooth for a tooth; blood for blood; measure for measure; love for love. — Give and it shall be given you. — He that watereth shall be watered himself. — What will you have? quoth God; pay for it and take it. — Nothing venture, nothing have. — Thou shalt be paid exactly for what thou hast done, no more, no less. — Who doth not work shall not eat. — Harm watch, harm catch. — Curses always recoil on the head of him who imprecates them. — If you put a chain around the neck of a slave, the other end fastens itself around your own. — Bad counsel confounds the adviser. — The devil is an ass.

It is thus written, because it is thus in life. Our action is overmastered and characterized above our will by the law of nature. We aim at a petty end quite aside from the public good, but our act arranges itself by irresistible magnetism in a line with the poles of the world.

A man cannot speak but he judges himself. With his will, or against his will, he draws his portrait to the eye of his companions by every word. Every opinion reacts on him who utters it. It is a thread-ball thrown at a mark, but the other end remains in the thrower's bag. Or, rather, it is a harpoon hurled at the whale, unwinding, as it flies, a coil of cord in the boat, and if the harpoon is not good, or not well thrown, it will go nigh to cut the steersman in twain, or to sink the boat.

You cannot do wrong without suffering wrong. "No man had ever a point of pride that was not injurious to him," said Burke. The exclusive in fashionable life does not see that he excludes himself from enjoyment, in the attempt to appropriate it. The exclusionist in religion does not see that he shuts the door of heaven on himself, in striving to shut out others. Treat men as pawns and ninepins, and you shall suffer as well as they. If you leave out their heart, you shall lose your own. The senses would make things of all persons; of women, of children, of the poor. The vulgar proverb, "I will get it from his purse or get it from his skin," is sound philosophy.

All infractions of love and equity in our social relations are speedily punished. They are punished by Fear. Whilst I stand in simple relations to my fellow man, I have no displeasure in meeting him. We meet as water meets water, or as two currents of air mix, with perfect diffusion and interpenetration of nature. But as soon as there is any departure from simplicity, and attempt at halfness, or good for me that is not good for him, my neighbor feels the wrong; he shrinks from me as far as I have shrunk from him; his eyes no longer seek mine; there is war between us; there is hate in him and fear in me.

All the old abuses in society, universal and particular, all unjust accumulations of property and power, are avenged in the same manner. Fear is an instructer of great sagacity, and the herald of all revolutions. One thing he teaches, that there is rottenness where he appears. He is a carrion crow, and though you see not well what he hovers for, there is death somewhere. Our property is timid, our laws are timid, our cultivated classes are timid. Fear for ages has boded and mowed and gibbered over government and property. That obscene bird is not there for nothing. He indicates great wrongs which must be revised.

Of the like nature is that expectation of change which instantly follows the suspension of our voluntary activity. The terror of cloudless noon, the emerald of Polycrates, the awe of prosperity, the instinct which leads every generous soul to impose on itself tasks of a noble asceticism and vicarious virtue, are the tremblings of the balance of justice through the heart and mind of man.

Experienced men of the world know very well that it is best to pay scot and lot as they go along, and that a man often pays dear for a small frugality. The borrower runs in his own debt. Has a man gained any thing who has received a hundred favors and rendered none? Has he gained by borrowing, through indolence or cunning, his neighbor's wares, or horses, or money? There arises on the deed the instant acknowledgment of benefit on the one part, and of debt on the other; that is, of superiority and inferiority. The transaction remains in the memory of himself and his neighbor; and every new transaction alters, according to its nature, their relation to each other. He may soon come to see that he had better have broken his own bones than to have ridden in his neighbor's coach, and that "the highest price he can pay for a thing is to ask for it."

A wise man will extend this lesson to all parts of life, and know that it is the part of prudence to face every claimant, and pay every just demand on your time, your talents, or your heart. Always pay; for, first or last, you must pay your entire debt. Persons and events may stand for a time between you and justice, but it is only a postponement. You must pay at last your own debt. If you are wise, you will dread a prosperity which only loads you with more. Benefit is the end of nature. But for every benefit which you receive, a tax is levied. He is great who confers the most benefits. He is base, — and that is the one base thing in the universe, — to receive favors and render none. In the order of nature we cannot render benefits to those from whom we receive them, or only seldom. But the benefit we receive must be rendered again, line for line, deed for deed, cent for cent, to somebody. Beware of too much good staying in your hand. It will fast corrupt and worm worms. Pay it away quickly in some sort.

Labor is watched over by the same pitiless laws. Cheapest, say the prudent, is the dearest labor. What we buy in a broom, a mat, a wagon, a knife, is some application of good sense to a common want. It is best to pay in your land a skilful gardener, or to buy good sense applied to gardening; in your sailor, good sense applied to navigation; in the house, good sense applied to cooking, sewing, serving; in your agent, good sense applied to accounts and affairs. So do you multiply your presence, or spread yourself throughout your estate. But because of the dual constitution of things, in labor as in life there can be no cheating. The thief steals from himself. The swindler swindles himself. For the real price of labor is knowledge and virtue, whereof wealth and credit are signs. These signs, like paper money, may be counterfeited or stolen, but that which they represent, namely, knowledge and virtue, cannot be counterfeited or stolen. These ends of labor cannot be answered but by real exertions of the mind, and in obedience to pure motives. The cheat, the defaulter, the gambler, cannot extort the knowledge of material and moral nature which his honest care and pains yield to the operative. The law of nature is, Do the thing, and you shall have the power: but they who do not the thing have not the power.

Human labor, through all its forms, from the sharpening of a stake to the construction of a city or an epic, is one immense illustration of the perfect compensation of the universe. The absolute balance of Give and Take, the doctrine that every thing has its price, — and if that price is not paid, not that thing but something else is obtained, and that it is impossible to get any thing without its price, — is not less sublime in the columns of a leger than in the budgets of states, in the laws of light and darkness, in all the action and reaction of nature. I cannot doubt that the high laws which each man sees implicated in those processes with which he is conversant, the stern ethics which sparkle on his chisel-edge, which are measured out by his plumb and foot-rule, which stand as manifest in the footing of the shop-bill as in the history of a state, — do recommend to him his trade, and though seldom named, exalt his business to his imagination.

The league between virtue and nature engages all things to assume a hostile front to vice. The beautiful laws and substances of the world persecute and whip the traitor. He finds that things are arranged for truth and benefit, but there is no den in the wide world to hide a rogue. Commit a crime, and the earth is made of glass. Commit a crime, and it seems as if a coat of snow fell on the ground, such as reveals in the woods the track of every partridge and fox and squirrel and mole. You cannot recall the spoken word, you cannot wipe out the foot track, you cannot draw up the ladder, so as to leave no inlet or clew. Some damning circumstance always transpires. The laws and substances of nature — water, snow, wind, gravitation — become penalties to the thief.

On the other hand, the law holds with equal sureness for all

right action. Love, and you shall be loved. All love is mathematically just, as much as the two sides of an algebraic equation.
The good man has absolute good, which like fire turns every thing
to its own nature, so that you cannot do him any harm; but as
the royal armies sent against Napoleon, when he approached, cast
down their colors and from enemies became friends, so disasters of
all kinds, as sickness, offence, poverty, prove benefactors: —

> "Winds blow and waters roll
> Strength to the brave, and power and deity,
> Yet in themselves are nothing."

The good are befriended even by weakness and defect. As no
man had ever a point of pride that was not injurious to him, so
no man had ever a defect that was not somewhere made useful to
him. The stag in the fable admired his horns and blamed his
feet, but when the hunter came, his feet saved him, and afterwards, caught in the thicket, his horns destroyed him. Every man
in his lifetime needs to thank his faults. As no man thoroughly
understands a truth until he has contended against it, so no man
has a thorough acquaintance with the hindrances or talents of
men, until he has suffered from the one, and seen the triumph of
the other over his own want of the same. Has he a defect of
temper that unfits him to live in society? Thereby he is driven
to entertain himself alone, and acquire habits of self-help; and
thus, like the wounded oyster, he mends his shell with pearl.

Our strength grows out of our weakness. The indignation
which arms itself with secret forces does not awaken until we are
pricked and stung and sorely assailed. A great man is always
willing to be little. Whilst he sits on the cushion of advantages,
he goes to sleep. When he is pushed, tormented, defeated, he
has a chance to learn something; he has been put on his wits, on
his manhood; he has gained facts; learns his ignorance; is cured
of the insanity of conceit; has got moderation and real skill. The
wise man throws himself on the side of his assailants. It is more
his interest than it is theirs to find his weak point. The wound
cicatrizes and falls off from him, like a dead skin, and when they

would triumph, lo! he has passed on invulnerable. Blame is safer than praise. I hate to be defended in a newspaper. As long as all that is said, is said against me, I feel a certain assurance of success. But as soon as honied words of praise are spoken for me, I feel as one that lies unprotected before his enemies. In general, every evil to which we do not succumb, is a benefactor. As the Sandwich Islander believes that the strength and valor of the enemy he kills, passes into himself, so we gain the strength of the temptation we resist.

The same guards which protect us from disaster, defect, and enmity, defend us, if we will, from selfishness and fraud. Bolts and bars are not the best of our institutions, nor is shrewdness in trade a mark of wisdom. Men suffer all their life long, under the foolish superstition that they can be cheated. But it is as impossible for a man to be cheated by any one but himself, as for a thing to be, and not to be, at the same time. There is a third silent party to all our bargains. The nature and soul of things takes on itself the guaranty of the fulfilment of every contract, so that honest service cannot come to loss. If you serve an ungrateful master, serve him the more. Put God in your debt. Every stroke shall be repaid. The longer the payment is withholden, the better for you; for compound interest on compound interest is the rate and usage of this exchequer.

The history of persecution is a history of endeavors to cheat nature, to make water run up hill, to twist a rope of sand. It makes no difference whether the actors be many or one, a tyrant or a mob. A mob is a society of bodies voluntarily bereaving themselves of reason and traversing its work. The mob is man voluntarily descending to the nature of the beast. Its fit hour of activity is night. Its actions are insane like its whole constitution. It persecutes a principle; it would whip a right; it would tar and feather justice, by inflicting fire and outrage upon the houses and persons of those who have these. It resembles the prank of boys who run with fire-engines to put out the ruddy aurora streaming to the stars. The inviolate spirit turns their spite against the wrongdoers. The martyr cannot be dishonored. Every lash inflicted is a tongue of fame; every prison a more illustrious abode;

every burned book or house enlightens the world; every suppressed or expunged word reverberates through the earth from side to side. Hours of sanity and consideration are always arriving to communities, as to individuals, when the truth is seen, and the martyrs are justified.

Thus do all things preach the indifferency of circumstances. The man is all. Every thing has two sides, a good and an evil. Every advantage has its tax. I learn to be content. But the doctrine of compensation is not the doctrine of indifferency. The thoughtless say, on hearing these representations, — What boots it to do well? there is one event to good and evil; if I gain any good, I must pay for it; if I lose any good, I gain some other; all actions are indifferent.

There is a deeper fact in the soul than compensation, to wit, its own nature. The soul is not a compensation, but a life. The soul *is*. Under all this running sea of circumstance, whose waters ebb and flow with perfect balance, lies the aboriginal abyss of real Being. Essence, or God, is not a relation, or a part, but the whole. Being is the vast affirmative, excluding negation, self-balanced, and swallowing up all relations, parts and times, within itself. Nature, truth, virtue are the influx from thence. Vice is the absence or departure of the same. Nothing, Falsehood, may indeed stand as the great Night or shade, on which, as a background, the living universe paints itself forth; but no fact is begotten by it; it cannot work; for it is not. It cannot work any good; it cannot work any harm. It is harm inasmuch as it is worse not to be than to be.

We feel defrauded of the retribution due to evil acts, because the criminal adheres to his vice and contumacy, and does not come to a crisis or judgment anywhere in visible nature. There is no stunning confutation of his nonsense before men and angels. Has he therefore outwitted the law? Inasmuch as he carries the malignity and the lie with him, he so far deceases from nature. In some manner there will be a demonstration of the wrong to the understanding also; but should we not see it, this deadly deduction makes square the eternal account.

Neither can it be said, on the other hand, that the gain of rectitude must be bought by any loss. There is no penalty to virtue; no penalty to wisdom; they are proper additions of being. In a virtuous action, I properly *am;* in a virtuous act, I add to the world; I plant into deserts conquered from Chaos and Nothing, and see the darkness receding on the limits of the horizon. There can be no excess to love; none to knowledge; none to beauty, when these attributes are considered in the purest sense. The soul refuses limits, and always affirms an Optimism, never a Pessimism.

Man's life is a progress, and not a station. His instinct is trust. Our instinct uses "more" and "less" in application to him, of the *presence of the soul,* and not of its absence; the brave man is greater than the coward; the true, the benevolent, the wise, is more a man and not less, than the fool and knave. There is no tax on the good of virtue; for, that is the incoming of God himself, or absolute existence, without any comparative. Material good has its tax, and if it came without desert or sweat, has no root in me and the next wind will blow it away. But all the good of nature is the soul's, and may be had, if paid for in nature's lawful coin, that is, by labor which the heart and the head allow. I no longer wish to meet a good I do not earn, for example, to find a pot of buried gold, knowing that it brings with it new burdens. I do not wish more external goods, — neither possessions, nor honors, nor powers, nor persons. The gain is apparent: the tax is certain. But there is no tax on the knowledge that the compensation exists, and that it is not desirable to dig up treasure. Herein I rejoice with a serene eternal peace. I contract the boundaries of possible mischief. I learn the wisdom of St. Bernard, — "Nothing can work me damage except myself; the harm that I sustain, I carry about with me, and never am a real sufferer but by my own fault."

In the nature of the soul is the compensation for the inequalities of condition. The radical tragedy of nature seems to be the distinction of More and Less. How can Less not feel the pain; how not feel indignation or malevolence towards More? Look at those who have less faculty, and one feels sad, and knows not well what to make of it. He almost shuns their eye; he fears they will

71

upbraid God. What should they do? It seems a great injustice. But see the facts nearly, and these mountainous inequalities vanish. Love reduces them, as the sun melts the iceberg in the sea. The heart and soul of all men being one, this bitterness of *His* and *Mine* ceases. His is mine. I am my brother, and my brother is me. If I feel overshadowed and outdone by great neighbors, I can yet love; I can still receive; and he that loveth, maketh his own the grandeur he loves. Thereby I make the discovery that my brother is my guardian, acting for me with the friendliest designs, and the estate I so admired and envied, is my own. It is the nature of the soul to appropriate all things. Jesus and Shakspeare are fragments of the soul, and by love I conquer and incorporate them in my own conscious domain. His virtue, — is not that mine? His wit, — if it cannot be made mine, it is not wit.

Such, also, is the natural history of calamity. The changes which break up at short intervals the prosperity of men, are advertisements of a nature whose law is growth. Every soul is by this intrinsic necessity quitting its whole system of things, its friends, and home, and laws, and faith, as the shell-fish crawls out of its beautiful but stony case, because it no longer admits of its growth, and slowly forms a new house. In proportion to the vigor of the individual, these revolutions are frequent, until in some happier mind they are incessant, and all worldly relations hang very loosely about him, becoming, as it were, a transparent fluid membrane through which the living form is seen, and not as in most men an indurated heterogeneous fabric of many dates, and of no settled character, in which the man is imprisoned. Then there can be enlargement, and the man of to-day scarcely recognizes the man of yesterday. And such should be the outward biography of man in time, a putting off of dead circumstances day by day, as he renews his raiment day by day. But to us, in our lapsed estate, resting, not advancing, resisting, not coöperating with the divine expansion, this growth comes by shocks.

We cannot part with our friends. We cannot let our angels go. We do not see that they only go out, that archangels may come in. We are idolaters of the old. We do not believe in the riches of the soul, in its proper eternity and omnipresence. We do not

believe there is any force in to-day to rival or re-create that beautiful yesterday. We linger in the ruins of the old tent, where once
we had bread and shelter and organs, nor believe that the spirit
can feed, cover, and nerve us again. We cannot again find aught
so dear, so sweet, so graceful. But we sit and weep in vain. The
voice of the Almighty saith, 'Up and onward forevermore!' We
cannot stay amid the ruins. Neither will we rely on the New;
and so we walk ever with reverted eyes, like those monsters who
look backwards.

And yet the compensations of calamity are made apparent to the
understanding also, after long intervals of time. A fever, a mutila-
tion, a cruel disappointment, a loss of wealth, a loss of friends
seems at the moment unpaid loss, and unpayable. But the sure
years reveal the deep remedial force that underlies all facts. The
death of a dear friend, wife, brother, lover, which seemed nothing
but privation, somewhat later assumes the aspect of a guide or
genius; for it commonly operates revolutions in our way of life,
terminates an epoch of infancy or of youth which was waiting to
be closed, breaks up a wonted occupation, or a household, or style
of living, and allows the formation of new ones more friendly to
the growth of character. It permits or constrains the formation
of new acquaintances, and the reception of new influences that
prove of the first importance to the next years; and the man or
woman who would have remained a sunny garden flower, with no
room for its roots and too much sunshine for its head, by the falling of the walls and the neglect of the gardener, is made the banian
of the forest, yielding shade and fruit to wide neighborhoods of
men.

SPIRITUAL LAWS

The living Heaven thy prayers respect,
House at once and architect,
Quarrying man's rejected hours,
Builds therewith eternal towers;
Sole and self-commanded works,
Fears not undermining days,
Grows by decays,
And, by the famous might that lurks
In reaction and recoil,
Makes flame to freeze, and ice to boil;
Forging, through swart arms of Offence,
The silver seat of Innocence.

SPIRITUAL LAWS

When the act of reflection takes place in the mind, when we look at ourselves in the light of thought, we discover that our life is embosomed in beauty. Behind us, as we go, all things assume pleasing forms, as clouds do far off. Not only things familiar and stale, but even the tragic and terrible are comely, as they take their place in the pictures of memory. The river-bank, the weed at the water-side, the old house, the foolish person, — however neglected in the passing, — have a grace in the past. Even the corpse that has lain in the chambers has added a solemn ornament to the house. The soul will not know either deformity or pain. If in the hours of clear reason we should speak the severest truth, we should say, that we had never made a sacrifice. In these hours the mind seems so great, that nothing can be taken from us that seems much. All loss, all pain is particular: the universe remains to the heart unhurt. Neither vexations nor calamities abate our trust. No man ever stated his griefs as lightly as he might. Allow for exaggeration in the most patient and sorely ridden hack that ever was driven. For it is only the finite that has wrought and suffered; the infinite lies stretched in smiling repose.

The intellectual life may be kept clean and healthful, if man will live the life of nature, and not import into his mind difficulties which are none of his. No man need be perplexed in his speculations. Let him do and say what strictly belongs to him, and though very ignorant of books, his nature shall not yield him any intellectual obstructions and doubts. Our young people are diseased with the theological problems of original sin, origin of

77

evil, predestination, and the like. These never presented a practical difficulty to any man, — never darkened across any man's road, who did not go out of his way to seek them. These are the soul's mumps and measles, and whooping-coughs, and those who have not caught them, cannot describe their health or prescribe the cure. A simple mind will not know these enemies. It is quite another thing that he should be able to give account of his faith, and expound to another the theory of his self-union and freedom. This requires rare gifts. Yet without this self-knowledge, there may be a sylvan strength and integrity in that which he is. "A few strong instincts and a few plain rules" suffice us.

My will never gave the images in my mind the rank they now take. The regular course of studies, the years of academical and professional education have not yielded me better facts than some idle books under the bench at the Latin school. What we do not call education is more precious than that which we call so. We form no guess at the time of receiving a thought, of its comparative value. And education often wastes its effort in attempts to thwart and baulk this natural magnetism, which is sure to select what belongs to it.

In like manner, our moral nature is vitiated by any interference of our will. People represent virtue as a struggle, and take to themselves great airs upon their attainments, and the question is everywhere vexed, when a noble nature is commended, whether the man is not better who strives with temptation. But there is no merit in the matter. Either God is there, or he is not there. We love characters in proportion as they are impulsive and spontaneous. The less a man thinks or knows about his virtues, the better we like him. Timoleon's victories are the best victories; which ran and flowed like Homer's verses, Plutarch said. When we see a soul whose acts are all regal, graceful and pleasant as roses, we must thank God that such things can be and are, and not turn sourly on the angel, and say, 'Crump is a better man with his grunting resistance to all his native devils.'

Not less conspicuous is the preponderance of nature over will in all practical life. There is less intention in history than we ascribe to it. We impute deep-laid, far-sighted plans to Cæsar and

Napoleon; but the best of their power was in nature, not in them. Men of an extraordinary success, in their honest moments, have always sung, 'Not unto us, not unto us.' According to the faith of their times, they have built altars to Fortune or to Destiny, or to St. Julian. Their success lay in their parallelism to the course of thought, which found in them an unobstructed channel; and the wonders of which they were the visible conductors, seemed to the eye their deed. Did the wires generate the galvanism? It is even true that there was less in them on which they could reflect, than in another; as the virtue of a pipe is to be smooth and hollow. That which externally seemed will and immovableness, was willingness and self-annihilation. Could Shakspeare give a theory of Shakspeare? Could ever a man of prodigious mathematical genius convey to others any insight into his methods? If he could communicate that secret, it would instantly lose its exaggerated value, blending with the daylight and the vital energy, the power to stand and to go.

The lesson is forcibly taught by these observations that our life might be much easier and simpler than we make it; that the world might be a happier place than it is; that there is no need of struggles, convulsions, and despairs, of the wringing of the hands and the gnashing of the teeth; that we miscreate our own evils. We interfere with the optimism of nature, for, whenever we get this vantage ground of the past, or of a wiser mind in the present, we are able to discern that we are begirt with laws which execute themselves.

The face of external nature teaches the same lesson. Nature will not have us fret and fume. She does not like our benevolence or our learning, much better than she likes our frauds and wars. When we come out of the caucus, or the bank, or the Abolition convention, or the Temperance meeting, or the Transcendental club, into the fields and woods, she says to us, 'So hot? my little Sir.'

We are full of mechanical actions. We must needs intermeddle, and have things in our own way, until the sacrifices and virtues of society are odious. Love should make joy; but our benevolence is unhappy. Our Sunday schools and churches and pauper-societies are yokes to the neck. We pain ourselves to please nobody. There are natural ways of arriving at the same ends at which these aim, but do not arrive. Why should all virtue work in one and the same way? Why should all give dollars? It is very inconvenient to us country folk, and we do not think any good will come of it. We have not dollars; merchants have; let them give them. Farmers will give corn; poets will sing; women will sew; laborers will lend a hand; the children will bring flowers. And why drag this dead weight of a Sunday school over the whole Christendom? It is natural and beautiful that childhood should inquire, and maturity should teach; but it is time enough to answer questions, when they are asked. Do not shut up the young people against their will in a pew, and force the children to ask them questions for an hour against their will.

If we look wider, things are all alike; laws, and letters, and creeds and modes of living, seem a travestie of truth. Our society is encumbered by ponderous machinery which resembles the endless aqueducts which the Romans built over hill and dale, and which are superseded by the discovery of the law that water rises to the level of its source. It is a Chinese wall which any nimble Tartar can leap over. It is a standing army, not so good as a peace. It is a graduated, titled, richly appointed Empire, quite superfluous when Town-meetings are found to answer just as well.

Let us draw a lesson from nature, which always works by short ways. When the fruit is ripe, it falls. When the fruit is despatched, the leaf falls. The circuit of the waters is mere falling. The walking of man and all animals is a falling forward. All our manual labor and works of strength, as prying, splitting, digging, rowing, and so forth, are done by dint of continual falling, and the globe, earth, moon, comet, sun, star, fall forever and ever.

The simplicity of the universe is very different from the simplicity of a machine. He who sees moral nature out and out, and thoroughly knows how knowledge is acquired and character formed, is a pedant. The simplicity of nature is not that which may easily be read, but is inexhaustible. The last analysis can no wise be made. We judge of a man's wisdom by his hope, knowing that the perception of the inexhaustibleness of nature is an immortal youth. The wild fertility of nature is felt in comparing our rigid names and reputations with our fluid consciousness. We pass in the world for sects and schools, for erudition and piety, and we are all the time jejune babes. One sees very well how Pyrrhonism grew up. Every man sees that he is that middle point whereof every thing may be affirmed and denied with equal reason. He is old, he is young, he is very wise, he is altogether ignorant. He hears and feels what you say of the seraphim, and of the tin-pedlar. There is no permanent wise man, except in the figment of the stoics. We side with the hero, as we read or paint, against the coward and the robber; but we have been ourselves that coward and robber, and shall be again, not in the low circumstance, but in comparison with the grandeurs possible to the soul.

A little consideration of what takes place around us every day would show us, that a higher law than that of our will regulates events; that our painful labors are unnecessary, and fruitless; that only in our easy, simple, spontaneous action are we strong, and by contenting ourselves with obedience we become divine. Belief and love, — a believing love will relieve us of a vast load of care. O my brothers, God exists. There is a soul at the centre of nature, and over the will of every man, so that none of us can wrong the universe. It has so infused its strong enchantment into nature, that we prosper when we accept its advice, and when we struggle to wound its creatures, our hands are glued to our sides, or they beat our own breasts. The whole course of things goes to teach us faith. We need only obey. There is guidance for each of us, and by lowly listening we shall hear the right word. Why need you choose so painfully your place, and occupation, and associates, and modes of action, and of entertainment? Certainly there is a possible right for you that precludes the need of balance and wilful election. For you there is a reality, a fit place and congenial duties. Place yourself in the middle of the stream of power and wisdom which animates all whom it floats, and you are without effort impelled to truth, to right, and a perfect contentment. Then you put all gainsayers in the wrong. Then you are the world, the measure of right, of truth, of beauty. If we will not be mar-plots with our miserable interferences, the work, the society, letters, arts, science, religion of men, would go on far better than now, and the Heaven predicted from the beginning of the world, and still predicted from the bottom of the heart, would organize itself, as do now the rose and the air and the sun.

I say, *do not choose;* but that is a figure of speech by which I would distinguish what is commonly called *choice* among men, and which is a partial act, the choice of the hands, of the eyes, of the appetites, and not a whole act of the man. But that which I call right or goodness, is the choice of my constitution; and that which I call heaven, and inwardly aspire after, is the state or circumstance desirable to my constitution; and the action which I in all my years tend to do, is the work for my faculties. We must hold a man amenable to reason for the choice of his daily craft or profession. It is not an excuse any longer for his deeds that they are the custom of his trade. What business has he with an evil trade? Has he not a *calling* in his character.

Each man has his own vocation. The talent is the call. There is one direction in which all space is open to him. He has faculties silently inviting him thither to endless exertion. He is like a ship in a river; he runs against obstructions on every side but one; on that side, all obstruction is taken away, and he sweeps serenely over a deepening channel into an infinite sea. This talent and this call depend on his organization, or the mode in which the general soul incarnates itself in him. He inclines to do something which is easy to him, and good when it is done, but which no other man can do. He has no rival. For the more truly he consults his own powers, the more difference will his work exhibit from the work of any other. His ambition is exactly proportioned to his powers. The height of the pinnacle is determined by the breadth of the base. Every man has this call of the power to do somewhat unique, and no man has any other call. The pretence that he has another call, a summons by name and personal election and outward "signs that mark him extraordinary, and not in the roll of common men," is fanaticism, and betrays obtuseness to perceive that there is one mind in all the individuals, and no respect of persons therein.

By doing his work, he makes the need felt which he can supply, and creates the taste by which he is enjoyed. By doing his own work, he unfolds himself. It is the vice of our public speaking, that it has not abandonment. Somewhere, not only every orator but every man should let out all the length of all the reins; should find or make a frank and hearty expression of what force and meaning is in him. The common experience is, that the man fits himself as well as he can to the customary details of that work or trade he falls into, and tends it as a dog turns a spit. Then is he a part of the machine he moves; the man is lost. Until he can manage to communicate himself to others in his full stature and proportion, he does not yet find his vocation. He must find in that an outlet for his character, so that he may justify his work to their eyes. If the labor is mean, let him by his thinking and character, make it liberal. Whatever he knows and thinks, whatever in his apprehension is worth doing, that let him communicate, or men will never know and honor him aright. Foolish, whenever you take the meanness and formality of that thing you do, instead of converting it into the obedient spiracle of your character and aims.

We like only such actions as have already long had the praise of men, and do not perceive that any thing man can do, may be divinely done. We think greatness entailed or organized in some places or duties, in certain offices or occasions, and do not see that Paganini can extract rapture from a catgut, and Eulenstein from a jews-harp, and a nimble-fingered lad out of shreds of paper with his scissors, and Landseer out of swine, and the hero out of the pitiful habitation and company in which he was hidden. What we call obscure condition or vulgar society, is that condition and society whose poetry is not yet written, but which you shall presently make as enviable and renowned as any. In our estimates, let us take a lesson from kings. The parts of hospitality, the connection of families, the impressiveness of death, and a thousand other things, royalty makes its own estimate of, and a royal mind will. To make habitually a new estimate, — that is elevation.

What a man does, that he has. What has he to do with hope or fear? In himself is his might. Let him regard no good as solid, but that which is in his nature, and which must grow out of him as long as he exists. The goods of fortune may come and go like summer leaves; let him scatter them on every wind as the momentary signs of his infinite productiveness.

He may have his own. A man's genius, the quality that differences him from every other, the susceptibility to one class of influences, the selection of what is fit for him, the rejection of what is unfit, determines for him the character of the universe. A man is a method, a progressive arrangement; a selecting principle, gathering his like to him, wherever he goes. He takes only his own, out of the multiplicity that sweeps and circles round him. He is like one of those booms which are set out from the shore on rivers to catch drift-wood, or like the loadstone amongst splinters of steel.

Those facts, words, persons which dwell in his memory without his being able to say why, remain, because they have a relation to him not less real for being as yet unapprehended. They are symbols of value to him, as they can interpret parts of his consciousness which he would vainly seek words for in the conventional images of books and other minds. What attracts my attention shall have it, as I will go to the man who knocks at my door, whilst a thousand persons, as worthy, go by it, to whom I give no regard. It is enough that these particulars speak to me. A few anecdotes, a few traits of character, manners, face, a few incidents have an emphasis in your memory out of all proportion to their apparent significance, if you measure them by the ordinary standards. They relate to your gift. Let them have their weight, and do not reject them and cast about for illustration and facts more usual in literature. What your heart thinks great, is great. The soul's emphasis is always right.

Over all things that are agreeable to his nature and genius, the man has the highest right. Everywhere he may take what belongs to his spiritual estate, nor can he take any thing else, though all doors were open, nor can all the force of men hinder him from taking so much. It is vain to attempt to keep a secret from one who has a right to know it. It will tell itself. That mood into which a friend can bring us, is his dominion over us. To the thoughts of that state of mind, he has a right. All the secrets of that state of mind, he can compel. This is a law which statesmen use in practice. All the terrors of the French Republic, which held Austria in awe, were unable to command her diplomacy. But Napoleon sent to Vienna M. de Narbonne, one of the old noblesse, with the morals, manners and name of that interest, saying, that it was indispensable to send to the old aristocracy of Europe, men of the same connexion, which, in fact, constitutes a sort of free-masonry. M. de Narbonne, in less than a fortnight, penetrated all the secrets of the Imperial Cabinet.

Nothing seems so easy as to speak and to be understood. Yet a man may come to find *that* the strongest of defences and of ties, — that he has been understood; and he who has received an opinion, may come to find it the most inconvenient of bonds.

If a teacher have any opinion which he wishes to conceal, his pupils will become as fully indoctrinated into that as into any which he publishes. If you pour water into a vessel twisted into coils and angles, it is vain to say, I will pour it only into this or that; — it will find its level in all. Men feel and act the consequences of your doctrine, without being able to show how they follow. Show us an arc of the curve, and a good mathematician will find out the whole figure. We are always reasoning from the seen to the unseen. Hence the perfect intelligence that subsists between wise men of remote ages. A man cannot bury his meanings so deep in his book, but time and like-minded men will find them. Plato had a secret doctrine, had he? What secret can he conceal from the eyes of Bacon? of Montaigne? of Kant? Therefore, Aristotle said of his works, "They are published and not published."

No man can learn what he has not preparation for learning, however near to his eyes is the object. A chemist may tell his most precious secrets to a carpenter, and he shall be never the wiser, — the secrets he would not utter to a chemist for an estate. God screens us evermore from premature ideas. Our eyes are holden that we cannot see things that stare us in the face, until the hour arrives when the mind is ripened; then we behold them, and the time when we saw them not, is like a dream.

Not in nature but in man is all the beauty and worth he sees. The world is very empty, and is indebted to this gilding, exalting soul for all its pride. "Earth fills her lap with splendors" *not her own*. The vale of Tempe, Tivoli, and Rome are earth and water, rocks and sky. There are as good earth and water in a thousand places, yet how unaffecting!

People are not the better for the sun and moon, the horizon and the trees; as it is not observed that the keepers of Roman galleries, or the valets of painters have any elevation of thought, or that librarians are wiser men than others. There are graces in the demeanor of a polished and noble person, which are lost upon the eye of a churl. These are like the stars whose light has not yet reached us.

He may see what he maketh. Our dreams are the sequel of our waking knowledge. The visions of the night bear some proportion to the visions of the day. Hideous dreams are exaggerations of the sins of the day. We see our evil affections embodied in bad physiognomies. On the Alps, the traveller sometimes beholds his own shadow magnified to a giant, so that every gesture of his hand is terrific. "My children," said an old man to his boys scared by a figure in the dark entry, "my children, you will never see any thing worse than yourselves." As in dreams, so in the scarcely less fluid events of the world, every man sees himself in colossal, without knowing that it is himself. The good, compared to the evil which he sees, is as his own good to his own evil. Every quality of his mind is magnified in some one acquaintance, and every emotion of his heart in some one. He is like a quincunx of trees, which counts five, east, west, north, or south; or, an initial, medial, and terminal acrostic. And why not? He cleaves to one person, and avoids another, according to their likeness or unlikeness to himself, truly seeking himself in his associates, and moreover in his trade, and habits, and gestures, and meats, and drinks; and comes at last to be faithfully represented by every view you take of his circumstances.

He may read what he writes. What can we see or acquire, but what we are? You have observed a skilful man reading Virgil. Well, that author is a thousand books to a thousand persons.

Take the book into your two hands, and read your eyes out; you will never find what I find. If any ingenious reader would have a monopoly of the wisdom or delight he gets, he is as secure now the book is Englished, as if it were imprisoned in the Pelews' tongue. It is with a good book as it is with good company. Introduce a base person among gentlemen: it is all to no purpose: he is not their fellow. Every society protects itself. The company is perfectly safe, and he is not one of them, though his body is in the room.

What avails it to fight with the eternal laws of mind, which adjust the relation of all persons to each other, by the mathematical measure of their havings and beings? Gertrude is enamored of Guy; how high, how aristocratic, how Roman his mien and manners! to live with him were life indeed: and no purchase is too great; and heaven and earth are moved to that end. Well, Gertrude has Guy: but what now avails how high, how aristocratic, how Roman his mien and manners, if his heart and aims are in the senate, in the theatre, and in the billiard room, and she has no aims, no conversation that can enchant her graceful lord?

He shall have his own society. We can love nothing but nature. The most wonderful talents, the most meritorious exertions really avail very little with us; but nearness or likeness of nature, — how beautiful is the ease of its victory! Persons approach us famous for their beauty, for their accomplishments, worthy of all wonder for their charms and gifts: they dedicate their whole skill to the hour and the company, with very imperfect result. To be sure, it would be ungrateful in us not to praise them loudly. Then, when all is done, a person of related mind, a brother or sister by nature, comes to us so softly and easily, so nearly and intimately, as if it were the blood in our proper veins, that we feel as if some one was gone, instead of another having come: we are utterly relieved and refreshed: it is a sort of joyful solitude. We foolishly think, in our days of sin, that we must court friends by compliance to the customs of society, to its dress, its breeding and its estimates. But only that soul can be my friend, which I encounter on the line of my own march, that soul to which I do not decline, and which does not decline to me, but, native of the same celestial latitude, repeats in its own all my experience. The scholar forgets himself, and apes the customs and costumes of the man of the world, to deserve the smile of beauty, and follows some giddy girl, not yet taught by religious passion to know the noble woman with all that is serene, oracular and beautiful in her soul. Let him be great, and love shall follow him. Nothing is more deeply punished than the neglect of the affinities by which alone society should be formed, and the insane levity of choosing associates by others' eyes.

He may set his own rate. It is a maxim worthy of all acceptation, that a man may have that allowance he takes. Take the place and attitude which belong to you, and all men acquiesce. The world must be just. It leaves every man, with profound unconcern, to set his own rate. Hero or driveller, it meddles not in the matter. It will certainly accept your own measure of your doing and being, whether you sneak about and deny your own name, or, whether you see your work produced to the concave sphere of the heavens, one with the revolution of the stars.

The same reality pervades all teaching. The man may teach by doing, and not otherwise. If he can communicate himself, he can teach, but not by words. He teaches who gives, and he learns who receives. There is no teaching until the pupil is brought into the same state or principle in which you are; a transfusion takes place: he is you, and you are he; then is a teaching, and by no unfriendly chance or bad company can he ever quite lose the benefit. But your propositions run out of one ear as they ran in at the other. We see it advertised that Mr. Grand will deliver an oration on the Fourth of July, and Mr. Hand before the Mechanics' Association, and we do not go thither, because we know that these gentlemen will not communicate their own character and experience to the company. If we had reason to expect such a confidence, we should go through all inconvenience and opposition. The sick would be carried in litters. But a public oration is an escapade, a non-committal, an apology, a gag, and not a communication, not a speech, not a man.

A like Nemesis presides over all intellectual works. We have yet to learn, that the thing uttered in words is not therefore affirmed. It must affirm itself, or no forms of logic or of oath can give it evidence. The sentence must also contain its own apology for being spoken.

The effect of any writing on the public mind is mathematically measurable by its depth of thought. How much water does it draw? If it awaken you to think, if it lift you from your feet with the great voice of eloquence, then the effect is to be wide, slow, permanent, over the minds of men; if the pages instruct you not, they will die like flies in the hour. The way to speak and write what shall not go out of fashion, is, to speak and write sincerely. The argument which has not power to reach my own practice, I may well doubt, will fail to reach yours. But take Sidney's maxim: — "Look in thy heart, and write." He that writes to himself, writes to an eternal public. That statement only is fit to be made public which you have come at in attempting to satisfy your own curiosity. The writer who takes his subject from his ear and not from his heart, should know that he has lost as much as he seems to have gained, and when the empty book has gathered all its praise, and half the people say, 'What poetry! what genius!' it still needs fuel to make fire. That only profits which is profitable. Life alone can impart life; and though we should burst, we can only be valued as we make ourselves valuable. There is no luck in literary reputation. They who make up the final verdict upon every book, are not the partial and noisy readers of the hour when it appears; but a court as of angels, a public not to be bribed, not to be entreated, and not to be overawed, decides upon every man's title to fame. Only those books come down which deserve to last. Gilt edges, vellum, and morocco, and presentation-copies to all the libraries will not preserve a book in circulation beyond its intrinsic date. It must go with all Walpole's Noble and Royal Authors to its fate. Blackmore, Kotzebue, or Pollok may endure for a night, but Moses and Homer stand forever. There are not in the world at any one time more than a dozen persons who read and understand Plato: — never enough to pay for an edition of his works; yet to every generation these come duly down, for the sake of those few persons, as if God brought them in his hand. "No book," said Bentley, "was ever written down by any but itself." The permanence of all books is fixed by no effort friendly or hostile, but by their own specific gravity, or the intrinsic importance of their contents to the constant mind of man. "Do not trouble yourself too much about the light on your statue," said Michel Angelo to the young sculptor; "the light of the public square will test its value."

In like manner the effect of every action is measured by the depth of the sentiment from which it proceeds. The great man knew not that he was great. It took a century or two, for that fact to appear. What he did, he did because he must; it was the most natural thing in the world, and grew out of the circumstances of the moment. But now, every thing he did, even to the lifting of his finger, or the eating of bread, looks large, all-related, and is called an institution.

These are the demonstrations in a few particulars of the genius of nature: they show the direction of the stream. But the stream is blood: every drop is alive. Truth has not single victories: all things are its organs, — not only dust and stones, but errors and lies. The laws of disease, physicians say, are as beautiful as the laws of health. Our philosophy is affirmative, and readily accepts the testimony of negative facts, as every shadow points to the sun. By a divine necessity, every fact in nature is constrained to offer its testimony.

Human character evermore publishes itself. The most fugitive deed and word, the mere air of doing a thing, the intimated purpose, expresses character. If you act, you show character; if you sit still, if you sleep, you show it. You think because you have spoken nothing, when others spoke, and have given no opinion on the times, on the church, on slavery, on marriage, on socialism, on secret societies, on the college, on parties and persons, that your verdict is still expected with curiosity as a reserved wisdom. Far otherwise; your silence answers very loud. You have no oracle to utter, and your fellow men have learned that you cannot help them; for, oracles speak. Doth not wisdom cry, and understanding put forth her voice?

Dreadful limits are set in nature to the powers of dissimulation.

Truth tyrannizes over the unwilling members of the body. Faces never lie, it is said. No man need be deceived, who will study the changes of expression. When a man speaks the truth in the spirit of truth, his eye is as clear as the heavens. When he has base ends, and speaks falsely, the eye is muddy and sometimes asquint.

I have heard an experienced counsellor say, that he never feared the effect upon a jury, of a lawyer who does not believe in his heart that his client ought to have a verdict. If he does not believe it, his unbelief will appear to the jury, despite all his protestations, and will become their unbelief. This is that law whereby a work of art, of whatever kind, sets us in the same state of mind wherein the artist was, when he made it. That which we do not believe, we cannot adequately say, though we may repeat the words never so often. It was this conviction which Swedenborg expressed, when he described a group of persons in the spiritual world endeavoring in vain to articulate a proposition which they did not believe: but they could not, though they twisted and folded their lips even to indignation.

A man passes for that he is worth. Very idle is all curiosity concerning other people's estimate of us, and all fear of remaining unknown is not less so. If a man know that he can do any thing, — that he can do it better than any one else, — he has a pledge of the acknowledgment of that fact by all persons. The world is full of judgment days, and into every assembly that a man enters, in every action he attempts, he is gauged and stamped. In every troop of boys that whoop and run in each yard and square, a new comer is as well and accurately weighed in the course of a few days, and stamped with his right number, as if he had undergone a formal trial of his strength, speed, and temper. A stranger comes from a distant school, with better dress, with trinkets in his pockets, with airs and pretensions: an older boy says to himself, 'It 's of no use: we shall find him out tomorrow.' 'What has he done?' is the divine question which searches men, and transpierces every false reputation. A fop may sit in any chair of the world, nor be distinguished for his hour from Homer and Washington; but there need never be any doubt concerning the respective ability of human beings. Pretension may sit still, but cannot act. Pretension never feigned an act of real greatness. Pretension never wrote an Iliad, nor drove back Xerxes, nor christianized the world, nor abolished slavery.

As much virtue as there is, so much appears; as much goodness as there is, so much reverence it commands. All the devils respect virtue. The high, the generous, the self-devoted sect will always instruct and command mankind. Never was a sincere word utterly lost. Never a magnanimity fell to the ground, but there is some heart to greet and accept it unexpectedly. A man passes for that he is worth. What he is, engraves itself on his face, on his form, on his fortunes, in letters of light. Concealment avails him nothing; boasting, nothing. There is confession in the glances of our eyes; in our smiles; in salutations; and the grasp of hands. His sin bedaubs him, mars all his good impression. Men know not why they do not trust him; but they do not trust him. His vice glasses his eye, cuts lines of mean expression in his cheek, pinches the nose, sets the mark of the beast on the back of the head, and writes O fool! fool! on the forehead of a king.

If you would not be known to do any thing, never do it. A man may play the fool in the drifts of a desert, but every grain of sand shall seem to see. He may be a solitary eater, but he cannot keep his foolish counsel. A broken complexion, a swinish look, ungenerous acts, and the want of due knowledge, — all blab. Can a cook, a Chiffinch, an Iachimo be mistaken for Zeno or Paul? Confucius exclaimed, — "How can a man be concealed! How can a man be concealed!"

On the other hand, the hero fears not, that if he withhold the avowal of a just and brave act, it will go unwitnessed and unloved. One knows it, — himself, — and is pledged by it to sweetness of peace, and to nobleness of aim, which will prove in the end a better proclamation of it than the relating of the incident. Virtue is the adherence in action to the nature of things, and the nature of things makes it prevalent. It consists in a perpetual substitution of being for seeming, and with sublime propriety God is described as saying, I AM.

The lesson which these observations convey is, Be, and not

seem. Let us acquiesce. Let us take our bloated nothingness out of the path of the divine circuits. Let us unlearn our wisdom of the world. Let us lie low in the Lord's power, and learn that truth alone makes rich and great.

If you visit your friend, why need you apologize for not having visited him, and waste his time and deface your own act? Visit him now. Let him feel that the highest love has come to see him, in thee its lowest organ. Or why need you torment yourself and friend by secret self-reproaches that you have not assisted him or complimented him with gifts and salutations heretofore? Be a gift and a benediction. Shine with real light, and not with the borrowed reflection of gifts. Common men are apologies for men; they bow the head, excuse themselves with prolix reasons, and accumulate appearances, because the substance is not.

We are full of these superstitions of sense, the worship of magnitude. We call the poet inactive, because he is not a president, a merchant, or a porter. We adore an institution, and do not see that it is founded on a thought which we have. But real action is in silent moments. The epochs of our life are not in the visible facts of our choice of a calling, our marriage, our acquisition of an office, and the like, but in a silent thought by the way-side as we walk; in a thought which revises our entire manner of life, and says, — 'Thus hast thou done, but it were better thus.' And all our after years, like menials, serve and wait on this, and, according to their ability, execute its will. This revisal or correction is a constant force, which, as a tendency, reaches through our lifetime. The object of the man, the aim of these moments is to make daylight shine through him, to suffer the law to traverse his whole being without obstruction, so that, on what point soever of his doing your eye falls, it shall report truly of his character, whether it be his diet, his house, his religious forms, his society, his mirth, his vote, his opposition. Now he is not homogeneous, but heterogeneous, and the ray does not traverse; there are no thorough lights: but the eye of the beholder is puzzled, detecting many unlike tendencies, and a life not yet at one.

Why should we make it a point with our false modesty to disparage that man we are, and that form of being assigned to us?

93

A good man is contented. I love and honor Epaminondas, but I do not wish to be Epaminondas. I hold it more just to love the world of this hour, than the world of his hour. Nor can you, if I am true, excite me to the least uneasiness by saying, 'he acted, and thou sittest still.' I see action to be good, when the need is, and sitting still to be also good. Epaminondas, if he was the man I take him for, would have sat still with joy and peace, if his lot had been mine. Heaven is large, and affords space for all modes of love and fortitude. Why should we be busy-bodies and super-serviceable? Action and inaction are alike to the true. One piece of the tree is cut for a weathercock, and one for the sleeper of a bridge; the virtue of the wood is apparent in both.

I desire not to disgrace the soul. The fact that I am here, certainly shows me that the soul had need of an organ here. Shall I not assume the post? Shall I skulk and dodge and duck with my unseasonable apologies and vain modesty, and imagine my being here impertinent? less pertinent than Epaminondas or Homer being there? and that the soul did not know its own needs? Besides, without any reasoning on the matter, I have no discontent. The good soul nourishes me, and unlocks new magazines of power and enjoyment to me every day. I will not meanly decline the immensity of good, because I have heard that it has come to others in another shape.

Besides, why should we be cowed by the name of Action? 'T is a trick of the senses, — no more. We know that the ancestor of every action is a thought. The poor mind does not seem to itself to be any thing, unless it have an outside badge, — some Gentoo diet, or Quaker coat, or Calvinistic prayer-meeting, or philanthropic society, or a great donation, or a high office, or, any how, some wild contrasting action to testify that it is somewhat. The rich mind lies in the sun and sleeps, and is Nature. To think is to act.

Let us, if we must have great actions, make our own so. All action is of an infinite elasticity, and the least admits of being inflated with the celestial air until it eclipses the sun and moon. Let us seek *one* peace by fidelity. Let me heed my duties. Why need I go gadding into the scenes and philosophy of Greek and

Italian history, before I have justified myself to my benefactors? How dare I read Washington's campaigns, when I have not answered the letters of my own correspondents? Is not that a just objection to much of our reading? It is a pusillanimous desertion of our work to gaze after our neighbors. It is peeping. Byron says of Jack Bunting, —

"He knew not what to say, and so, he swore."

I may say it of our preposterous use of books, — He knew not what to do, and so, *he read.* I can think of nothing to fill my time with, and I find the Life of Brant. It is a very extravagant compliment to pay to Brant, or to General Schuyler, or to General Washington. My time should be as good as their time, — my facts, my net of relations as good as theirs, or either of theirs. Rather let me do my work so well that other idlers, if they choose, may compare my texture with the texture of these and find it identical with the best.

This over-estimate of the possibilities of Paul and Pericles, this under-estimate of our own, comes from a neglect of the fact of an identical nature. Bonaparte knew but one Merit, and rewarded in one and the same way the good soldier, the good astronomer, the good poet, the good player. The poet uses the names of Cæsar, of Tamerlane, of Bonduca, of Belisarius; the painter uses the conventional story of the Virgin Mary, of Paul, of Peter. He does not, therefore, defer to the nature of these accidental men, of these stock heroes. If the poet write a true drama, then he is Cæsar, and not the player of Cæsar; then the selfsame strain of thought, emotion as pure, wit as subtle, motions as swift, mounting, extravagant, and a heart as great, self-sufficing, dauntless, which on the waves of its love and hope can uplift all that is reckoned solid and precious in the world, — palaces, gardens, money, navies, kingdoms, — marking its own incomparable worth by the slight it casts on these gauds of men, — these all are his, and by the power of these he rouses the nations. Let a man believe in God, and not in names and places and persons. Let the great soul incarnated in some woman's form, poor and sad and single, in some Dolly or

Joan, go out to service, and sweep chambers and scour floors, and its effulgent daybeams cannot be muffled or hid, but to sweep and scour will instantly appear supreme and beautiful actions, the top and radiance of human life, and all people will get mops and brooms; until, lo, suddenly the great soul has enshrined itself in some other form, and done some other deed, and that is now the flower and head of all living nature.

We are the photometers, we the irritable goldleaf and tinfoil that measure the accumulations of the subtle element. We know the authentic effects of the true fire through every one of its million disguises.

LOVE

"I was as a gem concealed;
Me my burning ray revealed."

Koran.

LOVE

Every promise of the soul has innumerable fulfilments: each of its joys ripens into a new want. Nature, uncontainable, flowing, forelooking, in the first sentiment of kindness anticipates already a benevolence which shall lose all particular regards in its general light. The introduction to this felicity is in a private and tender relation of one to one, which is the enchantment of human life; which, like a certain divine rage and enthusiasm, seizes on man at one period, and works a revolution in his mind and body; unites him to his race, pledges him to the domestic and civic relations, carries him with new sympathy into nature, enhances the power of the senses, opens the imagination, adds to his character heroic and sacred attributes, establishes marriage, and gives permanence to human society.

The natural association of the sentiment of love with the heyday of the blood, seems to require that in order to portray it in vivid tints which every youth and maid should confess to be true to their throbbing experience, one must not be too old. The delicious fancies of youth reject the least savor of a mature philosophy, as chilling with age and pedantry their purple bloom. And, therefore, I know I incur the imputation of unnecessary hardness and stoicism from those who compose the Court and Parliament of Love. But from these formidable censors I shall appeal to my seniors. For, it is to be considered that this passion of which we speak, though it begin with the young, yet forsakes not the old, or rather suffers no one who is truly its servant to grow old, but makes the aged participators of it, not less than the tender maiden, though in a different and nobler sort. For, it is a fire that, kindling its first embers in the narrow nook of a private bosom, caught from a wandering spark out of another private heart, glows and enlarges until it warms and beams upon multitudes of men and women, upon the universal heart of all, and so lights up the whole world and all nature with its generous flames. It matters not, therefore, whether we attempt to describe the passion at twenty, at thirty, or at eighty years. He who paints it at the first period, will lose some of its later, he who paints it at the last, some of its earlier traits. Only it is to be hoped that by patience and the muses' aid, we may attain to that inward view of the law, which shall describe a truth ever young and beautiful, so central that it shall commend itself to the eye at whatever angle beholden.

And the first condition is, that we must leave a too close and lingering adherence to facts, and study the sentiment as it appeared in hope and not in history. For, each man sees his own life defaced and disfigured, as the life of man is not, to his imagination. Each man sees over his own experience a certain stain of error, whilst that of other men looks fair and ideal. Let any man go back to those delicious relations which make the beauty of his life, which have given him sincerest instruction and nourishment, he will shrink and moan. Alas! I know not why, but infinite compunctions embitter in mature life the remembrances of budding joy, and cover every beloved name. Every thing is beautiful seen from the point of the intellect, or as truth. But all is sour, if seen as experience. Details are melancholy; the plan is seemly and noble. In the actual world — the painful kingdom of time and place — dwell care, and canker, and fear. With thought, with the ideal, is immortal hilarity, the rose of joy. Round it all the muses sing. But grief cleaves to names, and persons, and the partial interests of to-day and yesterday.

The strong bent of nature is seen in the proportion which this topic of personal relations usurps in the conversation of society. What do we wish to know of any worthy person so much as how he has sped in the history of this sentiment? What books in the circulating libraries circulate? How we glow over these novels of passion, when the story is told with any spark of truth and nature! And what fastens attention, in the intercourse of life, like any passage betraying affection between two parties? Perhaps we never saw them before, and never shall meet them again. But we see them exchange a glance, or betray a deep emotion, and we are no longer strangers. We understand them, and take the warmest interest in the development of the romance. All mankind love a lover. The earliest demonstrations of complacency and kindness are nature's most winning pictures. It is the dawn of civility and grace in the coarse and rustic. The rude village boy teazes the girls about the school house door; — but to-day he comes running into the entry, and meets one fair child disposing her satchel: he holds her books to help her, and instantly it seems to him as if she removed herself from him infinitely, and was a sacred precinct. Among the throng of girls he runs rudely enough, but one alone distances him: and these two little neighbors that were so close just now, have learned to respect each other's personality. Or who can avert his eyes from the engaging, half-artful, half-artless ways of school girls who go into the country shops to buy a skein of silk or a sheet of paper, and talk half an hour about nothing, with the broad-faced, good-natured shop-boy. In the village, they are on a perfect equality, which love delights in, and without any coquetry the happy, affectionate nature of woman flows out in this pretty gossip. The girls may have little beauty, yet plainly do they establish between them and the good boy the most agreeable, confiding relations, what with their fun and their earnest, about Edgar, and Jonas, and Almira, and who was invited to the party, and who danced at the dancing school, and when the singing school would begin, and other nothings concerning which the parties cooed. By and by that boy wants a wife, and very truly and heartily will he know where to find a sincere and sweet mate, without any risk such as Milton deplores as incident to scholars and great men.

I have been told, that in some public discourses of mine my reverence for the intellect has made me unjustly cold to the personal relations. But now I almost shrink at the remembrance of such disparaging words. For persons are love's world, and the coldest philosopher cannot recount the debt of the young soul wandering here in nature to the power of love, without being tempted to unsay as treasonable to nature, aught derogatory to the social instincts. For, though the celestial rapture falling out of heaven seizes only upon those of tender age, and although a beauty overpowering all analysis or comparison, and putting us quite beside ourselves, we can seldom see after thirty years, yet the remembrance of these visions outlasts all other remembrances, and is a wreath of flowers on the oldest brows. But here is a strange fact; it may seem to many men in revising their experience, that they have no fairer page in their life's book than the delicious memory of some passages wherein affection contrived to give a witchcraft surpassing the deep attraction of its own truth to a parcel of accidental and trivial circumstances. In looking backward, they may find that several things which were not the charm, have more reality to this groping memory than the charm itself which embalmed them. But be our experience in particulars what it may, no man ever forgot the visitations of that power to his heart and brain, which created all things new; which was the dawn in him of music, poetry and art; which made the face of nature radiant with purple light, the morning and the night varied enchantments; when a single tone of one voice could make the heart bound, and the most trivial circumstance associated with one form, is put in the amber of memory: when he became all eye when one was present, and all memory when one was gone; when the youth becomes a watcher of windows, and studious of a glove, a veil, a ribbon, or the wheels of a carriage; when no place is too solitary, and none too silent for him who has richer company and sweeter conversation in his new thoughts, than any old friends, though best and purest, can give him; for, the figures, the motions, the words of the beloved object are not like other images written in water, but, as Plutarch said, "enamelled in fire," and make the study of midnight.

> "Thou art not gone being gone, where'er thou art,
> Thou leav'st in him thy watchful eyes, in him thy loving
>   heart."

In the noon and the afternoon of life, we still throb at the recollection of days when happiness was not happy enough, but must be drugged with the relish of pain and fear; for he touched the secret of the matter, who said of love, —

"All other pleasures are not worth its pains:"

and when the day was not long enough, but the night too must be consumed in keen recollections; when the head boiled all night on the pillow with the generous deed it resolved on; when the moonlight was a pleasing fever, and the stars were letters, and the flowers ciphers, and the air was coined into song; when all business seemed an impertinence, and all the men and women running to and fro in the streets, mere pictures.

The passion rebuilds the world for the youth. It makes all things alive and significant. Nature grows conscious. Every bird on the boughs of the tree sings now to his heart and soul. The notes are almost articulate. The clouds have faces, as he looks on them. The trees of the forest, the waving grass and the peeping flowers have grown intelligent; and he almost fears to trust them with the secret which they seem to invite. Yet nature soothes and sympathizes. In the green solitude he finds a dearer home than with men.

> "Fountain heads and pathless groves,
> Places which pale passion loves,
> Moonlight walks, when all the fowls
> Are safely housed, save bats and owls,
> A midnight bell, a passing groan, —
> These are the sounds we feed upon."

Behold there in the wood the fine madman! He is a palace of sweet sounds and sights; he dilates; he is twice a man; he walks with arms akimbo; he soliloquizes; he accosts the grass and the trees; he feels the blood of the violet, the clover and the lily in his veins; and he talks with the brook that wets his foot.

The heats that have opened his perceptions of natural beauty, have made him love music and verse. It is a fact often observed, that men have written good verses under the inspiration of passion, who cannot write well under any other circumstances.

The like force has the passion over all his nature. It expands the sentiment; it makes the clown gentle, and gives the coward heart. Into the most pitiful and abject it will infuse a heart and courage to defy the world, so only it have the countenance of the beloved object. In giving him to another, it still more gives him to himself. He is a new man, with new perceptions, new and keener purposes, and a religious solemnity of character and aims. He does not longer appertain to his family and society; *he* is somewhat; *he* is a person; *he* is a soul.

And here let us examine a little nearer the nature of that influence which is thus potent over the human youth. Beauty, whose revelation to man we now celebrate, welcome as the sun wherever it pleases to shine, which pleases everybody with it and with themselves, seems sufficient to itself. The lover cannot paint his maiden to his fancy poor and solitary. Like a tree in flower, so much soft, budding, informing loveliness is society for itself, and she teaches his eye why Beauty was pictured with Loves and Graces attending her steps. Her existence makes the world rich. Though she extrudes all other persons from his attention as cheap and unworthy, she indemnifies him by carrying out her own being into somewhat impersonal, large, mundane, so that the maiden stands to him for a representative of all select things and virtues. For that reason the lover never sees personal resemblances in his mistress to her kindred or to others. His friends find in her a likeness to her mother, or her sisters, or to persons not of her blood. The lover sees no resemblance except to summer evenings and diamond mornings, to rainbows and the song of birds.

The ancients called beauty the flowering of virtue. Who can analyze the nameless charm which glances from one and another face and form? We are touched with emotions of tenderness and complacency, but we cannot find whereat this dainty emotion, this wandering gleam, points. It is destroyed for the imagination by any attempt to refer it to organization. Nor does it point to any relations of friendship or love known and described in society, but, as it seems to me, to a quite other and unattainable sphere, to relations of transcendant delicacy and sweetness, to what roses and violets hint and foreshow. We cannot approach beauty.

Its nature is like opaline doves'-neck lustres, hovering and evanescent. Herein it resembles the most excellent things, which all have this rainbow character, defying all attempts at appropriation and use. What else did Jean Paul Richter signify, when he said to music, "Away! away! thou speakest to me of things which in all my endless life I have found not, and shall not find." The same fluency may be observed in every work of the plastic arts. The statue is then beautiful, when it begins to be incomprehensible, when it is passing out of criticism, and can no longer be defined by compass and measuring wand, but demands an active imagination to go with it, and to say what it is in the act of doing. The god or hero of the sculptor is always represented in a transition *from* that which is representable to the senses, *to* that which is not. Then first it ceases to be a stone. The same remark holds of painting. And of poetry, the success is not attained when it lulls and satisfies, but when it astonishes and fires us with new endeavors after the unattainable. Concerning it, Landor inquires "whether it is not to be referred to some purer state of sensation and existence."

In like manner, personal beauty is then first charming and itself, when it dissatisfies us with any end; when it becomes a story without an end; when it suggests gleams and visions, and not earthly satisfactions; when it makes the beholder feel his unworthiness; when he cannot feel his right to it, though he were Cæsar; he cannot feel more right to it, than to the firmament and the splendors of a sunset.

Hence arose the saying, "If I love you, what is that to you?" We say so, because we feel that what we love, is not in your will, but above it. It is not you, but your radiance. It is that which you know not in yourself, and can never know.

This agrees well with that high philosophy of Beauty which the ancient writers delighted in; for they said, that the soul of man, embodied here on earth, went roaming up and down in quest of that other world of its own, out of which it came into this, but was soon stupefied by the light of the natural sun, and unable to see any other objects than those of this world, which are but shadows of real things. Therefore, the Deity sends the glory of youth before the soul, that it may avail itself of beautiful bodies as aids to its recollection of the celestial good and fair; and the man beholding such a person in the female sex, runs to her, and finds the highest joy in contemplating the form, movement, and intelligence of this person, because it suggests to him the presence of that which indeed is within the beauty, and the cause of the beauty.

If, however, from too much conversing with material objects, the soul was gross, and misplaced its satisfaction in the body, it reaped nothing but sorrow; body being unable to fulfil the promise which beauty holds out; but if, accepting the hint of these visions and suggestions which beauty makes to his mind, the soul passes through the body, and falls to admire strokes of character, and the lovers contemplate one another in their discourses and their actions, then, they pass to the true palace of Beauty, more and more inflame their love of it, and by this love extinguishing the base affection, as the sun puts out the fire by shining on the hearth, they become pure and hallowed. By conversation with that which is in itself excellent, magnanimous, lowly and just, the lover comes to a warmer love of these nobilities, and a quicker apprehension of them. Then, he passes from loving them in one, to loving them in all, and so is the one beautiful soul only the door through which he enters to the society of all true and pure souls. In the particular society of his mate, he attains a clearer sight of any spot, any taint, which her beauty has contracted from this world, and is able to point it out, and this with mutual joy that they are now able without offence to indicate blemishes and hindrances in each other, and give to each all help and comfort in curing the same. And, beholding in many souls the traits of the divine beauty, and separating in each soul that which is divine from the taint which it has contracted in the world, the lover ascends to the highest beauty, to the love and knowledge of the Divinity, by steps on this ladder of created souls.

Somewhat like this have the truly wise told us of love in all ages. The doctrine is not old, nor is it new. If Plato, Plutarch and Apuleius taught it, so have Petrarch, Angelo, and Milton. It awaits a truer unfolding in opposition and rebuke to that subterranean prudence which presides at marriages with words that take hold of the upper world, whilst one eye is prowling in the cellar, so that its gravest discourse has a savor of hams and powdering-tubs. Worst, when this sensualism intrudes into the education of young women, and withers the hope and affection of human nature, by teaching, that marriage signifies nothing but a housewife's thrift, and that woman's life has no other aim.

But this dream of love, though beautiful, is only one scene in our play. In the procession of the soul from within outward, it enlarges its circles ever, like the pebble thrown into the pond, or the light proceeding from an orb. The rays of the soul alight first on things nearest, on every utensil and toy, on nurses and domestics, on the house and yard and passengers, on the circle of household acquaintance, on politics, and geography, and history. But things are ever grouping themselves according to higher or more interior laws. Neighborhood, size, numbers, habits, persons, lose by degrees their power over us. Cause and effect, real affinities, the longing for harmony between the soul and the circumstance, the progressive, idealizing instinct, predominate later, and the step backward from the higher to the lower relations is impossible. Thus even love, which is the deification of persons, must become more impersonal every day. Of this at first it gives no hint. Little think the youth and maiden who are glancing at each other across crowded rooms, with eyes so full of mutual intelligence, of the precious fruit long hereafter to proceed from this new, quite external stimulus. The work of vegetation begins first in the irritability of the bark and leaf-buds. From exchanging glances, they advance to acts of courtesy, of gallantry, then to fiery passion, to plighting troth and marriage. Passion beholds its object as a perfect unit. The soul is wholly embodied, and the body is wholly ensouled.

> "Her pure and eloquent blood
>   Spoke in her cheeks, and so distinctly wrought,
>   That one might almost say her body thought."

Romeo, if dead, should be cut up into little stars to make the heavens fine. Life, with this pair, has no other aim, asks no more

than Juliet, — than Romeo. Night, day, studies, talents, kingdoms, religion, are all contained in this form full of soul, in this
soul which is all form. The lovers delight in endearments, in
avowals of love, in comparisons of their regards. When alone,
they solace themselves with the remembered image of the other.
Does that other see the same star, the same melting cloud, read
the same book, feel the same emotion that now delight me?
They try and weigh their affection, and adding up costly advantages, friends, opportunities, properties, exult in discovering that
willingly, joyfully, they would give all as a ransom for the beautiful, the beloved head, not one hair of which shall be harmed.
But the lot of humanity is on these children. Danger, sorrow,
and pain arrive to them, as to all. Love prays. It makes covenants with Eternal Power, in behalf of this dear mate. The union which is thus effected, and which adds a new value to every
atom in nature, for it transmutes every thread throughout the
whole web of relation into a golden ray, and bathes the soul in a
new and sweeter element, is yet a temporary state. Not always
can flowers, pearls, poetry, protestations, nor even home in another heart, content the awful soul that dwells in clay. It arouses
itself at last from these endearments, as toys, and puts on the har-
ness, and aspires to vast and universal aims. The soul which is
in the soul of each, craving a perfect beatitude, detects incongruities, defects, and disproportion in the behavior of the other.
Hence arise surprise, expostulation, and pain. Yet that which
drew them to each other was signs of loveliness, signs of virtue:
and these virtues are there, however eclipsed. They appear and
reappear, and continue to attract; but the regard changes, quits
the sign, and attaches to the substance. This repairs the wounded
affection. Meantime, as life wears on, it proves a game of permu-
tation and combination of all possible positions of the parties, to
employ all the resources of each, and acquaint each with the
strength and weakness of the other. For, it is the nature and end
of this relation, that they should represent the human race to each
other. All that is in the world which is or ought to be known, is
cunningly wrought into the texture of man, of woman.

Love

"The person love does to us fit,
Like manna, has the taste of all in it."

The world rolls: the circumstances vary, every hour. The angels that inhabit this temple of the body appear at the windows, and the gnomes and vices also. By all the virtues, they are united. If there be virtue, all the vices are known as such; they confess and flee. Their once flaming regard is sobered by time in either breast, and losing in violence what it gains in extent, it becomes a thorough good understanding. They resign each other, without complaint, to the good offices which man and woman are severally appointed to discharge in time, and exchange the passion which once could not lose sight of its object, for a cheerful, disengaged furtherance, whether present or absent, of each other's designs. At last they discover that all which at first drew them together, — those once sacred features, that magical play of charms, — was deciduous, had a prospective end, like the scaffolding by which the house was built; and the purification of the intellect and the heart, from year to year, is the real marriage, foreseen and prepared from the first, and wholly above their consciousness. Looking at these aims with which two persons, a man and a woman, so variously and correlatively gifted, are shut up in one house to spend in the nuptial society forty or fifty years, I do not wonder at the emphasis with which the heart prophesies this crisis from early infancy, at the profuse beauty with which the instincts deck the nuptial bower, and nature and intellect and art emulate each other in the gifts and the melody they bring to the epithalamium.

Thus are we put in training for a love which knows not sex, nor person, nor partiality, but which seeks virtue and wisdom everywhere, to the end of increasing virtue and wisdom. We are by nature observers, and thereby learners. That is our permanent state. But we are often made to feel that our affections are but tents of a night. Though slowly and with pain, the objects of the affections change, as the objects of thought do. There are moments when the affections rule and absorb the man, and make his happiness dependent on a person or persons. But in health the mind is presently seen again, — its overarching vault, bright with galaxies of immutable lights, and the warm loves and fears that swept over us as clouds, must lose their finite character, and blend with God, to attain their own perfection. But we need not fear that we can lose any thing by the progress of the soul. The soul may be trusted to the end. That which is so beautiful and attractive as these relations, must be succeeded and supplanted only by what is more beautiful, and so on for ever.

FRIENDSHIP

A ruddy drop of manly blood
The surging sea outweighs,
The world uncertain comes and goes,
The lover rooted stays.
I fancied he was fled,
And, after many a year,
Glowed unexhausted kindliness
Like daily sunrise there.
My careful heart was free again, —
O friend, my bosom said,
Through thee alone the sky is arched,
Through thee the rose is red,
All things through thee take nobler form,
And look beyond the earth,
The mill-round of our fate appears
A sun-path in thy worth.
Me too thy nobleness has taught
To master my despair;
The fountains of my hidden life
Are through thy friendship fair.

ESSAY VI

FRIENDSHIP

We have a great deal more kindness than is ever spoken. Maugre all the selfishness that chills like east winds the world, the whole human family is bathed with an element of love like a fine ether. How many persons we meet in houses, whom we scarcely speak to, whom yet we honor, and who honor us! How many we see in the street, or sit with in church, whom, though silently, we warmly rejoice to be with! Read the language of these wandering eye-beams. The heart knoweth.

The effect of the indulgence of this human affection is a certain cordial exhilaration. In poetry, and in common speech, the emotions of benevolence and complacency which are felt towards others, are likened to the material effects of fire; so swift, or much more swift, more active, more cheering are these fine inward irradiations. From the highest degree of passionate love, to the lowest degree of good will, they make the sweetness of life.

Our intellectual and active powers increase with our affection. The scholar sits down to write, and all his years of meditation do not furnish him with one good thought or happy expression; but it is necessary to write a letter to a friend, — and, forthwith, troops of gentle thoughts invest themselves, on every hand, with chosen words. See in any house where virtue and self-respect abide, the palpitation which the approach of a stranger causes. A commended stranger is expected and announced, and an uneasiness betwixt pleasure and pain invades all the hearts of a household. His arrival almost brings fear to the good hearts that would welcome him. The house is dusted, all things fly into their places, the old coat is exchanged for the new, and they must get up a dinner if they can. Of a commended stranger, only the good report is told by others, only the good and new is heard by us. He stands to us for humanity. He is, what we wish. Having imagined and invested him, we ask how we should stand related in conversation and action with such a man, and are uneasy with fear. The same idea exalts conversation with him. We talk better than we are wont. We have the nimblest fancy, a richer memory, and our dumb devil has taken leave for the time. For long hours we can continue a series of sincere, graceful, rich communications, drawn from the oldest, secretest experience, so that they who sit by, of our own kinsfolk and acquaintance, shall feel a lively surprise at our unusual powers. But as soon as the stranger begins to intrude his partialities, his definitions, his defects, into the conversation, it is all over. He has heard the first, the last and best, he will ever hear from us. He is no stranger now. Vulgarity, ignorance, misapprehension, are old acquaintances. Now, when he comes, he may get the order, the dress, and the dinner, — but the throbbing of the heart, and the communications of the soul, no more.

What is so pleasant as these jets of affection which make a young world for me again? What so delicious as a just and firm encounter of two, in a thought, in a feeling? How beautiful, on their approach to this beating heart, the steps and forms of the gifted and the true! The moment we indulge our affections, the earth is metamorphosed: there is no winter, and no night: all tragedies, all ennuis vanish, — all duties even; nothing fills the proceeding eternity but the forms all radiant of beloved persons. Let the soul be assured that somewhere in the universe it should rejoin its friend, and it would be content and cheerful alone for a thousand years.

I awoke this morning with devout thanksgiving for my friends, the old and the new. Shall I not call God the Beautiful, who daily showeth himself so to me in his gifts? I chide society, I embrace solitude, and yet I am not so ungrateful as not to see the wise, the lovely, and the noble-minded, as from time to time they pass my gate. Who hears me, who understands me, becomes mine, — a possession for all time. Nor is nature so poor, but she gives me this joy several times, and thus we weave social threads of our own, a new web of relations; and, as many thoughts in succession substantiate themselves, we shall by and by stand in a new world of our own creation, and no longer strangers and pilgrims in a traditionary globe. My friends have come to me unsought. The great God gave them to me. By oldest right, by the divine affinity of virtue with itself, I find them, or rather, not I, but the Deity in me and in them derides and cancels the thick walls of individual character, relation, age, sex, circumstance, at which he usually connives, and now makes many one. High thanks I owe you, excellent lovers, who carry out the world for me to new and noble depths, and enlarge the meaning of all my thoughts. These are new poetry of the first Bard, — poetry without stop, — hymn, ode, and epic, poetry still flowing, Apollo and the Muses chanting still. Will these too separate themselves from me again, or some of them? I know not, but I fear it not; for my relation to them is so pure, that we hold by simple affinity, and the Genius of my life being thus social, the same affinity will exert its energy on whomsoever is as noble as these men and women, wherever I may be.

I confess to an extreme tenderness of nature on this point. It is almost dangerous to me to "crush the sweet poison of misused wine" of the affections. A new person is to me a great event, and hinders me from sleep. I have often had fine fancies about persons which have given me delicious hours; but the joy ends in the day: it yields no fruit. Thought is not born of it; my action is very little modified. I must feel pride in my friend's accomplishments as if they were mine, — and a property in his virtues. I feel as warmly when he is praised, as the lover when he hears applause of his engaged maiden. We overestimate the conscience of our friend. His goodness seems better than our goodness, his nature finer, his temptations less. Every thing that is his, — his name, his form, his dress, books, and instruments, — fancy enhances. Our own thought sounds new and larger from his mouth.

Yet the systole and diastole of the heart are not without their analogy in the ebb and flow of love. Friendship, like the immortality of the soul, is too good to be believed. The lover, beholding his maiden, half knows that she is not verily that which he worships; and in the golden hour of friendship, we are surprised with shades of suspicion and unbelief. We doubt that we bestow on our hero the virtues in which he shines, and afterwards worship the form to which we have ascribed this divine inhabitation. In strictness, the soul does not respect men as it respects itself. In strict science, all persons underlie the same condition of an infinite remoteness. Shall we fear to cool our love by mining for the metaphysical foundation of this Elysian temple? Shall I not be as real as the things I see? If I am, I shall not fear to know them for what they are. Their essence is not less beautiful than their appearance, though it needs finer organs for its apprehension. The root of the plant is not unsightly to science, though for chaplets and festoons we cut the stem short. And I must hazard the production of the bald fact amidst these pleasing reveries, though it should prove an Egyptian skull at our banquet. A man who stands united with his thought, conceives magnificently of himself. He is conscious of a universal success, even though bought by uniform particular failures. No advantages, no powers, no gold or force can be any match for him. I cannot choose but rely on my own poverty, more than on your wealth. I cannot make your consciousness tantamount to mine. Only the star dazzles; the planet has a faint, moon-like ray. I hear what you say of the admirable parts and tried temper of the party you praise, but I see well that for all his purple cloaks I shall not like him, unless he is at last a poor Greek like me. I cannot deny it, O friend, that the vast shadow of the Phenomenal includes thee, also, in its pied and painted immensity, — thee, also, compared with whom all else is shadow. Thou art not Being, as Truth is, as Justice is, — thou art not my soul, but a picture and effigy of that. Thou hast come to me lately, and already thou art seizing thy hat and cloak. Is it not that the soul puts forth friends, as the tree puts forth leaves, and presently, by the germination of new buds, extrudes the old leaf? The law of nature is alternation forevermore. Each electrical state superinduces the opposite. The soul environs itself with friends, that it may enter into a grander self-acquaintance or solitude; and it goes alone, for a season, that it may exalt its conversation or society. This method betrays itself along the whole history of our personal relations. The instinct of affection revives the hope of union with our mates, and the returning sense of insulation recalls us from the chase. Thus every man passes his life in the search after friendship, and if he should record his true sentiment, he might write a letter like this, to each new candidate for his love.

Dear Friend: —

If I was sure of thee, sure of thy capacity, sure to match my mood with thine, I should never think again of trifles, in relation to thy comings and goings. I am not very wise: my moods are quite attainable: and I respect thy genius: it is to me as yet unfathomed; yet dare I not presume in thee a perfect intelligence of me, and so thou art to me a delicious torment. Thine ever, or never.

Yet these uneasy pleasures and fine pains are for curiosity, and not for life. They are not to be indulged. This is to weave cobweb, and not cloth. Our friendships hurry to short and poor conclusions, because we have made them a texture of wine and dreams, instead of the tough fibre of the human heart. The laws of friendship are austere and eternal, of one web with the laws of nature and of morals. But we have aimed at a swift and petty benefit, to suck a sudden sweetness. We snatch at the slowest fruit in the whole garden of God, which many summers and many winters must ripen. We seek our friend not sacredly, but with an adulterate passion which would appropriate him to ourselves. In vain. We are armed all over with subtle antagonisms, which, as soon as we meet, begin to play, and translate all poetry into stale prose. Almost all people descend to meet. All association must be a compromise, and, what is worst, the very flower and aroma of the flower of each of the beautiful natures disappears as they approach each other. What a perpetual disappointment is actual society, even of the virtuous and gifted! After interviews have been compassed with long foresight, we must be tormented presently by baffled blows, by sudden, unseasonable apathies, by epilepsies of wit and of animal spirits, in the heyday of friendship and thought. Our faculties do not play us true, and both parties are relieved by solitude.

I ought to be equal to every relation. It makes no difference how many friends I have, and what content I can find in conversing with each, if there be one to whom I am not equal. If I have shrunk unequal from one contest, the joy I find in all the rest becomes mean and cowardly. I should hate myself, if then I made my other friends my asylum.

> "The valiant warrior famoused for fight,
> After a hundred victories, once foiled,
> Is from the book of honor razed quite,
> And all the rest forgot for which he toiled."

Our impatience is thus sharply rebuked. Bashfulness and apathy are a tough husk in which a delicate organization is protected from premature ripening. It would be lost if it knew itself before any of the best souls were yet ripe enough to know and own it. Respect the *naturlangsamkeit* which hardens the ruby in a million years, and works in duration, in which Alps and Andes come and go as rainbows. The good spirit of our life has no heaven which is the price of rashness. Love, which is the essence of God, is not for levity, but for the total worth of man. Let us not have this childish luxury in our regards, but the austerest worth; let us approach our friend with an audacious trust in the truth of his heart, in the breadth, impossible to be overturned, of his foundations.

The attractions of this subject are not to be resisted, and I leave, for the time, all account of subordinate social benefit, to speak of that select and sacred relation which is a kind of absolute, and which even leaves the language of love suspicious and common, so much is this purer, and nothing is so much divine.

I do not wish to treat friendships daintily, but with roughest courage. When they are real, they are not glass threads or frostwork, but the solidest thing we know. For now, after so many ages of experience, what do we know of nature, or of ourselves? Not one step has man taken toward the solution of the problem of his destiny. In one condemnation of folly stand the whole universe of men. But the sweet sincerity of joy and peace, which I draw from this alliance with my brother's soul, is the nut itself whereof all nature and all thought is but the husk and shell. Happy is the house that shelters a friend! It might well be built, like a festal bower or arch, to entertain him a single day. Happier, if he know the solemnity of that relation, and honor its law! He who offers himself a candidate for that covenant, comes up, like an Olympian, to the great games, where the first-born of the world are the competitors. He proposes himself for contests where Time, Want, Danger are in the lists, and he alone is victor who has truth enough in his constitution to preserve the delicacy of his beauty from the wear and tear of all these. The gifts of fortune may be present or absent, but all the speed in that contest depends on intrinsic nobleness, and the contempt of trifles. There are two elements that go to the composition of friendship, each so sovereign, that I can detect no superiority in either, no reason why either should be first named. One is Truth. A friend is a person with whom I may be sincere. Before him, I may think aloud. I am arrived at last in the presence of a man so real and equal, that I may drop even those undermost garments of dissimulation, courtesy, and second thought, which men never put off, and may deal with him with the simplicity and wholeness, with which one chemical atom meets another. Sincerity is the luxury allowed, like diadems and authority, only to the highest rank, *that* being permitted to speak truth, as having none above it to court or conform unto. Every man alone is sincere. At the entrance of a second person, hypocrisy begins. We parry and fend the approach of our fellow man by compliments, by gossip, by amusements, by affairs. We cover up our thought from him under a hundred folds. I knew a man who, under a certain religious frenzy, cast off this drapery, and omitting all compliment and commonplace, spoke to the conscience of every person he encountered, and that with great insight and beauty. At first he was resisted, and all men agreed he was mad. But persisting, as indeed he could not help doing, for some time in this course, he attained to the advantage of bringing every man of his acquaintance into true relations with him. No man would think of speaking falsely with him, or of putting him off with any chat of markets or reading-rooms. But every man was constrained by so much sincerity to the like plaindealing, and what love of nature, what poetry, what symbol of truth he had, he did certainly show him. But to most of us society shows not its face and eye, but its side and its back. To stand in true relations with men in a false age, is worth a fit of insanity, is it not? We can seldom go erect. Almost every man we meet requires some civility, — requires to be humored; he has some fame, some talent, some whim of religion or philanthropy in his head that is not to be questioned, and which spoils all conversation with him. But a friend is a sane man who exercises not my ingenuity but me. My friend gives me entertainment without requiring any stipulation on my part. A friend, therefore, is a sort of paradox in nature. I who alone am, I who see nothing in nature whose existence I can affirm with equal evidence to my own, behold now the semblance of my being in all its height, variety and curiosity, reiterated in a foreign form; so that a friend may well be reckoned the masterpiece of nature.

The other element of friendship is Tenderness. We are holden to men by every sort of tie, by blood, by pride, by fear, by hope, by lucre, by lust, by hate, by admiration, by every circumstance and badge and trifle, but we can scarce believe that so much character can subsist in another as to draw us by love. Can another be so blessed, and we so pure, that we can offer him tenderness? When a man becomes dear to me, I have touched the goal of fortune. I find very little written directly to the heart of this matter in books. And yet I have one text which I cannot choose but remember. My author says, — "I offer myself faintly and bluntly to those whose I effectually am, and tender myself least to him to whom I am the most devoted." I wish that friendship should have feet, as well as eyes and eloquence. It must plant itself on the ground, before it vaults over the moon. I wish it to be a little of a citizen, before it is quite a cherub. We chide the citizen because he makes love a commodity. It is an exchange of gifts, of useful loans; it is good neighborhood; it watches with the sick; it holds the pall at the funeral; and quite loses sight of the delicacies and nobility of the relation. But though we cannot find the god under this disguise of a sutler, yet, on the other hand, we cannot forgive the poet if he spins his thread too fine, and does not substantiate his romance by the municipal virtues of justice, punctuality, fidelity and pity. I hate the prostitution of the name of friendship to signify modish and worldly alliances. I much prefer the company of plough-boys and tin-pedlars, to the silken and perfumed amity which celebrates its days of encounter by a frivolous display, by rides in a curricle, and dinners at the best taverns. The end of friendship is a commerce the most strict and homely that can be joined; more strict than any of which we have experience. It is for aid and comfort through all the relations and passages of life and death. It is fit for serene days, and graceful gifts, and country rambles, but also for rough roads and hard fare, shipwreck, poverty, and persecution. It keeps company with the sallies of the wit and the trances of religion. We are to dignify to each other the daily needs and offices of man's life, and embellish it by courage, wisdom and unity. It should never fall into something usual and settled, but should be alert and inventive, and add rhyme and reason to what was drudgery.

Friendship may be said to require natures so rare and costly, each so well tempered and so happily adapted, and withal so circumstanced, (for even in that particular, a poet says, love demands that the parties be altogether paired,) that its satisfaction can very seldom be assured. It cannot subsist in its perfection, say some of those who are learned in this warm lore of the heart, betwixt more than two. I am not quite so strict in my terms, perhaps because I have never known so high a fellowship as others. I please my imagination more with a circle of godlike men and women variously related to each other, and between whom subsists a lofty intelligence. But I find this law of *one to one*, peremptory for conversation, which is the practice and consummation of friendship. Do not mix waters too much. The best mix as ill as good and bad. You shall have very useful and cheering discourse at several times with two several men, but let all three of you come together, and you shall not have one new and hearty word. Two may talk and one may hear, but three cannot take part in a conversation of the most sincere and searching sort. In good company there is never such discourse between two, across the table, as takes place when you leave them alone. In good company, the individuals merge their egotism into a social soul exactly coextensive with the several consciousnesses there present. No partialities of friend to friend, no fondnesses of brother to sister, of wife to husband, are there pertinent, but quite otherwise. Only he may then speak who can sail on the common thought of the party, and not poorly limited to his own. Now this convention, which good sense demands, destroys the high freedom of great conversation, which requires an absolute running of two souls into one.

No two men but being left alone with each other, enter into simpler relations. Yet it is affinity that determines *which* two shall converse. Unrelated men give little joy to each other; will never suspect the latent powers of each. We talk sometimes of a great talent for conversation, as if it were a permanent property in some individuals. Conversation is an evanescent relation, — no more. A man is reputed to have thought and eloquence; he cannot, for all that, say a word to his cousin or his uncle. They accuse his silence with as much reason as they would blame the insignificance of a dial in the shade. In the sun it will mark the hour. Among those who enjoy his thought, he will regain his tongue.

Friendship requires that rare mean betwixt likeness and unlikeness, that piques each with the presence of power and of consent in the other party. Let me be alone to the end of the world, rather than that my friend should overstep by a word or a look his real sympathy. I am equally baulked by antagonism and by compliance. Let him not cease an instant to be himself. The only joy I have in his being mine, is that the *not mine* is *mine*. I hate, where I looked for a manly furtherance, or at least a manly resistance, to find a mush of concession. Better be a nettle in the side of your friend than his echo. The condition which high friendship demands, is, ability to do without it. That high office requires great and sublime parts. There must be very two, before there can be very one. Let it be an alliance of two large formidable natures, mutually beheld, mutually feared, before yet they recognize the deep identity which beneath these disparities unites them.

He only is fit for this society who is magnanimous; who is sure that greatness and goodness are always economy; who is not swift to intermeddle with his fortunes. Let him not intermeddle with this. Leave to the diamond its ages to grow, nor expect to accelerate the births of the eternal. Friendship demands a religious treatment. We talk of choosing our friends, but friends are self-elected. Reverence is a great part of it. Treat your friend as a spectacle. Of course he has merits that are not yours, and that you cannot honor, if you must needs hold him close to your person. Stand aside; give those merits room; let them mount and expand. Are you the friend of your friend's buttons, or of his thought? To a great heart he will still be a stranger in a thousand particulars, that he may come near in the holiest ground. Leave it to girls and boys to regard a friend as property, and to suck a short and all-confounding pleasure, instead of the noblest benefit.

Let us buy our entrance to this guild by a long probation. Why should we desecrate noble and beautiful souls by intruding on them? Why insist on rash personal relations with your friend? Why go to his house, or know his mother and brother and sisters? Why be visited by him at your own? Are these things material to our covenant? Leave this touching and clawing. Let him be to me a spirit. A message, a thought, a sincerity, a glance from him, I want, but not news, nor pottage. I can get politics, and chat, and neighborly conveniences, from cheaper companions. Should not the society of my friend be to me poetic, pure, universal, and great as nature itself? Ought I to feel that our tie is profane in comparison with yonder bar of cloud that sleeps on the horizon, or that clump of waving grass that divides the brook? Let us not vilify but raise it to that standard. That great defying eye, that scornful beauty of his mien and action, do not pique yourself on reducing, but rather fortify and enhance. Worship his superiorities; wish him not less by a thought, but hoard and tell them all. Guard him as thy counterpart. Let him be to thee forever a sort of beautiful enemy, untamable, devoutly revered, and not a trivial conveniency to be soon outgrown and cast aside. The hues of the opal, the light of the diamond, are not to be seen, if the eye is too near. To my friend I write a letter, and from him I receive a letter. That seems to you a little. It suffices me. It is a spiritual gift worthy of him to give and of me to receive. It profanes nobody. In these warm lines the heart will trust itself, as it will not to the tongue, and pour out the prophecy of a godlier existence than all the annals of heroism have yet made good.

Respect so far the holy laws of this fellowship as not to prejudice its perfect flower by your impatience for its opening. We must be our own, before we can be another's. There is at least this satisfaction in crime, according to the Latin proverb; — you can speak to your accomplice on even terms. *Crimen quos inquinat, æquat.* To those whom we admire and love, at first we cannot. Yet the least defect of self-possession vitiates, in my judgment, the entire relation. There can never be deep peace between two spirits, never mutual respect until, in their dialogue, each stands for the whole world.

What is so great as friendship, let us carry with what grandeur of spirit we can. Let us be silent, — so we may hear the whisper of the gods. Let us not interfere. Who set you to cast about what you should say to the select souls, or how to say any thing to such? No matter how ingenious, no matter how graceful and bland. There are innumerable degrees of folly and wisdom, and for you to say aught is to be frivolous. Wait, and thy heart shall speak. Wait until the necessary and everlasting overpowers you, until day and night avail themselves of your lips. The only reward of virtue, is virtue: the only way to have a friend, is to be one. You shall not come nearer a man by getting into his house. If unlike, his soul only flees the faster from you, and you shall never catch a true glance of his eye. We see the noble afar off, and they repel us; why should we intrude? Late — very late — we perceive that no arrangements, no introductions, no consuetudes, or habits of society, would be of any avail to establish us in such relations with them as we desire, — but solely the uprise of nature in us to the same degree it is in them: then shall we meet as water with water: and if we should not meet them then, we shall not want them, for we are already they. In the last analysis, love is only the reflection of a man's own worthiness from other men. Men have sometimes exchanged names with their friends, as if they would signify that in their friend each loved his own soul.

The higher the style we demand of friendship, of course the less easy to establish it with flesh and blood. We walk alone in the world. Friends, such as we desire, are dreams and fables. But a sublime hope cheers ever the faithful heart, that elsewhere, in other regions of the universal power, souls are now acting, enduring, and daring, which can love us, and which we can love. We may congratulate ourselves that the period of nonage, of follies, of blunders, and of shame, is passed in solitude, and when we are finished men, we shall grasp heroic hands in heroic hands. Only be admonished by what you already see, not to strike leagues of friendship with cheap persons, where no friendship can be. Our impatience betrays us into rash and foolish alliances which no God attends. By persisting in your path, though you forfeit the little, you gain the great. You demonstrate yourself, so as to put yourself out of the reach of false relations, and you draw to you the first-born of the world, — those rare pilgrims whereof only one or two wander in nature at once, and before whom the vulgar great, show as spectres and shadows merely.

It is foolish to be afraid of making our ties too spiritual, as if so we could lose any genuine love. Whatever correction of our popular views we make from insight, nature will be sure to bear us out in, and though it seem to rob us of some joy, will repay us with a greater. Let us feel, if we will, the absolute insulation of man. We are sure that we have all in us. We go to Europe, or we pursue persons, or we read books, in the instinctive faith that these will call it out and reveal us to ourselves. Beggars all.

The persons are such as we; the Europe, an old faded garment of dead persons; the books, their ghosts. Let us drop this idolatry. Let us give over this mendicancy. Let us even bid our dearest friends farewell, and defy them, saying, 'Who are you? Unhand me: I will be dependent no more.' Ah! seest thou not, O brother, that thus we part only to meet again on a higher platform, and only be more each other's, because we are more our own? A friend is Janus-faced: he looks to the past and the future. He is the child of all my foregoing hours, the prophet of those to come, and the harbinger of a greater friend.

I do then with my friends as I do with my books. I would have them where I can find them, but I seldom use them. We must have society on our own terms, and admit or exclude it on the slightest cause. I cannot afford to speak much with my friend. If he is great, he makes me so great that I cannot descend to converse. In the great days, presentiments hover before me in the firmament. I ought then to dedicate myself to them. I go in that I may seize them, I go out that I may seize them. I fear only that I may lose them receding into the sky in which now they are only a patch of brighter light. Then, though I prize my friends, I cannot afford to talk with them and study their visions, lest I lose my own. It would indeed give me a certain household joy to quit this lofty seeking, this spiritual astronomy, or search of stars, and come down to warm sympathies with you; but then I know well I shall mourn always the vanishing of my mighty gods. It is true, next week I shall have languid moods, when I can well afford to occupy myself with foreign objects; then I shall regret the lost literature of your mind, and wish you were by my side again. But if you come, perhaps you will fill my mind only with new visions, not with yourself but with your lustres, and I shall not be able any more than now to converse with you. So I will owe to my friends this evanescent intercourse. I will receive from them not what they have, but what they are. They shall give me that which properly they cannot give, but which emanates from them. But they shall not hold me by any relations less subtle and pure. We will meet as though we met not, and part as though we parted not.

Friendship

It has seemed to me lately more possible than I knew, to carry a friendship greatly, on one side, without due correspondence on the other. Why should I cumber myself with regrets that the receiver is not capacious? It never troubles the sun that some of his rays fall wide and vain into ungrateful space, and only a small part on the reflecting planet. Let your greatness educate the crude and cold companion. If he is unequal, he will presently pass away; but thou art enlarged by thy own shining, and, no longer a mate for frogs and worms, dost soar and burn with the gods of the empyrean. It is thought a disgrace to love unrequited. But the great will see that true love cannot be unrequited. True love transcends the unworthy object, and dwells and broods on the eternal, and when the poor, interposed mask crumbles, it is not sad, but feels rid of so much earth, and feels its independency the surer. Yet these things may hardly be said without a sort of treachery to the relation. The essence of friendship is entireness, a total magnanimity and trust. It must not surmise or provide for infirmity. It treats its object as a god, that it may deify both.

PRUDENCE

Theme no poet gladly sung,
Fair to old and foul to young,
Scorn not thou the love of parts,
And the articles of arts.
Grandeur of the perfect sphere
Thanks the atoms that cohere.

PRUDENCE

What right have I to write on Prudence, whereof I have little, and that of the negative sort? My prudence consists in avoiding and going without, not in the inventing of means and methods, not in adroit steering, not in gentle repairing. I have no skill to make money spend well, no genius in my economy, and whoever sees my garden, discovers that I must have some other garden. Yet I love facts, and hate lubricity, and people without perception. Then I have the same title to write on prudence, that I have to write on poetry or holiness. We write from aspiration and antagonism, as well as from experience. We paint those qualities which we do not possess. The poet admires the man of energy and tactics; the merchant breeds his son for the church or the bar: and where a man is not vain and egotistic, you shall find what he has not, by his praise. Moreover, it would be hardly honest in me not to balance these fine lyric words of Love and Friendship with words of coarser sound, and whilst my debt to my senses is real and constant, not to own it in passing.

Prudence is the virtue of the senses. It is the science of appearances. It is the outmost action of the inward life. It is God taking thought for oxen. It moves matter after the laws of matter. It is content to seek health of body by complying with physical conditions, and health of mind by the laws of the intellect.

The world of the senses is a world of shows; it does not exist for itself, but has a symbolic character; and a true prudence or law of shows recognizes the co-presence of other laws, and knows that its own office is subaltern; knows that it is surface and not centre where it works. Prudence is false when detached. It is legitimate when it is the Natural History of the soul incarnate; when it unfolds the beauty of laws within the narrow scope of the senses.

There are all degrees of proficiency in knowledge of the world. It is sufficient, to our present purpose, to indicate three. One class live to the utility of the symbol; esteeming health and wealth a final good. Another class live above this mark to the beauty of the symbol; as the poet, and artist, and the naturalist, and man of science. A third class live above the beauty of the symbol to the beauty of the thing signified; these are wise men. The first class have common sense; the second, taste; and the third, spiritual perception. Once in a long time, a man traverses the whole scale, and sees and enjoys the symbol solidly; then also has a clear eye for its beauty, and, lastly, whilst he pitches his tent on this sacred volcanic isle of nature, does not offer to build houses and barns thereon, reverencing the splendor of the God which he sees bursting through each chink and cranny.

The world is filled with the proverbs and acts and winkings of a base prudence, which is a devotion to matter as if we possessed no other faculties than the palate, the nose, the touch, the eye and ear; a prudence which adores the Rule of Three, which never subscribes, which never gives, which seldom lends, and asks but one question of any project— Will it bake bread? This is a disease like a thickening of the skin until the vital organs are destroyed. But culture, revealing the high origin of the apparent world, and aiming at the perfection of the man as the end, degrades every thing else, as health and bodily life, into means. It sees prudence not to be a several faculty, but a name for wisdom and virtue conversing with the body and its wants. Cultivated men always feel and speak so, as if a great fortune, the achievement of a civil or social measure, great personal influence, a graceful and commanding address had their value as proofs of the energy of the spirit. If a man lose his balance, and immerse himself in any trades or pleasures for their own sake, he may be a good wheel or pin, but he is not a cultivated man.

The spurious prudence, making the senses final, is the god of sots and cowards, and is the subject of all comedy. It is nature's joke, and therefore literature's. The true prudence limits this sensualism by admitting the knowledge of an internal and real world. This recognition once made, — the order of the world and the distribution of affairs and times being studied with the co-perception of their subordinate place, will reward any degree of attention. For our existence, thus apparently attached in nature to the sun and the returning moon and the periods which they mark, — so susceptible to climate and to country, so alive to social good and evil, so fond of splendor, and so tender to hunger and cold and debt, — reads all its primary lessons out of these books.

Prudence does not go behind nature, and ask whence it is. It takes the laws of the world whereby man's being is conditioned, as they are, and keeps these laws, that it may enjoy their proper good. It respects space and time, climate, want, sleep, the law of polarity, growth and death. There revolve to give bound and period to his being, on all sides, the sun and moon, the great for-malists in the sky: here lies stubborn matter, and will not swerve from its chemical routine. Here is a planted globe, pierced and belted with natural laws, and fenced and distributed externally with civil partitions and properties which impose new restraints on the young inhabitant.

We eat of the bread which grows in the field. We live by the air which blows around us, and we are poisoned by the air that is too cold or too hot, too dry or too wet. Time, which shows so va-cant, indivisible and divine in its coming, is slit and peddled into trifles and tatters. A door is to be painted, a lock to be repaired. I want wood, or oil, or meal, or salt; the house smokes, or I have a headache; then the tax; and an affair to be transacted with a man without heart or brains; and the stinging recollection of an injurious or very awkward word, — these eat up the hours. Do what we can, summer will have its flies: if we walk in the woods, we must feed musquitoes: if we go a fishing, we must expect a wet coat. Then climate is a great impediment to idle persons: we often resolve to give up the care of the weather, but still we regard the clouds and the rain.

We are instructed by these petty experiences which usurp the hours and years. The hard soil and four months of snow make the inhabitant of the northern temperate zone wiser and abler than his fellow who enjoys the fixed smile of the tropics. The islander may ramble all day at will. At night, he may sleep on a mat under the moon, and wherever a wild date-tree grows, nature has, without a prayer even, spread a table for his morning meal. The northerner is perforce a householder. He must brew, bake, salt and preserve his food, and pile wood and coal. But as it happens that not one stroke can labor lay to, without some new acquaintance with nature; and as nature is inexhaustibly significant, the inhabitants of these climates have always excelled the southerner in force. Such is the value of these matters, that a man who knows other things, can never know too much of these. Let him have accurate perceptions. Let him, if he have hands, handle; if eyes, measure and discriminate; let him accept and hive every fact of chemistry, natural history, and economics; the more he has, the less is he willing to spare any one. Time is always bringing the occasions that disclose their value. Some wisdom comes out of every natural and innocent action. The domestic man, who loves no music so well as his kitchen clock, and the airs which the logs sing to him as they burn on the hearth, has solaces which others never dream of. The application of means to ends, ensures victory and the songs of victory not less in a farm or a shop, than in the tactics of party, or of war. The good husband finds method as efficient in the packing of fire-wood in a shed, or in the harvesting of fruits in the cellar, as in Peninsular campaigns or the files of the Department of State. In the rainy day he builds a workbench, or gets his tool-box set in the corner of the barn-chamber, and stored with nails, gimlet, pincers, screwdriver, and chisel. Herein he tastes an old joy of youth and childhood, the cat-like love of garrets, presses, and corn-chambers, and of the conveniences of long housekeeping. His garden or his poultry-yard tells him many pleasant anecdotes. One might find argument for optimism, in the abundant flow of this saccharine element of pleasure, in every suburb and extremity of the good world. Let a man keep the law, — any law, — and his way will be strown with satisfactions. There is more difference in the quality of our pleasures than in the amount.

On the other hand, nature punishes any neglect of prudence. If you think the senses final, obey their law. If you believe in the soul, do not clutch at sensual sweetness before it is ripe on the slow tree of cause and effect. It is vinegar to the eyes, to deal with men of loose and imperfect perception. Dr. Johnson is reported to have said, — "If the child says, he looked out of this window, when he looked out of that, — whip him." Our American character is marked by a more than average delight in accurate perception, which is shown by the currency of the byword, "No mistake." But the discomfort of unpunctuality, of confusion of thought about facts, of inattention to the wants of to-morrow, is of no nation. The beautiful laws of time and space once dislocated by our inaptitude, are holes and dens. If the hive be disturbed by rash and stupid hands, instead of honey, it will yield us bees. Our words and actions to be fair, must be timely. A gay and pleasant sound is the whetting of the scythe in the mornings of June; yet what is more lonesome and sad than the sound of a whetstone or mower's rifle, when it is too late in the season to make hay? Scatter-brained and "afternoon men" spoil much more than their own affair, in spoiling the temper of those who deal with them. I have seen a criticism on some paintings, of which I am reminded, when I see the shiftless and unhappy men who are not true to their senses. The last Grand Duke of Weimar, a man of superior understanding, said: — "I have sometimes remarked in the presence of great works of art, and just now especially, in Dresden, how much a certain property contributes to the effect which gives life to the figures, and to the life an irresistible truth. This property is the hitting, in all the figures we draw, the right centre of gravity. I mean, the placing the figures firm upon their feet, making the hands grasp, and fastening the eyes on the spot where they should look. Even lifeless figures, as vessels and stools, — let them be drawn ever so correctly, lose all effect so soon as they lack the resting upon their centre of gravity, and have a certain swimming and oscillating appearance. The Raphael, in the Dresden gallery, (the only greatly affecting picture which I have seen,) is the quietest and most passionless piece you can imagine; a couple of saints who worship the Virgin and child. Nevertheless, it awakens a deeper impression than the contortions of ten crucified martyrs. For, beside all the resistless beauty of form, it possesses in the highest degree the property of the perpendicularity of all the figures." — This perpendicularity we demand of all the figures in this picture of life. Let them stand on their feet, and not float and swing. Let us know where to find them. Let them discriminate between what they remember and what they dreamed, use plain speech, give us facts, and honor their own senses with trust.

But what man shall dare tax another with imprudence? Who is prudent? The men we call greatest are least in this kingdom. There is a certain fatal dislocation in our relation to nature, distorting our modes of living, and making every law our enemy, which seems at last to have aroused all the wit and virtue in the world to ponder the question of Reform. We must call the highest prudence to counsel, and ask why health and beauty and genius should now be the exception, rather than the rule of human nature? We do not know the properties of plants and animals and the laws of nature through our sympathy with the same; but this remains the dream of poets. Poetry and prudence should be coincident. Poets should be lawgivers; that is, the boldest lyric inspiration should not chide and insult, but should announce and lead the civil code, and the day's work. But now the two things seem irreconcilably parted. We have violated law upon law, until we stand amidst ruins, and when by chance we espy a coincidence between reason and the phenomena, we are surprised. Beauty should be the dowry of every man and woman, as invariably as sensation; but it is rare. Health or sound organization should be universal. Genius should be the child of genius, and every child should be inspired; but now it is not to be predicted of any child, and nowhere is it pure. We call partial half-lights, by courtesy, genius; talent which converts itself to money, talent which glitters to-day, that it may dine and sleep well to-morrow; and society is officered by *men of parts*, as they are properly called, and not by divine men. These use their gifts to refine luxury, not to abolish it. Genius is always ascetic; and piety and love. Appetite shows to the finer souls as a disease, and they find beauty in rites and bounds that resist it.

Prudence

We have found out fine names to cover our sensuality withal, but no gifts can raise intemperance. The man of talent affects to call his transgressions of the laws of the senses trivial, and to count them nothing considered with his devotion to his art. His art never taught him lewdness, nor the love of wine, nor the wish to reap where he had not sowed. His art is less for every deduction from his holiness, and less for every defect of common sense. On him who scorned the world, as he said, the scorned world wreaks its revenge. He that despiseth small things, will perish by little and little. Goethe's Tasso is very likely to be a pretty fair historical portrait, and that is true tragedy. It does not seem to me so genuine grief when some tyrannous Richard III. oppresses and slays a score of innocent persons, as when Antonio and Tasso, both apparently right, wrong each other. One living after the maxims of this world, and consistent and true to them, the other fired with all divine sentiments, yet grasping also at the pleasures of sense, without submitting to their law. That is a grief we all feel, a knot we cannot untie. Tasso's is no infrequent case in modern biography. A man of genius, of an ardent temperament, reckless of physical laws, self-indulgent, becomes presently unfortunate, querulous, a "discomfortable cousin," a thorn to himself and to others.

The scholar shames us by his bifold life. Whilst something higher than prudence is active, he is admirable; when common sense is wanted, he is an incumbrance. Yesterday, Cæsar was not so great; to-day, the felon at the gallows' foot is not more miserable. Yesterday, radiant with the light of an ideal world, in which he lives, the first of men; and now oppressed by wants and by sickness, for which he must thank himself. He resembles the pitiful drivellers, whom travellers describe as frequenting the bazaars of Constantinople, who skulk about all day, yellow, emaciated, ragged, sneaking; and at evening, when the bazaars are open, slink to the opium shop, swallow their morsel, and become tranquil and glorified seers. And who has not seen the tragedy of imprudent genius, struggling for years with paltry pecuniary difficulties, at last sinking, chilled, exhausted, and fruitless, like a giant slaughtered by pins?

Is it not better that a man should accept the first pains and mortifications of this sort, which nature is not slack in sending him, as hints that he must expect no other good than the just fruit of his own labor and self-denial? Health, bread, climate, social position, have their importance, and he will give them their due. Let him esteem Nature a perpetual counsellor, and her perfections the exact measure of our deviations. Let him make the night, night, and the day, day. Let him control the habit of expense. Let him see that as much wisdom may be expended on a private economy, as on an empire, and as much wisdom may be drawn from it. The laws of the world are written out for him on every piece of money in his hand. There is nothing he will not be the better for knowing, were it only the wisdom of Poor Richard; or the State-street prudence of buying by the acre, to sell by the foot; or the thrift of the agriculturist, to stick a tree between whiles, because it will grow whilst he sleeps; or the prudence which consists in husbanding little strokes of the tool, little portions of time, particles of stock, and small gains. The eye of prudence may never shut. Iron, if kept at the ironmonger's, will rust; beer, if not brewed in the right state of the atmosphere, will sour; timber of ships will rot at sea, or, if laid up high and dry, will strain, warp, and dry-rot; money, if kept by us, yields no rent, and is liable to loss; if invested, is liable to depreciation of the particular kind of stock. Strike, says the smith, the iron is white; keep the rake, says the haymaker, as nigh the scythe as you can, and the cart as nigh the rake. Our Yankee trade is reputed to be very much on the extreme of this prudence. It takes bank notes, — good, bad, clean, ragged, — and saves itself by the speed with which it passes them off. Iron cannot rust, nor beer sour, nor timber rot, nor calicoes go out of fashion, nor money stocks depreciate, in the few swift moments in which the Yankee suffers any one of them to remain in his possession. In skating over thin ice, our safety is in our speed.

Let him learn a prudence of a higher strain. Let him learn that every thing in nature, even motes and feathers, go by law and not by luck, and that what he sows, he reaps. By diligence and self-command, let him put the bread he eats at his own disposal,

an identity of sentiment, assume that you are saying precisely that which all think, and in the flow of wit and love, roll out your paradoxes in solid column, with not the infirmity of a doubt. So at least shall you get an adequate deliverance. The natural motions of the soul are so much better than the voluntary ones, that you will never do yourself justice in dispute. The thought is not then taken hold of by the right handle, does not show itself proportioned, and in its true bearings, but bears extorted, hoarse, and half witness. But assume a consent, and it shall presently be granted, since, really, and underneath their external diversities, all men are of one heart and mind.

Wisdom will never let us stand with any man or men, on an unfriendly footing. We refuse sympathy and intimacy with people, as if we waited for some better sympathy and intimacy to come. But whence and when? To-morrow will be like to-day. Life wastes itself whilst we are preparing to live. Our friends and fellow-workers die off from us. Scarcely can we say, we see new men, new women approaching us. We are too old to regard fashion, too old to expect patronage of any greater, or more powerful. Let us suck the sweetness of those affections and consuetudes that grow near us. These old shoes are easy to the feet. Undoubtedly, we can easily pick faults in our company, can easily whisper names prouder, and that tickle the fancy more. Every man's imagination hath its friends; and life would be dearer with such companions. But, if you cannot have them on good mutual terms, you cannot have them. If not the Deity, but our ambition hews and shapes the new relations, their virtue escapes, as strawberries lose their flavor in garden beds.

Thus truth, frankness, courage, love, humility, and all the virtues range themselves on the side of prudence, or the art of securing a present well-being. I do not know if all matter will be found to be made of one element, as oxygen or hydrogen, at last, but the world of manners and actions is wrought of one stuff, and begin where we will, we are pretty sure in a short space, to be mumbling our ten commandments.

that he may not stand in bitter and false relations to other men; for the best good of wealth is freedom. Let him practise the minor virtues. How much of human life is lost in waiting! Let him not make his fellow creatures wait. How many words and promises are promises of conversation! Let his be words of fate. When he sees a folded and sealed scrap of paper float round the globe in a pine ship, and come safe to the eye for which it was written, amidst a swarming population, let him likewise feel the admonition to integrate his being across all these distracting forces, and keep a slender human word among the storms, distances, and accidents, that drive us hither and thither, and, by persistency, make the paltry force of one man reappear to redeem its pledge, after months and years, in the most distant climates.

We must not try to write the laws of any one virtue, looking at that only. Human nature loves no contradictions, but is symmetrical. The prudence which secures an outward well-being, is not to be studied by one set of men, whilst heroism and holiness are studied by another, but they are reconcilable. Prudence concerns the present time, persons, property, and existing forms. But as every fact hath its roots in the soul, and if the soul were changed, would cease to be, or would become some other thing, the proper administration of outward things will always rest on a just apprehension of their cause and origin, that is, the good man will be the wise man, and the single-hearted, the politic man. Every violation of truth is not only a sort of suicide in the liar, but is a stab at the health of human society. On the most profitable lie, the course of events presently lays a destructive tax; whilst frankness invites frankness, puts the parties on a convenient footing, and makes their business a friendship. Trust men, and they will be true to you; treat them greatly, and they will show themselves great, though they make an exception in your favor to all their rules of trade.

So, in regard to disagreeable and formidable things, prudence does not consist in evasion, or in flight, but in courage. He who wishes to walk in the most peaceful parts of life with any serenity, must screw himself up to resolution. Let him front the object of his worst apprehension, and his stoutness will commonly make his fear groundless. The Latin proverb says, that "in battles, the eye is first overcome." Entire self-possession may make a battle very little more dangerous to life than a match at foils or at football. Examples are cited by soldiers, of men who have seen the cannon pointed, and the fire given to it, and who have stepped aside from the path of the ball. The terrors of the storm are chiefly confined to the parlor and the cabin. The drover, the sailor, buffets it all day, and his health renews itself at as vigorous a pulse under the sleet, as under the sun of June.

In the occurrence of unpleasant things among neighbors, fear comes readily to heart, and magnifies the consequence of the other party; but it is a bad counsellor. Every man is actually weak, and apparently strong. To himself, he seems weak; to others, formidable. You are afraid of Grim; but Grim also is afraid of you. You are solicitous of the good will of the meanest person, uneasy at his ill will. But the sturdiest offender of your peace and of the neighborhood, if you rip up *his* claims, is as thin and timid as any; and the peace of society is often kept, because, as children say, one is afraid, and the other dares not. Far off, men swell, bully, and threaten: bring them hand to hand, and they are a feeble folk.

It is a proverb, that 'courtesy costs nothing;' but calculation might come to value love for its profit. Love is fabled to be blind; but kindness is necessary to perception; love is not a hood, but an eye-water. If you meet a sectary, or a hostile partisan, never recognize the dividing lines; but meet on what common ground remains, — if only that the sun shines, and the rain rains for both; the area will widen very fast, and ere you know it, the boundary mountains, on which the eye had fastened, have melted into air. If they set out to contend, Saint Paul will lie, and Saint John will hate. What low, poor, paltry, hypocritical people, an argument on religion will make of the pure and chosen souls! They will shuffle, and crow, crook, and hide, feign to confess here, only that they may brag and conquer there, and not a thought has enriched either party, and not an emotion of bravery, modesty, or hope. So neither should you put yourself in a false position with your contemporaries, by indulging a vein of hostility and bitterness. Though your views are in straight antagonism to theirs, assume

ESSAY VIII

HEROISM

In the elder English dramatists, and mainly in the plays of Beaumont and Fletcher, there is a constant recognition of gentility, as if a noble behavior were as easily marked in the society of their age, as color is in our American population. When any Rodrigo, Pedro, or Valerio enters, though he be a stranger, the duke or governor exclaims, This is a gentleman, — and proffers civilities without end; but all the rest are slag and refuse. In harmony with this delight in personal advantages, there is in their plays a certain heroic cast of character and dialogue, — as in Bonduca, Sophocles, the Mad Lover, the Double Marriage, — wherein the speaker is so earnest and cordial, and on such deep grounds of character, that the dialogue, on the slightest additional incident in the plot, rises naturally into poetry. Among many texts, take the following. The Roman Martius has conquered Athens, — all but the invincible spirits of Sophocles, the duke of Athens, and Dorigen, his wife. The beauty of the latter inflames Martius, and he seeks to save her husband; but Sophocles will not ask his life, although assured that a word will save him, and the execution of both proceeds.

> "*Valerius.* Bid thy wife farewell.
> *Soph.* No, I will take no leave. My Dorigen,
> Yonder, above, 'bout Ariadne's crown,
> My spirit shall hover for thee. Prithee, haste.
> *Dor.* Stay, Sophocles, — with this, tie up my sight;
> Let not soft nature so transformed be,

145

And lose her gentler sexed humanity,
To make me see my lord bleed.   So, 't is well;
Never one object underneath the sun
Will I behold before my Sophocles:
Farewell; now teach the Romans how to die.

   Mar.   Dost know what 't is to die?

   Soph.   Thou dost not, Martius,
And therefore, not what 't is to live; to die
Is to begin to live.   It is to end
An old, stale, weary work, and to commence
A newer, and a better.   'T is to leave
Deceitful knaves for the society
Of gods and goodness.   Thou, thyself, must part
At last, from all thy garlands, pleasures, triumphs,
And prove thy fortitude what then 't will do.

   Val.   But art not grieved nor vexed to leave thy life thus?

   Soph.   Why should I grieve or vex for being sent
To them I ever loved best?   Now I 'll kneel,
But with my back toward thee; 't is the last duty
This trunk can do the gods.

   Mar.   Strike, strike, Valerius,
Or Martius' heart will leap out at his mouth:
This is a man, a woman!   Kiss thy lord,
And live with all the freedom you were wont.
O love! thou doubly hast afflicted me
With virtue and with beauty.   Treacherous heart,
My hand shall cast thee quick into my urn,
Ere thou transgress this knot of piety.

   Val.   What ails my brother?

   Soph.   Martius, oh Martius,
Thou now hast found a way to conquer me.

   Dor.   O star of Rome! what gratitude can speak
Fit words to follow such a deed as this?

   Mar.   This admirable duke, Valerius,
With his disdain of fortune and of death,
Captived himself, has captivated me,
And though my arm hath ta'en his body here,

HEROISM

"Paradise is under the shadow of swords."

Mahomet.

Ruby wine is drunk by knaves,
Sugar spends to fatten slaves,
Rose and vine-leaf deck buffoons;
Thunderclouds are Jove's festoons,
Drooping oft in wreaths of dread
Lightning-knotted round his head;
The hero is not fed on sweets,
Daily his own heart he eats;
Chambers of the great are jails,
And head-winds right for royal sails.

avowal of the unschooled man, that he finds a quality in him that is negligent of expense, of health, of life, of danger, of hatred, of reproach, and knows that his will is higher and more excellent than all actual and all possible antagonists.

Heroism works in contradiction to the voice of mankind, and in contradiction, for a time, to the voice of the great and good. Heroism is an obedience to a secret impulse of an individual's character. Now to no other man can its wisdom appear as it does to him, for every man must be supposed to see a little farther on his own proper path, than any one else. Therefore, just and wise men take umbrage at his act, until after some little time be past: then, they see it to be in unison with their acts. All prudent men see that the action is clean contrary to a sensual prosperity; for every heroic act measures itself by its contempt of some external good. But it finds its own success at last, and then the prudent also extol.

Self-trust is the essence of heroism. It is the state of the soul at war, and its ultimate objects are the last defiance of falsehood and wrong, and the power to bear all that can be inflicted by evil agents. It speaks the truth, and it is just, generous, hospitable, temperate, scornful of petty calculations, and scornful of being scorned. It persists; it is of an undaunted boldness, and of a fortitude not to be wearied out. Its jest is the littleness of common life. That false prudence which dotes on health and wealth is the butt and merriment of heroism. Heroism, like Plotinus, is almost ashamed of its body. What shall it say, then, to the sugar-plums, and cats'-cradles, to the toilet, compliments, quarrels, cards, and custard, which rack the wit of all society. What joys has kind nature provided for us dear creatures! There seems to be no interval between greatness and meanness. When the spirit is not master of the world, then it is its dupe. Yet the little man takes the great hoax so innocently, works in it so headlong and believing, is born red, and dies gray, arranging his toilet, attending on his own health, laying traps for sweet food and strong wine, setting his heart on a horse or a rifle, made happy with a little gossip, or a little praise, that the great soul cannot choose but laugh at such earnest nonsense. "Indeed, these humble considerations make me out of love with greatness. What a disgrace is it to me to take note how many pairs of silk stockings thou hast, namely, these and those that were the peach-colored ones, or to bear the inventory of thy shirts, as one for superfluity, and one other for use."

Citizens, thinking after the laws of arithmetic, consider the inconvenience of receiving strangers at their fireside, reckon narrowly the loss of time and the unusual display: the soul of a better quality thrusts back the unseasonable economy into the vaults of life, and says, I will obey the God, and the sacrifice and the fire he will provide. Ibn Haukal, the Arabian geographer, describes a heroic extreme in the hospitality of Sogd, in Bukharia. "When I was in Sogd, I saw a great building, like a palace, the gates of which were open and fixed back to the wall with large nails. I asked the reason, and was told that the house had not been shut night or day, for a hundred years. Strangers may present themselves at any hour, and in whatever number; the master has amply provided for the reception of the men and their animals, and is never happier than when they tarry for some time. Nothing of the kind have I seen in any other country." The magnanimous know very well that they who give time, or money, or shelter, to the stranger — so it be done for love, and not for ostentation — do, as it were, put God under obligation to them, so perfect are the compensations of the universe. In some way, the time they seem to lose, is redeemed, and the pains they seem to take, remunerate themselves. These men fan the flame of human love and raise the standard of civil virtue among mankind. But hospitality must be for service, and not for show, or it pulls down the host. The brave soul rates itself too high to value itself by the splendor of its table and draperies. It gives what it hath, and all it hath, but its own majesty can lend a better grace to bannocks and fair water, than belong to city feasts.

The temperance of the hero, proceeds from the same wish to do no dishonor to the worthiness he has. But he loves it for its elegancy, not for its austerity. It seems not worth his while to be solemn, and denounce with bitterness flesh-eating, or wine-drinking, the use of tobacco, or opium, or tea, or silk, or gold. A great

His soul hath subjugated Martius' soul.
By Romulus, he is all soul, I think;
He hath no flesh, and spirit cannot be gyved;
Then we have vanquished nothing; he is free,
And Martius walks now in captivity."

I do not readily remember any poem, play, sermon, novel, or oration, that our press vents in the last few years, which goes to the same tune. We have a great many flutes and flageolets, but not often the sound of any fife. Yet, Wordsworth's Laodamia, and the ode of "Dion," and some sonnets, have a certain noble music; and Scott will sometimes draw a stroke like the portrait of Lord Evandale, given by Balfour of Burley. Thomas Carlyle, with his natural taste for what is manly and daring in character, has suffered no heroic trait in his favorites to drop from his biographical and historical pictures. Earlier, Robert Burns has given us a song or two. In the Harleian Miscellanies, there is an account of the battle of Lutzen, which deserves to be read. And Simon Ockley's History of the Saracens, recounts the prodigies of individual valor with admiration, all the more evident on the part of the narrator, that he seems to think that his place in Christian Oxford requires of him some proper protestations of abhorrence. But if we explore the literature of Heroism, we shall quickly come to Plutarch, who is its Doctor and historian. To him we owe the Brasidas, the Dion, the Epaminondas, the Scipio of old, and I must think we are more deeply indebted to him than to all the ancient writers. Each of his "Lives" is a refutation to the despondency and cowardice of our religious and political theorists. A wild courage, a stoicism not of the schools, but of the blood, shines in every anecdote, and has given that book its immense fame.

We need books of this tart cathartic virtue, more than books of political science, or of private economy. Life is a festival only to the wise. Seen from the nook and chimney-side of prudence, it wears a ragged and dangerous front. The violations of the laws of nature by our predecessors and our contemporaries, are punished in us also. The disease and deformity around us, certify the infraction of natural, intellectual, and moral laws, and often violation on violation to breed such compound misery. A lockjaw, that bends a man's head back to his heels, hydrophobia, that makes him bark at his wife and babes, insanity, that makes him eat grass; war, plague, cholera, famine, indicate a certain ferocity in nature, which, as it had its inlet by human crime, must have its outlet by human suffering. Unhappily, no man exists who has not in his own person become, to some amount, a stockholder in the sin, and so made himself liable to a share in the expiation.

Our culture, therefore, must not omit the arming of the man. Let him hear in season, that he is born into the state of war, and that the commonwealth and his own well-being, require that he should not go dancing in the weeds of peace, but warned, self-collected, and neither defying nor dreading the thunder, let him take both reputation and life in his hand, and with perfect urbanity, dare the gibbet and the mob by the absolute truth of his speech, and the rectitude of his behavior.

Towards all this external evil, the man within the breast assumes a warlike attitude, and affirms his ability to cope single-handed with the infinite army of enemies. To this military attitude of the soul, we give the name of Heroism. Its rudest form is the contempt for safety and ease, which makes the attractiveness of war. It is a self-trust which slights the restraints of prudence in the plenitude of its energy and power to repair the harms it may suffer. The hero is a mind of such balance that no disturbances can shake his will, but pleasantly, and, as it were, merrily, he advances to his own music, alike in frightful alarms, and in the tipsy mirth of universal dissoluteness. There is somewhat not philosophical in heroism; there is somewhat not holy in it; it seems not to know that other souls are of one texture with it; it has pride; it is the extreme of individual nature. Nevertheless, we must profoundly revere it. There is somewhat in great actions, which does not allow us to go behind them. Heroism feels and never reasons, and therefore is always right; and although a different breeding, different religion, and greater intellectual activity, would have modified, or even reversed the particular action, yet for the hero, that thing he does, is the highest deed, and is not open to the censure of philosophers or divines. It is the

should deck it with more than regal or national splendor, and act on principles that should interest man and nature in the length of our days.

We have seen or heard of many extraordinary young men, who never ripened, or whose performance in actual life, was not extraordinary. When we see their air and mien, when we hear them speak of society, of books, of religion, we admire their superiority, they seem to throw contempt on our entire polity and social state; theirs is the tone of a youthful giant, who is sent to work revolutions. But they enter an active profession, and the forming Colossus shrinks to the common size of man. The magic they used, was the ideal tendencies, which always make the Actual ridiculous; but the tough world had its revenge the moment they put their horses of the sun to plough in its furrow. They found no example and no companion, and their heart fainted. What then? The lesson they gave in their first aspirations is yet true; and a better valor and a purer truth shall one day organize their belief. Or why should a woman liken herself to any historical woman, and think, because Sappho, or Sévigné, or De Staël, or the cloistered souls who have had genius and cultivation, do not satisfy the imagination, and the serene Themis, none can, — certainly not she. Why not? She has a new and unattempted problem to solve, perchance that of the happiest nature that ever bloomed. Let the maiden, with erect soul, walk serenely on her way, accept the hint of each new experience, search in turn all the objects that solicit her eye, that she may learn the power and the charm of her new-born being, which is the kindling of a new dawn in the recesses of space. The fair girl, who repels interference by a decided and proud choice of influences, so careless of pleasing, so wilful and lofty, inspires every beholder with somewhat of her own nobleness. The silent heart encourages her; O friend, never strike sail to a fear. Come into port greatly, or sail with God the seas. Not in vain you live, for every passing eye is cheered and refined by the vision.

The characteristic of heroism is its persistency. All men have wandering impulses, fits and starts of generosity. But when you have chosen your part, abide by it, and do not weakly try to reconcile yourself with the world. The heroic cannot be the common, nor the common the heroic. Yet we have the weakness to expect the sympathy of people in those actions whose excellence is that they outrun sympathy, and appeal to a tardy justice. If you would serve your brother, because it is fit for you to serve him, do not take back your words when you find that prudent people do not commend you. Adhere to your own act, and congratulate yourself if you have done something strange and extravagant, and broken the monotony of a decorous age. It was a high counsel that I once heard given to a young person, — "Always do what you are afraid to do." A simple manly character need never make an apology, but should regard its past action with the calmness of Phocion, when he admitted that the event of the battle was happy, yet did not regret his dissuasion from the battle.

There is no weakness or exposure for which we cannot find consolation in the thought, — this is a part of my constitution, part of my relation and office to my fellow creature. Has nature covenanted with me that I should never appear to disadvantage, never make a ridiculous figure? Let us be generous of our dignity, as well as of our money. Greatness once and forever has done with opinion. We tell our charities, not because we wish to be praised for them, not because we think they have great merit, but for our justification. It is a capital blunder; as you discover, when another man recites his charities.

To speak the truth, even with some austerity, to live with some rigor of temperance, or some extremes of generosity, seems to be an asceticism which common good nature would appoint to those who are at ease and in plenty, in sign that they feel a brotherhood with the great multitude of suffering men. And not only need we breathe and exercise the soul by assuming the penalties of abstinence, of debt, of solitude, of unpopularity, but it behoves the wise man to look with a bold eye into those rarer dangers which sometimes invade men, and to familiarize himself with disgusting forms of disease, with sounds of execration, and the vision of violent death.

Times of heroism are generally times of terror, but the day never shines, in which this element may not work. The circum-

man scarcely knows how he dines, how he dresses, but without railing or precision, his living is natural and poetic. John Eliot, the Indian Apostle, drank water, and said of wine, — "It is a noble, generous liquor, and we should be humbly thankful for it, but, as I remember, water was made before it." Better still, is the temperance of king David, who poured out on the ground unto the Lord, the water which three of his warriors had brought him to drink, at the peril of their lives.

It is told of Brutus, that when he fell on his sword, after the battle of Philippi, he quoted a line of Euripides, — "O virtue, I have followed thee through life, and I find thee at last but a shade." I doubt not the hero is slandered by this report. The heroic soul does not sell its justice and its nobleness. It does not ask to dine nicely, and to sleep warm. The essence of greatness is the perception that virtue is enough. Poverty is its ornament. It does not need plenty, and can very well abide its loss.

But that which takes my fancy most, in the heroic class, is the good humor and hilarity they exhibit. It is a height to which common duty can very well attain, to suffer and to dare with solemnity. But these rare souls set opinion, success, and life, at so cheap a rate, that they will not soothe their enemies by petitions, or the show of sorrow, but wear their own habitual greatness. Scipio, charged with peculation, refuses to do himself so great a disgrace, as to wait for justification, though he had the scroll of his accounts in his hands, but tears it to pieces before the tribunes. Socrates' condemnation of himself to be maintained in all honor in the Prytaneum, during his life, and Sir Thomas More's playfulness at the scaffold, are of the same strain. In Beaumont and Fletcher's "Sea Voyage," Juletta tells the stout captain and his company, —

> "*Jul.* Why, slaves, 't is in our power to hang ye.
> *Master.*   Very likely,
> 'T is in our powers, then, to be hanged, and scorn ye."

These replies are sound and whole. Sport is the bloom and glow of a perfect health. The great will not condescend to take any thing seriously; all must be as gay as the song of a canary, though it were the building of cities or the eradication of old and foolish churches and nations, which have cumbered the earth long thousands of years. Simple hearts put all the history and customs of this world behind them, and play their own game in innocent defiance of the Blue-Laws of the world; and such would appear, could we see the human race assembled in vision, like little children frolicking together, though, to the eyes of mankind at large, they wear a stately and solemn garb of works and influences.

The interest these fine stories have for us, the power of a romance over the boy who grasps the forbidden book under his bench at school, our delight in the hero, is the main fact to our purpose. All these great and transcendent properties are ours. If we dilate in beholding the Greek energy, the Roman pride, it is that we are already domesticating the same sentiment. Let us find room for this great guest in our small houses. The first step of worthiness will be to disabuse us of our superstitious associations with places and times, with number and size. Why should these words, Athenian, Roman, Asia, and England, so tingle in the ear? Where the heart is, there the muses, there the gods sojourn, and not in any geography of fame. Massachusetts, Connecticut River, and Boston Bay, you think paltry places, and the ear loves names of foreign and classic topography. But here we are; and, if we will tarry a little, we may come to learn that here is best. See to it, only that thyself is here; — and art and nature, hope and fate, friends, angels, and the Supreme Being, shall not be absent from the chamber where thou sittest. Epaminondas, brave and affectionate, does not seem to us to need Olympus to die upon, nor the Syrian sunshine. He lies very well where he is. The Jerseys were handsome ground enough for Washington to tread, and London streets for the feet of Milton. A great man makes his climate genial in the imagination of men, and its air the beloved element of all delicate spirits. That country is the fairest, which is inhabited by the noblest minds. The pictures which fill the imagination in reading the actions of Pericles, Xenophon, Columbus, Bayard, Sidney, Hampden, teach us how needlessly mean our life is, that we, by the depth of our living,

THE OVER-SOUL

"But souls that of his own good life partake,
  He loves as his own self; dear as his eye
  They are to Him: He 'll never them forsake:
  When they shall die, then God himself shall die:
  They live, they live in blest eternity."

Henry More.

Space is ample, east and west,
But two cannot go abreast,
Cannot travel in it two:
Yonder masterful cuckoo
Crowds every egg out of the nest,
Quick or dead, except its own;
A spell is laid on sod and stone,
Night and Day were tampered with,
Every quality and pith
Surcharged and sultry with a power
That works its will on age and hour.

stances of man, we say, are historically somewhat better in this country, and at this hour, than perhaps ever before. More freedom exists for culture. It will not now run against an axe, at the first step out of the beaten track of opinion. But whoso is heroic, will always find crises to try his edge. Human virtue demands her champions and martyrs, and the trial of persecution always proceeds. It is but the other day, that the brave Lovejoy gave his breast to the bullets of a mob, for the rights of free speech and opinion, and died when it was better not to live.

I see not any road of perfect peace which a man can walk, but after the counsel of his own bosom. Let him quit too much association, let him go home much, and stablish himself in those courses he approves. The unremitting retention of simple and high sentiments in obscure duties, is hardening the character to that temper which will work with honor, if need be, in the tumult, or on the scaffold. Whatever outrages have happened to men, may befall a man again: and very easily in a republic, if there appear any signs of a decay of religion. Coarse slander, fire, tar and feathers, and the gibbet, the youth may freely bring home to his mind, and with what sweetness of temper he can, and inquire how fast he can fix his sense of duty, braving such penalties, whenever it may please the next newspaper, and a sufficient number of his neighbors to pronounce his opinions incendiary.

It may calm the apprehension of calamity in the most susceptible heart, to see how quick a bound nature has set to the utmost infliction of malice. We rapidly approach a brink over which no enemy can follow us.

> "Let them rave:
> Thou art quiet in thy grave."

In the gloom of our ignorance of what shall be, in the hour when we are deaf to the higher voices, who does not envy those who have seen safely to an end their manful endeavor? Who that sees the meanness of our politics, but inly congratulates Washington, that he is long already wrapped in his shroud, and forever safe; that he was laid sweet in his grave, the hope of humanity not yet subjugated in him? Who does not sometimes envy the good and brave, who are no more to suffer from the tumults of the natural world, and await with curious complacency the speedy term of his own conversation with finite nature? And yet the love that will be annihilated sooner than treacherous, has already made death impossible, and affirms itself no mortal, but a native of the deeps of absolute and inextinguishable being.

If we consider what happens in conversation, in reveries, in remorse, in times of passion, in surprises, in the instructions of dreams wherein often we see ourselves in masquerade, — the droll disguises only magnifying and enhancing a real element, and forcing it on our distinct notice, — we shall catch many hints that will broaden and lighten into knowledge of the secret of nature. All goes to show that the soul in man is not an organ, but animates and exercises all the organs; is not a function, like the power of memory, of calculation, of comparison, but uses these as hands and feet; is not a faculty, but a light; is not the intellect or the will, but the master of the intellect and the will; is the background of our being, in which they lie, — an immensity not possessed and that cannot be possessed. From within or from behind, a light shines through us upon things, and makes us aware that we are nothing, but the light is all. A man is the façade of a temple wherein all wisdom and all good abide. What we commonly call man, the eating, drinking, planting, counting man, does not, as we know him, represent himself, but misrepresents himself. Him we do not respect, but the soul, whose organ he is, would he let it appear through his action, would make our knees bend. When it breathes through his intellect, it is genius; when it breathes through his will, it is virtue; when it flows through his affection, it is love. And the blindness of the intellect begins, when it would be something of itself. The weakness of the will begins when the individual would be something of himself. All reform aims, in some one particular, to let the soul have its way through us; in other words, to engage us to obey.

Of this pure nature every man is at some time sensible. Language cannot paint it with his colors. It is too subtle. It is undefinable, unmeasurable, but we know that it pervades and contains us. We know that all spiritual being is in man. A wise old proverb says, "God comes to see us without bell:" that is, as there is no screen or ceiling between our heads and the infinite heavens, so is there no bar or wall in the soul where man, the effect, ceases, and God, the cause, begins. The walls are taken away. We lie open on one side to the deeps of spiritual nature, to all the attributes of God. Justice we see and know, Love, Freedom, Power.

These natures no man ever got above, but they tower over us, and most in the moment when our interests tempt us to wound them.

The sovereignty of this nature whereof we speak, is made known by its independency of those limitations which circumscribe us on every hand. The soul circumscribes all things. As I have said, it contradicts all experience. In like manner it abolishes time and space. The influence of the senses has, in most men, overpowered the mind to that degree, that the walls of time and space have come to look real and insurmountable; and to speak with levity of these limits, is, in the world, the sign of insanity. Yet time and space are but inverse measures of the force of the soul. The spirit sports with time —

> "Can crowd eternity into an hour,
> Or stretch an hour to eternity."

We are often made to feel that there is another youth and age than that which is measured from the year of our natural birth. Some thoughts always find us young and keep us so. Such a thought is the love of the universal and eternal beauty. Every man parts from that contemplation with the feeling that it rather belongs to ages than to mortal life. The least activity of the intellectual powers redeems us in a degree from the conditions of time. In sickness, in languor, give us a strain of poetry or a profound sentence, and we are refreshed; or produce a volume of Plato, or Shakspeare, or remind us of their names, and instantly we come into a feeling of longevity. See how the deep, divine thought reduces centuries, and millenniums, and makes itself present through all ages. Is the teaching of Christ less effective now than it was when first his mouth was opened? The emphasis of facts and persons in my thought has nothing to do with time. And so, always, the soul's scale is one; the scale of the senses and the understanding is another. Before the revelations of the soul, Time, Space and Nature shrink away. In common speech, we refer all things to time, as we habitually refer the immensely sundered stars to one concave sphere. And so we say that the Judg-

ESSAY IX

THE OVER-SOUL

There is a difference between one and another hour of life, in their authority and subsequent effect. Our faith comes in moments; our vice is habitual. Yet there is a depth in those brief moments, which constrains us to ascribe more reality to them than to all other experiences. For this reason, the argument, which is always forthcoming to silence those who conceive extraordinary hopes of man, namely, the appeal to experience, is forever invalid and vain. We give up the past to the objector, and yet we hope. He must explain this hope. We grant that human life is mean; but how did we find out that it was mean? What is the ground of this uneasiness of ours; of this old discontent? What is the universal sense of want and ignorance, but the fine innuendo by which the soul makes its enormous claim? Why do men feel that the natural history of man has never been written, but he is always leaving behind what you have said of him, and it becomes old, and books of metaphysics worthless? The philosophy of six thousand years has not searched the chambers and magazines of the soul. In its experiments there has always remained, in the last analysis, a residuum it could not resolve. Man is a stream whose source is hidden. Our being is descending into us from we know not whence. The most exact calculator has no prescience that somewhat incalculable may not baulk the very next moment. I am constrained every moment to acknowledge a higher origin for events than the will I call mine.

As with events, so is it with thoughts. When I watch that flowing river, which, out of regions I see not, pours for a season its streams into me, I see that I am a pensioner; not a cause, but a surprised spectator of this ethereal water; that I desire and look up, and put myself in the attitude of reception, but from some alien energy the visions come.

The Supreme Critic on the errors of the past and the present, and the only prophet of that which must be, is that great nature in which we rest, as the earth lies in the soft arms of the atmosphere; that Unity, that Over-Soul, within which every man's particular being is contained and made one with all other; that common heart, of which all sincere conversation is the worship, to which all right action is submission; that overpowering reality which confutes our tricks and talents, and constrains every one to pass for what he is, and to speak from his character and not from his tongue, and which evermore tends and aims to pass into our thought and hand, and become wisdom, and virtue, and power, and beauty. We live in succession, in division, in parts, in particles. Meantime within man is the soul of the whole; the wise silence; the universal beauty, to which every part and particle is equally related; the eternal ONE. And this deep power in which we exist, and whose beatitude is all accessible to us, is not only self-sufficing and perfect in every hour, but the act of seeing and the thing seen, the seer and the spectacle, the subject and the object, are one. We see the world piece by piece, as the sun, the moon, the animal, the tree; but the whole, of which these are the shining parts, is the soul. Only by the vision of that Wisdom can the horoscope of the ages be read, and by falling back on our better thoughts, by yielding to the spirit of prophecy which is innate in every man, we can know what it saith. Every man's words, who speaks from that life, must sound vain to those who do not dwell in the same thought on their own part. I dare not speak for it. My words do not carry its august sense; they fall short and cold. Only itself can inspire whom it will, and behold! their speech shall be lyrical, and sweet, and universal as the rising of the wind. Yet I desire, even by profane words, if I may not use sacred, to indicate the heaven of this deity, and to report what hints I have collected of the transcendent simplicity and energy of the Highest Law.

were. It arches over them like a temple, this unity of thought, in which every heart beats with nobler sense of power and duty, and thinks and acts with unusual solemnity. All are conscious of attaining to a higher self-possession. It shines for all. There is a certain wisdom of humanity which is common to the greatest men with the lowest, and which our ordinary education often labors to silence and obstruct. The mind is one, and the best minds who love truth for its own sake, think much less of property in truth. They accept it thankfully everywhere, and do not label or stamp it with any man's name, for it is theirs long beforehand, and from eternity. The learned and the studious of thought have no monopoly of wisdom. Their violence of direction in some degree disqualifies them to think truly. We owe many valuable observations to people who are not very acute or profound, and who say the thing without effort, which we want and have long been hunting in vain. The action of the soul is oftener in that which is felt and left unsaid, than in that which is said in any conversation. It broods over every society, and they unconsciously seek for it in each other. We know better than we do. We do not yet possess ourselves, and we know at the same time that we are much more. I feel the same truth how often in my trivial conversation with my neighbors, that somewhat higher in each of us overlooks this by-play, and Jove nods to Jove from behind each of us.

Men descend to meet. In their habitual and mean service to the world, for which they forsake their native nobleness, they resemble those Arabian Sheikhs, who dwell in mean houses and affect an external poverty, to escape the rapacity of the Pacha, and reserve all their display of wealth for their interior and guarded retirements.

As it is present in all persons, so it is in every period of life. It is adult already in the infant man. In my dealing with my child, my Latin and Greek, my accomplishments and my money, stead me nothing; but as much soul as I have avails. If I am wilful, he sets his will against mine, one for one, and leaves me, if I please, the degradation of beating him by my superiority of strength. But if I renounce my will, and act for the soul, setting that up as umpire between us two, out of his young eyes looks the same soul; he reveres and loves with me.

The soul is the perceiver and revealer of truth. We know truth when we see it, let skeptic and scoffer say what they choose. Foolish people ask you, when you have spoken what they do not wish to hear, 'How do you know it is truth, and not an error of your own?' We know truth when we see it, from opinion, as we know when we are awake that we are awake. It was a grand sentence of Emanuel Swedenborg, which would alone indicate the greatness of that man's perception, — "It is no proof of a man's understanding to be able to confirm whatever he pleases; but to be able to discern that what is true is true, and that what is false is false, this is the mark and character of intelligence." In the book I read, the good thought returns to me, as every truth will, the image of the whole soul. To the bad thought which I find in it, the same soul becomes a discerning, separating sword and lops it away. We are wiser than we know. If we will not interfere with our thought, but will act entirely, or see how the thing stands in God, we know the particular thing, and every thing, and every man. For, the Maker of all things and all persons, stands behind us, and casts his dread omniscience through us over things.

But beyond this recognition of its own in particular passages of the individual's experience, it also reveals truth. And here we should seek to reinforce ourselves by its very presence, and to speak with a worthier, loftier strain of that advent. For the soul's communication of truth is the highest event in nature, since it then does not give somewhat from itself, but it gives itself, or passes into and becomes that man whom it enlightens; or in proportion to that truth he receives, it takes him to itself.

We distinguish the announcements of the soul, its manifestations of its own nature, by the term *Revelation*. These are always attended by the emotion of the sublime. For this communication is an influx of the Divine mind into our mind. It is an ebb of the individual rivulet before the flowing surges of the sea of life. Every distinct apprehension of this central commandment agitates men with awe and delight. A thrill passes through all men at the reception of new truth, or at the performance of a

ment is distant or near, that the Millennium approaches, that a day of certain political, moral, social reforms is at hand, and the like, when we mean, that in the nature of things, one of the facts we contemplate is external and fugitive, and the other is permanent and connate with the soul. The things we now esteem fixed, shall, one by one, detach themselves, like ripe fruit, from our experience, and fall. The wind shall blow them none knows whither. The landscape, the figures, Boston, London, are facts as fugitive as any institution past, or any whiff of mist or smoke, and so is society, and so is the world. The soul looketh steadily forwards, creating a world before her, leaving worlds behind her. She has no dates, nor rites, nor persons, nor specialties, nor men. The soul knows only the soul; the web of events is the flowing robe in which she is clothed.

After its own law and not by arithmetic is the rate of its progress to be computed. The soul's advances are not made by gradation, such as can be represented by motion in a straight line; but rather by ascension of state, such as can be represented by metamorphosis, — from the egg to the worm, from the worm to the fly. The growths of genius are of a certain *total* character, that does not advance the elect individual first over John, then Adam, then Richard, and give to each the pain of discovered inferiority, but by every throe of growth, the man expands there where he works, passing, at each pulsation, classes, populations of men. With each divine impulse the mind rends the thin rinds of the visible and finite, and comes out into eternity, and inspires and expires its air. It converses with truths that have always been spoken in the world, and becomes conscious of a closer sympathy with Zeno and Arrian, than with persons in the house.

This is the law of moral and of mental gain. The simple rise as by specific levity, not into a particular virtue, but into the region of all the virtues. They are in the spirit which contains them all. The soul requires purity, but purity is not it; requires justice, but justice is not that; requires beneficence, but is somewhat better: so that there is a kind of descent and accommodation felt when we leave speaking of moral nature, to urge a virtue which it enjoins. To the well-born child, all the virtues are natural, and not painfully acquired. Speak to his heart, and the man becomes suddenly virtuous.

Within the same sentiment is the germ of intellectual growth, which obeys the same law. Those who are capable of humility, of justice, of love, of aspiration, stand already on a platform that commands the sciences and arts, speech and poetry, action and grace. For whoso dwells in this moral beatitude already anticipates those special powers which men prize so highly. The lover has no talent, no skill, which passes for quite nothing with his enamored maiden, however little she may possess of related faculty; and the heart which abandons itself to the Supreme Mind finds itself related to all its works and will travel a royal road to particular knowledges and powers. In ascending to this primary and aboriginal sentiment, we have come from our remote station on the circumference instantaneously to the centre of the world, where, as in the closet of God, we see causes, and anticipate the universe, which is but a slow effect.

One mode of the divine teaching is the incarnation of the spirit in a form, — in forms, like my own. I live in society; with persons who answer to thoughts in my own mind, or express a certain obedience to the great instincts to which I live. I see its presence to them. I am certified of a common nature; and these other souls, these separated selves, draw me as nothing else can. They stir in me the new emotions we call passion; of love, hatred, fear, admiration, pity; thence comes conversation, competition, persuasion, cities, and war. Persons are supplementary to the primary teaching of the soul. In youth we are mad for persons. Childhood and youth see all the world in them. But the larger experience of man discovers the identical nature appearing through them all. Persons themselves acquaint us with the impersonal. In all conversation between two persons, tacit reference is made as to a third party, to a common nature. That third party or common nature is not social; it is impersonal; is God. And so in groups where debate is earnest, and especially on high questions, the company become aware that the thought rises to an equal level in all bosoms, that all have a spiritual property in what was said, as well as the sayer. They all become wiser than they

By the same fire, vital, consecrating, celestial, which burns until it shall dissolve all things into the waves and surges of an ocean of light, we see and know each other, and what spirit each is of. Who can tell the grounds of his knowledge of the character of the several individuals in his circle of friends? No man. Yet their acts and words do not disappoint him. In that man, though he knew no ill of him, he put no trust. In that other, though they had seldom met, authentic signs had yet passed, to signify that he might be trusted as one who had an interest in his own character. We know each other very well, — which of us has been just to himself, and whether that which we teach or behold, is only an aspiration, or is our honest effort also.

We are all discerners of spirits. That diagnosis lies aloft in our life or unconscious power. The intercourse of society, — its trade, its religion, its friendships, its quarrels, — is one wide, judicial investigation of character. In full court, or in small committee, or confronted face to face, accuser and accused, men offer themselves to be judged. Against their will they exhibit those decisive trifles by which character is read. But who judges? and what? Not our understanding. We do not read them by learning or craft. No; the wisdom of the wise man consists herein, that he does not judge them; he lets them judge themselves, and merely reads and records their own verdict.

By virtue of this inevitable nature, private will is overpowered, and, maugre our efforts, or our imperfections, your genius will speak from you, and mine from me. That which we are, we shall teach, not voluntarily, but involuntarily. Thoughts come into our minds by avenues which we never left open, and thoughts go out of our minds through avenues which we never voluntarily opened. Character teaches over our head. The infallible index of true progress is found in the tone the man takes. Neither his age, nor his breeding, nor company, nor books, nor actions, nor talents, nor all together, can hinder him from being deferential to a higher spirit than his own. If he have not found his home in God, his manners, his forms of speech, the turn of his sentences, the build, shall I say, of all his opinions will involuntarily confess it, let him brave it out how he will. If he have found his centre, the Deity will shine through him, through all the disguises of ignorance, of ungenial temperament, of unfavorable circumstance. The tone of seeking, is one, and the tone of having is another.

The great distinction between teachers sacred or literary, — between poets like Herbert, and poets like Pope, — between philosophers like Spinoza, Kant, and Coleridge, and philosophers like Locke, Paley, Mackintosh, and Stewart, — between men of the world, who are reckoned accomplished talkers, and here and there a fervent mystic, prophesying, half-insane under the infinitude of his thought, — is, that one class speak *from within,* or from experience, as parties and possessors of the fact; and the other class, *from without,* as spectators merely, or perhaps as acquainted with the fact, on the evidence of third persons. It is of no use to preach to me from without. I can do that too easily myself. Jesus speaks always from within, and in a degree that transcends all others. In that, is the miracle. I believe beforehand that it ought so to be. All men stand continually in the expectation of the appearance of such a teacher. But if a man do not speak from within the veil, where the word is one with that it tells of, let him lowly confess it.

The same Omniscience flows into the intellect, and makes what we call genius. Much of the wisdom of the world is not wisdom, and the most illuminated class of men are no doubt superior to literary fame, and are not writers. Among the multitude of scholars and authors, we feel no hallowing presence; we are sensible of a knack and skill rather than of inspiration; they have a light, and know not whence it comes, and call it their own; their talent is some exaggerated faculty, some overgrown member, so that their strength is a disease. In these instances, the intellectual gifts do not make the impression of virtue, but almost of vice; and we feel that a man's talents stand in the way of his advancement in truth. But genius is religious. It is a larger imbibing of the common heart. It is not anomalous, but more like, and not less like other men. There is in all great poets, a wisdom of humanity, which is superior to any talents they exercise. The author, the wit, the partisan, the fine gentleman, does not take place of the man. Humanity shines in Homer, in Chaucer, in Spenser, in

great action, which comes out of the heart of nature. In these communications, the power to see, is not separated from the will to do, but the insight proceeds from obedience, and the obedience proceeds from a joyful perception. Every moment when the individual feels himself invaded by it, is memorable. By the necessity of our constitution, a certain enthusiasm attends the individual's consciousness of that divine presence. The character and duration of this enthusiasm varies with the state of the individual, from an extasy and trance and prophetic inspiration, — which is its rarer appearance, — to the faintest glow of virtuous emotion, in which form it warms, like our household fires, all the families and associations of men, and makes society possible. A certain tendency to insanity has always attended the opening of the religious sense in men, as if they had been "blasted with excess of light." The trances of Socrates, the "union" of Plotinus, the vision of Porphyry, the conversion of Paul, the aurora of Behmen, the convulsions of George Fox and his Quakers, the illumination of Swedenborg, are of this kind. What was in the case of these remarkable persons a ravishment, has, in innumerable instances in common life, been exhibited in less striking manner. Everywhere the history of religion betrays a tendency to enthusiasm. The rapture of the Moravian and Quietist; the opening of the internal sense of the Word, in the language of the New Jerusalem Church; the *revival* of the Calvinistic churches; the *experiences* of the Methodists, are varying forms of that shudder of awe and delight with which the individual soul always mingles with the universal soul.

The nature of these revelations is the same; they are perceptions of the absolute law. They are solutions of the soul's own questions. They do not answer the questions which the understanding asks. The soul answers never by words, but by the thing itself that is inquired after.

Revelation is the disclosure of the soul. The popular notion of a revelation, is, that it is a telling of fortunes. In past oracles of the soul, the understanding seeks to find answers to sensual questions, and undertakes to tell from God how long men shall exist, what their hands shall do, and who shall be their company, adding names, and dates, and places. But we must pick no locks. We must check this low curiosity. An answer in words is delusive; it is really no answer to the questions you ask. Do not require a description of the countries towards which you sail. The description does not describe them to you, and to-morrow you arrive there, and know them by inhabiting them. Men ask concerning the immortality of the soul, the employments of heaven, the state of the sinner, and so forth. They even dream that Jesus has left replies to precisely these interrogatories. Never a moment did that sublime spirit speak in their *patois*. To truth, justice, love, the attributes of the soul, the idea of immutableness is essentially associated. Jesus, living in these moral sentiments, heedless of sensual fortunes, heeding only the manifestations of these, never made the separation of the idea of duration from the essence of these attributes, nor uttered a syllable concerning the duration of the soul. It was left to his disciples to sever duration from the moral elements and to teach the immortality of the soul as a doctrine, and maintain it by evidences. The moment the doctrine of the immortality is separately taught, man is already fallen. In the flowing of love, in the adoration of humility, there is no question of continuance. No inspired man ever asks this question, or condescends to these evidences. For the soul is true to itself, and the man in whom it is shed abroad, cannot wander from the present, which is infinite, to a future, which would be finite.

These questions which we lust to ask about the future, are a confession of sin. God has no answer for them. No answer in words can reply to a question of things. It is not in an arbitrary "decree of God," but in the nature of man that a veil shuts down on the facts of to-morrow: for the soul will not have us read any other cipher than that of cause and effect. By this veil, which curtains events, it instructs the children of men to live in to-day. The only mode of obtaining an answer to these questions of the senses, is, to forego all low curiosity, and, accepting the tide of being which floats us into the secret of nature, work and live, work and live, and all unawares, the advancing soul has built and forged for itself a new condition, and the question and the answer are one.

Shakspeare, in Milton. They are content with truth. They use the positive degree. They seem frigid and phlegmatic to those who have been spiced with the frantic passion and violent coloring of inferior, but popular writers. For, they are poets by the free course which they allow to the informing soul, which through their eyes beholds again, and blesses the things which it hath made. The soul is superior to its knowledge; wiser than any of its works. The great poet makes us feel our own wealth, and then we think less of his compositions. His best communication to our mind, is, to teach us to despise all he has done. Shakspeare carries us to such a lofty strain of intelligent activity, as to suggest a wealth which beggars his own; and we then feel that the splendid works which he has created, and which in other hours, we extol as a sort of self-existent poetry, take no stronger hold of real nature than the shadow of a passing traveller on the rock. The inspiration which uttered itself in Hamlet and Lear, could utter things as good from day to day, forever. Why then should I make account of Hamlet and Lear, as if we had not the soul from which they fell as syllables from the tongue?

This energy does not descend into individual life, on any other condition than entire possession. It comes to the lowly and simple; it comes to whomsoever will put off what is foreign and proud; it comes as insight; it comes as serenity and grandeur. When we see those whom it inhabits, we are apprized of new degrees of greatness. From that inspiration the man comes back with a changed tone. He does not talk with men, with an eye to their opinion. He tries them. It requires of us to be plain and true. The vain traveller attempts to embellish his life by quoting my Lord, and the Prince, and the Countess, who thus said or did to *him*. The ambitious vulgar, show you their spoons, and brooches, and rings, and preserve their cards and compliments. The more cultivated, in their account of their own experience, cull out the pleasing poetic circumstance, — the visit to Rome, the man of genius they saw, the brilliant friend they know; still further on, perhaps, the gorgeous landscape, the mountain lights, the mountain thoughts, they enjoyed yesterday, — and so seek to throw a romantic color over their life. But the soul that ascends to wor-

171

ship the great God, is plain and true; has no rose-color, no fine
friends, no chivalry, no adventures; does not want admiration;
dwells in the hour that now is, in the earnest experience of the
common day, — by reason of the present moment and the mere
trifle having become porous to thought, and bibulous of the sea
of light.

Converse with a mind that is grandly simple, and literature
looks like word-catching. The simplest utterances are worthiest
to be written, yet are they so cheap, and so things of course, that
in the infinite riches of the soul, it is like gathering a few pebbles
off the ground, or bottling a little air in a phial, when the whole
earth, and the whole atmosphere are ours. Nothing can pass
there, or make you one of the circle, but the casting aside your
trappings, and dealing man to man in naked truth, plain confession and omniscient affirmation.

Souls, such as these, treat you as gods would; walk as gods in
the earth, accepting without any admiration, your wit, your
bounty, your virtue even, — say rather your act of duty, for your
virtue they own as their proper blood, royal as themselves, and
over-royal, and the father of the gods. But what rebuke their
plain fraternal bearing casts on the mutual flattery with which
authors solace each other, and wound themselves! These flatter
not. I do not wonder that these men go to see Cromwell, and
Christina, and Charles II., and James I., and the Grand Turk. For
they are in their own elevation, the fellows of kings, and must feel
the servile tone of conversation in the world. They must always
be a godsend to princes, for they confront them, a king to a king,
without ducking or concession, and give a high nature the refresh-
ment and satisfaction of resistance, of plain humanity, of even
companionship, and of new ideas. They leave them wiser and
superior men. Souls like these make us feel that sincerity is more
excellent than flattery. Deal so plainly with man and woman, as
to constrain the utmost sincerity, and destroy all hope of trifling
with you. It is the highest compliment you can pay. Their "highest praising," said Milton, "is not flattery, and their plainest advice
is a kind of praising."

Ineffable is the union of man and God in every act of the soul.

The simplest person, who in his integrity worships God, becomes God; yet forever and ever the influx of this better and universal self is new and unsearchable. It inspires awe and astonishment. How dear, how soothing to man, arises the idea of God, peopling the lonely place, effacing the scars of our mistakes and disappointments! When we have broken our god of tradition, and ceased from our god of rhetoric, then may God fire the heart with his presence. It is the doubling of the heart itself, nay, the infinite enlargement of the heart with a power of growth to a new infinity on every side. It inspires in man an infallible trust. He has not the conviction, but the sight that the best is the true, and may in that thought easily dismiss all particular uncertainties and fears, and adjourn to the sure revelation of time, the solution of his private riddles. He is sure that his welfare is dear to the heart of being. In the presence of law to his mind, he is overflowed with a reliance so universal, that it sweeps away all cherished hopes and the most stable projects of mortal condition in its flood. He believes that he cannot escape from his good. The things that are really for thee, gravitate to thee. You are running to seek your friend. Let your feet run, but your mind need not. If you do not find him, will you not acquiesce that it is best you should not find him? for there is a power, which, as it is in you, is in him also, and could therefore very well bring you together, if it were for the best. You are preparing with eagerness to go and render a service to which your talent and your taste invite you, the love of men, and the hope of fame. Has it not occurred to you, that you have no right to go, unless you are equally willing to be prevented from going? O believe, as thou livest, that every sound that is spoken over the round world, which thou oughtest to hear, will vibrate on thine ear. Every proverb, every book, every byword that belongs to thee for aid or comfort, shall surely come home through open or winding passages. Every friend whom not thy fantastic will, but the great and tender heart in thee craveth, shall lock thee in his embrace. And this, because the heart in thee is the heart of all; not a valve, not a wall, not an intersection is there anywhere in nature, but one blood rolls uninterruptedly, an endless circulation through all men, as the water of the globe is all one sea, and, truly seen, its tide is one.

Let man then learn the revelation of all nature, and all thought to his heart; this, namely; that the Highest dwells with him; that the sources of nature are in his own mind, if the sentiment of duty is there. But if he would know what the great God speaketh, he must 'go into his closet and shut the door,' as Jesus said. God will not make himself manifest to cowards. He must greatly listen to himself, withdrawing himself from all the accents of other men's devotion. Even their prayers are hurtful to him, until he have made his own. Our religion vulgarly stands on numbers of believers. Whenever the appeal is made, — no matter how indirectly, — to numbers, proclamation is then and there made, that religion is not. He that finds God a sweet, enveloping thought to him, never counts his company. When I sit in that presence, who shall dare to come in? When I rest in perfect humility, when I burn with pure love, — what can Calvin or Swedenborg say?

It makes no difference whether the appeal is to numbers or to one. The faith that stands on authority is not faith. The reliance on authority, measures the decline of religion, the withdrawal of the soul. The position men have given to Jesus, now for many centuries of history, is a position of authority. It characterizes themselves. It cannot alter the eternal facts. Great is the soul, and plain. It is no flatterer, it is no follower; it never appeals from itself. It believes in itself. Before the immense possibilities of man, all mere experience, all past biography, however spotless and sainted, shrinks away. Before that heaven which our presentiments foreshow us, we cannot easily praise any form of life we have seen or read of. We not only affirm that we have few great men, but absolutely speaking, that we have none; that we have no history, no record of any character or mode of living, that entirely contents us. The saints and demigods whom history worships, we are constrained to accept with a grain of allowance. Though in our lonely hours, we draw a new strength out of their memory, yet pressed on our attention, as they are by the thoughtless and customary, they fatigue and invade. The soul gives itself alone, original, and pure, to the Lonely, Original and Pure, who, on that condition, gladly inhabits, leads, and speaks through it. Then is it glad, young, and nimble. It is not wise, but it sees through all things. It is not called religious, but it is innocent. It calls the light its own, and feels that the grass grows, and the stone falls by a law inferior to, and dependent on its nature. Behold, it saith, I am born into the great, the universal mind. I the imperfect, adore my own Perfect. I am somehow receptive of the great soul, and thereby I do overlook the sun and the stars, and feel them to be the fair accidents and effects which change and pass. More and more the surges of everlasting nature enter into me, and I become public and human in my regards and actions. So come I to live in thoughts, and act with energies which are immortal. Thus revering the soul, and learning, as the ancient said, that "its beauty is immense," man will come to see that the world is the perennial miracle which the soul worketh, and be less astonished at particular wonders; he will learn that there is no profane history; that all history is sacred; that the universe is represented in an atom, in a moment of time. He will weave no longer a spotted life of shreds and patches, but he will live with a divine unity. He will cease from what is base and frivolous in his life, and be content with all places and with any service he can render. He will calmly front the morrow in the negligency of that trust which carries God with it, and so hath already the whole future in the bottom of the heart.

CIRCLES

Nature centres into balls,
And her proud ephemerals,
Fast to surface and outside,
Scan the profile of the sphere;
Knew they what that signified,
A new genesis were here.

CIRCLES

The eye is the first circle; the horizon which it forms is the second; and throughout nature this primary figure is repeated without end. It is the highest emblem in the cipher of the world. St. Augustine described the nature of God as a circle whose centre was everywhere, and its circumference nowhere. We are all our lifetime reading the copious sense of this first of forms. One moral we have already deduced in considering the circular or compensatory character of every human action. Another analogy we shall now trace; that every action admits of being outdone. Our life is an apprenticeship to the truth, that around every circle another can be drawn; that there is no end in nature, but every end is a beginning; that there is always another dawn risen on mid-noon, and under every deep a lower deep opens.

This fact, as far as it symbolizes the moral fact of the Unattainable, the flying Perfect, around which the hands of man can never meet, at once the inspirer and the condemner of every success, may conveniently serve us to connect many illustrations of human power in every department.

There are no fixtures in nature. The universe is fluid and volatile. Permanence is but a word of degrees. Our globe seen by God, is a transparent law, not a mass of facts. The law dissolves the fact and holds it fluid. Our culture is the predominance of an idea which draws after it this train of cities and institutions. Let us rise into another idea: they will disappear. The Greek sculpture is all melted away, as if it had been statues of ice: here and there a solitary figure or fragment remaining, as we see flecks and scraps of snow left in cold dells and mountain clefts, in June and July. For, the genius that created it, creates now somewhat else. The Greek letters last a little longer, but are already passing under the same sentence, and tumbling into the inevitable pit which the creation of new thought opens for all that is old. The new continents are built out of the ruins of an old planet: the new races fed out of the decomposition of the foregoing. New arts destroy the old. See the investment of capital in aqueducts, made useless by hydraulics; fortifications, by gunpowder; roads and canals, by railways; sails, by steam; steam by electricity.

You admire this tower of granite, weathering the hurts of so many ages. Yet a little waving hand built this huge wall, and that which builds, is better than that which is built. The hand that built, can topple it down much faster. Better than the hand, and nimbler, was the invisible thought which wrought through it, and thus ever behind the coarse effect, is a fine cause, which, being narrowly seen, is itself the effect of a finer cause. Every thing looks permanent until its secret is known. A rich estate appears to women a firm and lasting fact; to a merchant, one easily created out of any materials, and easily lost. An orchard, good tillage, good grounds, seem a fixture, like a gold mine, or a river, to a citizen; but to a large farmer, not much more fixed than the state of the crop. Nature looks provokingly stable and secular, but it has a cause like all the rest; and when once I comprehend that, will these fields stretch so immovably wide, these leaves hang so individually considerable? Permanence is a word of degrees. Every thing is medial. Moons are no more bounds to spiritual power than bat-balls.

The key to every man is his thought. Sturdy and defying though he look, he has a helm which he obeys, which is, the idea after which all his facts are classified. He can only be reformed by showing him a new idea which commands his own. The life of man is a self-evolving circle, which, from a ring imperceptibly small, rushes on all sides outwards to new and larger circles, and that without end. The extent to which this generation of circles, wheel without wheel will go, depends on the force or truth of the individual soul. For, it is the inert effort of each thought having formed itself into a circular wave of circumstance, — as, for instance, an empire, rules of an art, a local usage, a religious rite, — to heap itself on that ridge, and to solidify, and hem in the life. But if the soul is quick and strong, it bursts over that boundary on all sides, and expands another orbit on the great deep, which also runs up into a high wave, with attempt again to stop and to bind. But the heart refuses to be imprisoned; in its first and narrowest pulses, it already tends outward with a vast force, and to immense and innumerable expansions.

Every ultimate fact is only the first of a new series. Every general law only a particular fact of some more general law presently to disclose itself. There is no outside, no enclosing wall, no circumference to us. The man finishes his story, — how good! how final! how it puts a new face on all things! He fills the sky. Lo! on the other side rises also a man, and draws a circle around the circle we had just pronounced the outline of the sphere. Then already is our first speaker, not man, but only a first speaker. His only redress is forthwith to draw a circle outside of his antagonist. And so men do by themselves. The result of to-day which haunts the mind and cannot be escaped, will presently be abridged into a word, and the principle that seemed to explain nature, will itself be included as one example of a bolder generalization. In the thought of to-morrow there is a power to upheave all thy creed, all the creeds, all the literatures of the nations, and marshal thee to a heaven which no epic dream has yet depicted. Every man is not so much a workman in the world, as he is a suggestion of that he should be. Men walk as prophecies of the next age.

Step by step we scale this mysterious ladder: the steps are actions; the new prospect is power. Every several result is threatened and judged by that which follows. Every one seems to be contradicted by the new; it is only limited by the new. The new statement is always hated by the old, and, to those dwelling in the old, comes like an abyss of skepticism. But the eye soon gets wonted to it, for the eye and it are effects of one cause; then its innocency and benefit appear, and, presently, all its energy spent, it pales and dwindles before the revelation of the new hour.

Fear not the new generalization. Does the fact look crass and material, threatening to degrade thy theory of spirit? Resist it not; it goes to refine and raise thy theory of matter just as much.

There are no fixtures to men, if we appeal to consciousness. Every man supposes himself not to be fully understood; and if there is any truth in him, if he rests at last on the divine soul, I see not how it can be otherwise. The last chamber, the last closet, he must feel, was never opened; there is always a residuum unknown, unanalyzable. That is, every man believes that he has a greater possibility.

Our moods do not believe in each other. To-day, I am full of thoughts, and can write what I please. I see no reason why I should not have the same thought, the same power of expression to-morrow. What I write, whilst I write it, seems the most natural thing in the world: but, yesterday, I saw a dreary vacuity in this direction in which now I see so much; and a month hence, I doubt not, I shall wonder who he was that wrote so many continuous pages. Alas for this infirm faith, this will not strenuous, this vast ebb of a vast flow! I am God in nature; I am a weed by the wall.

The continual effort to raise himself above himself, to work a pitch above his last height, betrays itself in a man's relations. We thirst for approbation, yet cannot forgive the approver. The sweet of nature is love; yet if I have a friend, I am tormented by my imperfections. The love of me accuses the other party. If he were high enough to slight me, then could I love him, and rise by my affection to new heights. A man's growth is seen in the successive choirs of his friends. For every friend whom he loses for truth, he gains a better. I thought, as I walked in the woods and mused on my friends, why should I play with them this game of idolatry? I know and see too well, when not voluntarily blind, the speedy limits of persons called high and worthy. Rich, noble, and great they are by the liberality of our speech, but truth is sad. O blessed Spirit, whom I forsake for these, they are not thou! Every personal consideration that we allow, costs us heavenly state. We sell the thrones of angels for a short and turbulent pleasure.

How often must we learn this lesson? Men cease to interest us when we find their limitations. The only sin is limitation. As soon as you once come up with a man's limitations, it is all over

with him. Has he talents? has he enterprises? has he knowledge?
it boots not. Infinitely alluring and attractive was he to you
yesterday, a great hope, a sea to swim in; now, you have found
his shores, found it a pond, and you care not if you never see it
again.

Each new step we take in thought reconciles twenty seemingly
discordant facts, as expressions of one law. Aristotle and Plato
are reckoned the respective heads of two schools. A wise man will
see that Aristotle Platonizes. By going one step farther back in
thought, discordant opinions are reconciled, by being seen to be
two extremes of one principle, and we can never go so far back
as to preclude a still higher vision.

Beware when the great God lets loose a thinker on this planet.
Then all things are at risk. It is as when a conflagration has
broken out in a great city, and no man knows what is safe, or
where it will end. There is not a piece of science, but its flank
may be turned to-morrow; there is not any literary reputation, not
the so-called eternal names of fame, that may not be revised and
condemned. The very hopes of man, the thoughts of his heart,
the religion of nations, the manners and morals of mankind, are
all at the mercy of a new generalization. Generalization is always a new influx of the divinity into the mind. Hence the thrill
that attends it.

Valor consists in the power of self-recovery, so that a man cannot have his flank turned, cannot be outgeneralled, but put him
where you will, he stands. This can only be by his preferring
truth to his past apprehension of truth; and his alert acceptance
of it from whatever quarter; the intrepid conviction that his laws,
his relations to society, his christianity, his world, may at any time
be superseded and deccase.

There are degrees in idealism. We learn first to play with it
academically, as the magnet was once a toy. Then we see in the
heyday of youth and poetry that it may be true, that it is true in
gleams and fragments. Then, its countenance waxes stern and
grand, and we see that it must be true. It now shows itself ethical
and practical. We learn that God IS; that he is in me; and that
all things are shadows of him. The idealism of Berkeley is only

a crude statement of the idealism of Jesus, and that, again, is a crude statement of the fact that all nature is the rapid efflux of goodness executing and organizing itself. Much more obviously is history and the state of the world at any one time, directly dependent on the intellectual classification then existing in the minds of men. The things which are dear to men at this hour, are so on account of the ideas which have emerged on their mental horizon, and which cause the present order of things as a tree bears its apples. A new degree of culture would instantly revolutionize the entire system of human pursuits.

Conversation is a game of circles. In conversation we pluck up the *termini* which bound the common of silence on every side. The parties are not to be judged by the spirit they partake and even express under this Pentecost. To-morrow they will have receded from this high-water mark. To-morrow you shall find them stooping under the old packsaddles. Yet let us enjoy the cloven flame whilst it glows on our walls. When each new speaker strikes a new light, emancipates us from the oppression of the last speaker, to oppress us with the greatness and exclusiveness of his own thought, then yields us to another redeemer, we seem to recover our rights, to become men. O what truths profound and executable only in ages and orbs, are supposed in the announcement of every truth! In common hours, society sits cold and statuesque. We all stand waiting, empty, — knowing, possibly, that we can be full, surrounded by mighty symbols which are not symbols to us, but prose and trivial toys. Then cometh the god, and converts the statues into fiery men, and by a flash of his eye burns up the veil which shrouded all things, and the meaning of the very furniture, of cup and saucer, of chair and clock and tester, is manifest. The facts which loomed so large in the fogs of yesterday, — property, climate, breeding, personal beauty, and the like, have strangely changed their proportions. All that we reckoned settled, shakes and rattles; and literatures, cities, climates, religions, leave their foundations, and dance before our eyes. And yet here again see the swift circumscription. Good as is discourse, silence is better, and shames it. The length of the discourse indicates the distance of thought betwixt the speaker and the hearer. If they were at a perfect understanding in any part, no words would be necessary thereon. If at one in all parts, no words would be suffered.

Literature is a point outside of our hodiernal circle, through which a new one may be described. The use of literature is to afford us a platform whence we may command a view of our present life, a purchase by which we may move it. We fill ourselves with ancient learning; install ourselves the best we can in Greek, in Punic, in Roman houses, only that we may wiselier see French, English, and American houses and modes of living. In like manner, we see literature best from the midst of wild nature, or from the din of affairs, or from a high religion. The field cannot be well seen from within the field. The astronomer must have his diameter of the earth's orbit as a base to find the parallax of any star.

Therefore, we value the poet. All the argument, and all the wisdom, is not in the encyclopedia, or the treatise on metaphysics, or the Body of Divinity, but in the sonnet or the play. In my daily work I incline to repeat my old steps, and do not believe in remedial force, in the power of change and reform. But some Petrarch or Ariosto, filled with the new wine of his imagination, writes me an ode, or a brisk romance, full of daring thought and action. He smites and arouses me with his shrill tones, breaks up my whole chain of habits, and I open my eye on my own possibilities. He claps wings to the sides of all the solid old lumber of the world, and I am capable once more of choosing a straight path in theory and practice.

We have the same need to command a view of the religion of the world. We can never see christianity from the catechism: — from the pastures, from a boat in the pond, from amidst the songs of wood-birds, we possibly may. Cleansed by the elemental light and wind, steeped in the sea of beautiful forms which the field offers us, we may chance to cast a right glance back upon biography. Christianity is rightly dear to the best of mankind; yet was there never a young philosopher whose breeding had fallen into the christian church, by whom that brave text of Paul's, was not specially prized: — "Then shall also the Son be subject unto

Him who put all things under him, that God may be all in all."
Let the claims and virtues of persons be never so great and welcome, the instinct of man presses eagerly onward to the impersonal and illimitable, and gladly arms itself against the dogmatism
of bigots with this generous word, out of the book itself.

The natural world may be conceived of as a system of con-
centric circles, and we now and then detect in nature slight dis-
locations, which apprize us that this surface on which we now
stand, is not fixed, but sliding. These manifold tenacious qualities, this chemistry and vegetation, these metals and animals,
which seem to stand there for their own sake, are means and
methods only, — are words of God, and as fugitive as other words.
Has the naturalist or chemist learned his craft, who has explored
the gravity of atoms and the elective affinities, who has not yet
discerned the deeper law whereof this is only a partial or approximate statement, namely, that like draws to like; and that the
goods which belong to you, gravitate to you, and need not be
pursued with pains and cost? Yet is that statement approximate
also, and not final. Omnipresence is a higher fact. Not through
subtle, subterranean channels, need friend and fact be drawn to
their counterpart, but, rightly considered, these things proceed
from the eternal generation of the soul. Cause and effect are two
sides of one fact.

The same law of eternal procession ranges all that we call the
virtues, and extinguishes each in the light of a better. The great
man will not be prudent in the popular sense; all his prudence
will be so much deduction from his grandeur. But it behoves
each to see when he sacrifices prudence, to what god he devotes
it; if to ease and pleasure, he had better be prudent still: if to a
great trust, he can well spare his mule and panniers, who has a
winged chariot instead. Geoffrey draws on his boots to go
through the woods, that his feet may be safer from the bite of
snakes; Aaron never thinks of such a peril. In many years, neither
is harmed by such an accident. Yet it seems to me that with every
precaution you take against such an evil, you put yourself into the
power of the evil. I suppose that the highest prudence is the
lowest prudence. Is this too sudden a rushing from the centre

to the verge of our orbit? Think how many times we shall fall back into pitiful calculations, before we take up our rest in the great sentiment, or make the verge of to-day the new centre. Besides, your bravest sentiment is familiar to the humblest men. The poor and the low have their way of expressing the last facts of philosophy as well as you. "Blessed be nothing," and "the worse things are, the better they are," are proverbs which express the transcendentalism of common life.

One man's justice is another's injustice; one man's beauty, another's ugliness; one man's wisdom, another's folly; as one beholds the same objects from a higher point. One man thinks justice consists in paying debts, and has no measure in his abhorrence of another who is very remiss in this duty, and makes the creditor wait tediously. But that second man has his own way of looking at things; asks himself, which debt must I pay first, the debt to the rich, or the debt to the poor? the debt of money, or the debt of thought to mankind, of genius to nature? For you, O broker, there is no other principle but arithmetic. For me, commerce is of trivial import; love, faith, truth of character, the aspiration of man, these are sacred: nor can I detach one duty, like you, from all other duties, and concentrate my forces mechanically on the payment of moneys. Let me live onward: you shall find that, though slower, the progress of my character will liquidate all these debts without injustice to higher claims. If a man should dedicate himself to the payment of notes, would not this be injustice? Does he owe no debt but money? And are all claims on him to be postponed to a landlord's or a banker's?

There is no virtue which is final; all are initial. The virtues of society are vices of the saint. The terror of reform is the discovery that we must cast away our virtues, or what we have always esteemed such, into the same pit that has consumed our grosser vices.

> "Forgive his crimes, forgive his virtues too,
> Those smaller faults, half converts to the right."

It is the highest power of divine moments that they abolish our contritions also. I accuse myself of sloth and unprofitableness, day by day; but when these waves of God flow into me, I no longer reckon lost time. I no longer poorly compute my possible achievement by what remains to me of the month or the year; for these moments confer a sort of omnipresence and omnipotence, which asks nothing of duration, but sees that the energy of the mind is commensurate with the work to be done, without time.

And thus, O circular philosopher, I hear some reader exclaim, you have arrived at a fine pyrrhonism, at an equivalence and indifferency of all actions, and would fain teach us, that, *if we are true*, forsooth, our crimes may be lively stones out of which we shall construct the temple of the true God.

I am not careful to justify myself. I own I am gladdened by seeing the predominance of the saccharine principle throughout vegetable nature, and not less by beholding in morals that unrestrained inundation of the principle of good into every chink and hole that selfishness has left open, yea, into selfishness and sin itself; so that no evil is pure, nor hell itself without its extreme satisfactions. But lest I should mislead any when I have my own head, and obey my whims, let me remind the reader that I am only an experimenter. Do not set the least value on what I do, or the least discredit on what I do not, as if I pretended to settle anything as true or false. I unsettle all things. No facts are to me sacred; none are profane; I simply experiment, an endless seeker, with no Past at my back.

Yet this incessant movement and progression, which all things partake, could never become sensible to us, but by contrast to some principle of fixture or stability in the soul. Whilst the eternal generation of circles proceeds, the eternal generator abides. That central life is somewhat superior to creation, superior to knowledge and thought, and contains all its circles. Forever it labors to create a life and thought as large and excellent as itself, suggesting to our thought a certain development, as if that which is made, instructs how to make a better.

Thus there is no sleep, no pause, no preservation, but all things renew, germinate, and spring. Why should we import rags and relics into the new hour? Nature abhors the old, and old age seems the only disease: all others run into this one. We call it by

many names, — fever, intemperance, insanity, stupidity, and crime:
they are all forms of old age: they are rest, conservatism, appropriation, inertia, not newness, not the way onward. We grizzle
every day. I see no need of it. Whilst we converse with what is
above us, we do not grow old, but grow young. Infancy, youth,
receptive, aspiring, with religious eye looking upward, counts itself nothing, and abandons itself to the instruction flowing from
all sides. But the man and woman of seventy assume to know all,
they have outlived their hope, they renounce aspiration, accept
the actual for the necessary, and talk down to the young. Let
them then become organs of the Holy Ghost; let them be lovers;
let them behold truth; and their eyes are uplifted, their wrinkles
smoothed, they are perfumed again with hope and power. This
old age ought not to creep on a human mind. In nature, every
moment is new; the past is always swallowed and forgotten; the
coming only is sacred. Nothing is secure but life, transition, the
energizing spirit. No love can be bound by oath or covenant to
secure it against a higher love. No truth so sublime but it may
be trivial tomorrow in the light of new thoughts. People wish to
be settled: only as far as they are unsettled, is there any hope for
them.

Life is a series of surprises. We do not guess to-day the mood,
the pleasure, the power of to-morrow, when we are building up
our being. Of lower states, — of acts of routine and sense, — we
can tell somewhat; but the masterpieces of God, the total growths
and universal movements of the soul, he hideth; they are incalculable. I can know that truth is divine and helpful, but how it shall
help me, I can have no guess, for, *so to be* is the sole inlet of *so
to know*. The new position of the advancing man has all the
powers of the old, yet has them all new. It carries in its bosom
all the energies of the past, yet is itself an exhalation of the morning. I cast away in this new moment all my once hoarded knowledge, as vacant and vain. Now, for the first time, seem I to know
any thing rightly. The simplest words, — we do not know what
they mean, except when we love and aspire.

The difference between talents and character is adroitness to
keep the old and trodden round, and power and courage to make

a new road to new and better goals. Character makes an over-powering present, a cheerful, determined hour, which fortifies all the company, by making them see that much is possible and excellent, that was not thought of. Character dulls the impression of particular events. When we see the conqueror, we do not think much of any one battle or success. We see that we had exaggerated the difficulty. It was easy to him. The great man is not convulsible or tormentable; events pass over him without much impression. People say sometimes, 'See what I have overcome; see how cheerful I am; see how completely I have triumphed over these black events.' Not if they still remind me of the black event. True conquest is the causing the calamity to fade and disappear as an early cloud of insignificant result in a history so large and advancing.

The one thing which we seek with insatiable desire, is to forget ourselves, to be surprised out of our propriety, to lose our sempiternal memory, and to do something without knowing how or why; in short, to draw a new circle. Nothing great was ever achieved without enthusiasm. The way of life is wonderful: it is by abandonment. The great moments of history are the facilities of performance through the strength of ideas, as the works of genius and religion. "A man," said Oliver Cromwell, "never rises so high as when he knows not whither he is going." Dreams and drunkenness, the use of opium and alcohol are the semblance and counterfeit of this oracular genius, and hence their dangerous attraction for men. For the like reason, they ask the aid of wild passions, as in gaming and war, to ape in some manner these flames and generosities of the heart.

INTELLECT

Go, speed the stars of Thought
On to their shining goals; —
The sower scatters broad his seed, —
The wheat thou strew'st be souls.

ESSAY XI

INTELLECT

Every substance is negatively electric to that which stands above it in the chemical tables, positively to that which stands below it. Water dissolves wood, and iron, and salt; air dissolves water; electric fire dissolves air, but the intellect dissolves fire, gravity, laws, method, and the subtlest unnamed relations of nature in its resistless menstruum. Intellect lies behind genius, which is intellect constructive. Intellect is the simple power anterior to all action or construction. Gladly would I unfold in calm degrees a natural history of the intellect, but what man has yet been able to mark the steps and boundaries of that transparent essence? The first questions are always to be asked, and the wisest doctor is gravelled by the inquisitiveness of a child. How can we speak of the action of the mind under any divisions, as, of its knowledge, of its ethics, of its works, and so forth, since it melts will into perception, knowledge into act? Each becomes the other. Itself alone is. Its vision is not like the vision of the eye, but is union with the things known.

Intellect and intellection signify, to the common ear consideration of abstract truth. The considerations of time and place, of you and me, of profit and hurt, tyrannize over most men's minds. Intellect separates the fact considered from *you*, from all local and personal reference, and discerns it as if it existed for its own sake. Heraclitus looked upon the affections as dense and colored mists. In the fog of good and evil affections, it is hard for man to walk forward in a straight line. Intellect is void of affection, and sees an object as it stands in the light of science, cool and disengaged.

The intellect goes out of the individual, floats over its own personality, and regards it as a fact, and not as *I* and *mine*. He who is immersed in what concerns person or place, cannot see the problem of existence. This the intellect always ponders. Nature shows all things formed and bound. The intellect pierces the form, overleaps the wall, detects intrinsic likeness between remote things, and reduces all things into a few principles.

The making a fact the subject of thought, raises it. All that mass of mental and moral phenomena which we do not make objects of voluntary thought, come within the power of fortune; they constitute the circumstance of daily life; they are subject to change, to fear, and hope. Every man beholds his human condition with a degree of melancholy. As a ship aground is battered by the waves, so man, imprisoned in mortal life, lies open to the mercy of coming events. But a truth, separated by the intellect, is no longer a subject of destiny. We behold it as a god upraised above care and fear. And so any fact in our life, or any record of our fancies or reflections, disentangled from the web of our unconsciousness, becomes an object impersonal and immortal. It is the past restored, but embalmed. A better art than that of Egypt has taken fear and corruption out of it. It is eviscerated of care. It is offered for science. What is addressed to us for contemplation does not threaten us, but makes us intellectual beings.

The growth of the intellect is spontaneous in every expansion. The mind that grows could not predict the times, the means, the mode of that spontaneity. God enters by a private door into every individual. Long prior to the age of reflection, is the thinking of the mind. Out of darkness, it came insensibly into the marvellous light of to-day. In the period of infancy it accepted and disposed of all impressions from the surrounding creation after its own way. Whatever any mind doth or saith is after a law; and this native law remains over it after it has come to reflection or conscious thought. In the most worn, pedantic, introverted, self-tormentor's life, the greatest part is incalculable by him, unforeseen, unimaginable, and must be, until he can take himself up by his own ears. What am I? What has my will done to make me that I am?

Nothing. I have been floated into this thought, this hour, this connection of events, by secret currents of might and mind, and my ingenuity and wilfulness have not thwarted, have not aided to an appreciable degree.

Our spontaneous action is always the best. You cannot, with your best deliberation and heed, come so close to any question as your spontaneous glance shall bring you, whilst you rise from your bed, or walk abroad in the morning after meditating the matter before sleep, on the previous night. Our thinking is a pious reception. Our truth of thought is therefore vitiated as much by too violent direction given by our will, as by too great negligence. We do not determine what we will think. We only open our senses, clear away, as we can, all obstruction from the fact, and suffer the intellect to see. We have little control over our thoughts. We are the prisoners of ideas. They catch us up for moments into their heaven, and so fully engage us, that we take no thought for the morrow, gaze like children, without an effort to make them our own. By and by we fall out of that rapture, bethink us where we have been, what we have seen, and repeat, as truly as we can, what we have beheld. As far as we can recall these extasies, we carry away in the ineffaceable memory, the result, and all men and all the ages confirm it. It is called Truth. But the moment we cease to report, and attempt to correct and contrive, it is not truth.

If we consider what persons have stimulated and profited us, we shall perceive the superiority of the spontaneous or intuitive principle over the arithmetical or logical. The first contains the second, but virtual and latent. We want, in every man, a long logic; we cannot pardon the absence of it, but it must not be spoken. Logic is the procession or proportionate unfolding of the intuition; but its virtue is as silent method; the moment it would appear as propositions, and have a separate value, it is worthless.

In every man's mind, some images, words, and facts remain, without effort on his part to imprint them, which others forget, and afterwards these illustrate to him important laws. All our progress is an unfolding, like the vegetable bud. You have first an instinct, then an opinion, then a knowledge, as the plant has root, bud, and fruit. Trust the instinct to the end, though you can render no reason. It is vain to hurry it. By trusting it to the end, it shall ripen into truth, and you shall know why you believe.

Each mind has its own method. A true man never acquires after college rules. What you have aggregated in a natural manner, surprizes and delights when it is produced. For we cannot oversee each other's secret. And hence the differences between men in natural endowment are insignificant in comparison with their common wealth. Do you think the porter and the cook have no anecdotes, no experiences, no wonders for you? Every body knows as much as the savant. The walls of rude minds are scrawled all over with facts, with thoughts. They shall one day bring a lantern and read the inscriptions. Every man, in the degree in which he has wit and culture, finds his curiosity inflamed concerning the modes of living and thinking of other men, and especially of those classes whose minds have not been subdued by the drill of school education.

This instinctive action never ceases in a healthy mind, but becomes richer and more frequent in its informations through all states of culture. At last comes the era of reflection, when we not only observe, but take pains to observe; when we of set purpose, sit down to consider an abstract truth; when we keep the mind's eye open, whilst we converse, whilst we read, whilst we act, intent to learn the secret law of some class of facts.

What is the hardest task in the world? To think. I would put myself in the attitude to look in the eye an abstract truth, and I cannot. I blench and withdraw on this side and on that. I seem to know what he meant, who said, No man can see God face to face and live. For example, a man explores the basis of civil government. Let him intend his mind without respite, without rest, in one direction. His best heed long time avails him nothing. Yet thoughts are flitting before him. We all but apprehend, we dimly forebode the truth. We say, I will walk abroad, and the truth will take form and clearness to me. We go forth, but cannot find it. It seems as if we needed only the stillness and composed attitude of the library, to seize the thought. But we come in, and are as far from it as at first. Then, in a moment, and unannounced, the truth appears. A certain, wandering light appears, and is the distinction, the principle we wanted. But the oracle comes, because we had previously laid siege to the shrine. It seems as if the law of the intellect resembled that law of nature by which we now inspire, now expire the breath; by which the heart now draws in, then hurls out the blood, — the law of undulation. So now you must labor with your brains, and now you must forbear your activity, and see what the great Soul showeth.

The immortality of man is as legitimately preached from the intellections as from the moral volitions. Every intellection is mainly prospective. Its present value is its least. Inspect what delights you in Plutarch, in Shakspeare, in Cervantes. Each truth that a writer acquires, is a lantern which he turns full on what facts and thoughts lay already in his mind, and behold, all the mats and rubbish which had littered his garret, become precious. Every trivial fact in his private biography becomes an illustration of this new principle, revisits the day, and delights all men by its piquancy and new charm. Men say, where did he get this? and think there was something divine in his life. But no; they have myriads of facts just as good, would they only get a lamp to ransack their attics withal.

We are all wise. The difference between persons is not in wisdom but in art. I knew, in an academical club, a person who always deferred to me, who, seeing my whim for writing, fancied that my experiences had somewhat superior; whilst I saw that his experiences were as good as mine. Give them to me, and I would make the same use of them. He held the old; he holds the new; I had the habit of tacking together the old and the new, which he did not use to exercise. This may hold in the great examples. Perhaps if we should meet Shakspeare, we should not be conscious of any steep inferiority; no: but of a great equality, — only that he possessed a strange skill of using, of classifying his facts, which we lacked. For, notwithstanding our utter incapacity to produce anything like Hamlet and Othello, see the perfect reception this wit, and immense knowledge of life, and liquid eloquence find in us all.

If you gather apples in the sunshine, or make hay, or hoe corn, and then retire within doors, and shut your eyes, and press them with your hand, you shall still see apples hanging in the bright light, with boughs and leaves thereto, or the tasselled grass, or the corn-flags, and this for five or six hours afterwards. There lie the impressions on the retentive organ, though you knew it not. So lies the whole series of natural images with which your life has made you acquainted, in your memory, though you know it not, and a thrill of passion flashes light on their dark chamber, and the active power seizes instantly the fit image, as the word of its momentary thought.

It is long ere we discover how rich we are. Our history, we are sure, is quite tame: we have nothing to write, nothing to infer. But our wiser years still run back to the despised recollections of childhood, and always we are fishing up some wonderful article out of that pond; until, by and by, we begin to suspect that the biography of the one foolish person we know, is, in reality, nothing less than the miniature paraphrase of the hundred volumes of the Universal History.

In the intellect constructive, which we popularly designate by the word Genius, we observe the same balance of two elements, as in intellect receptive. The constructive intellect produces thoughts, sentences, poems, plans, designs, systems. It is the generation of the mind, the marriage of thought with nature. To genius must always go two gifts, the thought and the publication. The first is revelation, always a miracle, which no frequency of occurrence, or incessant study can ever familiarize, but which must always leave the inquirer stupid with wonder. It is the advent of truth into the world, a form of thought now, for the first time, bursting into the universe, a child of the old eternal soul, a piece of genuine and immeasurable greatness. It seems, for the time, to inherit all that has yet existed, and to dictate to the unborn. It affects every thought of man, and goes to fashion every institution. But to make it available, it needs a vehicle or art by which it is conveyed to men. To be communicable, it must become picture or sensible object. We must learn the language of facts. The most wonderful inspirations die with their subject, if he has no hand to paint them to the senses. The ray of light passes invisible through space, and only when it falls on an object is it seen. When the spiritual energy is directed on something outward, then it is a thought. The relation between it and you, first makes you, the value of you, apparent to me. The rich, inventive genius of the painter must be smothered and lost for want of the power of drawing, and in our happy hours, we should be inexhaustible poets, if once we could break through the silence into adequate rhyme. As all men have some access to primary truth, so all have some art or power of communication in their head, but only in the artist does it descend into the hand. There is an inequality whose laws we do not yet know, between two men and between two moments of the same man, in respect to this faculty. In common hours, we have the same facts as in the uncommon or inspired, but they do not sit for their portrait; they are not detached, but lie in a web. The thought of genius is spontaneous; but the power of picture or expression, in the most enriched and flowing nature, implies a mixture of will, a certain control over the spontaneous states, without which no production is possible. It is a conversion of all nature into the rhetoric of thought, under the eye of judgment, with a strenuous exercise of choice. And yet the imaginative vocabulary seems to be spontaneous also. It does not flow from experience only or mainly, but from a richer source. Not by any conscious imitation of particular forms are the grand strokes of the painter executed, but by repairing to the fountain-head of all forms in his mind. Who is the first drawing-master? Without instruction we know very well the ideal of the human form. A child knows if an arm or a leg be distorted in a picture, if the attitude be natural, or grand, or mean, though he has never received any instruction in drawing, or heard any conversation on the subject, nor can himself draw with correctness a single feature. A good form strikes all eyes pleasantly, long before they have any science on the subject, and a beautiful face sets twenty hearts in palpitation, prior to all consideration of the mechanical proportions of the features and head. We may owe to dreams some light on the fountain of this skill; for, as soon as we let our will go, and let the unconscious states ensue, see what cunning draughtsmen we are! We entertain ourselves with wonderful forms of men, of women, of animals, of gardens, of woods, and of monsters, and the mystic pencil wherewith we then draw, has no awkwardness or inexperience, no meagreness or poverty; it can design well, and group well; its composition is full of art, its colors are well laid on, and the whole canvas which it paints, is life-like, and apt to touch us with terror, with tenderness, with desire, and with grief. Neither are the artist's copies from experience, ever mere copies, but always touched and softened by tints from this ideal domain.

The conditions essential to a constructive mind, do not appear to be so often combined but that a good sentence or verse remains fresh and memorable for a long time. Yet when we write with ease, and come out into the free air of thought, we seem to be assured that nothing is easier than to continue this communication at pleasure. Up, down, around, the kingdom of thought has no enclosures, but the Muse makes us free of her city. Well, the world has a million writers. One would think, then, that good thought would be as familiar as air and water, and the gifts of each new hour would exclude the last. Yet we can count all our good books; nay, I remember any beautiful verse for twenty years. It is true that the discerning intellect of the world is always much in advance of the creative, so that there are many competent judges of the best book, and few writers of the best books. But some of the conditions of intellectual construction are of rare occurrence. The intellect is a whole, and demands integrity in every work. This is resisted equally by a man's devotion to a single thought, and by his ambition to combine too many.

Truth is our element of life, yet if a man fasten his attention on a single aspect of truth, and apply himself to that alone for a long time, the truth becomes distorted and not itself, but falsehood; herein resembling the air, which is our natural element, and the breath of our nostrils, but if a stream of the same be directed on the body for a time, it causes cold, fever, and even death. How wearisome the grammarian, the phrenologist, the political or religious fanatic, or indeed any possessed mortal, whose balance is lost by the exaggeration of a single topic. It is incipient insanity. Every thought is a prison also. I cannot see what you see, because I am caught up by a strong wind and blown so far in one direction, that I am out of the hoop of your horizon.

Is it any better, if the student, to avoid this offence, and to liberalize himself, aims to make a mechanical whole, of history, or science, or philosophy, by a numerical addition of all the facts that fall within his vision? The world refuses to be analyzed by addition and subtraction. When we are young, we spend much time and pains in filling our note-books with all definitions of Religion, Love, Poetry, Politics, Art, in the hope that in the course of a few years, we shall have condensed into our encyclopedia, the net value of all the theories at which the world has yet arrived. But year after year our tables get no completeness, and at last we discover that our curve is a parabola, whose arcs will never meet.

Neither by detachment, neither by aggregation, is the integrity of the intellect transmitted to its works, but by a vigilance which brings the intellect in its greatness and best state to operate every moment. It must have the same wholeness which nature has. Although no diligence can rebuild the universe in a model, by the best accumulation or disposition of details, yet does the world reappear in miniature in every event, so that all the laws of nature may be read in the smallest fact. The intellect must have the like perfection in its apprehension, and in its works. For this reason, an index or mercury of intellectual proficiency is the perception of identity. We talk with accomplished persons who appear to be strangers in nature. The cloud, the tree, the turf, the bird are not theirs, have nothing of them: the world is only their lodging and table. But the poet, whose verses are to be spheral and complete, is one whom nature cannot deceive, whatsoever face of strangeness she may put on. He feels a strict consanguinity, and detects more likeness than variety in all her changes. We are stung by the desire for new thought, but when we receive a new thought, it is only the old thought with a new face, and though we make it our own, we instantly crave another; we are not really enriched. For the truth was in us, before it was reflected to us from natural objects; and the profound genius will cast the likeness of all creatures into every product of his wit.

But if the constructive powers are rare, and it is given to few men to be poets, yet every man is a receiver of this descending holy ghost, and may well study the laws of its influx. Exactly parallel is the whole rule of intellectual duty, to the rule of moral duty. A self-denial, no less austere than the saint's, is demanded of the scholar. He must worship truth, and forego all things for that, and choose defeat and pain, so that his treasure in thought is thereby augmented.

God offers to every mind its choice between truth and repose. Take which you please, — you can never have both. Between these, as a pendulum, man oscillates. He in whom the love of repose predominates, will accept the first creed, the first philosophy, the first political party he meets, — most likely, his father's. He gets rest, commodity, and reputation; but he shuts the door of truth. He in whom the love of truth predominates, will keep himself aloof from all moorings and afloat. He will abstain from dogmatism, and recognize all the opposite negations between which, as walls, his being is swung. He submits to the inconvenience of suspense and imperfect opinion, but he is a candidate for truth, as the other is not, and respects the highest law of his being.

The circle of the green earth he must measure with his shoes, to find the man who can yield him truth. He shall then know that there is somewhat more blessed and great in hearing than in speaking. Happy is the hearing man: unhappy the speaking man. As long as I hear truth, I am bathed by a beautiful element, and am not conscious of any limits to my nature. The suggestions are thousandfold that I hear and see. The waters of the great deep have ingress and egress to the soul. But if I speak, I define, I confine, and am less. When Socrates speaks, Lysis and Menexenus are afflicted by no shame that they do not speak. They also are good. He likewise defers to them, loves them, whilst he speaks. Because a true and natural man contains and is the same truth which an eloquent man articulates: but in the eloquent man, because he can articulate it, it seems something the less to reside, and he turns to these silent beautiful with the more inclination and respect. The ancient sentence said, Let us be silent, for so are the gods. Silence is a solvent that destroys personality, and gives us leave to be great and universal. Every man's progress is through a succession of teachers, each of whom seems at the time to have a superlative influence, but it at last gives place to a new. Frankly let him accept it all. Jesus says, Leave father, mother, house and lands, and follow me. Who leaves all, receives more. This is as true intellectually, as morally. Each new mind we approach, seems to require an abdication of all our past and present possessions. A new doctrine seems, at first, a subversion of all our opinions, tastes, and manner of living. Such has Swedenborg, such has Kant, such has Coleridge, such has Hegel or his interpreter Cousin, seemed to many young men in this country. Take thankfully and heartily all they can give. Exhaust them, wrestle with them, let them not go until their blessing be won, and after a short season, the dismay will be overpast, the excess of influence withdrawn, and they will be no longer an alarming meteor, but one more bright star shining serenely in your heaven, and blending its light with all your day.

But whilst he gives himself up unreservedly to that which draws him, because that is his own, he is to refuse himself to that which draws him not, whatsoever fame and authority may attend it, because it is not his own. Entire self-reliance belongs to the intellect. One soul is a counterpoise of all souls, as a capillary column of water is a balance for the sea. It must treat things, and books, and sovereign genius, as itself also a sovereign. If Æschylus be that man he is taken for, he has not yet done his office, when he has educated the learned of Europe for a thousand years. He is now to approve himself a master of delight to me also. If he cannot do that, all his fame shall avail him nothing with me. I were a fool not to sacrifice a thousand Æschyluses to my intellectual integrity. Especially take the same ground in regard to abstract truth, the science of the mind. The Bacon, the Spinoza, the Hume, Schelling, Kant, or whosoever propounds to you a philosophy of the mind, is only a more or less awkward translator of things in your consciousness, which you have also your way of seeing, perhaps of denominating. Say then, instead of too timidly poring into his obscure sense, that he has not succeeded in rendering back to you your consciousness. He has not succeeded; now let another try. If Plato cannot, perhaps Spinoza will. If Spinoza cannot, then perhaps Kant. Anyhow, when at last it is done, you will find it is no recondite, but a simple, natural, common state, which the writer restores to you.

But let us end these didactics. I will not, though the subject might provoke it, speak to the open question between Truth and Love. I shall not presume to interfere in the old politics of the skies; — "The cherubim know most; the seraphim love most." The gods shall settle their own quarrels. But I cannot recite, even thus rudely, laws of the intellect, without remembering that lofty and sequestered class who have been its prophets and oracles, the high priesthood of the pure reason, the *Trismegisti*, the expounders of the principles of thought from age to age. When at long intervals, we turn over their abstruse pages, wonderful seems the calm and grand air of these few, these great spiritual lords, who have walked in the world, — these of the old religion, — dwelling in a worship which makes the sanctities of christianity look *parvenues* and popular; for "persuasion is in soul, but necessity is in intellect." This band of grandees, Hermes, Heraclitus, Empedocles, Plato, Plotinus, Olympiodorus, Proclus, Synesius, and the rest, have somewhat so vast in their logic, so primary in their thinking, that it seems antecedent to all the ordinary distinctions of rhetoric and literature, and to be at once poetry, and music, and dancing, and astronomy, and mathematics. I am present at the sowing of the seed of the world. With a geometry of sunbeams, the soul lays the foundations of nature. The truth and grandeur of their thought is proved by its scope and applicability, for it commands the entire schedule and inventory of things, for its illustration. But what marks its elevation, and has even a comic look to us, is the innocent serenity with which these babe-like Jupiters sit in their clouds, and from age to age prattle to each other, and to no contemporary. Well assured that their speech is intelligible, and the most natural thing in the world, they add thesis to thesis, without a moment's heed of the universal astonishment of the human race below, who do not comprehend their plainest argument; nor do they ever relent so much as to insert a popular or explaining sentence; nor testify the least displeasure or petulance at the dulness of their amazed auditory. The angels are so enamored of the language that is spoken in heaven, that they will not distort their lips with the hissing and unmusical dialects of men, but speak their own, whether there be any who understand it or not.

ART

Give to barrows, trays, and pans
Grace and glimmer of romance;
Bring the moonlight into noon
Hid in gleaming piles of stone;
On the city's paved street
Plant gardens lined with lilac sweet;
Let spouting fountains cool the air,
Singing in the sun-baked square;
Let statue, picture, park, and hall,
Ballad, flag, and festival,
The past restore, the day adorn,
And make each morrow a new morn.
So shall the drudge in dusty frock
Spy behind the city clock
Retinues of airy kings,
Skirts of angels, starry wings,
His fathers shining in bright fables,
His children fed at heavenly tables.
'T is the privilege of Art
Thus to play its cheerful part,
Man in Earth to acclimate,
And bend the exile to his fate,
And, moulded of one element
With the days and firmament,
Teach him on these as stairs to climb,
And live on even terms with Time;
Whilst upper life the slender rill
Of human sense doth overfill.

ART

Because the soul is progressive, it never quite repeats itself, but in every act attempts the production of a new and fairer whole. This appears in works both of the useful and the fine arts, if we employ the popular distinction of works according to their aim, either at use or beauty. Thus in our fine arts, not imitation, but creation is the aim. In landscapes, the painter should give the suggestion of a fairer creation than we know. The details, the prose of nature he should omit, and give us only the spirit and splendor. He should know that the landscape has beauty for his eye, because it expresses a thought which is to him good: and this, because the same power which sees through his eyes, is seen in that spectacle; and he will come to value the expression of nature, and not nature itself, and so exalt in his copy, the features that please him. He will give the gloom of gloom, and the sunshine of sunshine. In a portrait, he must inscribe the character, and not the features, and must esteem the man who sits to him as himself only an imperfect picture or likeness of the aspiring original within.

What is that abridgment and selection we observe in all spiritual activity, but itself the creative impulse? for it is the inlet of that higher illumination which teaches to convey a larger sense by simpler symbols. What is a man but nature's finer success in self-explication? What is a man but a finer and compacter landscape, than the horizon figures, — nature's eclecticism? and what is his speech, his love of painting, love of nature, but a still finer success? all the weary miles and tons of space and bulk left out, and the spirit or moral of it contracted into a musical word, or the most cunning stroke of the pencil?

But the artist must employ the symbols in use in his day and nation, to convey his enlarged sense to his fellow-men. Thus the new in art is always formed out of the old. The Genius of the Hour sets his ineffaceable seal on the work, and gives it an inexpressible charm for the imagination. As far as the spiritual character of the period overpowers the artist, and finds expression in his work, so far it will retain a certain grandeur, and will represent to future beholders the Unknown, the Inevitable, the Divine. No man can quite exclude this element of Necessity from his labor. No man can quite emancipate himself from his age and country, or produce a model in which the education, the religion, the politics, usages, and arts, of his times shall have no share. Though he were never so original, never so wilful and fantastic, he cannot wipe out of his work every trace of the thoughts amidst which it grew. The very avoidance betrays the usage he avoids. Above his will, and out of his sight, he is necessitated, by the air he breathes, and the idea on which he and his contemporaries live and toil, to share the manner of his times, without knowing what that manner is. Now that which is inevitable in the work, has a higher charm than individual talent can ever give, inasmuch as the artist's pen or chisel seems to have been held and guided by a gigantic hand to inscribe a line in the history of the human race. This circumstance gives a value to the Egyptian hieroglyphics, to the Indian, Chinese, and Mexican idols, however gross and shapeless. They denote the height of the human soul in that hour, and were not fantastic, but sprung from a necessity as deep as the world. Shall I now add that the whole extant product of the plastic arts has herein its highest value, *as history;* as a stroke drawn in the portrait of that fate, perfect and beautiful, according to whose ordinations all beings advance to their beatitude.

Thus, historically viewed, it has been the office of art to educate the perception of beauty. We are immersed in beauty, but our eyes have no clear vision. It needs, by the exhibition of single traits, to assist and lead the dormant taste. We carve and paint, or we behold what is carved and painted, as students of the mystery of Form. The virtue of art lies in detachment, in sequestering one object from the embarrassing variety. Until one thing comes out from the connection of things, there can be enjoyment, contemplation, but no thought. Our happiness and unhappiness are unproductive. The infant lies in a pleasing trance, but his individual character, and his practical power depend on his daily progress in the separation of things, and dealing with one at a time. Love and all the passions concentrate all existence around a single form. It is the habit of certain minds to give an all-excluding fulness to the object, the thought, the word, they alight upon, and to make that for the time the deputy of the world. These are the artists, the orators, the leaders of society. The power to detach, and to magnify by detaching, is the essence of rhetoric in the hands of the orator and the poet. This rhetoric, or power to fix the momentary eminency of an object, — so remarkable in Burke, in Byron, in Carlyle, — the painter and sculptor exhibit in color and in stone. The power depends on the depth of the artist's insight of that object he contemplates. For every object has its roots in central nature, and may of course be so exhibited to us as to represent the world. Therefore, each work of genius is the tyrant of the hour, and concentrates attention on itself. For the time, it is the only thing worth naming, to do that, — be it a sonnet, an opera, a landscape, a statue, an oration, the plan of a temple, of a campaign, or of a voyage of discovery. Presently we pass to some other object, which rounds itself into a whole, as did the first; for example, a well laid garden: and nothing seems worth doing but the laying out of gardens. I should think fire the best thing in the world, if I were not acquainted with air, and water, and earth. For it is the right and property of all natural objects, of all genuine talents, of all native properties whatsoever, to be for their moment the top of the world. A squirrel leaping from bough to bough, and making the wood but one wide tree for his pleasure, fills the eye not less than a lion, — is beautiful, self-sufficing, and stands then and there for nature. A good ballad draws my ear and heart whilst I listen, as much as an epic has done before. A dog, drawn by a master, or a litter of pigs, satisfies, and is a reality not less than the frescoes of Angelo. From this succession of excellent objects, we learn at last the immensity of the world, the opulence of human nature, which can run out to infinitude in any direction. But I also learn that what astonished and fascinated me in the first work, astonished me in the second work also, that excellence of all things is one.

The office of painting and sculpture seems to be merely initial. The best pictures can easily tell us their last secret. The best pictures are rude draughts of a few of the miraculous dots and lines and dyes which make up the ever-changing "landscape with figures" amidst which we dwell. Painting seems to be to the eye what dancing is to the limbs. When that has educated the frame to self-possession, to nimbleness, to grace, the steps of the dancing-master are better forgotten; so painting teaches me the splendor of color and the expression of form, and, as I see many pictures and higher genius in the art, I see the boundless opulence of the pencil, the indifferency in which the artist stands free to choose out of the possible forms. If he can draw every thing, why draw any thing? and then is my eye opened to the eternal picture which nature paints in the street with moving men and children, beggars, and fine ladies, draped in red, and green, and blue, and gray; long-haired, grizzled, white-faced, black-faced, wrinkled, giant, dwarf, expanded, elfish, — capped and based by heaven, earth, and sea.

A gallery of sculpture teaches more austerely the same lesson. As picture teaches the coloring, so sculpture the anatomy of form. When I have seen fine statues, and afterwards enter a public assembly, I understand well what he meant who said, "When I have been reading Homer, all men look like giants." I too see that painting and sculpture are gymnastics of the eye, its training to the niceties and curiosities of its function. There is no statue like this living man, with his infinite advantage over all ideal sculpture, of perpetual variety. What a gallery of art have I here! No mannerist made these varied groups and diverse original single figures. Here is the artist himself improvising, grim and glad, at his block. Now one thought strikes him, now another, and with each moment he alters the whole air, attitude and expression of his clay. Away with your nonsense of oil and easels, of marble and chisels: except to open your eyes to the masteries of eternal art, they are hypocritical rubbish.

The reference of all production at last to an Aboriginal Power, explains the traits common to all works of the highest art, — that they are universally intelligible; that they restore to us the simplest states of mind; and are religious. Since what skill is therein shown is the reappearance of the original soul, a jet of pure light, it should produce a similar impression to that made by natural objects. In happy hours, nature appears to us one with art; art perfected, — the work of genius. And the individual in whom simple tastes and susceptibility to all the great human influences overpower the accidents of a local and special culture, is the best critic of art. Though we travel the world over to find the beautiful, we must carry it with us, or we find it not. The best of beauty is a finer charm than skill in surfaces, in outlines, or rules of art can ever teach, namely, a radiation from the work of art of human character, — a wonderful expression through stone or canvas or musical sound of the deepest and simplest attributes of our nature, and therefore most intelligible at last to those souls which have these attributes. In the sculptures of the Greeks, in the masonry of the Romans, and in the pictures of the Tuscan and Venetian masters, the highest charm is the universal language they speak. A confession of moral nature, of purity, love, and hope, breathes from them all. That which we carry to them, the same we bring back more fairly illustrated in the memory. The traveller who visits the Vatican, and passes from chamber to chamber through galleries of statues, vases, sarcophagi, and candelabra, through all forms of beauty, cut in the richest materials, is in danger of forgetting the simplicity of the principles out of which they all sprung, and that they had their origin from thoughts and laws in his own breast. He studies the technical rules on these wonderful remains, but forgets that these works were not always thus constellated; that they are the contributions of many ages, and many countries; that each came out of the solitary workshop of one artist, who toiled perhaps in ignorance of the existence of other sculpture, created his work without other model, save life, household life, and the sweet and smart of personal relations, of beating hearts, and meeting eyes, of poverty, and necessity, and hope, and fear. These were his inspirations, and these are the effects he carries home to your heart and mind. In proportion to his force, the artist will find in his work an outlet for his proper character. He must not be in any manner pinched or hindered by his material, but through his necessity of imparting himself, the adamant will be wax in his hands, and will allow an adequate communication of himself in his full stature and proportion. He need not cumber himself with a conventional nature and culture, nor ask what is the mode in Rome or in Paris, but that house, and weather, and manner of living, which poverty and the fate of birth have made at once so odious and so dear, in the gray, unpainted wood cabin, on the corner of a New Hampshire farm, or in the log hut of the backwoods, or in the narrow lodging where he has endured the constraints and seeming of a city poverty, will serve as well as any other condition, as the symbol of a thought which pours itself indifferently through all.

I remember, when in my younger days, I had heard of the wonders of Italian painting, I fancied the great pictures would be great strangers; some surprising combination of color and form; a foreign wonder, barbaric pearl and gold, like the spontoons and standards of the militia, which play such pranks in the eyes and imaginations of school-boys. I was to see and acquire I knew not what. When I came at last to Rome, and saw with eyes the pictures, I found that genius left to novices the gay and fantastic and ostentatious, and itself pierced directly to the simple and true; that it was familiar and sincere; that it was the old, eternal fact I had met already in so many forms, — unto which I lived; that it was the plain *you and me* I knew so well, — had left at home in so many conversations. I had had the same experience already in a church at Naples. There I saw that nothing was changed with me but the place, and said to myself, — 'Thou foolish child, hast thou come out hither, over four thousand miles of salt water, to find that which was perfect to thee, there at home?' — that fact I saw again in the Academmia at Naples, in the chambers of sculpture, and yet again when I came to Rome, and to the paintings of Raphael, Angelo, Sacchi, Titian, and Leonardo da Vinci. "What, old mole! workest thou in the earth so fast?" It had travelled by my side: that which I fancied I had left in Boston, was here in the Vatican, and again at Milan, and at Paris, and made all travelling ridiculous as a treadmill. I now require this of all pictures, that they domesticate me, not that they dazzle me. Pictures must not be too picturesque. Nothing astonishes men so much as common sense and plain dealing. All great actions have been simple, and all great pictures are.

The Transfiguration, by Raphael, is an eminent example of this peculiar merit. A calm, benignant beauty shines over all this picture, and goes directly to the heart. It seems almost to call you by name. The sweet and sublime face of Jesus is beyond praise, yet how it disappoints all florid expectations! This familiar, simple, home-speaking countenance, is as if one should meet a friend. The knowledge of picture-dealers has its value, but listen not to their criticism when your heart is touched by genius. It was not painted for them, it was painted for you; for such as had eyes capable of being touched by simplicity and lofty emotions.

Yet when we have said all our fine things about the arts, we must end with a frank confession, that the arts, as we know them, are but initial. Our best praise is given to what they aimed and promised, not to the actual result. He has conceived meanly of the resources of man, who believes that the best age of production is past. The real value of the Iliad, or the Transfiguration, is as signs of power; billows or ripples they are of the stream of tendency; tokens of the everlasting effort to produce, which even in its worst estate, the soul betrays. Art has not yet come to its maturity, if it do not put itself abreast with the most potent influences of the world, if it is not practical and moral, if it do not stand in connection with the conscience, if it do not make the poor and uncultivated feel that it addresses them with a voice of lofty cheer. There is higher work for Art than the arts. They are abortive births of an imperfect or vitiated instinct. Art is the need to create; but in its essence, immense and universal, it is impatient of working with lame or tied hands, and of making cripples and monsters, such as all pictures and statues are. Nothing less than the creation of man and nature is its end. A man should find in it an outlet for his whole energy. He may paint and carve only as long as he can do that. Art should exhilarate, and throw down the walls of circumstance on every side, awakening in the beholder the same sense of universal relation and power which the work evinced in the artist, and its highest effect is to make new artists.

Already History is old enough to witness the old age and disappearance of particular arts. The art of sculpture is long ago perished to any real effect. It was originally a useful art, a mode of writing, a savage's record of gratitude or devotion, and among a people possessed of a wonderful perception of form, this childish carving was refined to the utmost splendor of effect. But it is the game of a rude and youthful people, and not the manly labor of a wise and spiritual nation. Under an oak tree loaded with leaves and nuts, under a sky full of eternal eyes, I stand in a thoroughfare; but in the works of our plastic arts, and especially of sculpture, creation is driven into a corner. I cannot hide from myself that there is a certain appearance of paltriness, as of toys, and the trumpery of a theatre, in sculpture. Nature transcends all our moods of thought, and its secret we do not yet find. But the gallery stands at the mercy of our moods, and there is a moment when it becomes frivolous. I do not wonder that Newton, with an attention habitually engaged on the paths of planets and suns, should have wondered what the Earl of Pembroke found to admire in "stone dolls." Sculpture may serve to teach the pupil how deep is the secret of form, how purely the spirit can translate its meanings into that eloquent dialect. But the statue will look cold and false before that new activity which needs to roll through all things, and is impatient of counterfeits, and things not alive. Picture and sculpture are the celebrations and festivities of form. But true art is never fixed, but always flowing. The sweetest music is not in the oratorio, but in the human voice when it speaks from its instant life, tones of tenderness, truth, or courage. The oratorio has already lost its relation to the morning, to the sun, and the earth, but that persuading voice is in tune with these. All works of art should not be detached, but extempore performances. A great man is a new statue in every attitude and action.

A beautiful woman is a picture which drives all beholders nobly mad. Life may be lyric or epic, as well as a poem or a romance.

A true announcement of the law of creation, if a man were found worthy to declare it, would carry art up into the kingdom of nature, and destroy its separate and contrasted existence. The fountains of invention and beauty in modern society are all but dried up. A popular novel, a theatre, or a ball-room makes us feel that we are all paupers in the alms-house of this world, without dignity, without skill, or industry. Art is as poor and low. The old tragic Necessity, which lowers on the brows even of the Venuses and the Cupids of the antique, and furnishes the sole apology for the intrusion of such anomalous figures into nature, — namely, that they were inevitable; that the artist was drunk with a passion for form which he could not resist, and which vented itself in these fine extravagances, — no longer dignifies the chisel or the pencil. But the artist, and the connoisseur, now seek in art the exhibition of their talent, or an asylum from the evils of life. Men are not well pleased with the figure they make in their own imaginations, and they flee to art, and convey their better sense in an oratorio, a statue, or a picture. Art makes the same effort which a sensual prosperity makes, namely, to detach the beautiful from the useful, to do up the work as unavoidable, and hating it, pass on to enjoyment. These solaces and compensations, this division of beauty from use, the laws of nature do not permit. As soon as beauty is sought not from religion and love, but for pleasure, it degrades the seeker. High beauty is no longer attainable by him in canvas or in stone, in sound, or in lyrical construction; an effeminate prudent, sickly beauty, which is not beauty, is all that can be formed; for the hand can never execute any thing higher than the character can inspire.

The art that thus separates, is itself first separated. Art must not be a superficial talent, but must begin farther back in man. Now men do not see nature to be beautiful, and they go to make a statue which shall be. They abhor men as tasteless, dull, and inconvertible, and console themselves with color-bags, and blocks of marble. They reject life as prosaic, and create a death which they call poetic. They despatch the day's weary chores, and fly to voluptuous reveries. They eat and drink, that they may afterwards execute the ideal. Thus is art vilified; the name conveys to the mind its secondary and bad senses; it stands in the imagination, as somewhat contrary to nature, and struck with death from the first. Would it not be better to begin higher up, — to serve the ideal before they eat and drink; to serve the ideal in eating and drinking, in drawing the breath, and in the functions of life? Beauty must come back to the useful arts, and the distinction between the fine and the useful arts be forgotten. If history were truly told, if life were nobly spent, it would be no longer easy or possible to distinguish the one from the other. In nature, all is useful, all is beautiful. It is therefore beautiful, because it is alive, moving, reproductive; it is therefore useful, because it is symmetrical and fair. Beauty will not come at the call of a legislature, nor will it repeat in England or America, its history in Greece. It will come, as always, unannounced, and spring up between the feet of brave and earnest men. It is in vain that we look for genius to reiterate its miracles in the old arts; it is its instinct to find beauty and holiness in new and necessary facts, in the field and roadside, in the shop and mill. Proceeding from a religious heart it will raise to a divine use, the railroad, the insurance office, the joint stock company, our law, our primary assemblies, our commerce, the galvanic battery, the electric jar, the prism, and the chemist's retort, in which we seek now only an economical use. Is not the selfish, and even cruel aspect which belongs to our great mechanical works, — to mills, railways, and machinery, — the effect of the mercenary impulses which these works obey? When its errands are noble and adequate, a steamboat bridging the Atlantic between Old and New England, and arriving at its ports with the punctuality of a planet, is a step of man into harmony with nature. The boat at St. Petersburgh, which plies along the Lena by magnetism, needs little to make it sublime. When science is learned in love, and its powers are wielded by love, they will appear the supplements and continuations of the material creation.

THE END.

NOTES

TEXTUAL APPARATUS

PARALLEL PASSAGES

INDEX

NOTES

The following informational notes are keyed to pages and lines of this text. The words introducing each note are those which begin and end the passage, sometimes a lengthy one, being annotated.

These notes are intended not just to guide scholars to Emerson's sources and to clarify obscurities but also to restore something of the context which existed for the reader of Emerson's time. Since, for example, few late-twentieth-century readers are steeped in Scripture, the notes include what once would have been unnecessary citations of chapter and verse. Because most readers are likely to ignore the instructions "See" and "Cf." and so not learn the words echoing in Emerson's mind, the notes often both cite and quote Scripture. Many once-famous lines of poetry are similarly treated, as is much of Shakespeare. Other kinds of contextual information—historical, biographical, geographical—tend to be copiously supplied, in the belief that understanding Emerson requires knowing what he knew.

Where no textual problem is involved, major writers, ancient and modern, are cited by specific book, chapter, and paragraph or in standard editions. Unless otherwise noted, translations of Greek and Latin quotations are from the Loeb Classical Library and are reprinted by permission of Harvard University Press and the Loeb Classical Library. Biblical quotations are from the King James Version.

3.10 WITHOUT HURRY, WITHOUT REST   Cf. Goethe's lines in "Zahme Xenien II": "Wie das Gestirn / Ohne Hast, / Aber ohne Rast" (*Goethes Sämtliche Werke* [Jubiläums-Ausgabe], 40 vols. [Stuttgart, Cotta, 1902–1907], IV, 43).

4.17 ASDRUBAL   Of the four Carthaginian generals named Asdrubal or Hasdrubal, Emerson probably had in mind the brother of Hannibal, who, after a distinguished career as soldier and ruler, died bravely in his first major battle on Italian soil. The spelling suggests a Greek rather than a Latin source, Polybius for example, and perhaps an eighteenth-century translation like that of James Hampton: "Asdrubal, who had so often distinguished himself upon former occasions, displayed no less courage in this last action. . . . he considered also . . . in what manner . . . he might submit with dignity to his adverse fortune" (*The General History of Polybius*, 4 vols. [London, 1772–1773], IV, 3–5).

6.23 "WHAT IS HISTORY . . . FABLE AGREED UPON?" Cf. Count Emmanuel Augustin Dieudonne de Las Cases, *Mémorial de Sainte Hélène. Journal of the Private Life and Conversations of the Emperor Napoleon at Saint Helena*, 4 vols. (Boston, 1823), IV, vii, 124. See *JMN*, V, 508.

7.2 FERGUSON DISCOVERED . . . LONG BEEN KNOWN James Ferguson (1710–1776), a Scottish astronomer, made his rediscoveries, not in astronomy but in mechanics, when he was an unschooled shepherd boy in Banffshire.

7.10 SIDNEY Presumably not Sir Philip but his grandnephew Algernon (1622–1683), soldier, republican, and regicide judge, who was executed, on doubtful evidence, for complicity in the Rye House plot to assassinate Charles II.

7.10 MARMADUKE ROBINSON In the Centenary Edition, Edward Emerson reported Charles Eliot Norton's conjecture that Emerson had accidentally fused the names of two Quaker victims of Puritanism, Marmaduke Stevenson and William Robinson, who were hanged "on Boston Common in 1659." That Emerson was familiar with their names and their fate is clear from his 1835 lecture on George Fox (*EL*, I, 179).

7.12 ANIMAL MAGNETISM IN PARIS, OR IN PROVIDENCE Emerson had long known the report on hypnotism published by the Paris Academy of Medicine and had referred to it in his lecture "The Uses of Natural History" (*EL*, I, 10). In 1837 he wrote to his brother William: "The gossip of the city is of Animal Magnetism. . . . now Mrs. Gleason has come from Providence & I was bidden today to go & see her magnetised by M. Poyen, who *thinks* his command & she does it" (*L*, II, 55).

7.18 OHIO CIRCLES Many of the ancient Indian earthworks in southern Ohio, especially those near Chillicothe and Marietta, are circles.

7.21 BELZONI DIGS . . . PYRAMIDS OF THEBES Giovanni Battista Belzoni (1778–1823) excavated the necropolis of Thebes and discovered the central chamber of the second pyramid of Gizeh.

8.24 MONAD   Emerson usually employed this word to mean simply "unit" or "individual." See *JMN*, VII, 173.

9.2 IO, IN ÆSCHYLUS . . . LUNAR HORNS   See Plutarch, *Moralia*, "Of Isis and Osiris," 52, and *Prometheus Bound*, lines 671–682. Cf. *L*, II, 337.

9.20 SCULPTURE, THE "TONGUE ON THE BALANCE OF EXPRESSION"   This puzzling phrase is presumably the result of an error in transcription. Its source is J. J. Winckelmann, quoted in A. W. Schlegel's lectures *Ueber dramatische Kunst und Litteratur* (Uppsala, 1817), I, 113, where "die Schönheit" is "die Zunge an der Wage des Ausdrucks," but where Schlegel has been concerned for some paragraphs with sculpture. If Emerson knew the Schlegel lectures, as he probably did, in the translation of John Black, *A Course of Lectures on Dramatic Art and Literature* (Philadelphia, 1833), he found there the statement "beauty with the ancients was the tongue on the balance of expression" (p. 50) and used it that way in his journals (e.g., *JMN*, V, 18) and lectures (e.g., *EL*, I, 348). A tongue is the index on a balance scale.

9.27 THE LAST ACTIONS OF PHOCION   See Plutarch, *Moralia*, "Sayings of Kings and Commanders: Phocion," 17. When, on the way to execution, an enemy spat in his face, Phocion said to the officers, "Will not somebody make this man stop his bad manners?"   And in the *Lives*, "Phocion," XXXVI, Plutarch recorded that when the executioner ran out of poison and demanded twelve drachmas to prepare more, "Phocion called one of his friends, and, asking if a man could not even die at Athens without paying for the privilege, bade him give the executioner his money."

10.3 AN OLD SACHEM OF THE FOREST . . . OF THE ROCK   Emerson observed this resemblance in George Catlin's portrait of Joseph Brant, which was reproduced as the frontispiece to Vol. II of William L. Stone's *Life of Joseph Brant—Thayendanega, Including the Indian Wars of the American Revolution* (New York, 1838). See *JMN*, VII, 171–172.

10.10 GUIDO'S ROSPIGLIOSI AURORA . . . MORNING CLOUD   A print of Guido Reni's "Aurora" fresco in the Rospigliosi Palace in Rome was sent by Thomas Carlyle as a gift to Lidian Emerson in 1839 and hung thereafter in the parlor of the house in Concord.   Edward Emerson's note on this passage concludes: "Mr. Emerson used to point out to his children how the varied repetition of the manes, heads and prancing forefeet the horses were imitations of the curved folds of a great cumulus cloud" (*W*, II, 383).

10.15 A PAINTER TOLD ME . . . IN EVERY ATTITUDE   The journal passage from which this sentence was drawn indicates that the painter was Caroline Sturgis (*JMN*, VII, 214).

10.19 ROOS "ENTERED INTO THE INMOST NATURE OF A SHEEP" On February 26, 1824, Goethe showed Eckermann "some etchings by Roos, the famous painter of animals; they were all of sheep in different postures and situations . . . 'I am half frightened,' said Goethe, 'when I look at these beasts. . . . I feel as if I might become a sheep, and as if the artist must have been one. How could he enter so into the inmost character of these creatures? for their very soul looks through the bodies he has drawn' " (J. P. Eckermann, *Conversations with Goethe*, trans. S. M. Fuller [Boston, 1839], pp. 88–89; vol. IV of *Specimens of Foreign Standard Literature*, ed. George Ripley [Boston, 1838–1842]). There were many landscape-and-animal painters named Roos, but the most famous was Philipp Peter Roos (1655–1706), known as Rosa da Tivoli from his many years of residence in and near that town, who kept a menagerie to provide himself with models and who made a specialty of sheep and shepherds: G. K. Nagler, *Neues Allgemeines Künstler-Lexicon* (Munich, 1843). See also *JMN*, VII, 214.

10.20 A DRAUGHTSMAN . . . EXPLAINED TO HIM Francis Graeter, who taught drawing at Alcott's Temple School (*JMN*, V, 424; VII, 214).

10.28 "COMMON SOULS . . . THEY ARE" Not located.

10.37 SANTA CROCE In 1833 Emerson had thought Santa Croce "not a Florentine no nor an European church but a church built by & for the human race" (*JMN*, IV, 175).

11.1 STRASBURG CATHEDRAL . . . ERWIN OF STEINBACH In Emerson's journal translation of Goethe's essay on Erwin von Steinbach these sentences appear: "How oft did I . . . enjoy the giant spirit of our old brother in his works. . . . Then revealed itself to me in gentle whispers the soul of the great Architect" (*JMN*, VI, 307).

11.12 A LADY . . . WAYFARER HAS PASSED ONWARD The lady was Elizabeth Hoar, who had been betrothed to Emerson's late brother Charles; the occasion, an evening ride from Waltham to Concord, was recorded in Emerson's journal on August 31, 1838 (*JMN*, VII, 61).

11.18 PRESENT LIKE AN ARCHANGEL . . . OF THE WORLD Cf. *Paradise Lost*, VII, 221–223: "Him all his train / Followed in bright procession to behold / Creation, and the wonders of his might."

11.20 MY COMPANION . . . SYMMETRICAL WINGS The day was in May 1838; the companion was John Sullivan Dwight, at that time a young Unitarian minister who had recently taken Emerson's place in the church at East Lexington (*JMN*, V, 504).

12.3 HEEREN . . . PILLARS OF THE INTERIOR?"   Arnold H. L. Heeren, *Historical Researches into the Politics, Intercourse, and Trade of the Carthaginians, Ethiopians, and Egyptians*, trans. D. A. Talboys, 2 vols. (Oxford, 1832), I, 369. Emerson's quotation begins with "determined" rather than with "The custom." See *JMN*, VII, 49.

12.36 SLENDER SHAFTS AND CAPITALS . . . BABYLON FOR THE WINTER   Cf. Arnold H. L. Heeren, *Historical Researches into the Politics, Intercourse, and Trade of the Principal Nations of Antiquity*, 3 vols. (Oxford, 1833): "The columns of Persepolis shoot upwards with a slender yet firm elevation, conveying a fit image of the stems of the lotus and palm" (I, 237); and "The spring was spent at Ecbatana, the three summer months at Susa, the autumn and winter in Babylon" (I, 401). See *JMN*, VII, 46, 48.

13.11 THE NOMADS OF AFRICA . . . THE GADFLY OF ASTABORAS   The Astaboras, or Atbara, rises in the highlands of Ethiopia and flows through the Sudan to the Nile. This passage is drawn largely from Heeren's *Historical Researches . . . Carthaginians, Ethiopians, and Egyptians*, I, 316–318. See *JMN*, VII, 91.

14.4 THE FORE-WORLD, AS THE GERMANS SAY   The German word is "Vorwelt," which Emerson encountered in *Faust, Part I*, line 2695: "O nimm mich auf, der du die Vorwelt schon / Bei Freud' und Schmerz im offnen Arm empfangen!" (*Goethes Sämtliche Werke*, XIII, 114). He might also have found it in Herder, Klopstock, and Schleiermacher.

14.19 WHOSE EYESOCKETS ARE . . . THE WHOLE HEAD   In *JMN*, IV, 332, Emerson identifies the source of the description as "Abernethy . . . in his Hunter book." The passage is a slight paraphrase of John Abernethy's *Physiological Lectures exhibiting a general view of Mr. Hunter's physiology . . . in the year 1817* (London, 1817), pp. 86–87.

14.30 "AFTER THE ARMY . . . DID THE LIKE"   See Xenophon, *The Anabasis*, IV, 11–12.

15.20 A PERSON OF CHILDLIKE GENIUS . . . GREEK   For the conception of the Greek spirit as youthful or childlike, see Thomas Taylor's translation of *The Commentaries of Proclus on the Timaeus of Plato . . .* , 2 vols. (London, 1820), I, 87: "Juvenility of soul . . . is analogous to renovation of life. . . . the Greeks are always children. . . . there is no discipline with them hoary from its existence in former periods of time."

15.22 LOVE OF NATURE IN THE PHILOCTETES . . . AND WAVES   See, for example, Philoctetes' farewell to Lemnos in his final speech.

Notes

16.15 MENU   In the Hindu scriptures there are many Menus, or Manus, but Emerson's frequent references are always to the son of Brahma, who dictated, as Sir William Jones put it, "a tract *On Religious and Civil Duties . . .* to the first inhabitants of the earth." "The laws ascribed to MENU," Jones wrote, "in whatever age they might have been promulgated, could not have received the form in which we now see them above *three thousand* years ago" (*Dissertations and Miscellaneous Pieces Relating to the History and Antiquities, the Arts, Sciences, and Literature, of Asia*, 2 vols. [London, 1792], I, 280, 340).   During the summer of 1840 Emerson had borrowed Jones's translations of *Institutes of Hindu Law; or, The Ordinances of Menu* and filled some ten pages of his journal with transcriptions (*JMN*, VI, 392–397).

16.22 THE THEBAIS, AND THE FIRST CAPUCHINS   "Thebais" is the Latin name for southern Egypt, where the first Christian monastic communities were established.   For Emerson's comments on Capuchin beggars of his own time, see *JMN*, IV, 138–139.

16.33 HOW BELUS WAS WORSHIPPED . . . MOUNDS OF CHOLULA   By Belus, Emerson presumably meant the Babylonian god Bel, or Baal, who was worshiped also in Egypt.   Jean François Champollion (1790–1832) was the first important Egyptologist.   In Cholula, near Puebla in Mexico, an enormous pyramid supported a temple of Quetzalcoatl.   Emerson's lecture "The Individual" of 1837, from which this paragraph is drawn, refers more accurately to "the mound of Cholula" (*EL*, II, 178).

17.8 "DOCTOR . . . VERY SELDOM?"   "Die Doctorin saget zu ihm 'Herr Doctor, wie kömmets, dass wir in Papstthum so hitzig, emsig, und so oft gebetet haben, jtzt aber ist unser Gebet ganz kalt, ja wir beten selten?'" (Luthers *Werke*, Kritische Gesamtausgabe, "Tischreden," IV, 569 [Weimar, Böhlau, 1912–1921]).   Emerson entered this speech, in English, into his journal in August 1836 (*JMN*, V, 191) and used it in a lecture the following year (*EL*, II, 178).   Where he found it is not so clear.   It may have caught his eye as he read—for "lustres"—in the *Tischreden*, though that seems unlikely.   It does appear in Henry Bell's translation of the *Tischreden, Colloquia Mensalia* (London, 1652), p. 240, but Bell's language is very different from Luther's and Emerson's.   It appears also, rather literally translated, in Jules Michelet's *Mémoires de Luther, ecrit par lui-même* (Paris, 1835), II, 165, which was warmly reviewed in *Blackwood's*, 39 (December 1835), 749–762; perhaps Emerson read Michelet and either translated the French or sought out the original German.

17.21 CREATIONS OF THE IMAGINATION AND NOT OF THE FANCY   In the years after Coleridge devised the term "esemplastic" to express the shaping-into-one power of the imagination and to elevate it above the lowly and merely associative power of the fancy (*Biographia Literaria*, ch. XIII), the two faculties had been carefully distinguished. What they meant in the 1840s was perhaps best said by Ruskin in *Modern Painters* (vol. II, pt. III, sec. II, no. 7): "The fancy sees the outside, and is able to give a portrait of the outside, clear, brilliant, and full of detail. The imagination sees the heart and inner nature, and makes them felt, but is often obscure, mysterious, and interrupted, in its giving of outer detail."

18.4 APOLLO KEPT THE FLOCKS OF ADMETUS In Euripides' *Alcestis*, Apollo, under sentence of Zeus and disguised as a herdsman, serves King Admetus of Pherae. See *PP* for other references to this legend.

19.7 GOETHE'S HELENA . . . LEDA The Helen of Troy episode of *Faust, Part II*, eventually to become Act III, was published in 1827 as *Helena / klassisch-romantische / Phantasmagorie / Zwischenspiel zu Faust*. The following year it was the subject of an essay-review by Carlyle, "Goethe's Helena." Perhaps for that reason Emerson thought of all of *Faust, Part II* under the title of the section which he had first known. Phorkyas is actually a character in "Helena": she is Mephistopheles, transformed into the ugly stewardess of the palace of Menelaus. But Chiron, the Griffins, and Faust's dream about Leda appear in Act II, the classical Walpurgisnacht.

19.23 PLATO SAID . . . THEMSELVES UNDERSTAND" Cf. *Apology*, 22. Jowett's translation reads: "They are like diviners or soothsayers who also say many fine things but do not understand the meaning of them." Edward Emerson recorded the following anecdote as a note to this passage: "When asked by one of his children whether some verse of Shakspeare, or perhaps it was a picture by Michelangelo, really was meant to carry with it the significance attributed to it, Mr. Emerson answered: 'Every one has a right to be credited with whatever of good another can find in his work.'" (*W*, II, 387).

19.33 "TO BEND THE SHOWS OF THINGS TO THE DESIRES OF THE MIND" Cf. Francis Bacon's *Advancement of Learning*, bk. II, ch. iv, para. 2: "poesy serveth and conferreth to magnanimity, morality, and to delectations. And therefore it was ever thought to have some participation of divineness, because it doth raise and erect the mind, by submitting the shows of things to the desires of the mind." See *JMN*, VI, 41n, for a list of other places where Emerson uses this sentence of Bacon.

19.35 IN PERCEFOREST . . . THE GENTLE GENELAS Cf. Richard Price's Preface to Thomas Warton's *History of English Poetry*, 3 vols. (London, 1840), I, 46–47: "In Perceforest and in Amadis, a garland and rose, which 'bloom on the head of her who is faithful, and fade upon the brow of the inconstant,' are proofs of the appellant's purity: and in the ballad published by Dr.

Percy, of the Boy and the Mantle, where the same test is introduced." Price's quotation is from John Colin Dunlap's *The History of Fiction . . . from the earliest Greek Romances to the Novels of the Present Age*, 3 vols. (Edinburgh, 1814), I, 240. In Percy's version of "The Boy and the Mantle," a boy, by the aid of a magic mantle, a drinking horn, and a knife, reveals the falsity of all but one of the ladies of Arthur's court; she is identified only as "Craddockes ladye" (*Reliques of Ancient English Poetry*, 3 vols. [Philadelphia, 1823], III, 41–49). Emerson seems to have confused her with Genelas, the heroine of a "foolish German fairy tale, 'the Short Mantle,' " which he had read in translation many years before and which, when he reread it in 1835, made his "cheeks glow again and almost the gracious drops fall at the triumph of the chaste & gentle Genelas" (*JMN*, V, 35; see also *JMN*, V, 89, and *EL*, I, 260–261). It is highly unlikely that he knew *Perceforest* at first hand, but he might well have read the first four books of *Amadis de Gaul* in Southey's translation, where he could have found the garland story in chs. XIV and XV of bk. II. The garland is, in Southey's words, "a head-dress of flowers, the half whereof were as beautiful and fresh as though they had just then been cut from the living stem; the other half so withered and dry, that it seemed they would crumble at a touch"; set on the head of a lady like Oriana, the beloved of Amadis, who with "surpassing love doth love her husband or friend, the dry flowers . . . again become fresh and green" (*Amadis of Gaul*, 4 vols. [London, 1803], II, 216).

20.7 THE NEWEST ROMANCE . . . LAMMERMOOR *The Bride of Lammermoor* (1819) was hardly "the newest romance," even for a man who read little fiction. In the lecture known as "The Age of Fable," probably delivered November 19, 1835, from which this and the preceding paragraph are adapted, Emerson wrote: "These remarks are capable of the most extensive application to romantic literature, even in its latest form the modern novel. I have before me Scott's fine novel *The Bride of Lammermoor*" (*EL*, I, 260). See also *JMN*, III, 247.

20.36 TALBOT'S SHADOW . . . HENRY VI Cf. Shakespeare's *Henry VI, Part I*, II, iii, 50–56. The fourth line of Emerson's quotation was doubtless deliberately abridged: "I tell you, madam, were the whole frame here" would have been distracting.

21.12 GAY-LUSSAC The French chemist Joseph-Louis Gay-Lussac (1778–1850) formulated the law of combining volumes. Emerson had heard him lecture at the Sorbonne in the summer of 1833 (*JMN*, IV, 197).

21.16 WHITTEMORE Amos Whittemore (1759–1828), a gunsmith of Cambridge, Massachusetts, invented devices important in the carding of cotton and wool.

22.5 THE TEMPLE OF FAME . . . THAT VARIEGATED VEST   Hesiod, Sophocles, Ovid, Vergil, and Chaucer all described Fame's house but not her robe.

25.1 "NE TE QUAESIVERIS EXTRA"   Persius, *Satires*, I, 7: "Look to no one outside yourself."   In the original the first word is "nec"; perhaps Emerson's alteration was intended to make the injunction more emphatic, but probably he just misremembered.   See *JMN*, IV, 318, and PP.

27.1 AN EMINENT PAINTER   Washington Allston.   On September 20, 1837, Emerson wrote in his journal: "I read this morning some lines by Mr Allston to Mrs Jameson, on the Diary of the Ennuyée, very good & entirely self-taught, original, not conventional" (*JMN*, V, 377).   The poem, "To the Author of 'The Diary of an Ennuyée,'" was published in Allston's posthumous volume *Lectures on Art, and Poems* (New York, 1850), pp. 377–380.

28.19 THAT IRON STRING   Emerson, like many of his contemporaries, used the words "iron" and "steel" interchangeably.   See two letters of the summer of 1839 in which he apologized for his "pen of steel" and his "iron pen" (*L*, II, 206, 219).

28.29 ADVANCING ON CHAOS AND THE DARK   A phrase in a letter from Emerson to Carlyle, "carrying forward & planting the standard of Oromasdes so many leagues farther on into the envious Dark" (*CEC*, 108), suggests that this metaphor is Zoroastrian as well as Miltonic.

30.21 ABOLITION . . . LAST NEWS FROM BARBADOES   Slavery was abolished in Barbados in 1834.

30.31 I SHUN FATHER AND MOTHER . . . GENIUS CALLS ME   Cf. Matthew 10:37: "He that loveth father or mother more than me is not worthy of me."

30.33 LINTELS OF THE DOOR-POST   Cf. Exodus 12:23: "For the Lord will pass through to smite the Egyptians; and when he seeth the blood upon the lintel, and on the two side posts, the Lord will pass over the door, and will not suffer the destroyer to come in unto your houses to smite you."

32.30 "THE FOOLISH FACE OF PRAISE"   Cf. Alexander Pope's *Epistle to Dr. Arbuthnot*, line 212.   See *JMN*, II, 239, and PP.

34.1 PYTHAGORAS WAS MISUNDERSTOOD   Possibly because when Pythagoras at the age of fifty-six returned to Samos after long years of study in Egypt, "no one was genuinely desirous of those disciplines which he endeavoured by all means to introduce among the Greeks"; possibly because later "they numbered him with the Gods" (*Iamblichus' Life of Pythagoras . . . translated from the Greek by Thomas Taylor* [London, 1818], pp. 13–14).

34.9 AN ACROSTIC OR ALEXANDRIAN STANZA . . . SAME THING Greek poets of the Alexandrian period were much given to the use of acrostics and, in the stern judgment of Professor Charles Anthon of Columbia College, to "such things as anagrams, *jeux de mots,* and other frivolities, which correct taste condemns." They also "occasionally indulged," he wrote, "in a singular species of trifling . . . *carmina figurata;* that is, pieces in which the lines are so arranged as to make the whole poem resemble the form of some object" (*A Manual of Greek Literature* [New York, 1853], pp. 363, 376). However, not even Professor Anthon charged the Alexandrians with the construction of palindromes, and, according to Karl Preisendanz ("Palindrom," *Paulys Real-Encyclopädie der Classischen Altertumswissenschaft* [Stuttgart, Metzler, 1949], XVIII, iii, 133–139), that species of frivolity did not flourish until the Byzantine period. Perhaps Emerson knew the Latin "Sator-palindrom" which was once believed—erroneously, Preisendanz says—to go back to the "alexandrinische Tradition" (p. 138), and which throughout the nineteenth century was widely used by the German peasantry for purposes of magic (Albrecht Dieterich, "ABC-Denkmäler," *Rheinisches Museum für Philologie,* 1901, third series, LVI, 90). The "sator" palindrome is quoted in *Thesaurus Linguae Latinae,* II, 506: "sator arepo tenet opera rotas"; it *may* be translated, "Seed-sower Half-acre controls the wheels by his labor." Arranged in what Emerson perhaps meant by the phrase "an acrostic or Alexandrian stanza," it spells the same things forward, backward, and across: S A T O R
A R E P O
T E N E T
O P E R A
R O T A S

35.37 SCIPIO, MILTON CALLED "THE HEIGHT OF ROME" In *Paradise Lost,* IX, 510.

36.14 FABLE OF THE SOT . . . HAD BEEN INSANE Cf. the Induction to *The Taming of the Shrew.*

36.27 SCANDERBEG, AND GUSTAVUS George Castriota (1403–1468), leader of the Albanian rebellion against the Turks, held before his defection the Turkish title of Iskander Bey. By "Gustavus" Emerson presumably meant Gustavus Adolphus (1594–1632), King of Sweden and leader of interventionist forces in the Thirty Years' War.

41.6 TAKE THE SHOES . . . WITHIN Cf. Exodus 3:5: "And he said, draw not nigh hither: but put off thy shoes from off thy feet, for the place whereon thou standest is holy ground."

41.25 'COME OUT UNTO US' Cf. Isaiah 36:16: "Hearken not to Hezekiah: for thus saith the king of Assyria, Make an agreement with me by a present, and come out to me."

41.28 "WHAT WE LOVE . . . OF THE LOVE" In a journal entry of 1839 Emerson quoted this sentence as a "great sentiment . . . which Schiller said, or said the like" (*JMN*, VII, 214). It is interestingly unlike the sentiment of Schiller's epigram "Liebe und Begierde": "Recht gesagt, Schlosser! Man liebt, was man hat; man begehrt, was man nicht hat; / Denn nur das reiche Gemüt liebt, nur das arme begehrt" (*Sämtliche Werke / Säkular-Ausgabe in 16 Bänden* [Stuttgart, Cotta, 1904–1905], II, 93). Emerson may have read an accurate translation of the poem in his friend John Sullivan Dwight's *Selected Minor Poems, Translated from the German of Goethe and Schiller*, which was published in Boston in 1839, but this paraphrase suggests a recollection of the original German.

43.37 THE WORD MADE . . . TO THE NATIONS Cf. John 1:14: "And the Word was made flesh, and dwelt among us"; and Revelation 22:2: "and the leaves of the tree were for the healing of the nations."

44.22 PRAYER IN ALL ACTION Edward Emerson's note to this passage says that, while a theological student, Emerson "worked in his uncle's hayfield beside a Methodist farm-hand . . . This man maintained that men are always praying" (*W*, II, 394). It was on the theme of "acted prayers" that Emerson wrote his first sermon, "Pray without Ceasing."

44.26 THE GOD Audate . . . OUR BEST GODS" Cf. *Bonduca*, III, 1. Few divinities have undergone more metamorphoses at the hands of printers and editors than this bloody war-god of the Britons. In the First Folio of Beaumont and Fletcher's *Comedies and Tragedies* (London, 1647), pt. V, p. 57, he was called "Audate" and was, not surprisingly, masculine. The Second Folio, *Fifty Comedies and Tragedies* (London, 1679), which was corrected by "an ingenious and worthy gentleman" who had known both of the authors, changed the name to "Andate" and the sex to feminine: "Her hidden meaning dwels in our endeavours" ([i] and pt. II, p. 33). She remained Andate in the libretto devised for Purcell's music in 1695 and in Jacob Tonson's seven-volume *Works* of 1711. In 1750, however, a "Mr. Sympson of Gainsborough," editing the play for the ten-volume *Works* begun by Lewis Theobald and continued by Thomas Seward, argued on historical grounds that the "real name of this Goddess . . . is not *Andate* but *Andrasta*; and so . . . ventured to alter the Text" (VI, 308). In 1778 George Colman, though convinced by Sympson's historical argument that the divinity was indeed a goddess, retained her Second Folio name (VI, 319–320). Not until 1812 was there a return to the First Folio. In that year Henry Weber, Sir Walter Scott's assistant and secretary, published in Edinburgh a fourteen-volume edition of the *Works* based on the principle that "Strict fidelity to the oldest text, wherever it affords sense" is the editor's "first and most obvious duty" (I, cxiii-cxiv). In *Bonduca* he rejected Sympson's Andrasta-emendation as "scarce warrantable," and, though he chided Fletcher for being "not very skilled in the British mythology," he restored the war-god's masculinity. He did not, however, restore his original name! What edition did Emerson use? Name and gender and his ownership of a copy of the First Folio suggest that he was more faithful than Weber to the oldest text; his American spellings and his substitution of "lies" for "dwels" suggest that he had the book in his memory and not on his library table as he wrote. However, see *JMN*, VII, 188 and 212, where the god's name has been transcribed as "Andate"; possibly Emerson knew Weber's edition.

45.8 "To THE PERSEVERING . . . SWIFT" This sentence appears among "The Chaldaean Oracles of Zoroaster" in Isaac Preston Cory's *Ancient Fragments of the Phoenician, Chaldaean . . . and Other Writers* (London, 1832), p. 271.

45.12 'LET NOT GOD . . . WE WILL OBEY' Cf. Exodus 20:19.

45.17 HUTTON James Hutton (1726–1797), Scottish geologist whose *Theory of the Earth* (1785) was the first statement of the naturalistic theory later popularized by Playfair and developed by Lyell.

46.5 AS ON THE FIRST MORNING An allusion perhaps to the speech of Raphael which begins the "Prolog im Himmel," *Faust I*: "Die Sonne tönt . . . Die unbegreiflich hohen Werke / Sind herrlich wie am ersten Tag" (*Goethes Sämtliche Werke*, XIII, 12).

47.31 THOUSAND-CLOVEN TONGUE Cf. Acts 2:1–4: "And when the day of Pentecost was fully come, they were all with one accord in one place. . . . And there appeared unto them cloven tongues like as of fire . . . And they were all filled with the Holy Ghost, and began to speak with other tongues, as the Spirit gave them utterance."

48.10 THE NAKED NEW ZEALANDER . . . SOFT PITCH If the source of this passage is, as the details about nakedness, weapons, mat, and shed suggest, Cook's account of his first visit to New Zealand, Emerson exaggerated the severity of the wound. Cook cited as evidence that "human nature" among the Maoris was "untainted with disease" and that health was "perfect and uninterrupted" the rapid healing of a warrior whose arm had been pierced by an English musket-ball. See *The Three Voyages of Captain James Cook Round the World*, 7 vols. (London, 1821), II, 34–48.

Compensation

49.8 Parry and Franklin   Sir William Edward Parry (1790–1855) and Sir John Franklin (1786–1847) were the best-known of contemporary explorers.

49.19 The Emperor . . . bake his bread himself"   Cf. Las Cases, *Mémorial de Sainte Hélène*, IV, vii, 97.

50.8 "Thy lot . . . seeking after it"   This is the fifteenth of the "Sentences of Ali, Son-in-Law of Mahomet, and his Fourth Successor." It appears on p. 2 of the appendix to Simon Ockley's *The History of the Saracens*, 2 vols. (London, 1718), II. See *JMN*, VI, 388, and VII, 400.

55.1 Ever since I was a boy . . . Compensation   Emerson's first extended treatment of this theme, from which half a dozen sentences of the 1841 essay were drawn, was written in his journal in 1826 (*JMN*, II, 340–346). See also *JMN*, II, 71, 99, 116, 117, 145, and 260. In 1835 he had written to Carlyle about "the compensations of the Universe, the equality and the coexistence of action and reaction, that all prayers are granted, that every debt is paid" (*CEC*, 121).

57.10 In the equation . . . animal body   Early in 1847 Emerson, reading and rereading Swedenborg for a new lecture, was so struck by a phrase which he found in the recently published translation by Augustus Clissold of *The Economy of the Animal Kingdom* (London, 1845) that he copied it into his journal (*JMN*, X, 36), in quotation marks, and inserted it without quotation marks into the new edition of his essays. Swedenborg himself had italicized the phrase: "While I have been dwelling on these stupendous mysteries . . . the idea has offered itself, of *a certain equation of quantity and quality in the fluids*." What he meant was that wherever "an excess of one species of liquid is consumed, thither, of course a supply of the same species must flow." This is why, for example, "the power of venery is encreased by its exercise, why the breasts and teats overflow while the infant sucks; and why habit becomes second nature" (I, 188–189).

57.13 electricity, galvanism   During the nineteenth century the word "electricity" was sometimes used to mean electric current produced by frictional means and was distinguished from "galvanism," electric current produced by chemical means, as in a battery.

58.10 they are increased that use them   Not a metaphor but a statement of family and social fact: Emerson's own modest inheritance was almost wholly committed to a large and increasing number of dependents. He had observed the experience in the lives of others and recorded it in his journal in 1831: "When riches are increased they are increased that eat them. There are no large estates . . . Few men have any disposable means. Claims are commensurate with fortunes" (*JMN*, III, 222).

59.7 Res nolunt diu male administrari On April 5, 1729, in a letter to Pope and Bolingbroke, Swift asked the name of the author of this Latin sentence: "the commonness," he wrote, "makes me not know . . . but sure he must be some Modern" (*The Correspondence of Jonathan Swift*, ed. Harold Williams, 5 vols. [Oxford, The Clarendon Press, 1963–1965], III, 329). See *JMN*, V, 280, and PP.

59.25 The naturalist sees . . . a rooted man Emerson's "naturalist" was probably a composite of many comparative anatomists — Buffon, Cuvier, Hunter, Home — whom he had read, and read about. If he had an individual in mind, he may well have been remembering the eighteenth-century Dutch scientist Pieter Camper, whose work he had learned of in Goethe's posthumously published "Vorträge über vergleichende Anatomie" and had described in his own lecture "Humanity of Science" of 1836 (*EL*, II, 28). Goethe had written: "Eingenommen von der aufgefassten Idee, wagte Camper, auf der schwarzen Lehrtafel durch Kreidestriche den Hund in ein Pferd, das Pferd in einen Menschen, die Kuh in einen Vogel zu verwandeln" (*Goethes Sämtliche Werke*, XXXIX, 166). The corresponding sentence of Emerson's lecture is interestingly altered: "Camper, the physiologist, was wont to draw on his blackboard the man, and by a few strokes transform him into a horse, then into an ox, into a bird, into a fish."

60.10 "It is in the world . . . by it" Cf. John 1:10: "He was in the world, and the world was made by him, and the world knew him not."

60.13 The dice of God are always loaded The standard text of this much-quoted fragment of Sophocles is ἀεὶ γὰρ εὖ πίπτουσιν οἱ Διὸς κύβοι (Augustus Nauck, *Tragicorum Graecorum Fragmenta* [Hildesheim, Olms, 1964], p. 320). Emerson's translation is colloquial and presumably ironic. According to A. C. Pearson in *The Fragments of Sophocles* (3 vols. [Cambridge, Cambridge University Press, 1917], III, 84), εὖ πίπτουσιν "must mean 'yield a good throw' to the player, who in this case is Zeus." For other uses by Emerson see PP.

61.14 All things shall be added unto it Cf. Luke 12:31: "But rather seek ye the kingdom of God; and all these things shall be added unto you."

61.30 "Drive out nature . . . she comes running back" Cf. Horace, *Epistles*, I, x, 24. See *JMN*, VII, 45.

62.10 "How secret art thou . . . unbridled desires" This is the only quotation in the first edition for which Emerson wrote a footnote. It is the conclusion of Augustine's chapter XVIII.

62.23 "OF ALL THE GODS . . . HIS THUNDERS SLEEP" Aeschylus, *The Furies*, lines 894–896. Emerson's quotation is, with slight alterations, from the translation of Robert Potter in *The Tragedies of Aeschylus*, 2 vols. (London, 1779), II, 288–289. See *JMN*, V, 401.

63.1 THERE IS A CRACK . . . GOD HAS MADE The sentence "There's a crack in every thing God has made except Reason" appears in Emerson's notebook "Encyclopedia" under the heading "My Proverbs" (*JMN*, VI, 198). Presumably it is of his own composition. See also PP.

63.9 THE FURIES . . . WOULD PUNISH HIM Cf. Plutarch, *Moralia*, "On Exile," 11: "for 'the Sun will not transgress his bounds,' says Heracleitus; 'else the Erinyes, ministers of Justice, will find him out.' " See *JMN*, VI, 218.

63.13 THE BELT WHICH AJAX . . . AJAX FELL Cf. Sophocles, *Ajax*, lines 1029–1034. See *JMN*, VI, 218, and PP.

63.17 THE THASIANS . . . BENEATH ITS FALL Cf. Thomas Brown, *Lectures on the Philosophy of the Human Mind*, 4 vols. (Edinburgh, 1820), III, 553: "When a statue had been erected by his fellow-citizens of Thasos to Theagenes, a celebrated victor in the public games of Greece, we are told, that it excited so strongly the envious hatred of one of his rivals, that he went to it every night, and endeavoured to throw it down by repeated blows, till at last, unfortunately successful, he was able to move it from its pedestal, and was crushed to death beneath it on its fall. This, if we consider the self-consuming misery of envy, is truly what happens to every envious man." See *JMN*, VI, 169, and PP.

64.9 ALL THINGS ARE DOUBLE . . . DEVIL IS AN ASS Emerson had collected most of this flight of proverbs in the notebook he called "Encyclopedia" (*JMN*, VI, 115–234). See esp. pp. 143, 215–218, and 224.

64.29 A HARPOON . . . SINK THE BOAT Edward Emerson, in his note to this passage (*W*, II, 399), wrote that his father often told "anecdotes of peril and accident" which he had heard while preaching in New Bedford or lecturing on Nantucket.

64.33 "NO MAN . . . SAID BURKE "A man never can have any point of pride that is not pernicious to him," Burke wrote in a letter to the painter James Barry, about a painter who had failed to study the Dutch and Italian masters. James Prior, *Memoir of the Life and Character of the Right Hon. Edmund Burke* (London, 1824), p. 130. See also *JMN*, VI, 157, and PP.

65.25 OBSCENE Presumably used here in its old sense of "ill-omened."

65.29 THE EMERALD OF POLYCRATES Polycrates, tyrant of Samos, worried by constant prosperity, threw his most valued possession, an emerald ring, into the sea as a propitiatory sacrifice. It was ominously returned to him the following day in the belly of a fish. Revolution, wars, and the crucifixion of Polycrates followed. See Herodotus, *History*, III, 40–43, and *JMN*, V, 94.

66.8 "THE HIGHEST PRICE . . . TO ASK FOR IT" Cf. Walter Savage Landor, "Eschines and Phocion," *Imaginary Conversations of Literary Men and Statesmen*, 3 vols. (London, 1826–1829), I, 116. See *JMN*, VI, 217. Edward Emerson wrote that "this maxim was a household word with Mr. Emerson. He was loath to place himself under obligation" (*W*, II, 400). The sentence appears also among the quotations which "enrich" the last pages of Emerson's essay on Landor in *The Dial*, 2 (October 1841), 270.

68.4 AS THE ROYAL ARMIES . . . BECAME FRIENDS Many vivid anecdotes of the defection of Bourbon troops during Napoleon's march from Antibes to Paris in March 1815 appear in Las Cases, *Mémorial de Sainte Hélène*, III, vi, 82–88.

68.8 "WINDS BLOW . . . ARE NOTHING" Lines 10–12 of Wordsworth's sonnet "September 1802. Near Dover," which begins "Inland, within a hollow vale, I stood," and which is usually printed among the "Sonnets Dedicated to Liberty."

68.14 THE STAG IN THE FABLE . . . HORNS DESTROYED HIM Aesop's "The Stag Drinking" appears in Robert Dodsley, *Select Fables of Aesop and other Fabulists* (London, 1809), pp. 19–20. See *JMN*, IV, 66, 329.

69.6 THE SANDWICH ISLANDER . . . HIMSELF The source of Emerson's information has not been located.

69.25 TO TWIST A ROPE OF SAND This metaphor for an impossible task is at least as old as Butler's *Hudibras* (I, i, 157–158) and seems to derive from medieval tales about demons for whom it was necessary to find endless employment: see for example Scott's footnote to *The Lay of the Last Minstrel*, II, xiii. In Emerson's frequent references to the legend, the demon is usually Asmodeus. See PP, esp. *JMN*, V, 186.

71.5 I PLANT INTO DESERTS . . . HORIZON See above, note to 28.29.

71.28 ST. BERNARD . . . FAULT" Cf. *The Meditations of St. Augustine . . . With Select Contemplations from St. Anselm and St. Bernard*, trans. George Stanhope (London, 1818), p. 401, a volume which was in Emerson's library. See *JMN*, III, 339, and PP.

72.34 OUR ANGELS GO . . . THAT ARCHANGELS MAY COME IN   Cf. in "Give All To Love" the lines "When half-gods go, / The gods arrive" (*W*, IX, 92).

73.8 THOSE MONSTERS WHO LOOK BACKWARDS   Whom or what did Emerson have in mind? Epimetheus, brother of Prometheus and husband of Pandora, was a Titan, but an "after-thinking" rather than a retrospective one. Lot's wife looked backward, but was hardly a monster. Cuvier and other naturalists had written of dinosaurs with easily revertible eyes, but the present tense was unsuitable for them. Perhaps the simile merely refers to the stalk-eyed crabs and lobsters of New England coastal waters.

73.26 THE BANIAN OF THE FOREST   Cf. Carlyle, *Sartor Resartus*, bk. I, ch. v, para. 7: "thy Act, thy Word . . . will be found flourishing as a Banyan-grove (perhaps, alas, as a Hemlock-forest!) after a thousand years."

78.10 "A FEW STRONG INSTINCTS AND A FEW PLAIN RULES"   See the concluding lines of Wordsworth's "Alas! What Boots the Long Laborious Quest," one of his "Sonnets Dedicated to Liberty": "and may not we with sorrow say, / A few strong instincts and a few plain rules, / Among the herdsmen of the Alps, have wrought / More for mankind at this unhappy day / Than all the pride of intellect and thought?"

78.29 TIMOLEON'S VICTORIES . . . PLUTARCH SAID   In his "Life of Timoleon," para. XXXVI. See *JMN*, V, 151, and PP.

78.33 'CRUMP IS A BETTER MAN . . . DEVILS'   In the journal entry from which this passage is drawn "Crump" is Jonathan Peele Dabney, a contemporary clergyman (*JMN*, VII, 67). See also *English Traits* (*W*, V, 144), where "Mr. Crump" represents the English eccentric.

79.3 'NOT UNTO US . . . US'   Cf. Psalms 115:1: "Not unto us, O Lord, not unto us, but unto thy name give glory."

79.5 ST. JULIAN   There are many saints named Julian. Emerson was probably thinking of the patron saint of hospitality, whose name he would have known from Chaucer ("General Prologue," line 340), and whose story he doubtless encountered in Warton's summary of the *Gesta Romanorum* (*History of English Poetry*, I, cxlviii). "A knight named Julian," Warton wrote, returned unexpectedly to his castle and slew two occupants of his bed in the belief that they were "his wife and her adulterer." Almost immediately he learned from his wife that they were his parents, who had long been seeking him and whom she had honored with a place in his own bed. In penance he "founded a sumptuous hospital for the accomodation of travellers, on the banks of a dangerous river."

82.34 "SIGNS THAT MARK HIM . . . COMMON MEN"   Cf. the speech of Glendower in *Henry IV, Part I*, I, iii, 41–43: "These signs have mark'd me extraordinary; / And all the courses of my life do show / I am not in the roll of common men."

82.36 NO RESPECT OF PERSONS   Cf. Acts 10:34–35: "I perceive that God is no respecter of persons: But in every nation he that feareth him, and worketh righteousness, is accepted with him."

83.25 EULENSTEIN FROM A JEWS-HARP   During his first concert tour in England, the young jew's-harp virtuoso Charles Eulenstein (1802–1890) was described as using "twelve or fourteen of these humble instruments, playing on two at a time, and changing them at pleasure with a rapidity truly astonishing" (*The Harmonicon, a Journal of Music*, 4 [June 1826], 132).   He was giving concerts in Scotland when Emerson was there in 1833, and he continued to astonish audiences until late in the century.   *The Concord Freeman* published a front-page article about him on May 14, 1841.

84.2 THE GOODS OF FORTUNE . . . ON EVERY WIND   Cf. Scott's *Old Mortality*, ch. 43, para. beginning "Thou art deceived": "Lord Evandale is a malignant, of heart like flint, and brow like adamant; the goods of the world fall on him like leaves on the frost-bound earth, and unmoved he will see them whirled off by the first wind." Edward Emerson, in his note to this passage (*W*, II, 406), wrote: "Mr. Emerson often repeated the speech with something of the pleasure it had given him in his boyhood."

84.8 A MAN IS A METHOD, A PROGRESSIVE ARRANGEMENT   Journal entries, esp. *JMN*, III, 299, and VI, 222, make it clear that this passage derives from Coleridge's *The Friend*.   In Essay VII of the Second Section, Coleridge wrote: "improgressive arrangement is not method"; and in Essay V of the same section, somewhat more clearly: "method implies a progressive transition . . . without continuous transition there can be no method . . . The term, method, can not therefore . . . be applied to a mere dead arrangement, containing in itself no principle of progression" (*The Complete Works of Samuel Taylor Coleridge*, ed. W. G. T. Shedd, 7 vols. [New York, 1854], II, 430, 416–417). See also PP.

85.5 NAPOLEON SENT TO VIENNA . . . IMPERIAL CABINET   Cf. Las Cases, *Mémorial de Sainte Hélène*, II, iii, 42–43: "In less than a fortnight M. de Narbonne penetrated all the secrets of the Vienna cabinet."   See also *JMN*, V, 486.

85.28 ARISTOTLE SAID . . . NOT PUBLISHED"   Plutarch, in his life of Alexander, vii, paraphrased a reply by Aristotle to a letter from Alexander which had chided him for publishing his lectures. Aristotle's defense was that they were in fact "both published and not published" because they were written in such a manner that they could be understood only by readers who had been taught by a master. See *JMN*, IV, 337.

85.34 OUR EYES ARE HOLDEN THAT WE CANNOT SEE Cf. Luke 24:13–16: "And, behold, two of them went that same day to a village called Emmaus . . . And it came to pass, that, while they communed together and reasoned, Jesus himself drew near and went with them. But their eyes were holden that they should not know him."

86.3 "EARTH FILLS HER LAP . . . NOT HER OWN Cf. line 77 of Wordsworth's "Ode: Intimations of Immortality": "Earth fills her lap with pleasures of her own."

86.20 "MY CHILDREN," SAID AN OLD MAN . . . YOURSELVES" In the journal entry from which this sentence is drawn, Emerson attributed it to "my Grandfather" (*JMN*, IV, 212). Edward Emerson's note in the first edition of the journals (*J*, III, 234) suggests, in addition to the two grandfathers, one great-grandfather, Joseph Emerson, but not, surprisingly, Emerson's step-grandfather, Ezra Ripley. See also *EL*, III, 156.

86.27 A QUINCUNX OF TREES . . . SOUTH A quincunx is a square marked by one point at each corner and a fifth at the center. Used singly or continuously, it was, as Charles Anthon wrote in his note to ch. XVII, para. 59, of Cicero's *De Senectute* (New York, 1850), p. 184, "the favorite mode of planting trees among the Romans, these being arranged in such a way, that, from whatever side they were viewed, they represented the Roman numeral V." Since lines in continuous quincuncial plantings may total more or fewer than five trees, Emerson's metaphor probably refers to the Roman numerals as seen from the central tree trunk of a single quincunx. For other ancient uses of the word see Varro, *Rerum Rusticarum*, I, vii, 2, and Caesar, *De Bello Gallico*, VII, 73.

86.28 AN INITIAL, MEDIAL, AND TERMINAL ACROSTIC That is, a triply repeated acrostic. Perhaps Emerson remembered the essay by Addison, *The Spectator*, No. 60, which included acrostics, chronograms, and rebuses among the varieties of false wit produced by idle monks and blockheads: "I have seen some of them where the verses have not only been edged by a name at each extremity, but have had the same name running down like a seam through the middle of the poem."

88.9 INSANE LEVITY . . . OTHERS' EYES Edward Emerson's note to this passage (*W*, II, 406) reads: "When somewhat importunately urged to be presented to a person for whom he felt no affinity, Mr. Emerson said, 'Whom God hath put asunder, let no man put together.' "

88.11 MAXIM WORTHY OF ALL ACCEPTATION Cf. I Timothy 1:15 and 4:9: "This is a faithful saying and worthy of all acceptation."

88.22 HE TEACHES WHO GIVES . . . RECEIVES A translation of the Latin maxim "Solus docet qui dat, et discit qui recipit," which Emerson found in *The Select Works of Robert Leighton*, 2 vols. (London, 1823), I, 444. See *JMN*, V, 408, and PP.

89.14 "LOOK IN THY HEART, AND WRITE" *Astrophel and Stella*, I, 14.

89.22 WE CAN ONLY BE VALUED . . . VALUABLE Cf. Vicesimus Knox, *Elegant Extracts . . . in Prose*, 7th ed., 2 vols. (London, 1797), II, 1028. See *JMN*, IV, 15, 17.

89.31 WALPOLE'S NOBLE AND ROYAL AUTHORS . . . POLLOK Among royal or noble authors Emerson seems to have had in mind not Henry the Eighth or Henry Howard, Earl of Surrey, but, say, Mildmay Fane, Earl of Westmoreland, of whom Walpole wrote: "All I can find of this Lord, is, that he wrote 'a very small book of poems' which he gave to, and is preserved in, the library of Emanuel-College Cambridge" (Horace Walpole, *A Catalogue of the Royal and Noble Authors of England, with Lists of their Works* [Strawberry Hill, 1758], I, 205). The best-known work of Sir Richard Blackmore (c. 1650–1729), physician to William III and Queen Anne, was a 350-page philosophical poem entitled *Creation* (1712). August Friedrich Ferdinand von Kotzebue (1761–1819) wrote over two hundred plays. By 1840 *The Course of Time*, a 330-page poem by Robert Pollok (1798–1827), was in its 15th edition.

89.37 "NO BOOK," SAID BENTLEY . . . BUT ITSELF" Cf. James Henry Monk, *The Life of Richard Bentley, D.D.*, 2 vols. (London, 1833), I, 116. See *JMN*, VI, 217, and PP.

90.4 "DO NOT TROUBLE . . . TEST ITS VALUE" Paraphrased from Thomas Roscoe, "The Life of Michael Angelo Buonaroti," in *Lives of Eminent Persons* (London, 1833), p. 72. See *JMN*, IV, 369, and PP.

90.20 THE LAWS OF DISEASE . . . OF HEALTH In *JMN*, V, 503, Emerson attributed this sentiment to his brother-in-law, Dr. Charles T. Jackson. See also PP.

90.35 DOTH NOT WISDOM . . . HER VOICE Proverbs 8:1.

91.7 AN EXPERIENCED COUNSELLOR . . . THEIR UNBELIEF Edward Emerson (*W*, II, 406) identified this counselor as his father's "honored friend, Samuel Hoar, Esq." Hoar (1778–1856), who practiced law in Concord, was a distinguished member of Congress and one of the founders of the Republican Party.

91.15 SWEDENBORG . . . INDIGNATION Here Emerson was paraphrasing and quoting from a "Memorable Relation" by Swedenborg. "On one occasion," Swedenborg reported, "there was a numerous assembly in the spiritual world, who were discoursing on this subject and saying, that not to be able to speak but as one thinks, must be a hard thing." Some of the clergy, among them "papists and monks," disagreed, and so an experiment was tried. They were enjoined to say, " 'Divine Human;' but as this thought was not rooted in the acknowledgment that the Lord was God as to his human nature also, therefore they could not; they twisted and folded their lips even to indignation, and would have forced their mouths to utter and extort it, but it was not in their power" (*The Apocalypse Revealed* . . . , 3 vols. [Boston, 1836], I, 253–255). See *JMN*, IV, 342–343, and PP.

92.8 NEVER WAS A SINCERE WORD UTTERLY LOST Cf. Baroness Staël Holstein, *Germany*, 3 vols. (London, 1813), III, 401: "With whatever atmosphere we may be surrounded, a sincere word was never completely lost." See *JMN*, VI, 61, and PP.

92.18 THE MARK OF THE BEAST Cf. Revelation 13:15–16: "And he had power to . . . cause that as many as would not worship the image of the beast should be killed. And he causeth all . . . to receive a mark in their right hand, or in their foreheads."

92.20 IF YOU WOULD NOT BE KNOWN . . . NEVER DO IT Cf. Vicesimus Knox, *Elegant Extracts*, II, 1032. See *JMN*, IV, 17, 21.

92.25 A CHIFFINCH, AN IACHIMO Chiffinch in Scott's *Peveril of the Peak* is "the well-known minister of [King] Charles's pleasures," a "dishonorable rascal," and a "base wretch" (chapter 27). Iachimo is the treacherous pseudo-seducer of Imogen in *Cymbeline*.

92.26 CONFUCIUS EXCLAIMED . . . CONCEALED" *Analects*, II, x, 4. Emerson used Joshua Marshman's translation, *The Works of Confucius* (Serampore, 1809), p. 103. See *JMN*, V, 120.

92.35 GOD . . . I AM Exodus 3:14.

93.3 LIE LOW IN THE LORD'S POWER In his lecture "The Heart" of 1838 Emerson had written, "as George Fox would say, 'Lie low in the Lord's power' " (*EL*, II, 292–293). He seems not to have meant the sentence as a quotation, but the phrases "keep low" and "in the Lord's power" appear very frequently in Fox's journals and letters.

93.33 THOROUGH LIGHTS An obsolete architectural term meaning windows placed opposite each other so that the daylight may shine through.

94.1 EPAMINONDAS Theban general in the wars against Sparta. In his lecture on Martin Luther, Emerson spoke of Epaminondas as "the greatest (some have thought) of the Greeks" (*EL*, I, 140).

94.24 THE NAME OF ACTION *Hamlet*, III, i, 88.

94.31 TO THINK IS TO ACT In 1831 and again in 1836 Emerson had entered this sentence in his journal as a quotation but had given no indication of its source (*JMN*, III, 298; V, 4).

95.5 BYRON . . . SWORE" Cf. *The Island*, III, v, 12. The swearer is Jack Skyscrape; it is Ben Bunting who hears Skyscrape's " 'G–d damn!' — those syllables intense, — / Nucleus of England's native eloquence." See *JMN*, II, 386, and PP.

95.10 THE LIFE OF BRANT Presumably Stone's *Life of Joseph Brant*, which Emerson had read in 1839. See above, note to 10.3.

95.19 BONAPARTE KNEW BUT MERIT . . . PLAYER Cf. Las Cases, *Mémorial de Sainte Hélène*, IV, vii, 120: "the same titles and the same decorations, were awarded equally to the ecclesiastic, the soldier, the artist, the philosopher, and the man of letters." See *JMN*, V, 507.

95.21 THE POET . . . OF BONDUCA, OF BELISARIUS John Fletcher wrote a play about Bonduca, the British queen and rebel against the Romans who is usually known as Boadicea; Jean François Marmontel wrote a romance about Justinian's great general Belisarius.

95.34 LET THE GREAT SOUL . . . MOPS AND BROOMS This passage, Oliver Wendell Holmes wrote, "is not any the worse for being the flowering out of a poetical bud of George Herbert's": *Ralph Waldo Emerson* (Boston, 1884), p. 170. Holmes was thinking presumably of these lines of "The Elixir": "A servant with this clause / Makes drudgerie divine: / Who sweeps a room, as for thy laws, / Makes that and th' action fine."

96.8 WE ARE THE PHOTOMETERS . . . TINFOIL In the middle 1840s either goldleaf or tinfoil was an essential element in an electrometer. Cf. Coleridge's *Aids to Reflection* (*Complete Works*, ed. Shedd, I, 414): "The electrometer will instantly show an electricity in the gold-leaf, similar to that of the cylinder which had been brought into contact with it."

97.1 "I WAS AS A GEM . . . REVEALED" On p. 51 of Emerson's manuscript notebook numbered "L" and entitled "Camadeva" the following lines appear: "I was as a treasure concealed; / then I loved that I might be known. / Koran." Immediately below are the steps by which Emerson turned them into a couplet: "I was as a gem concealed / <I burned with love & was revealed> / Me my burning <ray> love revealed" (angle brackets indicate cancellations). They do not come from *The Koran* but from *Practical Philosophy of the Muhammedan People . . . a Translation of the Akhlak-I-Jalaly . . .* (London, 1839). There the sentence is referred to as a text — "affection being the source of creation; as we learn from the text, I was as a . . ." — and appears in four places, pp. 92n, 145, 233, and 416, in slightly varying versions. What Emerson copied into his notebook is in the footnote on p. 92.

99.14 THE HEYDAY OF THE BLOOD Cf. *Hamlet*, III, iv, 68–70: "You cannot call it love, for at your age / The hey-day in the blood is tame, it's humble, / And waits upon the judgment."

101.30 RISK SUCH AS MILTON DEPLORES . . . GREAT MEN See *The Doctrine and Discipline of Divorce*, ch. III, para. 2.

102.16 CREATED ALL THINGS NEW Cf. Revelation 21:5: "And he that sat upon the throne said, Behold, I make all things new. And he said unto me, Write."

102.28 IMAGES WRITTEN IN WATER Cf. Shakespeare, *Henry VIII*, IV, ii, 45–46: "Men's evil manners live in brass; their virtues / We write in water." Cf. also Keats's epitaph.

102.29 PLUTARCH SAID, "ENAMELLED IN FIRE" Cf. *Moralia*, "The Dialogue on Love," 16. Emerson's phrase resembles that of the seventeenth-century translation by John Phillips, most readily available in the edition of William W. Goodwin (Boston, 1870), IV, 280: "the imaginations of lovers, being as it were enamelled by fire, leave the images of things imprinted in the memory."

102.31 "THOU ART NOT GONE . . . THY LOVING HEART" John Donne, "Epithalamion," 202–203.

103.3 "ALL OTHER PLEASURES . . . PAINS" Quoted by Charles de Marguetel de Saint-Denys de Saint-Evremont (1610–1703) in the following context: "We may seriously say of [the Christian religion], what has been gallantly said of Love" (*The Works of Mr. de St. Evremont* [London, 1770], I, 398). Edward

Emerson noted (*W*, II, 409) that this was a "favorite line" of his father's. See *JMN*, III, 249, and PP.

103.20 "Fountain heads and pathless groves . . . feed upon" John Fletcher (probably in collaboration with Thomas Middleton), *The Nice Valour; or, The Passionate Mad-man*, Act III. This is part of the Madman's song in praise of melancholy, which begins "Hence, all you vain delights" and was surely one of the sources of "Il Penseroso." Emerson seems to have been quoting from memory rather than from his copy of the 1647 First Folio of Beaumont and Fletcher, but he was essentially accurate except for "safely" in line 23, which should have been "warmly," and "passing" in line 24, which should have been "parting."

104.28 the flowering of virtue Cf. Plutarch, *Moralia*, "The Dialogue on Love," 21, and especially the translation by John Phillips in the Goodwin edition, IV, 300: "To be sure they say that beauty is the 'flower of virtue.'" See also *JMN*, III, 147, and PP.

105.4 Jean Paul Richter . . . shall not find" One of the "scraps" that Emerson found "in Chorley's Mrs Hemans" (*JMN*, V, 346–347). The sentence was quoted by Felicia Hemans in a letter to an unidentified correspondent which was published in Henry F. Chorley's *Memorials of Mrs. Hemans* (London, 1836), I, 282.

105.17 Landor inquires . . . existence" Cf. in "Duke de Richelieu, Sir Fire Coats, and Lady Glengrin," *Imaginary Conversations* (London, 1828), III, 206, the speech of the Sailor: "poetry, the knowledge of which, like other most important truths, seems to be reserved for a purer state of sensation and existence." See *JMN*, V, 43.

105.27 "If I love you, what is that to you?" In *Wilhelm Meisters Lehrjahre* Philine says to Wilhelm, "Und wenn ich dich lieb habe, was geht's dich an?" (*Goethes Sämtliche Werke*, XVII, 273). Emerson might also have found the "saying," thus translated, in Sarah Austin's *Characteristics of Goethe . . .*, 3 vols. (London, 1833), II, 195. See *CEC*, pp. 97–98, and PP.

105.36 but shadows of real things Cf. Plato's *Phaedrus*, esp. 246–249, and *Republic*, VII, 514–517.

106.34 Plato, Plutarch . . . and Milton In "platonic notions," Thomas Roscoe wrote in *Lives of Eminent Persons* (London, 1833), p. 58, Michaelangelo as poet "trod in the path of Dante and Petrarch, his great masters." For Plutarch on these notions see *Moralia*, "The Dialogue on Love," 19; for

Apuleius, *De Dogmate Platonis*, bk. II; for Milton, *Paradise Lost*, VIII, 588–594.

107.31 "HER PURE AND ELOQUENT BLOOD . . . BODY THOUGHT" See Donne's "The Second Anniversarie," lines 244–246, in *Of the Progress of the Soule.*

107.34 ROMEO . . . INTO LITTLE STARS Cf. *Romeo and Juliet*, III, ii, 22.

109.1 "THE PERSON . . . TASTE OF ALL IN IT" See Abraham Cowley's "Resolved to be Beloved," lines 23–24, in *The Mistress.*

109.25 DECK THE NUPTIAL BOWER See *Paradise Lost*, VIII, 510–511: "To the nuptial bower / I led her blushing like the morn," and IV, 708–710: "Here in close recess / With flowers, garlands, and sweet-smelling herbs / Espo)uséd Eve decked first her nuptial bed."

113.8 THE HEART KNOWETH Cf. Proverbs 14:10: "The heart knoweth his own bitterness."

115.5 STRANGERS AND PILGRIMS Cf. Hebrews 11:13–14: "and confessed that they were strangers and pilgrims on the earth. For they that say such things declare plainly that they seek a country."

115.23 "CRUSH THE SWEET POISON OF MISUSED WINE" Cf. *Comus*, line 47.

116.5 DOUBT Used here in its old sense of "suspect" or "fear."

116.18 AN EGYPTIAN SKULL AT OUR BANQUET Cf. Plutarch, *Moralia*, "The Dinner of the Seven Wise Men," 2: "the skeleton which in Egypt they are wont, with fair reason, to bring in and expose at their parties, urging the guests to remember that what it is now, they soon shall be."

117.19 COBWEB, AND NOT CLOTH Cf. Ben Jonson, *The Sad Shepherd*, III, v, 9–11: "But you must wait occasions, and obey them; / Sail in an Egg shell, make a Straw your Mast, / A Cobweb all your Cloth, and pass unseen." See *JMN*, IV, 13, and PP.

118.12 "THE VALIANT WARRIOR . . . FOR WHICH HE TOILED" Cf. Shakespeare, *Sonnets*, XXV, 9–12: "valiant" should have been "painful."

118.20 NATURLANGSAMKEIT This rare word occurs among Goethe's "nachgelassene Werke" in *Zur Farbenlehre*: "Stationäre Völker behandeln ihre Technik mit Religion. . . . Sie gehen mit einer Art von Naturlangsamkeit zu Werke" (*Goethes Sämtliche Werke*, XL, 126). In 1838 Emerson had written to William Henry Furness: "I have just read with great satisfaction . . . the Historical part of Goethe's Farbenlehre" (*Records of a Lifelong Friendship*, ed. H. H. Furness [Boston, Houghton Mifflin, 1910], p. 8). And in 1839 he had written to Margaret Fuller: "We are strangely impatient of the secular crystallizations of nature in Cavern or in Man, of that which Goethe distinguishes by the grand word *Naturlangsamkeit*" (*L*, II, 192).

119.34 I KNEW A MAN . . . DID CERTAINLY SHOW   Jones Very, undoubtedly, of whom Emerson wrote in a letter to Elizabeth Peabody late in 1838: "I wish the whole world were as mad as he. . . . If it shall prove that his peculiarities are fixed, it can never alter the value of the truth & illumination he communicates, if you deal with him with perfect sincerity" (*L*, II, 171).

120.33 "I OFFER MYSELF . . . MOST DEVOTED"   Cf. Montaigne, "A Consideration upon Cicero," *Essays*, I, xxxix; the quotation is, approximately, from the Cotton translation (London, 1693), I, 399.   In the early summer of 1840 Emerson had written in his journal: "I must find the fine things my old Montaigne said so little Parisian, so English about his familiars to balance my fine jaunty gauze stuffs on Friendship — 'I offer myself poorly but proudly to those whose I effectually am &c.'   Here it is . . . 'I offer myself faintly & bluntly' " (*JMN*, VII, 378).

123.3 VERY   Used here in its old sense of "truly."

124.8 TO MY FRIEND I WRITE A LETTER . . . RECEIVE   This passage, somewhat shortened, was used by Charles Eliot Norton as an epigraph to his edition of *The Correspondence of Thomas Carlyle and Ralph Waldo Emerson*, 2 vols. (Boston, 1883), I, title page.

124.19 CRIMEN QUOS INQUINAT, AEQUAT   Cf. Lucan, *Pharsalia* (or *The Civil War*), V, 290: "facinus, quos inquinat, aequat"; ("crime levels those whom it pollutes").   See *JMN*, VI, 55, and PP.

135.5 DR. JOHNSON IS REPORTED . . . WHIP HIM"   Cf. Boswell's *Life of Johnson* for March 31, 1778 (ed. George Birkbeck Hill, rev. and enlarged by L. F. Powell [Oxford, The Clarendon Press, 1934], III, 228), where Johnson is reported to have said "check" rather than "whip."

135.9 THE BYWORD, "NO MISTAKE"   The *OED* records "and no mistake" as a colloquial synonym for "undoubtedly" in a manuscript of 1818 ("He is the real thing and no mistake"), but has no recorded appearance in print before 1837.   According to John S. Farmer's *Americanisms — Old and New* (London, 1889), p. 368, the byword was much used in the United States: "At one time it rounded off almost every phrase."

135.19 "AFTERNOON MEN" The *OED* defines "afternoon man" as "tippler" and cites a passage in Burton's *Anatomy of Melancholy* ("Beroaldus will have drunkards, afternoon men, and such as more than ordinarily delight in drink, to be mad") which seems to support that definition. Another sentence, however, a few pages further on in *The Anatomy*, suggests a less limited meaning and one closer to Emerson's: "they are giddy-heads, afternoon men" (Robert Burton, *The Anatomy of Melancholy*, ed. Floyd Dell and Paul Jordan-Smith [New York, Farrar and Rinehart, 1927], pp. 62, 99). Emerson generally used the word to suggest fecklessness, procrastination, or some other manifestation of imprudence, as in *JMN*, V, 375: "I have among my kinsmen a man to whom more than any one I have known I may apply the phrase 'an afternoon man.' He rolls and riots in delays." See PP.

135.23 THE LAST GRAND DUKE OF WEIMAR . . . ALL THE FIGURES" Part of a letter from *Briefe an Johann Heinrich Merck von Göthe, Herder, Wieland und andern bedeutenden Zeitgenossen* (Darmstadt, 1835), pp. 362–363, which Emerson had translated and entered in his journal in April 1837 (*JMN*, V, 300–301). The Grand Duke was Karl August, Grossherzog von Sachsen-Weimar, Goethe's patron, who had died in 1828 and had been succeeded by his son Karl Friedrich. Merck (1741–1791) was a poet and critic who had published Goethe's *Götz von Berlichingen* at his own expense.

137.5 WISH TO REAP WHERE HE HAD NOT SOWED Cf. Matthew 25:26–27: "His lord answered and said unto him, Thou wicked and slothful servant, thou knewest that I reap where I sowed not . . . Thou oughtest therefore to have put my money to the exchangers, and then at my coming I should have received mine own with usury." See also below, note to 138.36.

137.8 ON HIM WHO SCORNED THE WORLD . . . REVENGE Emerson was probably thinking of Byron's scornful lines in *Childe Harold*, III, 113, 1–2: "I have not loved the World nor the World me; / I have not flattered its rank breath"; and of the hostility with which the fashionable world reacted to his separation from Lady Byron.

137.9 DESPISETH SMALL THINGS . . . LITTLE Cf. Ecclesiasticus 9:1. Emerson found the verse in Jeremy Taylor's *The Rule and Exercises of Holy Dying*, ch. II, sec. ii, where it concludes a paragraph on hindering "the journey of little sins into a heap." See PP.

137.10 GOETHE'S TASSO . . . LAW In *Torquato Tasso* the poet is passionate, rash, and madly suspicious; his antagonist, Antonio Montecatino, State Secretary to the Duke of Ferrara, is calm, prudent, and mature. In the final speech of the play Tasso exclaims, "O edler Mann! Du stehest fest und still, /

Ich scheine nur die sturmbewegte Welle" (*Goethes Sämtliche Werke*, XII, 220).

137.21 "DISCOMFORTABLE COUSIN"   This is Richard II's chiding exclamation to Aumerle, who has reminded him that Bolingbroke "Grows strong and great in substance and in friends" (*Richard II*, III, ii, 125).   See *EL*, II, 316.

137.30 PITIFUL DRIVELLERS . . . GLORIFIED SEERS   See, for example, the description of "the bazaars of the opium-eaters" in N. P. Willis's *Pencillings by the Way* (London, 1835), II, 260–265.   Emerson's first version of this sentence, in a journal entry of 1836, began: "I am like those opium-eaters of Constantinople" (*JMN*, V, 173).   See also PP.

138.7 MAKE THE NIGHT, NIGHT, AND THE DAY, DAY   In a journal of 1832 Emerson listed this among "Spanish Proverbs"; he had found it in Knox's *Elegant Extracts . . . in Prose*, II, 1036.   See *JMN*, IV, 17, and PP.

138.15 TO STICK A TREE . . . WHILST HE SLEEPS   Cf. the deathbed admonition of the Laird of Dumbiedikes to his son (*The Heart of Midlothian*, ch. VIII): "Jock, when ye hae naething else to do, ye may be aye sticking in a tree; it will be growing, Jock, when ye're sleeping."   Emerson entered a somewhat altered version of this speech in his journal in 1831 (*JMN*, III, 314) and used it in his 1838 lecture "Prudence" (*EL*, II, 317).

138.36 WHAT HE SOWS, HE REAPS   Cf. Galatians 6:7: "Be not deceived; God is not mocked: for whatsoever a man soweth, that shall he also reap."

140.1 "IN BATTLES, THE EYE IS FIRST OVERCOME"   Cf. Tacitus, *Germania*, 43.   See *JMN*, V, 439, and PP.

141.21 THESE OLD SHOES ARE EASY TO THE FEET   In his journal of 1832 Emerson wrote: "King James liked old friends best, as he said his old shoes were easiest to his feet," a paraphrase of two sentences from John Selden's *Table Talk* (ed. Edward Arber [London, 1869], p. 51).   See *JMN*, IV, 19; VI, 161.   By 1838 in the lecture "Prudence" (*EL*, II, 321) the sentence had assumed its present form.

141.24 LIFE WOULD BE DEARER . . . LOSE THEIR FLAVOR   This passage was preceded in the journal entry for July 27, 1837, by the sentence: "A letter today from Carlyle rejoiced me" (*JMN*, V, 346).   Carlyle had written: "Almost a month ago there went a copy of a Book called *French Revolution* with your address on it over to Red-Lion Square" (*CEC*, p. 164).

143.1 "PARADISE IS UNDER THE SHADOW OF SWORDS." MAHOMET   In Simon Ockley's *The History of the Saracens* (2 vols. [London, 1718]), Abdo'llah Ebn

Jaafar is quoted as saying, "The Apostle of God has said, That Paradise is under the Shadow of Swords" (I, 164). See *JMN*, VI, 388, and PP.

145.5 RODRIGO, PEDRO, OR VALERIO . . . A GENTLEMAN Characters with these and similar names abound in the plays of Beaumont and Fletcher. In *The Coxcomb*, for example, there are gentlemen named Ricardo, Pedro, and Valerio; in *The Pilgrim*, the last scene of which might have been in Emerson's memory, the main action involves Roderigo, Pedro, and the Governor.

145.15 SOPHOCLES Sophocles, Duke of Athens, is the main character in "The Triumph of Honour," the first of *Four Plays, or Moral Representations, in One*. It is "The Triumph of Honour" which Emerson summarizes and quotes from — with two minor omissions — on pp. 145–147.

147.11 SCOTT WILL SOMETIMES . . . BURLEY See above, note to 84.2

147.16 IN THE HARLEIAN MISCELLANIES . . . TO BE READ *The Harleian Miscellany*, ed. J. Malham, 12 vols. (London, 1808–1811), IV, 183–200. On November 14, 1839, Emerson wrote to Margaret Fuller: "I have read an admirable tract in the Harleian Miscellany an account of the Battle of Lutzen & the death of Gustavus. It is as fine as Plutarch" (*L*, II, 235).

147.18 SIMON OCKLEY'S HISTORY . . . ABHORRENCE Simon Ockley, B.D. (1678–1720), was "Professor of Arabick in the University of Cambridge." The following sentence is characteristic of the partisan tone of his preface, though not of his history: "Mahomet and his successors soon rooted out Idolatry, and united those jarring Tribes in the Profession of that new Superstition, which he pretended to have received by Inspiration from God" (*The History of the Saracens* [London, 1718], I, xii-xiii).

147.31 LIFE IS A FESTIVAL ONLY TO THE WISE Cf. the saying of Diogenes recorded in Plutarch's *Moralia*, "On Tranquillity of Mind," 20: "Does not a good man consider every day a festival?" See *JMN*, V, 119.

148.1 A LOCKJAW . . . THAT MAKES HIM EAT GRASS Tetanus does sometimes produce spasmodic contractions so severe that the victim is doubled up backward, and in late stages of human rabies breathing becomes so difficult that it sounds like barking. For Nebuchadnezzar's madness and eating of grass, see Daniel 4:33.

149.25 HEROISM . . . IS ALMOST ASHAMED OF ITS BODY A paraphrase of the first sentence of Porphyry's life of Plotinus. See *JMN*, III, 251, and PP.

149.37 "INDEED, THESE HUMBLE CONSIDERATIONS . . . ONE OTHER FOR USE"
Cf. *Henry IV, Part II*, II, ii. 13–19. This is an abridgment of Hal's speech
to Poins.

150.10 GOD . . . WILL PROVIDE Cf. Genesis 22:7–8: "And Abraham said,
My son, God will provide himself a lamb for a burnt offering."

150.11 IBN HAUKAL . . . OTHER COUNTRY" Cf. Ebn Haukal, *Oriental Geography*, trans. Sir William Ouseley (London, 1800), pp. 234–235. Ebn Haukal,
of whom almost nothing is known, published his book in 977. See *JMN*, VI,
322, and PP.

151.2 JOHN ELIOT . . . MADE BEFORE IT" William Allen, *An American Biographical and Historical Dictionary* (Boston, 1832), p. 371. See *JMN*, V,
155n, and PP.

151.6 TEMPERANCE OF KING DAVID . . . PERIL OF THEIR LIVES See I Chronicles
11:17–19: "Shall I drink the blood of these men that have put their lives in
jeopardy?"

151.9 IT IS TOLD OF BRUTUS . . . BUT A SHADE" See the *Roman History*
of Dio Cassius, bk. xlvii, para. 49, where Brutus is said to have quoted a
speech of Hercules. There is no evidence that the lines are by Euripides: in
Nauck's *Fragmenta Tragicorum Graecorum*, p. 910, they appear among the
anonymous fragments. Presumably Emerson was thinking of the *Hercules
Furens* of Euripides.

151.23 SCIPIO, CHARGED WITH PECULATION . . . BEFORE THE TRIBUNES Livy,
bk. xxxviii, para. 55. Emerson might also have found the story in Montaigne's "Of Conscience," para. 6 (*Essays*, bk. II, ch. v). See *EL*, II, 334.

151.26 SOCRATES' CONDEMNATION . . . DURING HIS LIFE See Plato, "Apology,"
36. The Prytaneum was the civic center of Athens, where distinguished citizens were sometimes maintained as guests of the state. Socrates proposes —
seriously, he says — that he be condemned to such maintenance rather than
to the death which Meletus has demanded.

151.27 SIR THOMAS MORE'S PLAYFULNESS AT THE SCAFFOLD After More had
laid his head on the block, he moved his beard, saying that it at least had
not committed treason. For many years Emerson had linked the names of
Socrates and More because of "their . . . renowned deaths": see *JMN*, IV,
356, and V, 10.

151.28 BEAUMONT AND FLETCHER'S "SEA VOYAGE," . . . SCORN YE" Act IV,
scene iii.

152.6 BLUE-LAWS   A term made notorious by the Reverend Samuel Peters in his *General History of Connecticut* (London, 1781), which listed forty-five laws of extraordinary ferocity or absurdity — "Adultery shall be punished with death. . . . Every male shall have his hair cut round according to a cap" — and attributed them especially to the colony of New Haven, with the result that Connecticut suffered for many years under the nickname of "the Blue Law State."   The affair was fully discussed by Walter F. Prince in "An Examination of Peters's 'Blue Laws,'" *Annual Report of the American Historical Association for the Year 1898* (Washington, 1899), pp. 97–138.

152.10 THE POWER OF A ROMANCE . . . UNDER HIS BENCH AT SCHOOL   Cf. this sentence from the journal of 1836: "The four College years & the three years of Divinity have not yielded me so many grand facts as some idle books under the bench at Latin School" (*JMN*, V, 226).

152.29 SYRIAN   Something of the connotation this word had for Emerson appears in a passage of a letter he wrote from Nantasket Beach in July 1841: "the lassitude of this Syrian summer . . . more and more draws the cords of Will out of my thought and leaves me nothing but perpetual observation, perpetual acquiescence and perpetual thankfulness" (*Letters from Ralph Waldo Emerson to a Friend*, ed. Charles Eliot Norton [Boston, 1899], p. 35).

154.10 "ALWAYS DO WHAT YOU ARE AFRAID TO DO"   An injunction of Mary Moody Emerson, Emerson's aunt.   See his biographical sketch of her in *W*, X, 405–406.

154.12 THE CALMNESS OF PHOCION . . . FROM THE BATTLE   Recounted in Plutarch's "Life of Phocion," sec. XXIII, and Montaigne, *Essays*, bk. III, ch. 2, para. 18.   See *JMN*, IV, 351, and PP.

155.7 IT IS BUT THE OTHER DAY, THAT THE BRAVE LOVEJOY . . . NOT TO LIVE   It was on November 7, 1837, eleven weeks before Emerson gave his Boston lecture entitled "Heroism," that Elijah Lovejoy was murdered by a pro-slavery mob in Alton, Illinois.   See *JMN*, V, 437, and *EL*, II, 327.

155.28 "LET THEM RAVE . . . IN THY GRAVE"   Cf. Tennyson's "A Dirge" of *Poems, Chiefly Lyrical* (1830), lines 4 and 6.   When Emerson entered this passage in his journal in 1834, shortly after he had learned of the death of his brother Edward in Puerto Rico, he treated only the first line as a quotation; the second seemed to be, as it is, a paraphrase.   See *JMN*, IV, 325.

157.1 "BUT SOULS . . . IN BLEST ETERNITY"   These are the opening lines of stanza 19, canto II, of Henry More's "Psychozoia, or, the life of the Soul," in *Philosophical Poems* (Cambridge, 1647).   Emerson entitled them "Euthanasia" when he included them in his anthology *Parnassus*.

161.32 "GOD COMES TO SEE US WITHOUT BELL" Cf. Vicesimus Knox, *Elegant Extracts*, II, 1035, where it appears among "Old Spanish Proverbs." See *JMN*, IV, 16.

162.14 "CAN CROWD ETERNITY . . . TO ETERNITY" From a speech by Lucifer in Byron's *Cain*, I, i, 536–537. Line 535 reads: "With us acts are exempt from time, and we . . ." See *JMN*, VII, 140.

163.7 THE WIND SHALL BLOW THEM NONE KNOWS WHITHER Cf. John 3:8: "The wind bloweth where it listeth, and thou hearest the sound thereof, but canst not tell whence it cometh, and whither it goeth"; and Isaiah 41:16: "and the wind shall carry them away."

163.29 ZENO AND ARRIAN Presumably Emerson meant Zeno the Stoic rather than Zeno the Eleatic and was thinking of Arrian as disciple of Epictetus rather than as historian; in his early journals he had listed both writers among the Stoics (*JMN*, I, 226) and had twice coupled their names (*JMN*, I, 258, 346).

166.10 "IT IS NO PROOF . . . INTELLIGENCE" This sentence is a paraphrase of Swedenborg by Caleb Reed which appeared in "The Nature and Character of True Wisdom and Intelligence," *The New Jerusalem Magazine*, 3 (January 1830), 151. For the original Swedenborg passage see *The Doctrine of the New Jerusalem concerning the Sacred Scripture* (Boston, 1795), p. 147 (sec. 91). See *JMN*, VI, 342.

167.14 "BLASTED WITH EXCESS OF LIGHT" A reference to Milton in Gray's "Progress of Poesy," line 101.

167.15 THE TRANCES OF SOCRATES . . . SWEDENBORG For an account of what might be called a trance of Socrates see the speech of Alcibiades in *Symposium*, 220. Plotinus, in Thomas Taylor's translation, *Select Works of Plotinus* (London, 1817), says that God "is one alone" (p. 272) and that "beyond being there is *the one*" (p. 279). Taylor, in his introduction to the *Select Works* (pp. xv, lvii–lxix), quotes Porphyry on his own and Plotinus' vision of and union with God. The title page of Jakob Böhme's *Aurora* (London, 1656), which Emerson copied into his journal, says that the dawn is "the root or mother of Philosophy, Astrology & Theology" (*JMN*, V, 75). All the enthusiasts here mentioned were considered in the same order, and more extensively, by Emerson in his lecture "Religion" (*EL*, II, 91–92).

167.22 THE OPENING OF THE INTERNAL SENSE OF THE WORD . . . CHURCH The anonymous author of the Preface to Swedenborg's *The Doctrine of the New Jerusalem concerning the Sacred Scripture* (Boston, 1795) says that from "the following treatise of our illuminated author" the reader may learn "the *internal* or *spiritual sense* of the scriptures" (p. v), and Swedenborg writes: "it hath pleased the Lord to reveal to me the internal sense" (p. 12).

172.24 THE GRAND TURK No seventeenth-century sultan of Turkey is likely to have attracted European visitors. If Emerson had in mind a particular Grand Turk, he probably meant Suleiman the Magnificent, whose reign (1520–1566) was marked by a flowering of poetry and architecture, or perhaps Ahmed III, who reigned from 1703 till 1736 and encouraged tulip gardening and lyric poetry.

172.34 THEIR "HIGHEST PRAISING . . . PRAISING" Cf. *Areopagitica*, para. 4. See *EL*, III, 285.

174.6 'GO INTO HIS CLOSET AND SHUT THE DOOR' Cf. Matthew 6:6: "when thou prayest, enter into thy closet, and when thou hast shut thy door, pray to thy Father which is in secret."

175.14 "ITS BEAUTY IS IMMENSE" In the introduction to Taylor's translation of *Select Works of Plotinus* this sentence from Plotinus' "On Beauty" appears: "All the Gods are venerable and beautiful, their beauty is immense" (p. lxxix). In *JMN*, V, 385, the sentence "The beauty of the Soul is immense" appears without quotation marks.

175.19 OF SHREDS AND PATCHES *Hamlet*, III, iv, 102.

175.23 THE WHOLE FUTURE . . . HEART In his notebook "Encyclopedia" Emerson entered the sentence "The whole future is in the bottom of the heart" under the heading "My Proverbs" (*JMN*, VI, 197). See PP.

179.4 ST. AUGUSTINE . . . CIRCUMFERENCE NOWHERE Saint Augustine wrote at length about the nature of God and about circles, but he seems not to have used this metaphor. Emerson read it in John Norris, *An Essay Towards the Theory of the Ideal or Intelligible World*, 2 vols. (London, 1701–1704), I, 389, where it refers not to God but to Truth, "whose Center is every where and whose Circumference is no where." He copied it into his journal immediately before some "admirable passages" which Norris had "quoted from St. Augustine" about the city of God (*JMN*, V, 57) and was perhaps later misled by the juxtaposition. Or perhaps he remembered Bonaventure's version in *Itinerarium Mentis ad Deum*, ch. V, para. 8: "est sphaera intelligibilis, cujus centrum est ubique, et circumferentia nusquam" and attributed it to the wrong saint. Surely he knew it also from Browne's *Religio Medici*, I, sec. x, where it is attributed to Hermes Trismegistus; and from Coleridge's *Aids to Reflection*, where it appears without attribution or quotation marks and immediately after the words of Jesus, "Before Abraham was, I am," as an example of a paradox incomprehensible to the Understanding (*Complete Works*, ed. Shedd, I, 252). In Lorenz Oken's *Elements of Physiophilosophy* (London, 1847), p. 32, it has become simply a "profound saying." The Swiss intellectual historian Georges Poulet, who seems to have read every circular philosopher and poet except Emerson, cites in *The Metamorphoses of the Circle* (Baltimore, Johns Hopkins Press, 1966) a score of medieval, renaissance, and baroque users of the metaphor, but none is earlier than the twelfth century and none attributes it to Augustine. Probably the safest attribution is that of the fourteenth-century mystic Heinrich Suso: "Es sagt ein weiser Meister" (Poulet, p. 352).

179.12 ANOTHER DAWN RISEN ON MID-NOON   Cf. *Paradise Lost*, V, 308–311: "Haste hither, Eve, and, worth thy sight, behold / Eastward among those trees what glorious Shape / Comes this way moving; seems another morn / Risen on mid-noon."

182.19 RAISE HIMSELF ABOVE HIMSELF . . . A MAN'S RELATIONS   Cf. Samuel Daniel's Epistle "To the Lady Margaret, Countess of Cumberland," lines 98 and 99: "unless above himself he can / Erect himself, how poor a thing is man!" The passage was a favorite with Coleridge, who had quoted it twice in *Aids to Reflection* (*Complete Works*, ed. Shedd, I, 120 and 181) in "Aphorisms" dealing with "Self-Superintendence" and the striving of "all things . . . to ascend" and had used it as the epigraph to Essay XIV of *The Friend* (II, 96). See *JMN*, VI, 103, and PP.

184.13 THE SPIRIT THEY PARTAKE . . . THE CLOVEN FLAME   Cf. Acts 2:1–4. See above, note to 47.31.

185.36 THAT BRAVE TEXT OF PAUL'S . . . ALL IN ALL"   Cf. I Corinthians 15:28.

187.33 "FORGIVE HIS CRIMES . . . CONVERTS TO THE RIGHT"   Cf. Edward Young, *The Complaint; or, Night Thoughts*, IX, 2316–2317. See *JMN*, III, 274, and PP.

188.10 LIVELY STONES . . . THE TRUE GOD   Cf. I Peter 2:5: "Ye also, as lively stones, are built up a spiritual house, an holy priesthood, to offer up spiritual sacrifices, acceptable to God by Jesus Christ."

188.17 NOR HELL ITSELF WITHOUT ITS EXTREME SATISFACTIONS   In a journal entry of 1840 Emerson attributed this odd belief to Swedenborg: "The good Swedenborg was aware, I believe . . . that the hells were not without their extreme satisfactions" (*JMN*, VII, 521). Swedenborg did write that "the delights of every one's life after death are turned into corresponding delights," but the satisfactions of his hells, though extreme, were not as "saccharine" as Emerson remembered them: "Those who have passed life in mere pleasures . . . in the other life love excrementitious things and privies, which to them are objects of delight, because such pleasures are spiritual filth" (Emanuel Swedenborg, *Concerning Heaven and Its Wonders and Concerning Hell* [Boston, 1837], pp. 328–329).

190.18 NOTHING GREAT WAS EVER ACHIEVED WITHOUT ENTHUSIASM   See Coleridge's *The Stateman's Manual*, para. 18 (*Complete Works*, ed. Shedd, I, 433): "histories incomparably more authentic than Mr. Hume's . . . confirm by irrefragable evidence the aphorism of ancient wisdom, that nothing great was ever achieved without enthusiasm.   For what is enthusiasm but the oblivion and swallowing up of self in an object dearer than self, or in an idea more vivid?"   See also *JMN*, V, 15, where Emerson enclosed the sentence in quotation marks.

190.22 "A MAN," SAID OLIVER CROMWELL . . . WHITHER HE IS GOING"   According to Bishop William Warburton, who annotated Clarendon's *History of the Rebellion and Civil Wars in England*, Cromwell made this remark to "Bellievre, the French minister."   See the Boston edition of 1827, which Emerson owned, bk. VIII, p. 1831.   See also *JMN*, VI, 93, and PP.

193.23 HERACLITUS . . . FORWARD IN A STRAIGHT LINE   No such statement, or metaphor, appears among the Fragments of Heraclitus (G. S. Kirk, *Heraclitus: The Cosmic Fragments* [Cambridge, Cambridge University Press, 1962]) or in the chapter on Heraclitus in Heinrich Ritter's *The History of Ancient Philosophy*, 2 vols. (London, 1838), from which Emerson drew most of his Heraclitan quotations (see *JMN*, VI, 378–380).   Ritter did, however, write that Heraclitus "accounted for the ignorance and incapacity of the drunkard, by his having a moist soul; whereas the dry soul is the wisest and best" (I, 258); and in the lecture from which this paragraph is drawn (*EL*, II, 249) Emerson wrote: "Heraclitus said, 'Dry light makes the best souls,' looking upon the affections as moist and colored mists."   Perhaps Emerson later attributed his own metaphor to Heraclitus.   Perhaps he had in mind a passage in Bacon's *Advancement of Learning* (bk. I, ch. i, para. 3) which says that the *"Lumen siccum"* of Heraclitus "becometh *lumen madidum*, or *maceratum*, being steeped and infused in the humours of the affections."

195.16 TAKE NO THOUGHT FOR THE MORROW   Matthew 6:34.

196.29 NO MAN CAN SEE GOD FACE TO FACE AND LIVE   Cf. Exodus 33:17–20: "And the Lord said unto Moses . . . Thou canst not see my face: for there shall no man see me, and live."

197.7 THE LAW OF UNDULATION For an earlier, fuller statement of this "law" see "The American Scholar" in *CW*, I, 61.10. See also *JMN*, IV, 87, and V, 189.

198.18 THE HUNDRED VOLUMES OF THE UNIVERSAL HISTORY Johannes von Müller's *Universal History*, which Emerson owned, had only four volumes; but he had read about a new French compilation called *Panthéon Littéraire*, which was a "Collection universelle des Chefs-d'oeuvre de l'Esprit humaine" and was expected "to consist of 100 thick volumes" (*Foreign Quarterly Review*, 17 [July 1836], 269; *JMN*, XII, 83). By 1845, when *Panthéon Littéraire* was complete, it consisted of 135 volumes.

199.7 IN OUR HAPPY HOURS . . . ADEQUATE RHYME The journal version of this passage was "when I walk in Walden wood as on 4 July I seem to myself an inexhaustible poet, if only I could once break thro' the fence of silence, & vent myself in adequate rhyme" (*JMN*, VII, 228).

201.8 WHEN WE ARE YOUNG . . . OUR ENCYCLOPEDIA An autobiographical sentence. One of Emerson's most important notebooks, which he used from 1824 to 1836, was in fact called "Encyclopedia" (*JMN*, VI, 115–234).

202.19 A CANDIDATE FOR TRUTH This is an allusion to — or, rather, what Emerson called a "lustre" from — Francis Bacon. In 1824, probably, Emerson copied into his "Encyclopedia" this abridgment of a sentence from *The Advancement of Learning*: "Silence is the candidate for truth" and later in lectures made the final phrase his own (*JMN*, VI, 121, and PP). Bacon's sentence appears in bk. VI, ch. iii, as one of the "Examples of Antitheta" under the heading "Loquacity." See the Bohn edition of *The Physical and Metaphysical Works of Lord Bacon* (London, 1858), I, 256.

202.30 WHEN SOCRATES SPEAKS . . . DO NOT SPEAK See Plato's *Lysis*, esp. 211.

202.37 LET US BE SILENT, FOR SO ARE THE GODS Cf. Plutarch, *Moralia*, "Concerning Talkativeness," 8: "in speaking we have men as teachers, but in keeping silent we have gods."

203.5 LEAVE FATHER . . . RECEIVES MORE Cf. Matthew 19:28–29: "every one that hath forsaken houses, or brethren, or sisters, or father, or mother, or wife, or children, or lands, for my name's sake, shall receive an hundredfold, and shall inherit everlasting life."

203.11 HEGEL OR HIS INTERPRETER COUSIN In Heidelberg in 1817 Victor Cousin, a young teacher of philosophy and a follower of Kant and Schelling, "accidentally and without seeking it met with Hegel," who was not at that time widely known. "From our first conversation," Cousin wrote in *Fragments Philosophiques*, "I divined what he was, I comprehended his whole reach, I felt that I was in the presence of a superior man; and when I continued my journey from Heidelberg into other parts of Germany, I proclaimed him wherever I went, I prophesied him, as it were" (*Philosophical Miscellanies . . .* , trans. George Ripley, 2 vols. [Boston, 1838], I, 86, in *Specimens of Foreign Standard Literature*). The Hegelian element in Cousin's Eclecticism was most apparent in his philosophy of history, which Emerson knew from his *Introduction to the History of Philosophy*, trans. Henning Gotfried Linberg (Boston, 1832).

203.14 WRESTLE WITH THEM . . . UNTIL THEIR BLESSING BE WON   Cf. Genesis 32:24–29, esp. 26: "And he said, I will not let thee go, except thou bless me."

204.9 "THE CHERUBIM KNOW MOST; THE SERAPHIM LOVE MOST"   The first statement of this distinction was made in the fifth or the sixth century by Dionysius the Pseudo-Areopagite, whose *Concerning the Celestial Hierarchy* became the foundation of medieval angelology. Emerson might have encountered it almost anywhere in the patristic writings, in the *Summa Theologica* of Aquinas, for example: "the Cherubim have the excellence of science and the Seraphim the excellence of ardor" (Question 108, Article 5, *Basic Writings of Saint Thomas Aquinas* [New York, Random House, 1945], I, 1004). But he is certain to have seen it in Bacon's *Advancement of Learning* (bk. I, ch. vi, para. 3): "the first place or degree is given to the angels of love, which are termed seraphim; the second to the angels of light, which are termed cherubim." The quoted version apparently comes from a speech by Adah in Byron's *Cain*, I, i, 420–421: "I have heard it said, / The Seraphs *love most* — Cherubim *know most*."

204.13 TRISMEGISTI   As Emerson used this variation on a rare word, it did not refer only to the Greco-Egyptian and Neoplatonic mystics who considered themselves followers of Hermes (i.e., Thoth) Trismegistus (thrice-great), but could include, in addition to the "band of grandees" listed seven lines below, such "spiritual lords" as Moses, Confucius, Jesus, and Spinoza. See *JMN*, VII, 37.

204.19 "PERSUASION IS IN SOUL, BUT NECESSITY IS IN INTELLECT"   Cf. "Enneades" in *Select Works of Plotinus*, trans. Taylor, p. 417. See *JMN*, VII, 413.

205.4 THE HISSING AND UNMUSICAL DIALECTS OF MEN   Cf. the metamorphosis of the fallen angels in Book X of *Paradise Lost*, lines 504–577: "On all sides from innumerable tongues / A dismal universal hiss."

211.27 I SHOULD THINK FIRE . . . WATER, AND EARTH   The opening of Emerson's lecture "Water" (*EL*, I, 50) makes it clear that in this sentence he is alluding to the first line of the first of Pindar's *Olympian Odes*: "Water is best."   See also PP.

211.36 A DOG, DRAWN BY A MASTER . . . THE FRESCOES OF ANGELO   In Emerson's journal this sentence reads: "A dog drawn by Landseer or a litter of pigs satisfies & is a reality not less than the Transfiguration" (*JMN*, VII, 200).

212.27 "WHEN I HAVE BEEN READING HOMER, ALL MEN LOOK LIKE GIANTS" The writer, or speaker, of this sentence is unidentified.

214.21 BARBARIC PEARL AND GOLD   Milton, *Paradise Lost,* II, 1–5: "High on a throne of royal state, which far / Outshone the wealth of Ormus and of Ind / Or where the gorgeous East with richest hand / Show'rs on her kings barbaric pearl and gold, / Satan exalted sat."

214.37 SACCHI   On April 15, 1833, Emerson had written in his journal: "Few pictures please me more than the Vision of St Romoaldo by Andrea Sacchi in the Vatican" (*JMN*, IV, 159).

214.37 "WHAT, OLD MOLE . . . IN THE EARTH SO FAST?"   Cf. *Hamlet*, I, v, 162.

216.22 NEWTON . . . "STONE DOLLS"   Cf. Joseph Spence, *Observations, Anecdotes and Characters of Books and Men* (Oxford, The Clarendon Press, 1966), I, 350: "Let him have but a stone doll and he's satisfied."   See *JMN*, V, 87, and PP.

218.31 THE BOAT AT ST. PETERSBURGH . . . ALONG THE LENA BY MAGNETISM "Lena" is perhaps a slip of the pen for "Neva," or perhaps a printer's misreading of Emerson's manuscript, but in all later editions the error went uncorrected.   "Magnetism" here means "electromagnetism."   After Faraday's theoretical publications of the early 1830s, European and American technologists turned eagerly to what the Potsdam physicist Moritz Hermann von Jacobi in an article of 1835 called "l'application de l'électromagnétisme au mouvement des machines" *(Allgemeine Deutsche Biographie).*   In 1836 the editor of the Philadelphia *Journal of the Franklin Institute* reported cautiously on a Belgian experiment: "A very successful trial of a locomotive impelled by magnetic force, is *said* to have been made by M. Lemaire of Brussels" (n.s., XVII, 365).   In 1837 Thomas Davenport, a learned blacksmith of Brandon, Vermont, applied for a patent on "an application of magnetism . . . for propelling machinery" (*ibid.*, XX, 340).   In the autumn of 1838 Jacobi, who had been called to a professorship in the Imperial Academy of Sciences in St. Petersburg, successfully conducted "experiments in navigation on the Neva, with a ten-oared shallop furnished with paddle-wheels, which were put into motion by an electromagnetic machine" (*The Selected Correspondence of Michael Faraday*, ed. L. Pearce Williams, 2 vols. [Cambridge, The University Press, 1971], I, 345).

News of Jacobi's triumph spread slowly even among European scientists. Faraday himself did not learn of it until Jacobi wrote to him early in the following summer (*ibid.*, 343), and Emerson probably knew nothing of the St. Petersburg experiments until February 1841, when he was correcting and revising the last proofsheets of this book. In that month *The Journal of the Franklin Institute* first carried news of what "Professor Jacobi of St. Petersburg" had accomplished with "magnetism developed by the application of the galvanic current." The editor's report was detailed: "In the last trials made in propelling a boat twenty-eight feet long, seven and a half wide, and drawing two feet and three quarters of water, on the Neva, a velocity of three miles an hour was kept up. The boat carried twelve to fourteen persons" (3rd series, I, 135).

TEXTUAL APPARATUS

For each essay in this volume the following textual material is appended: (1) a record of all emendations made within the copy-text, whether substantive or accidental; (2) a collation of all variants in substantives or in spelling made in later editions but rejected from this edition; and (3) a record of word-division changes from copy-text to the text printed here. To avoid duplication we do not have a separate section of textual notes. Rather, we include notes within the pertinent tables, so that any comment on the basis for change within the copy-text or for rejection of later variants occurs at the point of the decision. The editions collated are described in the textual introduction, but for convenience a table of collated editions is printed at the head of the record of emendations accepted within copy-text.

Emendations in the copy-text. The copy-text (the 1841 edition) may be recreated by the reader, since all emendations in it are recorded. The table of emendations reads as follows: at the left margin are the page and line number of this edition, then the reading here adopted (that is, the emendation in copy-text), a square bracket, and the date identifying the edition in which the adopted emendation was first printed. If, instead of an edition date, the initials RWE occur, the emendation comes from unpublished corrections and notes for revision by Emerson himself; if the abbreviation ed. appears, it is an emendation made by the editors of the present edition. The emendation and its identifying date are followed by a semicolon and then by the copy-text reading, identified with its date of 1841. Any further changes in later editions follow in chronological order. Whenever an entry warrants, a textual note of explanation is appended.

The collated editions are indicated by the date of publication on their title pages, even though in some cases the copyright date and the actual date of publication occurred in the prior year (for example, BAL 5370, the "Blue and Gold" edition, is dated 1865 on its title page but was printed in late 1864, and the *Prose Works*, BAL 5375, dated 1870, actually appeared in 1869). The Riverside edition of 1883–1893 and the Centenary edition of 1903–1904 have been collated and included within the record of substantive changes although they have no authority. They provide the texts most used in our era and fill out the historical record. They are marked respectively with the letters R and C rather than with dates. The 1841 and 1853 English editions have no authority, and, although they have been collated and their peculiarities noted in the textual introduction, they are not included.

For each entry we print the word preceding and following the emendation, except for changes in the form of a single word (spelling, hyphenation, changes in tense or case). An example of an emendation within copy-text and its readings follows:

13.9 America, these propensities still fight out] 1847; America, the contest of these propensities still fights out 1841

In the adopted revision Emerson avoids the tautology involved in having a "contest" that "fights out the old battle."

The entry indicates that the emendation of copy-text appears on page 13, line 9, of this edition, and that the accepted reading is "America, these propensities still fight out," which was first printed in the 1847 edition. The original reading from the 1841 copy-text is "America, the contest of these propensities still fights out." By not printing any further versions, the entry also indicates that all later editions carried the 1847 reading.

Rejected Substantives. All substantive changes and spelling changes appearing in authoritative editions as well as in the Riverside and Centenary editions that are not adopted by this edition are entered here. Since accidentals (changes in punctuation and capitalization) number in the thousands and usually indicate the practice of the publishing house or the printer rather than of Emerson, we have recorded only those accidentals in the 1847 revision (the one later edition that Emerson thoroughly revised, prepared for the press, and proofread) that are markedly significant to rhythm or syntax, such as end punctuation, dashes, and commas that alter or clarify syntax. All accidentals have been collated and a record kept by the editors. The basis for acceptance or rejection of variants has been described in the textual introduction. Explanations for specific exclusions are supplied in the form of a note following debatable instances. The historical record appears as part of each entry. Examples read as follows:

164.25   thence comes] thence come 1876
          The singular verb is probably Emerson's, since it also appears in the source passage (*EL*, III, 42).

At the left margin are the page and line numbers of this edition, followed by the copy-text reading retained in this edition. The reading is followed by a square bracket, but we print no date since the bracketed reading in this list is always from the 1841 copy-text, unless otherwise indicated. Then follows the record of further changes, listed in chronological order. Only those editions first printing a new version are recorded; each later edition can be assumed to accept the last recorded version unless listed otherwise. If only a single date appears, all later editions accept the variant printed here. In the above example the reading that appears in copy-text and this edition is "thence comes" followed by a square bracket and the 1876 variant, which was rejected for the reason given in the note. The entry indicates that the copy-text reading appears in all editions prior to 1876 (the 1847, 1865, and 1870 editions), and that the editions after 1876 (the Riverside and Centenary editions) carry the rejected variant. In another example, a later edition (here 1865) returned to the original copy-text reading and "rejected" the variant (here from the 1847 edition) as we do also.

133.30   the stinging recollection] the stringing recollection 1847; the stinging recollection 1865

The note that follows this entry explains the basis for rejecting the 1847 printing error, which was also corrected in the editions after 1865 (the 1870, 1876, Riverside, and Centenary editions).

Word-Division. Two lists are appended below to record line-end hyphenations. The first list shows the forms adopted here for possible compound words that were hyphenated at the line-end in the copy-text. On the basis of Emerson's usage in his journals, letters, and formal writing, the editors have decided whether to print copy-text hyphenations at the line-end as single words or as hyphenated compounds. The page and line numberings locate the word within the present text (referred to as *CW* for *Collected Works*).

The second list records the copy-text reading for possible compounds hyphenated at the line-end in this edition (*CW*). Any possible compound hyphenated at line-end in this edition occurs as an unhyphenated, solidly written word in copy-text if it is not in this list. Words coincidentally hyphenated at line-end both in this edition and in the copy-text are given in the form which would have been adopted had they fallen within the line here and are marked by a dagger (†). The symbol (/-/) indicates hyphenation at line end in the text being quoted.

I. *CW* forms of possible compounds which were hyphenated at line-end in the copy-text:

4.37	self-reliance	79.16	daylight
7.21	mummy-pits	83.18	whenever
13.12	gadfly	85.2	statesmen
14.19	eye-sockets	87.21	nothing
14.37	sharper-tongued	88.35	non-committal
18.30	roadside	91.14	cannot
20.23	market-town	94.28	prayer-meeting
20.29	foreshow	95.26	selfsame
21.9	thick-strown	99.3	forelooking
21.27	to-day	101.27	nothings
30.23	wood-chopper	101.28	By and by (emendation)
32.5	withdrawn	104.27	rainbows
32.7	reinforce	105.1	doves'-neck
32.8	blindman's-buff	106.36	subterranean
33.26	thousand-eyed	113.24	household
38.32	upright	114.12	kinsfolk
40.31	somewhat	114.26	metamorphosed
44.24	throughout	114.27	nothing
46.22	somewhat	115.4	by and by (emendation)
48.8	well-clad	115.31	overestimate
48.25	note-books	121.19	shipwreck
60.4	re-appears	123.10	intermeddle
62.8	mermaid's	123.10	intermeddle
64.7	omnipresent	126.4	farewell
64.28	thread-ball	126.8	Janus-faced
66.21	cannot	140.17	neighborhood
67.21	chisel-edge	148.1	lockjaw
67.21	foot-rule	148.2	hydrophobia
70.22	Falsehood	154.1	cannot
72.6	outdone	154.4	outrun
78.4	whooping-coughs	154.28	brotherhood
78.8	self-union	159.16	metaphysics

163.19	metamorphosis	187.27	landlord's
163.34	somewhat	189.22	to-day
165.34	nothing	196.28	withdraw
170.12	*without*	198.5	corn-flags
171.22	whomsoever	202.32	likewise
172.20	over-royal	203.21	whatsoever
174.8	withdrawing	203.33	whosoever
175.10	everlasting	204.10	cannot
181.23	to-morrow	212.21	long-haired
182.21	cannot	215.15	picture-dealers
183.25	outgeneralled (emendation)	217.8	alms-house
185.12	cannot		

II. Copy-text forms of possible compounds which are hyphenated at line-ends in *CW*.

11.5	sea-shell	99.14	heyday
11.24	wide-stretched	106.36	†subterranean
27.21	to-morrow	107.12	household
28.23	trustworthy	113.24	†household
29.30	everywhere	117.1	self-acquaintance
30.17	well-spoken	117.19	cobweb
30.23	†wood-chopper	118.35	frostwork
32.5	†withdrawn	120.22	masterpiece
32.18	handkerchief	123.13	self-elected
33.21	somewhat	133.5	co-perception
33.26	metaphysics	134.27	work-bench
40.1	self-existence	135.24	sometimes
42.8	cannot	136.30	half-lights
43.29	township	136.32	to-morrow
46.4	million-orbed	148.18	single-handed
48.6	something	149.26	sugar-plums
58.33	overlooks	154.28	†brotherhood
59.36	cannot	163.34	†somewhat
64.20	overmastered	164.27	Childhood
66.23	somebody	165.22	somewhat
67.14	something	167.20	Everywhere
70.23	background	173.30	byword
82.25	something	174.20	withdrawal
83.15	whatever	180.2	somewhat
91.29	undergone	183.24	cannot
92.22	cannot	190.1	overpowering
93.27	daylight	190.9	overcome
94.9	superserviceable	196.35	cannot

200.3	wherewith		212.12	dancing-master
200.31	falsehood		213.36	household
204.31	babe-like		216.15	thoroughfare
209.21	self-explication		218.1	afterwards

COLLATED EDITIONS

1841   *Essays.* Boston: James Munroe and Company, 1841.

1847   *Essays: First Series.* New edition. Boston: James Munroe and Company, 1847. (The first stereotyped edition, from whose plates newly dated impressions continued to be made through 1874, with only a single change.)

1865   *Essays: First and Second Series.* Boston: Ticknor and Fields, 1865. (Printed in the summer of 1864 and electrotyped as part of the Blue and Gold series.)

1870   *The Prose Works of Ralph Waldo Emerson.* New and revised edition, in two volumes. Boston: Fields, Osgood, and Company, 1870. (A third volume was added in 1878 or 1880. *Essays: First Series* was included in the first; the edition was published in the fall of 1869 but dated 1870.)

1876   *Essays: First Series.* New and revised edition. Boston: James R. Osgood and Company, late Ticknor & Fields, and Fields, Osgood, & Company, 1876. Little Classic Edition.

R   *Essays: First Series.* New and revised edition. Boston: Houghton, Mifflin and Company, 1884. (Volume II of the Riverside Edition, ed. James Elliot Cabot, 1883–1893.)

C   *Essays: First Series.* Boston and New York: Houghton, Mifflin and Company, 1903. (Volume II of the Centenary Edition, ed. Edward W. Emerson, 1903–1904.)

I. HISTORY

Emendations in Copy-Text

1.4   everywhere] 1847; every where 1841

Emerson's practice in writing compounds with "every" (every body, everyone, every thing, everywhere) is variable in his journals, although in the manuscript of *Representative Men* he tends to write them solid. "Every body" and "every thing" appear almost invariably as two words in copy-text; "everywhere" is written both ways, but is changed to the one-word version in the 1847 text. Although the change could be a printer's effort to make Emerson's spelling consistent, the 1847 form coincides with his more usual practice and so is accepted here and below (36.36, 78.24, 84.32, and 109.30). See also the Emendations note for "anywhere," at 70.30.

3.1   [¶] There is] ed.; [no ¶] THERE is 1841; [¶] THERE is 1847

Throughout the 1841 text the printer followed a convention of beginning each essay flush left rather than with a paragraph indentation. Here and throughout, this edition does not attempt to reproduce all lineation and printing conventions of copy-text. We do not, for example, reprint signature numbers found at the bottom of pages in copy-text, punctuate running titles, or print the first word of each essay in small capitals; nor do we keep copy-text's small capitals in two passages within essays (see the emendations at 57.7 and 117.10). We do, however, maintain the first edition's convention of separate half-title pages for each essay, the 1847 edition's format for the mottoes to each essay, and both editions' practice of carrying essay numbers and titles as running titles.

3.13   But the thought is always prior] 1847; But always the thought is prior 1841

3.20   are the] RWE, ed.; are merely the 1841

In the Abel Adams copy, Emerson marked this change with a large "x" in the margin of the text and listed it as one of his corrections on the back cover. Although the change did not appear in any of the printed versions of *Essays I*, it accords with his general practice for the 1847 revision of tempering the tone of the essays.

4.6   him. Each new fact in] 1847; him. Every step in 1841

4.15   priest and king] 1847; priest, and king 1841

Emerson strengthens the parallel structure of the phrases "priest and king" and "martyr and executioner" in the 1847 edition by dropping the comma in the first phrase.

4.16   shall learn nothing rightly. What] 1847; shall see nothing, learn nothing, keep nothing. What 1841

4.20   say, 'Under this mask did] 1847; say, 'Here is one of my coverings. Under this fantastic, or odious, or graceful mask, did 1841

4.22   our actions] 1847; our own actions 1841

4.24   lose their] 1847; lose all their 1841

In the 1847 edition Emerson often deletes strong, absolute adverbs and adjectives, such as "all," "always," "great," "ever," in an effort to modify somewhat the tone of the *Essays* (for further discussion, see the textual introduction).

4.27   is the universal] 1847; is this universal 1841

The 1847 revision avoids the awkward repetition of "this" in the following sentence.

4.30 reason; all express more or less distinctly some] 1847; reason, all express at last reverence for some 1841

4.37 which belong] 1847; which belongs 1841, 1865; which belong 1870

The change of the verb to agree with a plural antecedent ("heroism and grandeur") is characteristic of Emerson's care for grammar throughout the 1847 revision.

5.2 pictures— . . . genius—anywhere] 1847; pictures,— . . . genius, anywhere 1841

The addition or deletion of dashes is a type of change more likely to be made by an author than by a compositor. Although compositors regularly tinker with commas, semicolons, and colons, especially when they have a "house style" to go by, dashes are not so clearly subject to rules, and compositors are apt to leave them to the author's idiosyncracies. Throughout the 1847 edition dashes are added or deleted to improve and clarify Emerson's complicated syntax. Their use is often subtle, a matter of emphasis and even at times of explication of a passage. In most cases we accept such changes as Emerson's. Dashes are regularly added to set off parenthetical remarks or parallel examples, as in this entry. Single dashes are used as colons, to set off examples, or as semicolons, to link loosely two clauses. Dashes are often added before a quotation or saying, especially when it follows a form of "to say" (see the Emendations notes for 41.25 and 44.26). Dashes are also deleted, although less often, to improve syntax (see 44.2, 89.20, 107.23, 140.26, 160.1, 169.2, 214.15, and 218.30) or to improve parallel structure (see 9.17, 9.20, 161.9); they are occasionally replaced by semicolons (see 85.26, 140.26, 160.1).

5.4 for better men; but] 1847; for our betters, but 1841

5.5 strokes we] 1847; strokes, there we 1841

5.12 applauded. [¶] We have the same interest in condition] 1847; applauded. [¶] So is it in respect to condition 1841

In the 1847 edition Emerson typically alters passages with inverted order and rhetorical flourishes.

5.17 each reader his] 1847; each man his 1841

5.18 man. Books] 1847; man. All books 1841

5.19 which he finds] 1847; which the wise man finds 1841

5.20 the eloquent praise] 1847; the loud praise 1841

5.22 A true aspirant, therefore] 1847; A wise and good soul, therefore 1841

Here and above (5.19) Emerson revises in an effort to modify the paragraph's rhythmic repetition of "the wise man."

5.26 fact and circumstance,—in] 1847; fact that befalls,—in 1841

6.2 a wonderful] 1847; a most wonderful 1841

6.3 its own virtue] 1847; its whole virtue 1841

6.5 sit solidly at home, and] 1847; sit at home with might and main, and 1841

Emerson's 1847 revision provides a more vivid image and concentrated form in place of the rhetorical tag phrase.

6.17　Babylon, Troy, Tyre, Palestine, and even early Rome, have passed or are passing into] 1870; Babylon and Troy and Tyre and even early Rome are passing already into 1841; Babylon, Troy, Tyre, Palestine, and even early Rome, are passing already into 1847, R

The addition of "Palestine" to the list of countries in 1847, and the further qualification of the time factor in 1870, both seem clearly authorial emendations.

6.21　have made] 1847; have thus made 1841

6.23　upon?" This] 1847; upon?' This 1841

The single quotation mark, the only one in a passage which otherwise uses double marks, indicates a printer's error.

6.27　Greece, Asia, Italy] 1847; Greece, Palestine, Italy 1841

The substitution of "Asia" for "Palestine" may have been not only a reflection of Emerson's attempt to include the various Eastern great books as well as Hebraism and Christianity but a mark of his wish to avoid repetition resulting from inclusion of "Palestine" in the list of countries "passing into fiction" (see 6.17).

6.30　the emphatic facts of history] 1847; the facts that have moved us in history 1841

6.33　Every mind must] 1847; Every soul must 1841

This revision is the first of many Emerson made in an attempt to specify the meaning of "soul."

7.1　Somewhere, sometime, it] 1847; Somewhere or other, some time or other, it 1841

7.6　in ourselves see] 1847; in our own nature see 1841

7.7　reason of every] 1847; reason for every 1841

7.8　public and private] 1847; public, every private 1841

7.19　Memphis,—is] 1847; Memphis, is 1841

7.21　Now.　Belzoni] 1847; Now.　It is to banish the *Not me*, and supply the *Me*.　It is to abolish difference and restore unity.　Belzoni 1841

7.25　as he, so] 1847; as himself, so 1841

7.25　himself should] 1847; himself in given circumstances should 1841

7.26　is solved] 1847; is then solved 1841

7.28　all with] 1847; all like a creative soul, with 1841

7.33　and state] 1847; and historical state 1841

8.9　intellect is to the] 1847; intellect consists in the 1841

8.10　which neglects surface] 1847; which overlooks surface 1841

8.15　appearance. [¶] Upborne and surrounded as we are by] 1847; appearance. [¶] Why, being as we are surrounded by 1841

8.17　air, why should] 1847; air, should 1841

8.19　of figure?　The] 1847; of form?　The 1841

The substitution of "figure" for "form" avoids the awkward repetition, since "forms" ends the preceding sentence.

8.27 constant individual] 1847; constant type of the individual 1841

The 1847 revision clarifies and improves Emerson's original statement by avoiding the logical weakness of the copy-text version. By substituting "individual" for "type of the individual" Emerson avoids blurring the biological progression from individual through species and genus, to the "steadfast type" of 8.29.

8.32 moral. Through the bruteness and toughness of matter, a subtle spirit bends all things to its own will. The] 1847; moral. Beautifully shines a spirit through the bruteness and toughness of matter. Alone omnipotent, it converts all things to its own end. The 1841

8.34 into soft but] 1847; into softest but 1841

8.35 it, and, whilst] 1847; it, but, whilst 1841; its, and, whilst 1865; it, and whilst 1870

The substitution in 1847 and thereafter of "and" for "but" avoids the repetition of the conjunction five words earlier. From 1870 on the punctuation varies somewhat. The 1865 variant of "its" makes no grammatical sense and is certainly a printer's error.

8.36 changed again. Nothing] 1847; changed altogether. Nothing 1841

8.36 form; yet] 1847; form. Yet 1841

Throughout the 1847 edition Emerson alters the "spoken" style of copy-text by combining short sentences and fragments into longer, smoother units. He often revises such sentences by eliminating rhetorical repetition of subjects and verbs; frequently, as in this example, he combines sentences by merely changing a period to a semicolon.

8.37 the remains or] 1847; the rudiments or 1841

9.4 Osiris-Jove] 1847; Jove 1841

9.9 simplicity of] 1847; simplicity and unity of 1841

9.10 recognize] 1847; recognise 1841

Emerson usually uses the "z" spelling; in the manuscript of *Representative Men*, he wavers in words of this class, but he changes one "s" to "z" in his correction copy, and many similar changes are made in the 1870 edition. This word is spelled with a "z" six times in the journals of the period (*JMN*, V, 112; VII, 15, 106, 123, 202, 277). The "s" spelling occurs only once in the same journals (*JMN*, VII, 196) and once earlier in "Nature" (*CW*, I, 34.9). Webster gives only "recognize," though Worcester lists both forms. See also the Emendations notes for "apprize" (171.24) and "characterized" (64.21), and the Rejected Substantives notes for "enterprizes" (43.21) and "surprizes" (196.7).

9.10 character. Observe the] 1847; character. See the variety of the 1841

9.11 genius. We] 1847; genius. Thus at first we 1841

9.13   Xenophon, and Plutarch] 1847; Xenophon, Plutarch 1841

9.14   did. We have the same national mind expressed] 1847; did. Then we have the same soul expressed 1841

9.15   *literature*, in epic and lyric poems] 1847; *literature*; in poems 1841

9.16   philosophy; a] 1847; philosophy: a 1841

9.17   *architecture*, a beauty as of temperance itself, limited to the straight line and the square,—a builded geometry. Then] 1847; *architecture*, —the purest sensuous beauty,—the perfect medium never overstepping the limit of charming propriety and grace. Then 1841

9.19   once again in] 1847; once more in 1841

9.20   *sculpture*, the "tongue] 1847; *sculpture*,—"the tongue 1841

       The excision of the dash strengthens the parallel relationship of this passage with earlier revised passages at 9.15 and 9.17.

9.20   expression," a multitude of forms in the utmost freedom of action, and never transgressing the ideal serenity; like votaries performing some religious dance before the gods, and, though in convulsive pain or mortal combat, never daring to break the figure and decorum of their dance. Thus] 1847; expression," those forms in every action, at every age of life, ranging through all the scale of condition, from god to beast, and never transgressing the ideal serenity, but in convulsive exertion the liege of order and of law. Thus 1841

       This extensive revision partially serves to improve the parallel balance between the two appositives of "sculpture": "*the* tongue" and "*a* multitude."

9.26   representation: and] 1847; representation,—the most various expression of one moral thing: and 1841

9.28   Phocion? [¶] Every] 1847; Phocion? Yet do these varied external expressions proceed from one national mind. [¶] Every 1841

10.2   works; and delights] 1847; works. She delights 1841

10.22   him. [no ¶] In a certain . . . works. It] 1847; him. [¶] What is to be inferred from these facts but this; that in a certain . . . works? It 1841

10.24   By a deeper apprehension, and] 1847; By descending far down into the depths of the soul, and 1841

10.29   Because a profound nature awakens] 1847; Because a soul, living from a great depth of being, awakens 1841

10.32   pictures, addresses. [¶] Civil] 1847; pictures, are wont to animate. [¶] Civil 1841

10.33   Civil and natural history, the history of art and of literature, must] 1847; Civil history, natural history, the history of art, and the history of literature,—all must 1841

10.37   man. Santa] 1847; man. It is in the soul that architecture exists. Santa 1841

11.4   the reason] 1847; the sufficient reason 1841

11.11   things the] 1847; things for us also the 1841

11.12 heed. [no ¶] A] 1847; heed. Let me add a few examples, such as fall within the scope of every man's observation, of trivial facts which go to illustrate great and conspicuous facts. [¶] A 1841

11.15 onward: a thought] 1847; onward. This is precisely the thought 1841

11.19 remember one summer day, in the fields, my] 1847; remember that being abroad one summer day, my 1841

11.24 wide-stretched] 1847; wide stretched 1841

The word is written solid in the source passage (*JMN*, V, 504); another "wide" compound, "wide-related," is hyphenated at 23.5.

11.28 once showed to] 1847; once revealed to 1841

11.33 By surrounding ourselves with the original circumstances, we invent] 1847; By simply throwing ourselves into new circumstances we do continually invent 1841

11.36 temple preserves the] 1847; temple still presents the 1841

12.27 its locust, elm, oak, pine, fir, and spruce] 1847; its locust, its pine, its oak, its fir, its spruce 1841

By removing the pronoun "its" before each of the tree names, the 1847 revision emphasizes the triad ("its ferns, its spikes of flowers, its locust . . .") of fern, flower, and tree.

13.9 America, these propensities still fight out] 1847; America, the contest of these propensities still fights out 1841

In the adopted revision Emerson avoids the tautology involved in having a "contest" that "fights out the old battle."

13.10 in the nation and in the individual. The] 1847; in each individual. We are all rovers and all fixtures by turns, and pretty rapid turns. The 1841

13.11 Africa were constrained] 1847; Africa are constrained 1841

13.12 gadfly] 1870; gad/-/fly 1841; gad-fly 1865, R

Although the 1870 change could well be a printer's correction, Emerson wrote the word solid in the source passage for both here and 13.17 (*JMN*, VII, 91). Webster and Worcester list the word as "gadfly."

13.13 and to drive] 1847; and drive 1841

13.16 curiosity; a progress] 1847; curiosity. A progress 1841

13.17 gadfly] 1870; gad-fly 1841, R

13.17 Bay. Sacred cities, to which a periodical religious pilgrimage was enjoined, or stringent laws and customs, tending to invigorate the national bond, were the check on the old rovers; and the cumulative values of long residence are the restraints on the itinerary of the present day. The antagonism of the two tendencies is not less active in individuals, as the love of adventure or the love of repose happens to predominate. A man of rude health and flowing spirits has the faculty of rapid domestication, lives in his wagon, and roams through all latitudes as easily as a Calmuc. At sea, or in the forest, or in the snow, he sleeps as warm, dines with as good appetite, and associates as happily, as beside his own chimneys. Or perhaps his facility is deeper seated, in the increased range of his faculties of observation, which yield him points of interest wherever fresh objects meet his eyes. The pastoral nations were needy and hungry to desperation; and this intellectual nomadism, in its excess, bankrupts the mind, through the dissipation of power on a miscellany of objects. The home-keeping wit, on the other hand, is that continence or content which finds all the elements of life in its own soil; and which has its own perils of monotony and deterioration, if not stimulated by foreign infusions. [¶] Every thing] 1847; Bay. The difference between men in this respect is the faculty of rapid domestication, the power to find his chair and bed everywhere, which one man has, and another has not. Some men have so much of the Indian left, have constitutionally such habits of accommodation, that at sea, or in the forest, or in the snow, they sleep as warm, and dine with as good appetite, and associate as happily, as in their own house. And to push this old fact still one degree nearer, we may find it a representative of a permanent fact in human nature. The intellectual nomadism is the faculty of objectiveness or of eyes which everywhere feed themselves. Who hath such eyes, everywhere falls into easy relations with his fellow-men. Every man, every thing is a prize, a study, a property to him, and this love smooths his brow, joins him to men and makes him beautiful and beloved in their sight. His house is a wagon; he roams through all latitudes as easily as a Calmuc. [¶] Every thing 1841

14.4   world,—the] 1847; world, the 1841

14.11   later? What but this, that every man passes personally through a Grecian period. The] 1847; later? This period draws us because we are Greeks. It is a state through which every man in some sort passes. The 1841

14.21   head. [no ¶] The manners] 1847; head. [¶] The manners 1841

14.24   Luxury and elegance are not known. A] 1847; Luxury is not known, nor elegance. A 1841

14.32   ground covered] 1847; ground, covered 1841

    The excision of the comma, probably Emerson's change, clarifies the ambiguity in copy-text about whether the "snow" covers the "troops," or, more likely, the "ground."

14.35   army exists a] 1847; army seemed to be a 1841

    Except for the quotation from Xenophon, the whole paragraph is in the present tense until the intrusion of "seemed." Emerson's 1847 revision strengthens the sentence in style and statement.

15.9   reflective, but] 1847; reflective but 1841

    The comma, along with the substantive change at 15.10, clarifies the opposition of "reflective" to both perfect "senses" and perfect "health" (that is, "the natural" of the preceding sentence) rather than to just "senses" alone.

15.10   senses and in] 1847; senses, perfect in 1841

15.11   of children. They] 1847; of boys. They 1841

15.14   exists; but] 1847; exists, but 1841

The 1847 semicolon clarifies the syntax by distinguishing main clauses from subordinate phrases.

15.17   childhood. The] 1847; childhood. Our reverence for them is our reverence for childhood. Nobody can reflect upon an unconscious act with regret or contempt. Bard or hero cannot look down on the word or gesture of a child. It is as great as they. The 1841

15.19   besides that there are always individuals] 1847; beside that always there are individuals 1841

15.22   Hellas. I admire the love of nature in the Philoctetes. In reading] 1847; Hellas. A great boy, a great girl, with good sense, is a Greek. Beautiful is the love of nature in the Philoctetes. But in reading 1841

16.7   have, from] 1847; have always, from 1841

16.17   theirs. [¶] I] 1847; theirs. [¶] Then I 1841

17.2   he repeats step] 1847; he reacts step 1841

17.12   he has in literature] 1847; he hath in all literature 1841

17.17   him, dotted] 1847; him, yet dotted 1841

18.3   are the] 1847; are all the 1841

18.4   poets. When] 1847; poets. Every man is a divinity in disguise, a god playing the fool. It seems as if heaven had sent its insane angels into our world as to an asylum, and here they will break out into their native music and utter at intervals the words they have heard in heaven; then the mad fit returns, and they mope and wallow like dogs. When 1841

18.11   to solid] 1847; to all solid 1841

18.12   Orpheus. The] 1847; Orpheus, which was to his childhood an idle tale. The 1841

18.18   man agent or patient] 1847; man agent, or patient 1841; man, agent, or patient 1865; man agent or patient 1870

Although the meaning is slightly ambiguous no matter what the punctuation ("man, agent or patient" would perhaps have been clearest), the 1847 revision clarifies somewhat by not obscuring the contrast in "agent or patient."

18.21   souls is] 1847; souls: that too is 1841

18.26   Ah! brother, stop] 1847; Ah, brother, hold fast to the man and awe the beast; stop 1841

19.27   is a] 1847; is manifestly a 1841

20.3   annals,—that . . . like,—I] 1847; annals, that . . . like, I 1841

20.9   Castle a] 1847; Castle, a 1841

The copy-text carries no comma in the same position in the parallel clause that follows (that is, after "state"); the 1847 excision improves the parallel structure and clarifies that "Ravenswood Castle" is the subject of an implied "is."

20.18 nature. His power consists] 1847; nature. The power of man consists 1841

20.20 being. In old Rome the public roads beginning at the Forum proceeded north] 1847; being. In the age of the Cæsars, out from the Forum at Rome proceeded the great highways north 1841

20.27 world. His] 1847; world. All his 1841

20.28 him, and predict] 1847; him. All his faculties predict 1841

20.30 presuppose air. He] 1847; presuppose a medium like air. Insulate and you destroy him. He 1841

21.1 "His . . . / . . . it."] 1847; His . . . / . . . it. 1841

Here copy-text fails to use quotation marks on an indented and offset quotation. In the fifteen other examples of such indented and spaced quotations in copy-text, thirteen employ quotation marks and only two omit them (145.20-147.5 and 151.31-151.33). The 1847 revision of this and the two other examples makes them coincide with Emerson's frequent practice in the journals (see *JMN*, VII, 59, 136, 140, 186, 187).

21.11 Davy or of Gay-Lussac, from] 1847; Davy and Gay Lussac from 1841

The name is also hyphenated in the source passage (*EL*, II, 18).

21.12 exploring the] 1847; exploring always the 1841

21.18 wood? Do not the] 1847; wood? the 1841

21.31 One, and] 1847; One; and 1841

The semicolon in copy-text interrupts the parallel "that" clauses and so makes the sentence difficult to read. It seems a possible printer's error corrected in the 1847 revision.

21.34 pupil. He] 1847; pupil, for each new-born man. He 1841

22.24 As old . . . man,—perhaps older,—] 1847; As long . . . man—perhaps longer— 1841

22.27 other. What connection do the books show between the fifty or sixty chemical elements, and the historical eras? Nay] 1847; other. Nay 1841

23.9 nature. The] 1847; nature, but from it, rather. The 1841

23.10 boy, stand nearer to the light by which nature is to be read, than] 1847; boy, come much nearer to these,—understand them better than 1841

Rejected Substantives

3.20 application] applications 1870; application R

The 1870 and 1876 editions' grammatical changes rarely accord with Emerson's own practice and seem, as in this instance, more likely to be printer's corrections than the author's revisions (see also 36.9).

4.18   depravations] deprivations 1870; depravations R

The context of the passage and the reference to "Asdrubal or Cæsar Borgia" indicate that the 1870 and 1876 change was an error, corrected in the Riverside edition.

4.19   for you. Stand] for yon. Stand 1876; for you. Stand R

4.24   zodiack] zodiac 1847

Webster and Worcester list only "zodiac," but Emerson's own practice includes both spellings, with "zodiack" more frequent during the period of the *Essays*. The "zodiac" spelling occurs only in the original journal and lecture passages of this particular quotation (*JMN*, V, 256 and *EL*, II, 16) and in *CW*, I, 86; in the other noted occurrences of the word in the manuscript of *Representative Men* (18.16), and in journals and lectures of the period (*JMN*, VII, 275 and 276; *JMN*, IX, 311; *EL*, III, 233, 278, and 369) "zodiack" appears.

5.3   our ear] our ears 1865; our ear 1870

Since the 1870 edition changes "ears" back to a poetic singular, the 1865 change was probably a printer's correction in an edition Emerson apparently never saw to proofread.

5.6   Shakspeare] Shakespeare 1865; Shakspeare 1876

Although Emerson's most common spelling in his early journals, letters, and lectures is "Shakspear" (see *CW*, I, 294, note for 61.36), he prefers the spelling "Shakspeare" in the journals from 1841 on (*JMN*, VII and IX), in the manuscript and first edition of *Representative Men*, and throughout the 1841 edition of *Essays I*. In four cases in *Essays I* Emerson changes the spelling from the source passage's "Shakspear" (*JMN*, IV, 50; *JMN*, V, 357; *JMN*, VII, 185) to the copy-text's "Shakspeare." In each case in *Essays I* copy-text reads "Shakspeare," the 1865 and 1870 texts print "Shakespeare," and the 1876 text returns to copy-text spelling. "Shakspeare" appears at 18.6, 47.22, 47.25, 47.26, 63.33, 72.11, 79.12, 79.13, 162.25, 171.1, and 171.10.

6.11   forever] for ever 1847

Although Worcester gives "for-ever" as meaning "eternally" and "for ever" to mean "without end," Emerson normally spells the word and its variant, "forevermore," solid (see *JMN*, IV, 326; VII, 203, 370, 372, 506; *CW*, I, 293, note for 54.35). The word is spelled solid throughout copy-text (see 40.12, 80.30, 89.33, 124.5, 154.20, 155.34, 159.7, 171.17, 173.2, 188.30 for "forever," and 73.6, 116.36 for "forevermore").

7.34   forest dwellers] forest-dwellers 1847

The words appear without a hyphen in both source passages (*JMN*, V, 402, and *EL*, II, 268).

8.21   greybeards] graybeards 1847

In the journals covering the period 1838–1842, Emerson uses "grey" in various combinations five times (*JMN*, VII, 271, 340, 367, 396, 402), and we find no examples of "gray." In this volume of the *Essays*, however, "gray" does appear, though perhaps as a printer's substitution (see 214.12).

8.22   causal] casual 1865; causal 1876

Ruth Emerson's copy of *Essays: First Series* contains a note in Emerson's hand: "*casual* instead of *causal* in all new editions." The comment apparently was a late insertion to note that the "new editions" of 1865 and 1870 carried this misreading which was then corrected in 1876. The misreading of "casual" for "causal" appears a second time in the 1870 edition at 60.26.

9.36   well known] well-known 1847

In his journals Emerson writes modifying compounds with "well" as two words, hyphenated, or solid. He usually writes "well known" without a hyphen (see *JMN*, VII, 381, and V, 64). In copy-text such compounds appear either hyphenated ("well-spoken," 30.17, and "well-clad," 48.8) or as two words (see also "well laid," 211.26, and "well tempered," 121.26). All are hyphenated in the 1847 text (except "well tempered," which does not precede a noun), indicating a probable printer's revision although both versions accord with Emerson's practice. See also Emerson's instructions about making his spelling, "well nigh," conform with standard usage (*CW*, I, 292, note for 58.1).

12.18   the bareness of] the barrenness of 1847

Since the source passage (*EL*, II, 52) also carries the copy-text version, "bareness," the 1847 change (kept through all subsequent editions) is rejected as a probable printer's error. The copy-text reading makes more sense in the context, since it is only because the trees are *bare* of leaves that their limbs resemble the "Saxon" rather than the Gothic arch. The change to "barrenness" adds an unnecessary and jarring dimension of sterility. Emerson uses "bare" again at 12.22.

15.26   fellow beings] fellow-beings 1847

In his journals Emerson writes compounds with "fellow" (fellow beings, fellow creature, fellow man, fellow workers) solid (*JMN*, V, 334) or, more often, as two words (*JMN*, IV, 19; V, 322; VII, 96, and *EL*, II, 321). Worcester hyphenates such compounds; Webster gives them as one solid word. In copy-text most examples are printed as two words ("fellow man" at 65.9 and 119.32; "fellow men" at 90.34; "fellow creature(s)" at 139.4 and 154.17), then hyphenated in the 1847 revision, probably by a printer trying to make Emerson's practice consistent. Three examples are hyphenated in copy-text as well: "fellow-men" in a passage deleted in 1847 (see the Emendations note for 13.17), and at 210.4, and "fellow-workers" at 141.17.

17.14 described] describes 1865; described 1870

The 1865 change seems a probable printer's error. It is grammatically inaccurate and was corrected in the next (1870) edition.

18.2 skepticism] scepticism 1865; skepticism R

Emerson himself invariably spells the word "skepticism"; it appears thus throughout his letters, manuscript of *Representative Men*, lectures, and journals. Worcester prefers "skeptic," although he admits that "sceptic" (the "original" spelling) is "the probably more common orthography." The appearance of "sceptic" from the 1865 edition on, indicates a publisher's house-styling, revised back in the Riverside. "Skeptic" and its derivatives are similarly altered to "sceptic" in the 1870 and 1876 editions of *Representative Men*, then back to "skeptic" in the Riverside.

18.6 Shakspeare] Shakespeare 1865; Shakspeare 1876

18.30 roadside [hyphenated at line-end in copy-text]] road-side 1847; roadside 1870; road-side R

In his journals Emerson writes the word solid (*JMN*, IV, 70, and IX, 86), and it also appears solid later in copy-text (218.20). It is hyphenated in *CW*, I (14.9 and 22.28).

18.37 routine, the] routine the 1847; routine, the R

In the source passage (*EL*, III, 48) Emerson named *three* types of men, apparently intending them as a series of "men" created by "facts." Although copy-text's deletion of the third type obscures the series, the 1847 excision of the comma incorrectly changes the meaning, implying that "facts" turn "men of routine" into "men of *sense*."

19.33 endeavor] endeavour 1847; endeavor 1865

Emerson's practice in writing words ending in "or/our" is very inconsistent. He tended to use the "or" endings early in his career (see *CW*, I, 287, note for 40.1) and spells the words with "or" fairly consistently in the 1841 copy-text. In his journals and letters the "our" spelling appears more frequently from around 1844 on. "Our" endings appear throughout the manuscript of *Representative Men*, written about the same time Emerson revised *Essays I* for the 1847 edition. The 1847 spellings are also probably Emerson's, as are, probably, the copy-text spellings. Emerson's practice was, however, far too variable even within certain time periods to confirm any specific instance of an "or/our" word as his version. We, therefore, retain copy-text here and throughout the volume for the following "or" words changed in 1847 to "our": "behavior," "demeanor," "enamored," "endeavor" and its derivatives, "neighbor" and its derivatives, "parlor," "savor," and "succor." Most examples are changed back to "or" in the 1865 text in accord with "house styling." The few exceptions ("savor" at 99.18, and "enamored" at 87.12) are "corrected" in the 1870 edition. For another exception, see the Rejected Substantives note for 29.11.

20.2 Genelas] Venelas C

E. W. Emerson emended the name here and in "Domestic Life" (*W*, VII, 123, and 381) on the basis of its appearance in a French source. But R. W. Emerson seems to have taken the original story from a German fairytale (see *JMN*, V, 35) and in the manuscript references he clearly uses the form "Genelas" (*JMN*, V, 35 and 89; *EL*, I, 260).

20.10 disguise] disguised 1870; disguise R

The change from noun to participle in the editions of 1870 and 1876 alters the meaning from the passage's original context (see *JMN*, III, 247), since it emphasizes "Bunyan" rather than "disguise," and results in nonsense. It seems, therefore, a printer's correction and not Emerson's own.

21.9 thick-strown] thick-strewn 1847

Worcester and Webster both give "strow" and "strew" as acceptable. Emerson uses "strown" in "The American Scholar" in 1837 (*CW*, I, 65.36), and in that instance the later (1849) revision does not change the original.

22.37 neighboring] neighbouring 1847; neighboring 1865

23.1 succor] succour 1847; succor 1865

23.5 truelier] trulier 1847; truly 1870; trulier R

Emerson spells the superlative form "trueliest" in the manuscript and first edition of *Representative Men* (80.22). In the journals, he writes "more truly" (*JMN*, V, 19).

II. SELF-RELIANCE

Emendations in Copy-Text

25.1 "Ne . . . extra."] 1847; Ne . . . extra. 1841

The addition of quotation marks in the 1847 edition makes this phrase, a much-used quotation of Emerson's, accord with his normal punctuation practice, a practice he had already used for the second quotation on the page.

25.2 star; and . . . / . . . fate; / Nothing] 1847; star, and . . . / . . . fate, / Nothing 1841

Emerson wrote that he spent a lot of time "correcting and mottoing" his *Essays* for the 1847 revision (*L*, III, 417), and the changes in punctuation in one of the few "mottos" printed in copy-text are more likely his than a printer's.

25.4   Commands] 1847; Command 1841

In the 1647 First Folio of Beaumont and Fletcher which Emerson owned, he found "Command"; but the 1679 second edition and most later versions read "Commands," a reading which supplies a verb here for "soul." In the manuscript notebook for his anthology *Parnassus*, Emerson wrote "Command" (Houghton 124, p. 148), but he adopted the later reading in the published anthology (p. 156) and revised his copy of the First Folio.

26.2   teat; / Wintered] 1847; teat: / Wintered 1841

See the Emendations note for 25.2.

27.2   conventional. The soul always hears] 1847; conventional. Always the soul hears 1841

27.8   for the inmost in due time becomes] 1847; for always the inmost becomes 1841

27.17   recognize] 1847; recognise 1841

27.20   good-humored] 1847; good humored 1841

Emerson's practice with "good" compounds is highly irregular; he occasionally spells them two different ways in the same journal passage or letter (for example, "good looking" and "goodlooking," *L*, II, 216; "good natured" and "good-natured," *JMN*, VIII, 50; "good breeding" and "good-breeding," *Essays II*, 1844 edition, p. 148). He tends, however, to hyphenate the adjectival forms and to write the nouns as two words. In copy-text he hyphenates "good-natured" at 30.24 and 101.19.

28.8   none. This sculpture in the memory is not without preëstablished harmony. The] 1847; none. It is not without preëstablished harmony, this sculpture in the memory. The 1841

28.10   ray. We] 1847; ray. Bravely let him speak the utmost syllable of his confession. We 1841

28.14   cowards. A] 1847; cowards. It needs a divine man to exhibit any thing divine. A 1841

28.23   the absolutely trustworthy was seated at] 1847; the Eternal was stirring at 1841

28.27   not minors and invalids in a protected corner] 1847; not pinched in a corner 1841

28.28   but guides, redeemers, and benefactors, obeying the Almighty effort, and advancing on] 1847; but redeemers and benefactors, pious aspirants to be noble clay plastic under the Almighty effort, let us advance and advance on 1841

29.5   room his voice is sufficiently clear and emphatic. It] 1847; room, who spoke so clear and emphatic? Good Heaven! it is he! it is that very lump of bashfulness and phlegm which for weeks has done nothing but eat when you were by, that now rolls out these words like bell-strokes. It 1841

29.11 nature. A boy is in the parlour what the pit is in the playhouse; independent] 1847; nature. How is a boy the master of society; independent 1841

29.23 his neutrality! Who] 1847; his neutral, godlike independence! Who 1841

29.23 thus avoid all pledges, and] 1847; thus lose all pledge, and 1841

29.24 unbiassed] 1870; unbiased 1841, R

The word is also spelled "unbiassed" in the source passage (*JMN*, VII, 66). The 1870 and 1876 form appeared earlier in the unauthorized 1853 English edition as well.

29.25 formidable. He] 1847; formidable, must always engage the poet's and the man's regards. Of such an immortal youth the force would be felt. He 1841

30.2 of your own] 1847; of our own 1841

"Our" may have been a typographical error in copy-text, changed in 1847 to agree with "you," "yourself," and "you" in the next sentence.

30.9 replied, "They . . . Devil's child . . . Devil." No] 1847; replied, 'They . . . devil's child . . . devil.' No 1841

The capitals on "Devil's" and "Devil" appeared in the original source passage (*JMN*, V, 49) and may have been overlooked by the printer in the 1841 edition. The change from single to double quotation marks indicates that both the question of the friend and the response are to be thought of as real, not imaginary. Emerson normally uses single quotation marks for suppositious or manufactured remarks, double quotation marks for real sources.

31.9 by and by] 1847; by-and-by 1841

Emerson regularly spells the phrase without hyphens in his journals, usually writing it "by & by" (see *JMN*, V, 79, 428; VII, 159, 183, 212, 224).

31.17 life is for] 1847; life is not an apology, but a life. It is for 1841

31.20 bleeding. I] 1847; bleeding. My life should be unique; it should be an alms, a battle, a conquest, a medicine. I 1841

32.6 But do your work, and] 1847; But do your thing, and 1841

Both forms appear in earlier sources: "Do your thing" appears in 1839 (*JMN*, VII, 225) and "Do your work" in 1839 (*EL*, III, 102), in 1840 (*EL*, III, 309), and in *JMN*, XII, 149, 252, and 291. In an 1845 journal entry (*JMN*, IX, 342) Emerson wrote, "My doing my <thin> office entitles me to the benefit of your doing yours," and continued, "Work in thy place . . . and thy secretion to the spiritual body is made." This journal passage indicates a similar revision of "thing" to "work," here in the form of "office," and to "work" itself in the next statement. Since "Do your work" appears in the next sentence, the 1847 change may have been a printer's error caused by glancing ahead, but the change accords with Emerson's previous tinkerings with the passage, and is, therefore, accepted as an emendation.

32.15 side,—the] 1847; side; the 1841

The semicolon creates an unnecessary and confusing break in the sentence, especially since it divides "one side" from the specific example ("the permitted side"). Emerson's usual practice would have been to add a second dash *after* the parenthetical remark as well (see the Emendations note for 5.2), but the single dash improves the syntax somewhat, and is almost certainly the author's change.

32.30 mean "the] 1847; mean, "the 1841

Emerson frequently separates subject and verb by punctuation but very rarely verb and object. The comma may be a printer's almost instinctive punctuation before a quotation.

32.34 face with the most disagreeable sensation. [¶] For] 1847; face and make the most disagreeable sensation, a sensation of rebuke and warning which no brave young man will suffer twice. [¶] For 1841

32.36 nonconformity] 1847; non-conformity 1841

The word is spelled without a hyphen earlier in copy-text ("nonconformist" at 29.37), in *Essays II* (1844 edition, pp. 109 and 115), and in the journals (*JMN*, VII, 261).

33.5 cause, but] 1847; cause,—disguise no god, but 1841
33.21 this corpse] 1847; this monstrous corpse 1841
33.25 but to bring] 1847; but bring 1841
33.26 day. In] 1847; day. Trust your emotion. In 1841
33.34 wall. Speak what you think now in hard words, and] 1847; wall. Out upon your guarded lips! Sew them up with packthread, do. Else, if you would be a man, speak what you think to-day in words as hard as cannon balls, and 1841
33.36 to-day.—'Ah, so you shall be sure to be misunderstood.'—Is] 1847; to-day. Ah, then, exclaim the aged ladies, you shall be sure to be misunderstood. Misunderstood! It is a right fool's word. Is 1841

34.8 gauge] 1847; guage 1841

Worcester lists only the 1847 correction of this common Emersonian misspelling. The misspelling appears often in his journals (see *JMN*, V, 32, 174, 184, 426 and *JMN*, VIII, 118), and had to be corrected in later editions of his first published volume (see *CW*, I, 216.9 and 216.11) and of *Representative Men* (see "guaged" in the manuscript and 1850 edition at 64.18, corrected in the 1870 edition).

34.19 moment. [¶] There will be an agreement in] 1847; moment. [¶] Fear never but you shall be consistent in 1841
34.24 of at] 1847; of when seen at 1841
34.26 tacks. See] 1847; tacks. This is only microscopic criticism. See 1841

34.31   Greatness appeals] 1847; Greatness always appeals 1841
34.31   be firm enough to-day to] 1847; be great enough now to 1841
35.1   behind. They shed] 1847; behind. There they all stand and shed 1841
35.3   angels. That] 1847; angels to every man's eye. That 1841
35.14   us never bow and apologize more] 1847; us bow and apologize never more 1841
35.17   make it true] 1847; made it true 1841
        This evident typo in the copy-text was caught and corrected by the 1841 English edition as well as by the 1847 American edition.
35.21   Actor working wherever a man works; that] 1847; Actor moving wherever moves a man; that 1841
35.24   events. Ordinarily] 1847; events. You are constrained to accept his standard. Ordinarily 1841
35.26   else; it] 1847; else. It 1841
35.28   indifferent. Every] 1847; indifferent,—put all means into the shade. This all great men are and do. Every 1841
35.30   his design;—and] 1847; his thought;—and 1841
35.31   a train of clients. A] 1847; a procession. A 1841
35.35   as, Monachism, of the Hermit Antony; the Reformation] 1847; as, the Reformation 1841
36.18   insane, owes] 1847; insane,—owes 1841
36.23   imagination plays] 1847; imagination makes fools of us, plays 1841
36.30   with original views] 1847; with vast views 1841
36.33   has been] 1847; has indeed been 1841
36.36   everywhere] 1847; every where 1841
        See the Emendations note for 1.4.
37.13   genius, of virtue, and of life] 1847; genius, the essence of virtue, and the essence of life 1841
37.20   proceeds] 1847; proceedeth 1841
37.21   proceed] 1847; proceedeth 1841
        Emerson eliminated Biblical archaisms in the above two items and elsewhere (see 38.28 and 39.22) in the 1847 revision, but overlooked (or did not wish consistency) "giveth" in 37.25.
37.24   and of] 1847; and the fountain of 1841
37.25   wisdom, and which] 1847; wisdom, of that inspiration of man which 1841
37.27   us receivers of its truth and organs of its activity. When] 1847; us organs of its activity and receivers of its truth. When 1841
37.30   causes, all] 1847; causes,—all metaphysics, all 1841
37.32   man discriminates between] 1847; man discerns between 1841
37.33   perceptions, and knows that to his involuntary perceptions a perfect faith is] 1847; perceptions. And to his involuntary perceptions, he knows a perfect respect is 1841

37.36   disputed. My] 1847; disputed. All my 1841

37.37   the idlest reverie] 1847; the most trivial reverie 1841

37.37   emotion, command my curiosity and respect. Thoughtless] 1847; emotion are domestic and divine. Thoughtless 1841

38.15   wisdom, old] 1847; wisdom, then old 1841

38.18   one as] 1847; one thing as 1841

38.20   disappear. If] 1847; disappear. This is and must be. If 1841

38.26   and authority of] 1847; and majesty of 1841

38.28   makes] 1847; maketh 1841

38.32   apologetic; he . . . upright; he] 1847; apologetic. He . . . upright. He 1841

39.4   alike. But] 1847; alike. There is no time to it. But 1841

39.19   comes. If] 1847; comes. So was it with us, so will it be, if we proceed. If 1841

39.22   disburden] 1847; disburthen 1841

39.29   yourself, it] 1847; yourself,—it 1841

39.29   or accustomed way] 1847; or appointed way 1841

39.33   exclude example and experience. You] 1847; exclude all other being. You 1841

39.33   man, not] 1847; man not 1841

      Since Emerson normally uses a comma in such a situation, and since the comma would have come at a line-end in copy-text, its omission may be a printer's error.

39.34   its forgotten ministers. Fear] 1847; its fugitive ministers. There shall be no fear in it. Fear 1841

39.35   it. There] 1847; it. It asks nothing. There 1841

39.36   hope. In the hour of vision, there] 1847; hope. We are then in vision. There 1841

39.37   gratitude, nor] 1847; gratitude nor 1841

39.37   soul raised over passion beholds identity and eternal causation, perceives the self-existence of Truth and Right, and calms itself with knowing] 1847; soul is raised over passion. It seeth identity and eternal causation. It is a perceiving that Truth and Right are. Hence it becomes a Tranquillity out of the knowing 1841

40.3   nature, the] 1847; nature; the 1841

      Emerson occasionally revises the heavy punctuation of copy-text; the changes here and below simplify and clarify the syntax, and are almost certainly Emerson's.

40.4   Sea,—long intervals . . . centuries,—are] 1847; Sea; vast intervals . . . centuries, are 1841

40.5   feel underlay] 1847; feel, underlay 1841

40.5   underlay every former] 1847; underlay that former 1841

40.6   present, and what] 1847; present, and will always all circumstance, and what 1841

40.10 state, in . . . gulf, in] 1847; state; in . . . gulf; in 1841

Emerson's 1847 revision of semicolons to commas avoids the illogical paralleling of phrases with clauses, and returns to the punctuation of the original journal passage (*JMN*, VII, 518). He also revises the next sentence (40.12) in the same way to improve the parallel structure of the passage.

40.12 past, turns . . . poverty, all . . . shame, confounds . . . rogue, shoves] 1847; past; turns . . . poverty; all . . . shame; confounds . . . rogue; shoves 1841

40.18 more obedience than] 1847; more soul than 1841

The search for the precise word was extensive here; in the original journal passage (*JMN*, VII, 368) Emerson began with "self repose."

40.20 spirits. We] 1847; spirits; who has less, I rule with like facility. We 1841

40.26 ONE. Self-existence is the attribute of the Supreme Cause, and it constitutes the measure of good by the degree in which it enters into all lower forms. All] 1847; ONE. Virtue is the governor, the creator, the reality. All 1841

40.29 much virtue] 1847; much of virtue 1841

40.30 contain. Commerce, husbandry] 1847; contain. Hardship, husbandry 1841

40.32 of its presence] 1847; of the soul's presence 1841

The substitution of the pronoun for "soul" creates a referent in "virtue," although the reference is vague and may not have been intentional.

40.33 growth. Power is in nature the essential measure of right. Nature suffers nothing to remain in her kingdoms which cannot help itself. The genesis and maturation of a planet, its poise and orbit, the bended] 1847; growth. The poise of a planet, the bended 1841

40.37 every animal and vegetable, are] 1847; every vegetable and animal, are 1841

41.1 are demonstrations] 1847; are also demonstrations 1841

41.2 soul. [¶] Thus] 1847; soul. All history from its highest to its trivial passages is the various record of this power. [¶] Thus 1841

41.6 Bid the invaders take] 1847; Bid them take 1841

41.11 is his genius admonished] 1847; is the soul admonished 1841

41.13 of other men] 1847; of men 1841

41.13 alone. I] 1847; alone. Isolation must precede true society. I 1841

41.25 say,—'Come] 1847; say, 'Come 1841

Emerson frequently revises the punctuation between a form of "say" and a quotation from copy-text's usual comma to the 1847 edition's dash, or comma and dash.

41.25 us.' But keep thy state; come not into their] 1847; us.'—Do not spill thy soul; do not all descend; keep thy state; stay at home in thine own heaven; come not for a moment into their facts, into their hub/-/bub of conflicting appearances, but let in the light of thy law on their 1841

41.31   temptations; let] 1847; temptations, let 1841

The 1847 revision's shift from comma to semicolon establishes the parallel clauses and avoids misreading.

41.32   constancy, in] 1847; constancy in 1841

The change is likely Emerson's, made to indicate that "courage and constancy" is in apposition with the preceding phrase, and that "in our Saxon breasts" modifies both pairs, not just the second.

42.9   should. I will] 1847; should. I must be myself. I will 1841

43.3   taskmaster] 1847; task-master 1841

The word is also written solid in the source passage (*JMN*, IV, 283).

43.14   insolvent, cannot] 1847; insolvent; cannot 1841

Emerson usually separates items in series by commas, as he does in the rest of the sentence.

43.15   and do] 1847; and so do 1841

43.19   soldiers. We shun the rugged battle . . . born. [¶] If] 1847; soldiers. The rugged battle . . . born, we shun. [¶] If 1841

43.34   Stoic open the resources] 1847; stoic arise who shall reveal the resources 1841

44.2   window, we] 1847; window,—we 1841

The dash confuses the syntax by separating the dependent clause from its main clause and creates the misleading impression that the main clause is parenthetical.

44.6   self-reliance must] 1847; self-reliance,—a new respect for the divinity in man,—must 1841

44.15   commodity,—any . . . good,—is] 1847; commodity—any . . . good, is 1841

The dash balances the end with the beginning of the offset parenthetical remark. The added comma after "commodity" could be a printer's effort at making punctuation consistent, but Emerson may have added it to improve the balance.

44.19   is meanness and theft. It] 1847; is theft and meanness. It 1841

44.26   replies,— / "His] 1847; replies, / "His 1841

Emerson frequently adds a dash in the 1847 edition to set off quotations or sayings. At 89.13, for example, Emerson adds a dash to set off a "maxim"; at 124.18, a "proverb"; at 154.10, a "high counsel."

45.1   with their own reason. The] 1847; with the soul. The 1841

45.3   wide: him] 1847; wide. Him 1841

45.13   am hindered of] 1847; am bereaved of 1841

45.18   a Fourier, it] 1847; a Spurzheim, it 1841

The substitution of Fourier for Spurzheim may be the result of

Emerson's diminution of interest in phrenology by 1847 and the increase of interest in Fourier and communitarianism.

45.19   proportion to] 1847; proportion always to 1841

45.23   the elemental] 1847; the great elemental 1841

45.26   terminology, as a girl who] 1847; terminology that a girl does who 1841

45.27   botany in] 1847; botany, in 1841

     The substantive change and insertion of the comma earlier in the sentence (45.26) makes the deletion of the comma here necessary for parallel construction. The change is almost certainly Emerson's.

45.28   pupil will find] 1847; pupil will feel a real debt to the teacher,—will find 1841

45.29   of his master's] 1847; of his writings. This will continue until he has exhausted his master's 1841

45.37   that light, unsystematic] 1847; that, light unsystematic 1841

     The punctuation of the copy-text seems a possible printer's error, with a comma misplaced after "that" rather than after "light"—its normal position in Emerson's heavy punctuation.

46.7   the superstition of Travelling, whose idols are Italy, England, Egypt, retains its fascination for] 1847; the idol of Travelling, the idol of Italy, of England, of Egypt, remains for 1841

46.10   did so by sticking] 1847; did so not by rambling round creation as a moth round a lamp, but by sticking 1841

46.12   place. The] 1847; place, and that the merrymen of circumstance should follow as they may. The 1841

46.13   home, and] 1847; home with the soul, and 1841

46.14   still, and shall] 1847; still, and is not gadding abroad from himself, and shall 1841

46.26   paradise. Our first journeys discover to us the indifference of places. At] 1847; paradise. We owe to our first journeys the discovery that place is nothing. At 1841

     The revised version, although perhaps more awkward than the copy-text version, is more precise in its change of "nothing" to "indifference."

46.35   is a] 1847; is itself only a 1841

46.37   and our system] 1847; and the universal system 1841

47.4   our faculties, lean] 1847; our whole minds lean 1841

47.5   Distant. The] 1847; Distant, as the eyes of a maid follow her mistress. The 1841

47.23   Newton? Every] 1847; Newton. Every 1841

     The preceding sentence, also a direct question, ends with a question mark, and the change is probably Emerson's correction of an oversight in copy-text.

47.24   a unique] 1847; an unique 1841

47.25   borrow. Shakspeare] 1847; borrow. If any body will tell me whom the great man imitates in the original crisis when he performs a great act, I will tell him who else than himself can teach him. Shakspeare 1841

47.26   assigned you, and you cannot hope] 1847; assigned thee, and thou canst not hope 1841

47.28   moment for you an] 1847; moment, there is for me an 1841

47.28   utterance brave and]1847; utterance bare and 1841
         Although the source passage (*JMN*, VII, 186) also reads "bare," the 1847 substitution makes logical sense and could certainly have been one of Emerson's own revisions.

47.32   if you can] 1847; if I can 1841

47.33   surely you can] 1847; surely I can 1841

47.34   nature. Abide in] 1847; nature. Dwell up there in 1841

48.4   other. It] 1847; other. Its progress is only apparent, like the workers of a treadmill. It 1841

48.13   that the white man has lost his aboriginal strength. If] 1847; that his aboriginal strength the white man has lost. If 1841

48.19   but lacks so] 1847; but loses so 1841

48.20   has a] 1847; has got a 1841

48.20   he fails of the] 1847; he has lost the 1841

49.4   but will be his] 1847; but be wholly his 1841

49.10   of celestial phenomena than] 1847; of facts than 1841

49.19   Las Cases] C; Las Casas 1841
         Although Emerson often misspells the name (see *JMN*, V, 482; VI, 100; VII, 329), he spells it correctly in the manuscript of *Representative Men* (although it was changed in the first edition, 233.2, to "Las Casas"), and in his journals (see *JMN*, V, 310, 311, 474, 485, 486, 489, 507; VI, 154) . In *JMN*, V, 483, Emerson corrects the spelling by crossing out the "a" and inserting an "e": "Las Cas <a> es."

49.32   esteem the] 1847; esteem what they call the soul's progress, namely, the 1841

49.34   property. They] 1847; property They 1841
         In a printer's error, copy-text dropped the period at the line-end.

49.36   property, out] 1847; property, ashamed of what he has, out 1841

49.37   his nature. Especially] 1847; his being. Especially 1841

50.5   is living] 1847; is permanent and living 1841

50.8   man breathes. "Thy] 1847; man is put. "Thy 1841

50.17   multitude. Not so] 1847; multitude. But not so 1841

50.19   off all foreign support] 1847; off from himself all external support 1841

50.24   is inborn, that] 1847; is in the soul, that 1841

50.25   weak because] 1847; weak only because 1841

50.31   But do] 1847; Bu tdo 1841

This is another of the rare typographical errors of the copy-text.

50.34 shalt sit hereafter out of fear from her rotations. A] 1847; shalt always drag her after thee. A 1841

51.1 other favorable event] 1847; other quite external event 1841

51.2 it. Nothing] 1847; it. It can never be so. Nothing 1841

Rejected Substantives

25.9 *Fortune] Fortunes* 1876; *Fortune* R

The 1876 change was an error, corrected in the next edition.

28.21 connexion] connection 1847

Emerson usually spells the word in British style, "connexion"; it appears thus in *CW*, I, 32.4, 36.4, and 68.25, and in many journal passages from the early *JMN*, V, 431, and VII, 203, to a passage written in 1848 (*JMN*, X, 303). Worcester lists both forms. The American spelling, "connection," appears at 83.32.

28.32 behavior] behaviour 1847; behavior 1865

29.11 parlour] [1847; not in copy-text]; parlor 1865

Emerson uses both spellings, but the 1865 change is almost certainly a printer's house-styling. Although we usually follow copy-text spelling of "or/our" words (see the Rejected Substantives note for 19.33), here the word first appeared in the 1847 edition and we retain the "our" spelling as typical of Emerson's practice at that time.

33.1 bystanders] by-standers 1847

Although Emerson's practice with "by" words is somewhat variable (see "by-play" at 165.23, and in *JMN*, VII, 141; "byways" in *JMN*, VII, 313; and the Emendations note for "byword," 59.4), "bystanders" is also written solid in the source passage (*JMN*, VII, 69-70).

33.2 parlor] parlour 1847; parlor 1865

33.2 aversation] aversion C

Emerson also prefers the now archaic "aversation" in his 1863 essay on Thoreau: "his aversation from English and European manners and tastes almost reached contempt" (*W*, X, 459). Worcester lists both words, giving "aversion" the additional meaning of "cause of aversion."

34.30 you now. Greatness] you how. Greatness 1870; you now. Greatness 1876

35.30 posterity seem to] posterity seems to 1870; posterity seem to R

36.9 have] has 1876; have R

Emerson frequently treats a series with "or" as though it were an "and" series and so a plural subject, as he does in the source passage of this entry (*EL*, II, 223). Since only the 1870 and 1876 editions find the grammar unacceptable and since even in 1870 the change is made inconsistently throughout the sentence (see 36.10), the correction is probably a printer's.

36.10 seem] seems 1870; seem R

See the note for 36.9, above.

36.26 is] are 1870; is R

The correction of the verb to a plural confuses the real subject "total" with "both" and is probably a printer's error.

39.6 tiptoe] titpoe 1847; tiptoe 1865

The typographical error in the 1847 edition remains through all the many impressions from its plates. Even the 1869 impression still carries the misprint, though it was caught and corrected in the Blue and Gold (1865) edition as well as in the 1853 English edition.

39.26 far off] far-off 1847

The source passages (*JMN*, VII, 150, and *EL*, III, 143) also read "far off."

40.12 forever] for ever 1847

40.26 ever blessed] ever-blessed 1847

In his journals Emerson usually writes "ever" compounds as one solid word or as two words without a hyphen (for example, "evermore" in *JMN*, VII, 203, and VIII, 4, and "ever renewing" in *JMN*, VII, 377). In copy-text such compounds are printed hyphenated ("ever-changing," 212.9), solid ("evermore," 45.2, in a passage deleted in 1847 at 72.17, 90.25; and "everlasting," 124.32), and as two words. We retain copy-text in this case as more in agreement with Emerson's practice.

42.3 endeavor] endeavour 1847; endeavor 1865

42.32 neighbor] neighbour 1847; neighbor 1865

43.18 parlor] parlour 1847; parlor 1865

43.21 enterprizes] enterprises 1847

Copy-text spelling is kept here since Emerson spells the word almost equally with either a "z" or an "s" (see *CW*, I, 65.35; *JMN*, VII, 201; IX, 189, for "enterprise," and *CW*, I, 210.36; *JMN*, VII, 400; *L*, II, 286 and 305, for "enterprize").

44.1 acts from himself] acts for himself 1865; acts from himself 1870

The copy-text reading appears in both source passages (*JMN*, VII, 202, and *EL*, III, 265); the 1865 reading is almost certainly a printer's change.

44.27 endeavors] endeavours 1847; endeavors 1865

45.25 Swedenborgianism] Swedenborgism 1847

Though all American editions from 1847 on carry "Swedenborgism" and though Emerson occasionally uses that form in his later journals (*JMN*, VIII, 497; IX, 188), his normal usage is the copy-text form (*JMN*, IV, 17; V, 214; VII, 103, 127; *CEC*, 102, 109).

47.22 Shakspeare] Shakespeare 1865; Shakspeare 1876
47.25 Shakspeare . . . Shakspeare] Shakespeare . . . Shakespeare 1865; Shakspeare . . . Shakspeare 1876
48.26 insurance office] insurance-office 1847
    Copy-text form appears in Emerson's journals (*JMN*, VII, 420).
48.29 entrenched] intrenched 1865; entrenched R
    Worcester lists only "intrenched" and Emerson writes "intrenchments" in the manuscript and 1850 edition of *Representative Men* (232.24), but the source passage for this entry (*EL*, II, 175) carries "entrenched." Although the change accords with Emerson's varying practice, it is unlikely that he sent in spelling changes for the 1865 edition (which he probably did not see to proofread), and the change in this instance is likely a printer's correction.

III. COMPENSATION

Emendations in Copy-Text

53.1 COMPENSATION / The wings of Time are black and white, / Pied with morning and with night. / Mountain tall and ocean deep / Trembling balance duly keep. / In changing moon, in tidal wave, / Glows the feud of Want and Have. / Gauge of more and less through space / Electric star and pencil plays. / The lonely Earth amid the balls / That hurry through the eternal halls, / A makeweight flying to the void, / Supplemental asteroid, / Or compensatory spark, / Shoots across the neutral Dark.] 1847; COMPENSATION. / [not in 1841] 1841

54.1 Man's the elm, and Wealth the vine; / Stanch and strong the tendrils twine: / Though the frail ringlets thee deceive, / None from its stock that vine can reave. / Fear not, then, thou child infirm, / There's no god dare wrong a worm. / Laurel crowns cleave to deserts, / And power to him who power exerts; / Hast not thy share? On winged feet, / Lo! it rushes thee to meet; / And all that Nature made thy own, / Floating in air or pent in stone, / Will rive the hills and swim the sea, / And, like thy shadow, follow thee.] 1847; [not in 1841] 1841

55.8 dwelling-house, greetings, relations, debts] 1847; dwelling-house, the greetings, the relations, the debts 1841
56.14 draw was,—'We] 1847; draw, was; 'We 1841
    The 1847 edition's use of the comma and dash to avoid confusion of the dialogue clarifies the passage.
56.16 by and by] 1847; by-and-by 1841
56.24 falsehood. [¶] I] 1847; falsehood, and summoning the dead to its present tribunal. [¶] I 1841

57.7 Polarity] C; POLARITY 1841

> See the Emendations note for 3.1.

57.10 animals; in the equation of quantity and quality in the fluids of the
animal body; in the systole] 1847; animals; in the systole 1841

57.19 woman; odd, even; subjective] 1847; woman; subjective 1841

58.34 the charges of that eminence. With] 1847; the responsibility of over-
looking. With 1841

> Emerson's 1847 revision avoids the repetition of "overlooks" from
the previous line.

59.4 byword] 1847; by-word 1841

> The original journal passage (*JMN*, VII, 125) also reads "byword."
See also the Emendations note for 135.9.

59.5 nations. It is] 1847; nations. It will not be baulked of its end in
the smallest iota. It is 1841

59.11 convict. If the law is too mild, private vengeance comes in. If the
government is a terrific democracy, the pressure is resisted by an
overcharge of energy in the citizen, and life glows with a fiercer flame.
The] 1847; convict. Nothing arbitrary, nothing artificial can endure.
The 1841

59.17 circumstances] 1847; circumstance 1841

60.10 inspiration] 1847; inspirations 1841

60.10 strength. "It] 1847; strength. It is almighty. All nature feels its
grasp. "It 1841

60.11 it." Justice] 1847; it." It is eternal, but it enacts itself in time and
space. Justice 1841

60.12 postponed. A] 1847; postponed A 1841

> The dropped period occurred at lineend in most printings of the
1841 edition. The Abel Adams copy prints the period.

60.13 Οἱ κύβοι Διὸς ἀεὶ εὐπίπτουσι,—The] 1847; Οἱ κυβοι Διος ἀει εὐπίπτουσι.
The 1841

> The dash connecting the Greek quotation with its English transla-
tion clarifies the passage and seems more likely the author's change
than a compositor's addition.

61.1 partially, to sunder, to] 1847; partially; to sunder; to 1841

61.3 has always been dedicated to] 1847; has been dedicated always to 1841

61.20 to possess one] 1847; to get only one 1841

61.22 bitter. [¶] This dividing and detaching is steadily counteracted] 1847;
bitter. [¶] Steadily is this dividing and detaching counteracted 1841

61.27 things, as soon as we] 1847; things, the moment we 1841

61.34 know; that they] 1847; know; brags that they 1841

> In the 1847 edition Emerson apparently changed his mind about
the repetition of "brags," which he had added as an insertion in the
first version of the passage (*JMN*, VII, 124-125) and had included in
the lecture version (*EL*, III, 148).

61.37   is because he] 1847; is that he 1841
62.25   sleep." / [no ¶] A plain] 1847; sleep." [¶] A plain 1841
62.27   and it] 1847; and indeed it 1841
62.30   and though] 1847; and so though 1841
62.31   invulnerable; the sacred waters did not wash the heel by which
        Thetis held him. Siegfried] 1847; invulnerable; for Thetis held him
        by the heel when she dipped him in the Styx, and the sacred waters
        did not wash that part. Siegfried 1841
63.1   it must be. There] 1847; it always is. There 1841
63.1   made. It would seem, there is always this] 1847; made. Always, it
        would seem, there is this 1841
63.14   Hector dragged . . . Achilles, and . . . Ajax was] 1847; Hector, dragged
        . . . Achilles; and . . . Ajax, was 1841
            The 1847 change from semicolon to comma after "Achilles,"
        together with the deletion of commas after "Hector" and "Ajax,"
        improves the balance of clauses and is in keeping with Emerson's
        practice of sometimes revising copy-text's heavy punctuation.
63.23   it; that which he does not know; that] 1847; it. That is the best part
        of each, which he does not know, that 1841
63.29   embarrass] 1847; embarrasses 1841
            Both the source passage (*JMN*, VII, 185) and the 1841 edition give
        the double subject a singular verb. The correction is a good example
        of Emerson's usual concern for grammar in the 1847 revision.
64.6   and workshops by] 1847; and all languages by 1841
64.21   characterized] 1847; characterised 1841
64.29   harpoon hurled at] 1847; harpoon thrown at 1841
65.10   or as two currents of air mix, with] 1847; or a current of air meets
        another, with 1841
65.17   society, universal and particular] 1847; society, the great and universal
        and the petty and particular 1841
65.20   he teaches] 1847; he always teaches 1841
65.33   is best] 1847; is always best 1841
66.11   is the] 1847; is always the 1841
66.34   of things] 1847; of all things 1841
67.5   gambler, cannot] 1847; gambler cannot extort the benefit, cannot 1841
67.12   universe. The] 1847; universe. Every where and always this law is
        sublime. The 1841
67.14   price,—and] 1847; price; and 1841
67.16   price,—is] 1847; price,—this doctrine is 1841
67.19   sees implicated] 1847; sees ever implicated 1841
67.29   rogue. Commit] 1847; rogue. There is no such thing as conceal-
        ment. Commit 1841
67.33   word, you] 1847; word. you 1841
            The period, one of the few typographical errors in copy-text, was

probably overlooked in proofreading because it falls at the end of both line and page.

67.34 clew. Some damning circumstance always transpires] 1847; clew. Always some damning circumstance transpires 1841

67.35 nature—water . . . gravitation—become] 1847; nature, water . . . gravitation, become 1841

The 1847 punctuation clarifies the appositional nature of "water . . . gravitation."

68.6 so disasters] 1847; so do disasters 1841

68.7 benefactors:— / "Winds] 1847; benefactors. / "Winds 1841

68.20 until he] 1847; until first he 1841

68.25 weakness. The indignation which arms itself with secret forces does not awaken until we are pricked and stung and sorely assailed. A] 1847; weakness. Not until we are pricked and stung and sorely shot at, awakens the indignation which arms itself with secret forces. A 1841

68.33 man throws] 1847; man always throws 1841

69.36 wrongdoers] 1847; wrong doers 1841

"Wrongdoers" is written solid in the source passage (*EL*, II, 109) as well.

70.3 side. Hours of sanity and consideration are always arriving to communities, as to individuals, when the truth is seen, and the martyrs are justified. [¶] Thus] 1847; side. The minds of men are at last aroused; reason looks out and justifies her own, and malice finds all her work vain. It is the whipper who is whipped, and the tyrant who is undone. [¶] Thus 1841

70.18 Being. Essence, or] 1847; Being. Existence, or 1841

70.23 background] 1847; back-ground 1841

"Background" is written without a hyphen in Emerson's journals (*JMN*, VIII, 30, and 105), in "Nature" (*CW*, I, 14.6), and in *Essays II* (1844 edition, 189.10). Emerson also wrote it as two words without a hyphen (*JMN*, IV, 379). See also 161.12.

70.30 anywhere] 1847; any where 1841

Emerson's practice in writing compounds with "any" (anybody, anyhow, anyone, anything) is variable in his own journals, although he tends to write them solid, as he does throughout the manuscript of *Representative Men*. In the journal source passage here (*JMN*, V, 493), the word is written solid. Compounds with "any" are generally printed as two words in copy-text, probably according to a printer's designation. They are occasionally changed in the 1847 revision to accord with Emerson's most common practice, and, since the changes are made unsystematically, they are probably an author's corrections rather than across-the-board printer's changes.

71.8   refuses limits, and always affirms an] 1847; refuses all limits.   It affirms
        in man always an 1841

71.10   Man's life . . . application to him] 1876; His life . . . application to
        man 1841, R
            The rearrangement of noun and pronoun sharpens the sentences.
        Emerson said that he had made revisions in the 1876 text; this is one
        of the few apparent.

71.11   [him], of] 1847; [him], always of 1841
            The bracketed word is an emendation appearing only in the 1876
        edition (see the Emendations note for 71.10), where "man" appeared
        in other editions.

71.14   is no] 1847; is, therefore, no 1841

71.16   comparative.   Material good] 1847; comparative.   All external good
        1841

71.22   new burdens.   I] 1847; new responsibility.   I 1841

71.28   Bernard,—"Nothing] 1847; Bernard, "Nothing 1841

71.37   it.   He almost shuns their eye; he] 1847; it.   Almost he shuns their
        eye; almost he 1841

72.2   But see the facts nearly] 1847; But face the facts, and see them nearly
        1841

72.3   them, as] 1847; them all, as 1841

72.11   the nature] 1847; the eternal nature 1841

72.11   to appropriate all things.   Jesus] 1847; to appropriate and make all
        things its own.   Jesus 1841

72.17   growth.   Every] 1847; growth.   Evermore it is the order of nature to
        grow, and every 1841

72.25   the living form is seen] 1847; the form is alway seen 1841

72.29   recognizes] 1847; recognises 1841

72.32   resting, not . . . resisting, not] 1847; resting not . . . resisting not 1841
            The addition of the commas clarifies the reading of the sentence and
        is a change characteristic of Emerson's practice.

Rejected Substantives

56.17   tomorrow] to-morrow 1847
            In his journals and in the manuscript of *Representative Men*,
        Emerson writes "today" and "tomorrow" solid, without hyphens.   The
        words are hyphenated in most of his published works, but probably
        because of house-styling.   The 1841 reading here is probably a
        printer's failure to "correct" his copy; the 1847 reading is probably a
        printer's change.

59.2   that the world] that that world 1870; that the world 1876
            Since the 1870 version appears in no other edition and since the

source passage (*EL*, III, 146) also has the copy-text version, the change is probably a printer's.

60.4   re-appears [hyphenated at line-end in copy-text]] reappears 1847

Although "reappears" is printed solid at 108.28, and is written solid twice in the manuscript of *Representative Men*, Emerson usually hyphenates words with "re" as a prefix. See, for example, "re-unites" (61.25), "re-commencement" (*CW*, I 52.1), and "re-makes" (*Essays II*, 1844, 145). See also the Rejected Substantives note for "re-create," 73.1. An exception is "reinforce," which is hyphenated at line-end in copy-text (see the Word Division list for 32.7), but appears solid in the 1847 edition and in several source passages ("reinforce" in *EL*, III, 309, and "reinforcement" in *JMN*, VIII, 137).

60.26   causal] casual 1870; causal 1876

The confusion of "casual" for "causal" occurs in the 1870 edition in an earlier passage as well (see Rejected Substantives for 8.22); context in both cases indicates unmistakably a printer's error.

61.11   ends] end 1870; ends R

The change within the editions of 1870 and 1876 seems more probably a printer's error than authorial, since "ends" is the form used in the second half of the sentence.

61.25   re-unites] reunites 1847

63.18   endeavored] endeavoured 1847; endeavored 1865

63.33   Shakspeare] Shakespeare 1865; Shakspeare 1876

65.9   fellow man] fellow-man 1847

65.13   neighbor] neighbour 1847; neighbor 1865

65.19   instructer] instructor 1865

Emerson uses both "instructer" and "instructor"; Worcester accepts both spellings. The "er" spelling appears in the source passage (*JMN*, VII, 198), earlier in "The American Scholar" (*CW*, I, 59.32), and in the manuscript and first edition of *Representative Men* (20.6).

66.1   neighbor's] neighbour's 1847; neighbor's 1865

66.5   neighbor] neighbour 1847; neighbor 1865

66.8   neighbor's] neighbour's 1847; neighbor's 1865

67.16   leger] ledger 1865; leger R

Emerson's usual spelling when referring to his own accounts is "leger" (see Alterations note for 68.3, *CW*, I, 293). The 1865, 1870, 1876, and Centenary editions usually correct the spelling to "ledger," though in this case the Centenary does not.

69.4   honied] honeyed 1847

Neither Webster nor Worcester carries the participial form, but the *OED* gives both spellings, and Emerson uses "honied" in the source passage (*JMN*, VII, 95).

69.24   endeavors] endeavours 1847; endeavors 1865

70.19   Being is the] Being in the 1870; Being is the R

72.6   neighbors] neighbours 1847; neighbors 1865
73.1   re-create] recreate 1847
        The hyphen also appears in the source passage (*JMN*, VII, 202).
73.6   forevermore] for evermore 1847
73.24   garden flower] garden/-/flower 1847; garden-flower 1865
        Copy-text also prints "garden beds" as two words (141.28).
73.27   neighborhoods] neighbourhoods 1847; neighborhoods 1865

IV. SPIRITUAL LAWS

Emendations in Copy-Text

75.1   SPIRITUAL LAWS / The living Heaven thy prayers respect, / House at once and architect, / Quarrying man's rejected hours, / Builds therewith eternal towers; / Sole and self-commanded works, / Fears not undermining days, / Grows by decays, / And, by the famous might that lurks / In reaction and recoil, / Makes flame to freeze, and ice to boil; / Forging, through swart arms of Offence, / The silver seat of Innocence.] 1847; SPIRITUAL LAWS. / [not in 1841] 1841
77.15   unhurt. Neither vexations nor calamities abate] 1847; unhurt. Distress never, trifles never abate 1841
        The 1847 revision clarifies the dual subject of "abate."
78.19   magnetism, which is sure to select what belongs to it. [¶] In] 1847; magnetism which with sure discrimination selects its own. [¶] In 1841
78.24   everywhere] 1847; every where 1841
78.24   whether . . . temptation. But] 1847; Whether . . . temptation? But 1841
        Since the question is direct, the 1847 change of the question mark to a period makes more grammatical sense, and is typical of the kind of punctuation changes Emerson makes in the 1847 revision. See also 133.12, for the same kind of change.
79.15   secret, it would instantly lose its] 1847; secret, instantly it would lose all its 1841
79.19   it; that . . . is; that] 1847; it, that . . . is, that 1841
        The 1847 change makes the clauses parallel with the last clause in the sentence, punctuated with a semicolon (79.22) in copy-text.
79.25   with laws] 1847; with spiritual laws 1841
79.27   lesson. Nature] 1847; lesson with calm superiority. Nature 1841
79.32   us, 'So hot? my little Sir.'] 1847; us, "So hot? my little sir." 1841
        The single quotation marks of the 1847 edition are accepted to indicate Emerson's normal convention for imaginary instead of real quotation. See the Emendations note for 30.9.

80.6   dollars; merchants have; let] 1847; dollars. Merchants have. Let 1841

80.7   corn; poets . . . sing; women . . . sew; laborers . . . hand; the] 1847;
corn. Poets . . . sing. Women . . . sew. Laborers . . . hand. The
1841

81.15 day would . . . us, that . . . law than . . . will regulates] 1847; day,
would . . . us that . . . law, than . . . will, regulates 1841
The punctuation changes throughout the first part of this sentence
greatly improve the syntax and clarify the passage.

81.17 are unnecessary, and fruitless] 1847; are very unnecessary, and altogether fruitless 1841

81.21 O my brothers] 1847; O myb rothers 1841
This is one of the few typographical errors in copy-text.

81.34 which animates all whom it floats, and you] 1847; which flows into
you as life, place yourself in the full centre of that flood, then you 1841

82.23 over a deepening channel into] 1847; over God's depths into 1841

82.29 other. His] 1847; other. When he is true and faithful, his 1841

83.1   supply, and creates] 1847; supply. He creates 1841

83.2   enjoyed. By] 1847; enjoyed. He provokes the wants to which he
can minister. By 1841

83.12 proportion, he] 1847; proportion as a wise and good man, he 1841

83.13 justify his work to their eyes. If] 1847; justify himself to their eyes
for doing what he does. If 1841

83.14 is mean, let] 1847; is trivial, let 1841

83.27 scissors, and] 1847; scissors; and 1841
The semicolon creates a misleading division of the series into parts;
the change in 1847 is probably Emerson's.

83.31 any. In] 1847; any. Accept your genius, and say what you think.
In 1841

84.3   him scatter] 1847; him play with them, and scatter 1841

84.8   universe. A] 1847; universe. As a man thinketh, so is he, and as a
man chooseth, so is he and so is nature. A 1841

84.29 literature. What] 1847; literature. Respect them, for they have their
origin in deepest nature. What 1841

84.32 Everywhere] 1847; Every where 1841

85.9   M. de Narbonne] 1847; M. Narbonne 1841
Copy-text prints the name correctly in 85.5.

85.10 Cabinet. [¶] Nothing] 1847; Cabinet. [¶] A mutual understanding
is ever the firmest chain. Nothing 1841

85.19 its level] 1847; its own level 1841

85.36 ripened; then] 1847; ripened,—then 1841
The semicolon makes more syntactical sense than the dash.

86.15 night bear] 1847; night always bear 1841

86.16 are exaggerations] 1847; are only exaggerations 1841

86.17 our evil] 1847; our own evil 1841

86.18   sometimes beholds his] 1847; sometimes sees his 1841

86.24   himself. The good, compared] 1847; himself that he sees. The good
which he sees, compared 1841

86.35   writes] 1847; writeth 1841
Emerson often alters Biblical or archaic constructions in his 1847
text (see the Emendations note for 37.21), but apparently he overlooked the revision of "maketh" in the parallel lead sentence of the
preceding paragraph (86.14) .

86.36   have observed a] 1847; have seen a 1841

87.4   Pelews' tongue] 1847; Pelews tongue 1841
In the source passages (*JMN*, III, 327, and *EL*, II, 149) the apos-
trophe is properly used.

87.27   company, with] 1847; company; with 1841
The copy-text semicolon is a probable printer's error, since it
precedes a prepositional phrase.

87.28   be ungrateful] 1847; be very ungrateful 1841

87.28   them loudly] 1847; them very loudly 1841

87.36   But only] 1847; But later, if we are so happy, we learn that only 1841

88.3   scholar forgets himself, and apes the] 1847; scholar and the prophet
forget themselves, and ape the 1841

88.4   beauty, and follows] 1847; beauty. He is a fool and follows 1841;
beauty, and follow 1870; beauty, and follows R

88.5   girl, not yet taught by religious passion to know the noble woman]
1847; girl, and not with religious, ennobling passion, a woman 1841

88.11   is a maxim] 1847; is an universal maxim 1841

88.13   attitude which belong to you, and] 1847; attitude to which you see
your unquestionable right, and 1841

88.14   It leaves] 1847; It always leaves 1841

88.14   man, with . . . unconcern, to] 1847; man with . . . unconcern to 1841
The commas clarify the slight ambiguity in copy-text by indicating
that "with . . . unconcern" describes the world's attitude rather than
the man.

88.31   and experience to the company. If] 1847; and being to the audience.
If 1841

88.32   a confidence, we] 1847; a communication, we 1841

89.2   forms of logic or of oath can give it evidence. The] 1847; forms of
grammar and no plausibility can give it evidence, and no array of
arguments. The 1841

89.7   think, if . . . eloquence, then] 1847; think; if . . . eloquence; then 1841
Since Emerson does not normally separate introductory adverbial
clauses by semicolons, the 1847 revision was probably made by him.

89.13   maxim:—"Look] 1847; maxim: "Look 1841

89.20   say, 'What] 1847; say—'what 1841
Although Emerson usually *adds* dashes between forms of "say" and

quotations, here, because the quotation comes in the middle of a sentence, the lighter punctuation is more appropriate and the change is probably the author's.

89.28 last. Gilt edges, vellum, and morocco, and presentation-copies] 1847; last. All the gilt edges and vellum and morocco, all the presentation-copies 1841

90.6 Michel] 1847; Michael 1841

Emerson occasionally spells the painter's name "Michael" (see *JMN*, IV, 230), but his most common spelling is that of the 1847 edition: for example, in the manuscript and first edition of *Representative Men*, in his journals, and in his lecture manuscripts (see *JMN*, IV, 155, 160, 260, 356; VII, 16, 235; *EL*, I, 99n).

90.11 must; it] 1847; must: he used no election: it 1841

90.19 organs,—not] 1847; organs, not 1841

The dash clarifies the rhetorical pause in the sentence.

90.25 character evermore publishes itself. The] 1847; character does evermore publish itself. It will not be concealed. It hates darkness,—it rushes into light. The 1841

90.28 still, if] 1847; still, you show it; if 1841

90.30 slavery, on marriage, on socialism, on secret societies, on the college] 1847; slavery, on the college 1841

91.7 he never feared the] 1847; he feared never the 1841

91.21 and all fear of remaining unknown is not less so. If] 1847; and idle is all fear of remaining unknown. If 1841

91.26 gauged] 1847; guaged 1841

91.28 weighed in the course] 1847; weighed in the balance, in the course 1841

91.32 airs and pretensions] 1847; airs, and pretension 1841

91.32 an older boy says] 1847; an old boy sniffs thereat, and says 1841

91.33 has] 1847; hath 1841

91.37 there need never] 1847; there can never 1841

92.1 beings. Pretension] 1847; beings, when we seek the truth. Pretension 1841

92.4 slavery. [¶] As] 1847; slavery. [¶] Always as 1841

92.8 Never was a sincere word utterly] 1847; Never a sincere word was utterly 1841

92.9 ground, but there is some heart to greet and accept it] 1847; ground. Always the heart of man greets and accepts it 1841

92.12 light. Concealment] 1847; light which all men may read but himself. Concealment 1841

92.17 eye, cuts lines of mean expression in his] 1847; eye, demeans his 1841

92.26 exclaimed,—"How] 1847; exclaimed, "How 1841

92.37 which these] 1847; which all these 1841

92.37 convey is, Be, and] 1847; convey, is, Be and 1841

The 1847 changes improve the reading of the sentence and clarify the "lesson." They are likely to have been author's changes.

93.13   head, excuse . . . reasons, and accumulate] 1847; head, they excuse . . . reasons, they accumulate 1841

93.15   magnitude. We] 1847; magnitude. God loveth not size: whale and minnow are of like dimension. But we 1841

93.23   says,—'Thus] 1847; says, 'Thus 1841

93.24   menials, serve] 1847; menials, do serve 1841

93.25   ability, execute] 1847; ability, do execute 1841

94.20   me, and unlocks] 1847; me alway, unlocks 1841

94.36   me heed my] 1847; me do my 1841

95.1   have justified] 1847; have washed my own face, or justified 1841

95.1   my benefactors] 1847; my own benefactors 1841

95.6   Bunting,— / "He] 1847; Bunting, / "He 1841

95.8   books,—He] 1847; books: He 1841

95.10   and I] 1847; and so, without any constraint, I 1841

95.12   time,—my facts, my] 1847; time: my world, my facts, all my 1841

95.21   player. The] 1847; player. Thus he signified his sense of a great fact. The 1841

95.30   world,—palaces] 1847; world, palaces 1841

The dash sets off the examples of "all that is . . . solid and precious," completed by the second dash in the sentence ("kingdoms,—").

95.33   nations. Let] 1847; nations. But the great names cannot stead him, if he have not life himself. Let 1841

96.2   daybeams] 1847; day-beams 1841

Emerson writes "daybeams" as one word in the source passage (*JMN*, VII, 189).

Rejected Substantives

78.19   baulk] balk 1847

Although Worcester prefers "balk" and the word is so spelled throughout the 1847 edition, Emerson consistently spells the word "baulk" in the manuscript of *Representative Men*, and in his journals and letters (see *JMN*, VII, 180, 230, 307, 330; V, 8, 328; *L*, II, 80, 140, 157, 216; *CW*, I, 37.37).

79.12   Shakspeare . . . Shakspeare] Shakespeare . . . Shakespeare 1865; Shakspeare . . . Shakspeare 1876

79.24   vantage ground] vantage-ground 1847

In the source passage and elsewhere in the lectures (*EL*, III, 313, and 243), Emerson spells the phrase without a hyphen.

79.27   external nature] eternal nature 1870; external nature R

The source passage (*EL*, III, 299) also reads "external," indicating that the reading in the 1870 and 1876 editions is probably a printer's error.

79.30   Abolition convention . . . Temperance meeting] Abolition-convention
. . . Temperance-meeting 1847
Both examples appear without hyphens in the source passage
(*EL*, III, 299).

79.37   Sunday schools] Sunday-schools 1847
Emerson rarely hyphenates compounds with "school" (see the Rejected Substantives note for "dancing school" and "singing school"
at 101.26), and he was especially consistent in spelling "Sunday
school" (for an exception, see *L*, IV, 532). In his journals he writes
such examples without hyphens even when using them as adjectives
(see *JMN*, V, 45, and 173; *L*, V, 494, 499, and 534). Both here and
at 80.9, the hyphenated forms are rejected as probable printer's versions.

80.9   Sunday school] Sunday-school 1847

80.16   travestie] travesty 1870
Although Worcester lists only "travesty," Emerson characteristically
uses the older form (see *JMN*, VII, 204).

80.30   forever] for ever 1847

81.9   tin-pedlar] tin-pedler 1847
The source passage (*EL*, III, 292) reads "tin pedlar." The 1847
edition alters copy-text's spelling to "tin-peddlers" at 121.11.

83.20   aims. [¶] We like] aims. [no ¶] We like 1876; aims. [¶] We like R

84.14   steel. [¶] Those] steel. [no ¶] Those 1847
Since "steel" occurs at a line-end in the 1847 text, the lack of a
paragraph indentation in the next line could be a printer's error.

85.8   connexion] connection 1847

86.11   demeanor] demeanour 1847; demeanor 1865

87.12   enamored] enamoured 1847; enamored 1870

87.18   billiard room] billiard-room 1847
In his journals Emerson also writes "recitation rooms" without
a hyphen (*JMN*, VII, 238) but varies his spelling of other forms
of "room" compounds (for example, "reading-rooms" at 120.6;
"sittingroom" and "recitation-rooms" in *Essays II*, 1844 edition, 187.9,
and 282.7).

90.34   fellow men] fellow-men 1847

91.17   endeavoring] endeavouring 1847; endeavoring 1865

91.25   judgment days] judgment-days 1847
In the journals and lectures the phrase is usually unhyphenated
and capitalized (see *EL*, II, 301; *JMN*, X, 62, and 94).

91.28   new comer] new-comer 1847
The phrase also is unhyphenated in *Essays II* (1844 edition, p. 87).

91.33 tomorrow] to-morrow 1847

See the Rejected Substantives note for 56.17.

94.9 busy-bodies] busybodies 1847

95.5 neighbors] neighbours 1847; neighbors 1865

V. LOVE

Emendations in Copy-Text

97.1 LOVE / "I was as a gem concealed; / Me my burning ray revealed." *Koran*.] 1847; LOVE. [not in 1841] 1841

99.1 [¶] Every promise] ed.; [no ¶] EVERY soul is a celestial Venus to every other soul. The heart has its sabbaths and jubilees, in which the world appears as a hymeneal feast, and all natural sounds and the circle of the seasons are erotic odes and dances. Love is omnipresent in nature as motive and reward. Love is our highest word, and the synonym of God. Every promise 1841; [¶] EVERY promise 1847

100.1 that, kindling] 1847; that kindling 1841

The 1847 comma clarifies the syntax by signaling that "kindling" begins a nonrestrictive modifier.

100.12 young and beautiful] 1847; young, ever beautiful 1841

100.15 adherence to facts] 1847; adherence to the actual, to facts 1841

100.18 certain stain of] 1847; certain slime of 1841

100.22 shrink and moan. Alas] 1847; shrink and shrink. Alas 1841

100.23 life the] 1847; life all the 1841

100.24 budding joy, and] 1847; budding sentiment, and 1841

100.26 are melancholy] 1847; are always melancholy 1841

100.27 noble. In the actual world—the painful kingdom . . . place—dwell care] 1847; noble. It is strange how painful is the actual world,—the painful kingdom . . . place. There dwells care 1841

100.28 care, and canker, and] 1847; care and canker and 1841

Emerson's general practice in the journals and in the manuscript of *Representative Men* is not to put commas in this type of series. He occasionally does, however, and the changes here and in 100.30, where there appears a substantive change as well, are probably Emerson's.

100.30 But grief cleaves to names, and persons, and the partial interests of to-day and yesterday. [¶] The] 1847; But with names and persons and the partial interests of to-day and yesterday, is grief. [¶] The 1841

101.10 child disposing her] 1847; child arranging her 1841

101.28 By and by] 1847; By-and-by 1841

101.32   told, that in some public discourses of mine my reverence] 1847;
          told that my philosophy is unsocial, and, that in public discourses,
          my reverence 1841

101.33   intellect has made me] 1847; intellect makes me 1841

102.20   heart bound, and] 1847; heart beat, and 1841

102.21   when he became] 1847; when we became 1841

102.31   where'er] 1847; where e'er 1841
          Emerson wrote the word as solid in the source passage (*EL*, III, 57)
          and when he quoted the stanza in *Parnassus* (p. 62).

103.2   love,— / "All] 1847; love, / "All 1841

103.11   passion rebuilds the] 1847; passion re-makes the 1841

103.13   soul. The notes are almost articulate] 1847; soul. Almost the notes
          are articulate 1841

103.16   and he almost fears] 1847; and almost he fears 1841

103.24   groan,— / These] 1847; groan, / These 1841
          The lecture source passage (*EL*, III, 58) carries the copy-text punc-
          tuation, but since Emerson frequently adds dashes in similar cases in
          the 1847 revision, and since the dash also appears in the manuscript
          notebook for Emerson's anthology, *Parnassus* (Houghton 124, p. 108),
          the change is probably the author's.

103.31   The heats that have opened his] 1847; The causes that have sharpened
          his 1841

104.8   society; *he* . . . somewhat; *he* . . . person; *he*] 1847; society. *He* . . .
          somewhat. *He* . . . person. *He* 1841

104.11   youth. Beauty . . . celebrate, welcome . . . themselves, seems] RWE,
          1847; youth. Let us approach and admire Beauty . . . celebrate,—
          beauty, welcome . . . themselves. Wonderful is its charm. It seems
          1841
          In the Abel Adams copy, Emerson marked the excisions in brackets
          in the text and noted inside the back cover that the page was "cor-
          rected."

104.17   was pictured with] 1847; was ever painted with 1841

104.20   unworthy, she] 1847; unworthy, yet she 1841

104.23   lover never sees personal] 1847; lover sees never personal 1841

104.27   birds. [¶] The ancients called beauty the] 1847; birds. [¶] Beauty is
          ever that divine thing the ancients esteemed it. It is, they said, the
          1841

104.32   gleam, points] 1847; gleam point 1841
          Both the grammar (the pronoun referent "It" starting the next
          sentence) and the original source passage (*JMN*, V, 303) support the
          1847 change to a singular verb with an offsetting comma, although
          Emerson did use copy-text's form earlier in *EL*, III, 59.

104.34   love known and described in society, but] 1847; love that society
          knows and has, but 1841

104.36   sweetness, to] 1847; sweetness, a true faerie land; to 1841
104.37   cannot approach beauty] 1847; cannot get at beauty 1841
105.6   same fluency may] 1847; same fact may 1841
105.19   existence." [¶] In like manner, personal beauty is then first charming]
          1847; existence." [¶] So must it be with personal beauty, which love
          worships. Then first is it charming 1841
105.23   satisfactions; when it makes] 1847; satisfactions; when it seems / "too
          bright and good, / For human nature's daily food;" / when it makes
          1841
105.29   is not you, but your radiance. It] 1847; is the radiance of you and
          not you. It 1841
106.30   which it has contracted] 1847; which they have contracted 1841
106.31   ascends to] 1847; ascends ever to 1841
107.1   is prowling in the] 1847; is eternally boring down into the 1841
107.2   has a savor] 1847; has ever a slight savor 1841
107.3   when this] 1847; when the snout of this 1841
107.13   But things] 1847; But by the necessity of our constitution, things 1841
107.18   the progressive, idealizing instinct, predominate] 1847; the high pro-
          gressive idealizing instinct, these predominate 1841
107.18   and the] 1847; and ever the 1841
107.23   intelligence, of] 1847; intelligence,—of 1841
          The dash in copy-text is possibly a holdover from the source read-
          ings (*JMN*, V, 297, and *EL*, III, 64) where Emerson rhetorically
          repeated the beginning of the sentence ("[how] little think . . . ") and
          so needed the longer pause (though he did not use a dash in the
          lecture MS). Here the dash interrupts the syntactical flow of the sen-
          tence, and the revision is probably the author's.
108.6   star, the] 1847; star; the 1841
          Copy-text's semicolon awkwardly separates items in a series other-
          wise punctuated by commas.
108.8   up costly] 1847; up all costly 1841
108.23   craving a] 1847; craving for a 1841
108.25   arise] RWE, 1847; arises 1841
          The shift to a plural verb to agree with plural subjects is marked for
          correction in Emerson's hand in the Abel Adams copy of the 1841 edi-
          tion, indicating that it was his correction rather than a printer's
          revision. The "s" is deleted both in the text and in the margin with a
          delete sign.
108.31   to employ all] 1847; to extort all 1841
108.32   the strength] 1847; the whole strength 1841
109.3   hour. The] 1847; hour. All the 1841
109.5   and the] 1847; and all the 1841
109.29   seeks] RWE, 1847; seeketh 1841

In the Abel Adams copy, Emerson crossed out the verb ending
and put an "x" in the margin.

109.30 everywhere] 1847; every where 1841

Rejected Substantives

99.7 on man] on a man 1870; on man R

The 1870 and 1876 variant seems more probably a printer's change
than authorial.

99.18 savor] savour 1847; savor 1870

101.8 teazes] teases 1847

Since Emerson spells the word both ways (see *CEC*, 192, and *L*, II,
304 for "teaze"; *JMN*, VII, 171 for "teases"), we keep the copy-text
version. Worcester lists only "tease," but the *OED* gives both spellings
for Emerson's time.

101.9 school house] school-house 1847

The source passage (*JMN*, VII, 171) also reads "school house."
In his journals, Emerson spells compounds with "school" (school
boy, schoolmen, school girls) either as two words or solid (for example,
"schoolboys," *JMN*, VII, 222, and "schoolhouse," *JMN*, X, 18). The
hyphenated versions (see "school-boys" at 214.23) are probably
printer's spellings. See also the Rejected Substantives note for 101.17.

101.14 neighbors] neighbours 1847; neighbors 1865

101.17 school girls] school-girls 1847

The source passage (*EL*, III, 55) also reads "school girls."

101.26 dancing school . . . singing school] dancing-school . . . singing-school
1847

The source passage (*JMN*, VII, 159) spells both examples without
hyphens.

103.20 Fountain heads] Fountain-heads 1847

Although elsewhere in *Essays I* Emerson uses a hyphen in "fountain-
head" (199.26), in the earlier lecture version (*EL*, III, 58) and in the
manuscript notebook for the anthology *Parnassus* (Houghton 124,
p. 108) Emerson writes the word without a hyphen. The published
Parnassus incorrectly prints "Fountain-head" (p. 139).

104.36 transcendant] transcendent 1847

Worcester gives only "transcendent," the spelling that should
follow from the Latin root. Emerson, however, almost invariably
spells the word adjectively "transcendant," although he does not
misspell the cognate forms "transcendental" or "transcendentalist."
The word is spelled with an "a" throughout the journals and lectures
(see *EL*, III, 60, and *JMN*, V, 303), and several times in the manuscript of *Representative Men*, although elsewhere in *Essays I* (28.26,

152.13, and 160.36) it appears in the uncharacteristic spelling, perhaps corrected there by the publisher or printer. See also the note in *CW*, I for 135.34 (p. 302).

105.6   have found not, and] have not found, and 1847

The change of the inversion incorrectly alters Mrs. Hemans' translation of the excerpt from Richter (see the informational note for 105.4), and was probably made accidentally in Emerson's overall enthusiasm for altering inversions for the 1847 edition.

105.7   plastic] plastie 1847; plastic 1865

This printer's error remained in all later stereotype impressions of the 1847 text through 1869.

105.10   measuring wand] measuring-wand 1847

The source passage (*EL*, III, 60) also has no hyphen.

105.16   endeavors] endeavours 1847; endeavors 1865

107.15   Neighborhood] Neighbourhood 1847; Neighborhood 1865

108.24   behavior] behaviour 1847; behavior 1865

VI. FRIENDSHIP

Emendations in Copy-Text

111.1   FRIENDSHIP / A ruddy drop of manly blood / The surging sea outweighs, / The world uncertain comes and goes, / The lover rooted stays. / I fancied he was fled, / And, after many a year, / Glowed unexhausted kindliness / Like daily sunrise there. / My careful heart was free again,— / O friend, my bosom said, / Through thee alone the sky is arched, / Through thee the rose is red, / All things through thee take nobler form, / And look beyond the earth, / The mill-round of our fate appears / A sun-path in thy worth. / Me too thy nobleness has taught / To master my despair; / The fountains of my hidden life / Are through thy friendship fair.] 1870; FRIENDSHIP. / [not in 1841] 1841; FRIENDSHIP. / A ruddy . . . earth, / And is the mill-round of our fate / A sun-path . . . fair. 1847

114.20   more. [¶] What is so pleasant as these . . . which make a . . . again? What so delicious as a just . . . feeling? How] 1847; more. [¶] Pleasant are these . . . which relume a . . . again. Delicious is a just . . . feeling. How 1841

114.27   vanish,—all] 1847; vanish;—all 1841

The copy-text punctuation confuses the parallel nouns within the clause.

114.33   God the] 1847; God, the 1841

Copy-text's comma, which does not appear in the source passage

(*JMN*, VII, 212), changes the meaning of "call" from "give a name to" to "communicate with or summon," and makes "the Beautiful" an appositive. The reading does not make sense within the context of the sentence, and so we accept the 1847 edition's return to the original punctuation as probably an author's change.

115.4   by and by] 1847; by-and-by 1841

The source passage (*JMN*, VII, 212) reads "by & by."

115.9   them derides and cancels] 1847; them, both deride and cancel 1841

In the Abel Adams copy, Emerson changed "both" to "doth" by crossing out the "b" and marking a "d" in the margin, thus correcting a probable printer's error and restoring the reading found in the source passage (*JMN*, VII, 212). The 1847 revision, like the source version and the Abel Adams correction, clarifies the confused grammar by changing verb number. It also revises the archaic verb form of the original, as Emerson had already done in 1841 by replacing the journal's "conniveth" with "connives" (115.11). This emendation is part of extensive authorial revisions of the journal and copy-text versions (see 115.14 and 115.15).

115.10   sex, circumstance] 1847; sex and circumstance 1841

115.14   are new poetry of the first Bard,—poetry] RWE, 1847; are not stark and stiffened persons, but the new-born poetry of God,—poetry 1841

In the Abel Adams copy, Emerson bracketed the 1841 version from "These" through "but," part of which he then deleted in 1847.

115.15   flowing, Apollo] RWE, 1847; flowing, and not yet caked in dead books with annotation and grammar, but Apollo 1841

In the Abel Adams copy, Emerson bracketed the entire section deleted in 1847.

115.24   me a] 1847; me always a 1841

115.25   have often had fine fancies about persons which have] 1847; have had such fine fancies lately about two or three persons, as have 1841

115.29   mine,—and a property] 1847; mine,—wild, delicate, throbbing property 1841

115.33   his,—his . . . instruments,—fancy] 1847; his, his . . . instruments, fancy 1841

116.10   love by mining] 1847; love by facing the fact, by mining 1841

117.4   relations. The instinct] 1847; relations. Ever the instinct 1841

117.5   and the] 1847; and ever the 1841

117.10   Dear Friend] ed.; DEAR FRIEND 1841

See the Emendations note for 3.1.

117.10   [Friend]:— / If] 1847; FRIEND, / If 1841

For the brackets on "Friend," see the previous entry.

117.23   are austere and] 1847; are great, austere, and 1841

118.3   heyday] 1847; hey-day 1841

In the source passage (*JMN*, VII, 333) and elsewhere in the journals

(*JMN*, VII, 215, and 392), Emerson spells the word without a hyphen; it is also printed solid later in copy-text (183.33). Both Webster and Worcester give "heyday."

118.9   contest, the] 1847; contest, instantly the 1841

118.25 regards, but] 1847; regards; but 1841

   The semicolon in copy-text, which may have been a printer's error since it appears at the line-end, confuses the clausal structure of the sentence.

118.35 frostwork] 1847; frost-work 1841

   Emerson writes the word solid in a passage in his journals (*JMN*, IV, 74).

119.10 law! He] 1847; law! It is no idle band, no holiday engagement. He 1841

119.17 the speed in] RWE, 1847; the hap in 1841

   In the Abel Adams copy, Emerson crossed out "hap" in the text.

120.7   to the like plaindealing, and] 1847; to face him, and 1841; to the like plain dealing, and 1865; to the like plain-dealing, and 1870; to the like plaindealing, and R

120.12 civility,—requires . . . humored; he] 1847; civility, requires . . . humored;—he 1841

   In the 1847 version, the dash is moved from the position after a semicolon, where it is superfluous, to set off the parallel phrases ("requires . . . ,—requires . . .") from each other.

120.15 and which spoils] 1847; and so spoils 1841

120.17 requiring any stipulation on my part. A] 1847; requiring me to stoop, or to lisp, or to mask myself. A 1841

120.33 says,—"I] 1847; says, "I 1841

120.37 it vaults over] 1847; it walks over 1841

121.12 which celebrates] 1847; which only celebrates 1841

121.24 drudgery. [¶] Friendship may] 1847; drudgery. [¶] For perfect friendship it may 1841

121.25 costly, each so well tempered and] 1847; costly, so well tempered each, and 1841

121.28 that its satisfaction can very seldom be assured. It] 1847; that very seldom can its satisfaction be realized. It 1841

122.8   individuals merge] 1847; individuals at once merge 1841

122.9   coextensive] 1865; cöextensive 1841; co/-/extensive 1847; co-extensive R

   Emerson wrote the word solid without a diaeresis in the source passage (*JMN*, V, 374), as was his practice for this type of word in the manuscript of *Representative Men*. In any case, the 1841 diaeresis is placed over the wrong vowel.

122.35 *mine.* I hate, where] 1847; *mine.* It turns the stomach, it blots the daylight; where 1841

Friendship

In the Abel Adams copy, Emerson deleted the semicolon after "daylight" and inserted a comma and dash in the margin. He also noted the page number for this passage in his list of corrections inside the back cover, but evidently decided later to revise the entire passage.

123.2   it. That high office requires] 1847; it. To be capable of that high office, requires 1841

123.6   recognize] 1847; recognise 1841

123.8   magnanimous; who] 1847; magnanimous. He must be so, to know its law. He must be one who 1841

123.9   economy; who] 1847; economy. He must be one who 1841

123.10   not intermeddle] 1847; not dare to intermeddle 1841

123.13   treatment. We talk] 1847; treatment. We must not be wilful, we must not provide. We talk 1841

123.15   course he] 1847; course, if he be a man, he 1841

123.17   aside; give . . . room; let . . . expand. Are] 1847; aside. Give . . . room. Let . . . expand. Be not so much his friend that you can never know his peculiar energies, like fond mammas who shut up their boy in the house until he is almost grown a girl. Are 1841

Emerson marked this passage with a line in the margin of the Abel Adams copy.

123.22   pleasure, instead of the noblest benefit. [¶] Let] 1847; pleasure instead of the pure nectar of God. [¶] Let 1841

124.3   superiorities; wish] 1847; superiorities. Wish 1841

124.4   thy counterpart. Let] 1847; thy great counterpart; have a princedom to thy friend. Let 1841

124.9   little. It suffices me. It] 1847; little. Me it suffices. It 1841

Emerson marked this passage with a line in the margin of the Abel Adams copy.

124.18   proverb;—you] 1847; proverb; you 1841

124.28   or how to] 1847; or to 1841

124.31   thy heart shall] 1847; thy soul shall 1841

124.33   lips. The only reward] 1847; lips. The only money of God is God. He pays never with any thing less or any thing else. The only reward 1841

124.35   one. You shall not come] 1847; one. Vain to hope to come 1841

124.36   shall never catch a] 1847; shall catch never a 1841

125.25   great. You demonstrate] 1847; great. You become pronounced. You demonstrate 1841

126.9   come, and the . . . friend. [¶] I] 1847; come. He is the . . . friend. It is the property of the divine to be reproductive. [¶] I 1841

Emerson marked this passage (beginning at "A friend . . ." at 126.7) with a line in the margin of the Abel Adams copy.

126.16   before me in] 1847; before me, far before me in 1841

126.26   languid moods, when] 1847; languid times, when 1841

309

126.34 give, but which emanates from] 1847; give me, but which radiates from 1841

127.3 with regrets that] 1847; with the poor fact that 1841

127.8 away; but ... shining, and] 1847; away, but ... shining; and 1841
The revision improves the balance of the sentence by separating the main clauses with a semicolon and by changing the internal punctuation of the second clause to a comma.

127.12 transcends the] 1847; transcends instantly the 1841

Rejected Substantives

113.15 good will] good-will 1847
The source passage (*EL*, II, 282) reads "good will."

114.18 may get the] may find the 1876; may get the R
Since the copy-text version also appears in the source passage (*JMN*, VII, 76), and since the change appears only in the 1876 edition, we retain the copy-text.

115.31 overestimate [hyphenated at line-end in copy-text]] over-estimate 1847
Although Emerson hyphenates nouns with the prefix "over" (for example, "over-soul" at 160.8, and "over-estimate" at 95.17), he usually writes other forms as solid (for example, "overarching" at 110.1, and *JMN*, VII, 80; "overpowered" at 12.25, and *JMN*, VIII, 51; "overlooks" at 58.33, and *JMN*, VII, 125). In the source passage for this entry (*JMN*, V, 162) the word is solid. One exception is the hyphenation of "over-royal" at 172.20 (hyphenated at line-end in copy-text, 1847, and Riverside, and hyphenated in all other editions and in the source passage, *JMN*, VII, 120, and *EL*, III, 285).

116.36 forevermore] for evermore 1847
The source passage (*JMN*, VII, 372) spells the word solid.

119.32 fellow man] fellow-man 1847

121.3 neighborhood] neighbourhood 1847; neighborhood 1865

121.11 plough-boys] ploughboys 1847
In his journals Emerson writes the similar compound "plough-man" both hyphenated and as one solid word (*JMN*, VII, 414 and 526).

121.11 tin-pedlars] tin-peddlers 1847

122.33 baulked] balked 1847

123.17 those merits] these merits 1870; those merits R

123.27 house, or know] house, and know 1870; house, or know R

123.32 neighborly] neighbourly 1847; neighborly 1865

124.5 forever] for ever 1847
In the source (*JMN*, VII, 370), the word appears as "forever."

124.33 lips. [no ¶] The only] lips. [¶] The only 1865; lips. [no ¶] The only 1870

126.36 subtle] subtile 1847

Each instance of the word in *Essays I* is spelled "subtle" in copy-text and in the source passages (see 161.29 and 186.20; see also *JMN*, VII, 215 and 363, and *EL*, II, 85). Here and at 161.29, the 1847 text changes the spelling to "subtile," as it appears throughout the 1836 edition of "Nature" (see *CW*, I, 290, note for 32.4). Worcester gives different definitions for each spelling, and Emerson may have intended to differentiate his specific usage in each case. Therefore, although the 1847 changes could be Emerson's, we retain copy-text as more closely reflecting his intent.

VII. PRUDENCE

Emendations in Copy-Text

129.1 PRUDENCE / Theme no poet gladly sung, / Fair to old and foul to young, / Scorn not thou the love of parts, / And the articles of arts. / Grandeur of the perfect sphere / Thanks the atoms that cohere.] 1847; PRUDENCE. / [not in 1841] 1841

131.25 shows recognizes] 1847; shows, recognises 1841

The 1847 excision of the misleading comma, like the following emendation, improves the clarity and balance of the sentence.

131.25 laws, and] 1847; laws; and 1841

The 1847 revision strengthens the clause as one of three paired rhetorical contrasts in the sentence ("exist for itself" / "symbolic"; "co-presence of other laws" / "subaltern"; "surface" / "not centre").

132.7 live] 1847; lives 1841

In the source passage (*EL*, II, 311) and in the 1841 version of this paragraph, "class" is the subject of one singular verb ("lives") and three plural ones ("live" twice, and "have"). In the paragraph as revised, all four verbs are plural.

132.23 which never gives, which seldom lends, and] 1847; which gives never, which lends seldom, and 1841

133.7 For our existence, thus] 1847; For, our existence thus 1841

The 1847 revision clarifies the syntax by showing that "attached" is not a verb of which "existence" is the subject, but a participle modifying it.

133.9 mark,—so] 1847; mark; so 1841

The semicolon in copy-text confuses the relation between subject ("our existence") and verb ("reads"); the 1847 punctuation also accords with that at the end of the series ("debt,—reads").

133.12 ask whence it is. It] 1847; ask, whence it is? It 1841

Since the question is indirect, the 1847 excision of the comma and change of the question-mark to a period make more grammatical sense and are typical of the kind of punctuation changes Emerson makes in the 1847 revision.

133.29   headache] 1847; head ache 1841

The single-word version also appears in the source passage (*EL*, II, 313).

133.32   flies: if . . . [musquitoes]: if] 1847; flies. If . . . musquitoes. If 1841

Emerson typically revises short sentences into longer units, as he does in the next sentence as well (133.34). For the rejected 1847 spelling "mosquitos" (here replaced in brackets by the accepted copy-text spelling), see the Rejected Substantives note for 133.33.

133.34   persons: we] 1847; persons. We 1841

134.8   food, and pile] 1847; food. He must pile 1841

134.32   poultry-yard tells him] 1847; poultry-yard,—very paltry places, it may be,—tell him 1841

135.6   said,—"If] 1847; said, "If 1841

135.9   byword] 1847; by-word 1841

In the source passage (*JMN*, VII, 280) Emerson spells the word without a hyphen, but in the variant form, "byeword," as it also appears in *JMN*, VII, 268.

135.24   said:—"I] 1847; said; "I 1841

The semicolon in copy-text is probably a printer's error.

135.36   seen,) is] 1847; seen), is 1841

Emerson's practice in his letters and journals and in the MS of *Representative Men* is to place commas, and often even end punctuation, within the parenthesis mark (see *L*, II, 391, 409, 429).

136.7   remember and . . . dreamed, [. . .], give] 1847; remember, and . . . dreamed. Let them [. . .]. Let them give 1841

The 1847 excision of the comma after "remember" coincides with the overall revision in the passage of several short sentences into one longer unit. For the revision of the bracketed portions, see the next note.

136.7   dreamed, use plain speech, give] 1870; dreamed. Let them call a spade a spade. Let them give 1841; dreamed, call a spade a spade, give 1847, R

Emerson wrote that he made changes in the 1870 edition; this is one of the few apparent.

136.11   distorting our] 1847; distorting all our 1841

137.4   art. His art never] 1847; art. His art rebukes him. That never 1841

137.26   to-day, the felon at the gallows' foot is not more miserable] 1847; to-day, Job not so miserable 1841

137.28   men; and . . . wants and . . . himself. He] 1847; men, and . . . wants, and . . . himself, none is so poor to do him reverence. He 1841

In the preceding sentence, the semicolon is used to emphasize contrast. Its use here continues the contrast and, with the other excisions, clarifies the confused syntax.

137.29 resembles the pitiful drivellers, whom] 1847; resembles the opium eaters, whom 1841

137.31 day, yellow] 1847; day, the most pitiful drivellers, yellow 1841

137.32 ragged, sneaking; and at] 1847; ragged, and sneaking; then at 1841

137.33 open, slink] 1847; open, they slink 1841

137.34 tranquil and glorified seers. And] 1847; tranquil, glorious, and great. And 1841

The 1847 revision strengthens grammatically the contrast between "pitiful drivellers" (137.30) and "glorified seers."

138.20 rust; beer . . . sour; timber . . . dry-rot; money] 1847; rust. Beer . . . sour. Timber . . . dry-rot. Money 1841

138.24 white; keep] 1847; white. Keep 1841

138.27 prudence. It takes] 1847; prudence. It saves itself by its activity. It takes 1841

138.28 notes,—good . . . ragged,—and] 1847; notes—good . . . ragged, and 1841

Emerson probably added the dash after "ragged," as he does frequently in the 1847 edition to set off a parenthetical remark. Although the added comma after "notes" could be a printer's effort at making punctuation consistent, it is likely that Emerson himself added the comma to improve the balance of the parenthetical remark.

138.31 moments in which] 1847; moments which 1841

138.37 disposal, that] 1847; disposal, and not at that of others, that 1841

139.8 population, let] 1847; population; let 1841

The semicolon in copy-text, falling at the end of the line, may well have been a printer's error, for it separates a long subordinate adverbial clause from the main clause, which Emerson seldom does.

139.21 thing, the] 1847; thing, therefore, the 1841

139.28 frankness invites] 1847; frankness proves to be the best tactics, for it invites 1841

140.2 overcome." Entire] 1847; overcome." The eye is daunted, and greatly exaggerates the perils of the hour. Entire 1841

140.3 football] 1847; foot-ball 1841

In the source passage (*JMN*, V, 439) Emerson writes the word solid, as he did elsewhere in the journals with compounds with "foot" (for example, "footprints" at *JMN*, VII, 151). Such compounds are usually hyphenated in copy-text ("foot-prints" at 39.30 and "foot-track" at 67.33).

140.24 recognize] 1847; recognise 1841

140.26 both; the] 1847; both,—the 1841

The 1847 change to a semicolon clarifies the reading of the passage by indicating that the preceding subordinate clause ("if only . . .

both") modifies "what common ground remains," rather than what follows. The lecture source passage (*EL*, II, 321) also reconciles the ambiguity with a semicolon after "both."

140.29 If they set out to contend, Saint Paul will lie, and Saint John will] 1847; If he set out to contend, almost St. Paul will lie, almost St. John will 1841; [later editions follow 1847, except that in 1876 both occurrences of "Saint" are abbreviated "St." as in 1841.]

140.31 souls! They will shuffle, and] 1847; souls. Shuffle they will, and 1841

140.35 position with your] 1847; position to your 1841

141.10 underneath their] 1847; underneath all their 1841

141.24 and life would be dearer with] 1847; and pleasant would life be with 1841

Rejected Substantives

133.30 the stinging recollection] the stringing recollection 1847; the stinging recollection 1865

Emerson spoke of this proof-error of 1847 as the only error he had found in the edition and urged its correction in the 1853 English edition (*L*, III, 440). He also listed it as an erratum in his journals (see Index Major, Houghton 106, pp. 94-95). It was so corrected, but remained as an erratum in all impressions of the American stereotype plates until 1860, when Ticknor and Fields reprinted with some minor plate corrections.

133.33 musquitoes] mosquitos 1847; mosquitoes 1870; mosquitos R

The copy-text spelling appears in both source passages (*EL*, II, 313, and *JMN*, V, 49), and also in *JMN*, VII, 386. Worcester lists "musquetoe" and "mosquito," and adds a special note about the variety of spellings.

133.33 a fishing] a-fishing 1847

The source passages (*EL*, II, 313, and *JMN*, V, 49) also carry the copy-text version.

134.22 ensures] insures 1847

136.31 money, talent] money; talent 1847

The 1847 revision is an attempt to supply clarity through a punctuation change, but since neither version actually clarifies the meaning fully, the variant is not accepted.

137.12 Richard III.] Richard the Third 1847

137.25 incumbrance] encumbrance 1847

The copy-text spelling also appears in the source passage (*EL*, II, 316).

137.33 opium shop] opium-shop 1847

In the source passage (*JMN*, V, 17) Emerson writes the words "opium shop."

138.27   bank notes] bank-notes 1847
        Neither version accords with Emerson's practice in the manuscripts
    of his journals and lectures, which is to write compounds with "bank"
    as one solid word ("banknotes," *JMN*, V, 412, and *EL*, II, 243;
    "bankstock," *JMN*, VIII, 113). At 56.10, "bank-stock" appears in
    both copy-text and the 1847 revision, but the hyphenated version
    may well be a printer's spelling.
139.4   fellow creatures] fellow-creatures 1847
140.7   parlor] parlour 1847; parlor 1865
140.10   neighbors] neighbours 1847; neighbors 1865
140.15   good will] good-will 1847
140.16   ill will] ill-will 1847
        "Ill will" appears without a hyphen in both source passages (*EL*,
    II, 320, and *JMN*, V, 400).
140.17   neighborhood] neighbourhood 1847; neighborhood 1865
141.28   garden beds] garden-beds 1847

VIII. HEROISM

Emendations in Copy-Text

143.2   *Mahomet.* / Ruby wine is drunk by knaves, / Sugar spends to fatten
        slaves, / Rose and vine-leaf deck buffoons; / Thunderclouds are Jove's
        festoons, / Drooping oft in wreaths of dread / Lightning-knotted
        round his head; / The hero is not fed on sweets, / Daily his own
        heart he eats; / Chambers of the great are jails, / And head-winds
        right for royal sails.] 1847; *Mahomet.* / [not in 1841] 1841; *Mahomet.* /
        . . . Thunder-clouds . . . sails. 1870; *Mahomet.* / . . . Thunderclouds
        . . . sails. R
145.20   "*Valerius* . . . captivity."] 1847; *Valerius* . . . captivity. 1841, R
148.6   Unhappily, no] 1847; Unhappily, almost no 1841
148.6   exists who . . . person become, to] 1847; exists, who . . . person, be-
        come to 1841
        The 1847 edition's rearrangement of commas makes sense out of
    what is otherwise somewhat garbled syntax.
148.28   in it; it] 1847; in it: it 1841
        Since the other three places in the sentence where independent
    clauses join are marked by semicolons, the colon here appears to be
    an error.
148.30   has] 1847; hath 1841
148.33   right; and although] 1847; right, and, although 1841
149.3   and knows] 1847; and that he knows 1841

149.20 just, generous] 1847; just. It is generous 1841
149.24 wealth is the butt] 1847; wealth, is the foil, the butt 1841
149.28 all society] 1847; all human society 1841
149.31 then it is its] 1847; then is it its 1841
150.11 Haukal] C; Hankal 1841

    The correct spelling of Ibn Haukal was supplied first in the Centenary edition. The original misspelling may well have been a misreading of Emerson's hand in 1841 (his "u" and "n" frequently being almost indistinguishable).

151.3 wine,—"It] 1847; wine, "It 1841
151.10 Euripides,—"O] 1847; Euripides, "O 1841
151.15 ornament. It does not need plenty, and] 1847; ornament. Plenty, it does not need, and 1841
151.30 company,— / "*Jul.* . . . ye."] 1847; company, / *Jul.* . . . ye. 1841
152.5 own game in] 1847; own play in 1841
152.20 ear? Where] 1847; ear. Let us feel that where 1841
152.24 are; and] 1847; are;—that is a great fact, and 1841
152.26 and fate, friends] 1847; and dread, friends 1841
152.31 man makes] 1847; man illustrates his place, makes 1841
153.8 on our entire polity and social state; theirs] 1847; on the whole state of the world; theirs 1841
153.16 aspirations is . . . true; and . . . valor and . . . truth shall one day organize their belief. Or] 1847; aspirations, is . . . true, and . . . valor, and . . . truth, shall one day execute their will, and put the world to shame. Or 1841

    Emerson probably revised the excess punctuation of the sentence when he changed its ending. The changes improve the clarity and rhythm of the sentence.

153.25 experience, search in turn all the objects that solicit her eye, that] 1847; experience, try, in turn, all the gifts God offers her, that 1841
153.26 charm of her new-born being, which is the kindling of a new dawn in the recesses of space. The] 1847; charm, that like a new dawn radiating out of the deep of space, her new-born being is. The 1841
153.35 of heroism] 1847; of a genuine heroism 1841
153.37 have chosen your part, abide by it, and] 1847; have resolved to be great, abide by yourself, and 1841
154.7 you. Adhere to] 1847; you. Be true to 1841
154.10 person,—"Always] 1847; person, "Always 1841
155.10 peace which . . . walk, but after the counsel] 1847; peace, which . . . walk but to take counsel 1841

    The 1847 edition's shifting of the comma makes more syntactical sense by clarifying "but after the counsel" as the one example of a "road of perfect peace."

155.31 envy those who] 1847; envy them who 1841

Rejected Substantives

145.3   behavior] behaviour 1847; behavior 1865
146.30   Martius, oh Martius] Martius, O Martius 1847
         The copy-text reading appears in the 1647 edition of Beaumont
         and Fletcher that Emerson read.
147.16   Harleian] Harlein 1870; Harleian 1876
148.1   lockjaw [hyphenated at line-end in copy-text, 1847, and in Riverside]]
         lock-jaw C
         Emerson writes the word solid in the source passage (*JMN*, IV, 349).
148.16   behavior] behaviour 1847; behavior 1865
151.18   good humor] good-humor 1847
151.26   Socrates'] Socrates's 1847
         Emerson uses the copy-text form throughout the journals (see *JMN*,
         VI, 143, 324, and *JMN*, IX, 324, 412), and in the manuscript of *Repre-
         sentative Men*.
154.17   fellow creature] fellow-creature 1847
154.20   forever] for ever 1847
154.27   good nature] good-nature 1847
154.31   behoves] behooves 1847
         Emerson consistently uses the copy-text spelling in his manuscripts
         (see *JMN*, VII, 207, 270, 369; IX, 187; *EL*, III, 27; *L*, II, 138).
155.23   neighbors] neighbours 1847; neighbors 1865
155.32   endeavor] endeavour 1847; endeavor 1865
155.34   forever] for ever 1847

IX. THE OVER-SOUL

Emendations in Copy-Text

157.6   *Henry More.* / Space is ample, east and west, / But two cannot go
         abreast, / Cannot travel in it two: / Yonder masterful cuckoo / Crowds
         every egg out of the nest, / Quick or dead, except its own; / A spell
         is laid on sod and stone, / Night and Day were tampered with, /
         Every quality and pith / Surcharged and sultry with a power / That
         works its will on age and hour.] 1870; *Henry More.* / [not in 1841]
         1841; *Henry More.* / Space . . . Day 've been tampered . . . hour.
         1847, R
         The 1870 change ("Day were tampered") also appears in the Cen-
         tenary volume of *Poems* where E.W. Emerson reprinted many of the
         mottoes for the essays (*C*, IX, 278.8).

159.3   Yet there is a] 1847; Yet is there a 1841
159.8   vain. We] 1847; vain. A mightier hope abolishes despair. We 1841
159.12   innuendo] 1865; inuendo 1841
         Emerson regularly misspells "innuendo," ignoring the Latin deriva-
         tion (*innuere*) which necessitates the double "n" (see *JMN*, VII, 19,
         and *JMN*, XIII, 114). Webster lists only "innuendo"; Worcester prints
         "innuendo" only in the body of the text, but gives "inuendo" in his
         table of dubious or various orthography.
159.13   the soul] 1847; the great soul 1841
159.14   but he is always leaving] 1847; but always he is leaving 1841
159.20   hidden. Our] 1847; hidden. Always our 1841
160.1   me, I . . . pensioner; not] 1847; me,—I . . . pensioner,—not 1841
         The dashes in copy-text confuse the syntax and are replaced by
         Emerson's 1847 punctuation.
160.5   on the] 1847; on all the 1841
160.14   tongue, and] 1847; tongue; and 1841
         The original semicolon confuses the syntax by separating the last
         "which"-clause from its noun ("reality"), in contrast with the preced-
         ing "which"-clause.
160.21   seeing and] 1847; seeing, and 1841
         The 1847 change balances "seeing and the thing seen" with the
         other parallel pairs in the sentence.
160.25   soul. Only] 1847; soul. It is only 1841
160.25   Wisdom can the horoscope of the ages be read, and by] 1847; Wisdom,
         that the horoscope of the ages can be read, and it is only by 1841
160.28   man, we] 1847; man, that we 1841
160.34   if I may not use sacred, to] 1847; if sacred I may not use, to 1841
161.9   comparison, but] 1847; comparison,—but 1841
         The change balances the parallel series of oppositions in the sen-
         tence.
161.11   will; is] 1847; will;—is 1841
         The excision of this dash improves the sequence of ideas and helps
         to build to the climax of the summing comparison ("an immensity
         . . . possessed").
161.11   the background] 1847; the vast back-ground 1841
161.26   the soul] 1847; the great soul 1841
161.30   unmeasurable] 1847; unmeasureable 1841
         The source passage (*EL*, II, 85), Worcester, and Webster spell the
         word "unmeasurable."
162.1   but they] 1847; but always they 1841
162.6   circumscribes] 1847; circumscribeth 1841
162.10   look real] 1847; look solid, real 1841
162.12   soul. The] 1847; soul. A man is capable of abolishing them both.
         The 1841

162.22 the conditions of] 1847; the influences of 1841
162.27 thought reduces centuries] 1847; thought demolishes centuries 1841
162.30 persons in my thought has] 1847; persons to my soul has 1841; person in my thought has 1870; persons in my thought has R
162.32 the revelations] 1847; the great revelations 1841
163.11 world before her, leaving worlds behind] 1847; world alway before her, and leaving worlds alway behind 1841
163.13 only the soul; the web of events is the flowing robe in which she is clothed. [¶] After] 1847; only the soul. All else is idle weeds for her wearing. [¶] After 1841
163.33 all. The soul requires] 1847; all. The soul is superior to all the particulars of merit. The soul requires 1841
163.37 enjoins. To the well-born child, all] 1847; enjoins. For, to the soul in her pure action, all 1841
164.5   aspiration, stand already] 1847; aspiration, are already 1841
164.7   beatitude already anticipates] 1847; beatitude, does already anticipate 1841
164.8   highly. The] 1847; highly; just as love does justice to all the gifts of the object beloved. The 1841
164.10 faculty; and] 1847; faculty. And 1841
164.11 heart which . . . Mind finds] 1847; heart, which . . . Mind, finds 1841
        The 1847 edition's excision of the commas alters and clarifies the meaning of the passage by changing the clause from a nonrestrictive to a restrictive one. The 1847 version repeats the punctuation found in the source passage (*EL*, III, 300).
164.13 powers. In] 1847; powers. For, in 1841
164.20 or express a] 1847; or outwardly express to me a 1841
164.22 and these] 1847; and so these 1841
164.34 on high questions, the] 1847; on great questions of thought, the 1841
164.35 become aware that] 1847; become aware of their unity; aware that 1841
164.36 equal level in] 1847; equal height in 1841
164.37 all become wiser] 1847; all wax wiser 1841
165.9   truth. They accept it thankfully everywhere] 1847; truth. Thankfully they accept it everywhere 1841
165.11 beforehand, and from] 1847; beforehand. It is theirs from 1841
165.34 nothing; but] 1847; nothing. They are all lost on him: but 1841
165.34 have avails] 1847; have, avails 1841
        The 1847 excision of the comma is probably Emerson's change since he cuts the rest of the sentence so drastically.
165.34 am wilful, he sets] 1847; am merely wilful, he gives me a Rowland for an Oliver, sets 1841
166.11 to confirm . . . pleases; but] 1847; to affirm . . . pleases, but 1841; to affirm . . . pleases; but R

The passage, part of a quotation from Swedenborg and Caleb Reed in *The New Jerusalem Magazine*, and a favorite of Emerson's, is quoted correctly in *JMN*, VI, 342, and VII, 116 (where the "*confirm*" appears with italics), and in *EL*, III, 17.

166.26 nature, since it] 1847; nature, for it 1841

167.5 memorable. By] 1847; memorable. Always, I believe, by 1841

167.10 appearance,—to] 1847; appearance, to 1841

167.14 if they had been "blasted] 1847; if "blasted 1841

167.15 Socrates, the . . . Plotinus, the . . . Porphyry, the . . . Paul, the . . . Behmen, the . . . Quakers, the . . . Swedenborg, are] 1847; Socrates; the . . . Plotinus; the . . . Porphyry; the . . . Paul; the . . . Behmen; the . . . Quakers; the . . . Swedenborg; are 1841

Emerson generally punctuates series with commas, not semicolons. The last semicolon of the sentence, furthermore, falls between subject and verb, a punctuation rarely found in his manuscripts.

167.24 *revival* . . . churches . . . *experiences*] 1847; revival . . . Churches . . . experiences 1841

The italics and the lower case are Emerson's guide to the reader to take the terms as theologically technical, a guide he uses earlier in the essay when he refers to "the term *Revelation*" (166.31).

167.28 is the same; they] 1847; is always the same: they 1841

167.37 adding names] 1847; adding even names 1841

168.1 dates, and] 1847; dates and 1841

The comma is probably Emerson's addition, since his practice in the manuscript of *Representative Men* and in his lectures and journals is to put commas either after each item in this type of series (" . . . and . . . and . . . ") or after none.

168.3 not require a] 1847; not ask a 1841

168.6 ask concerning the] 1847; ask of the 1841

168.7 soul, the] 1847; soul, and the 1841

168.7 heaven, the] 1847; heaven, and the 1841

168.15 attributes, nor uttered] 1847; attributes; never uttered 1841

168.30 cipher than that] 1847; cipher but that 1841

168.37 one. [¶] By] 1847; one. [¶] Thus is the soul the perceiver and revealer of truth. By 1841

169.1 fire, vital, consecrating, celestial, which] 1847; fire, serene, impersonal, perfect, which 1841

169.3 light, we] 1847; light,—we 1841

The dash creates an unnecessary break between an introductory adverbial phrase and the subject.

169.14 power. The intercourse] 1847; power, not in the understanding. The whole intercourse 1841

169.14 society,—its] 1847; society, its 1841

The dash balances with the one after "quarrels" at the end of the parenthetical remark.

170.4 literary,—between . . . Pope,—between . . . Coleridge, and . . . Stewart,—between . . . thought,—is] 1847; literary; between . . . Pope; between . . . Coleridge,—and . . . Stewart; between . . . thought, is 1841

170.8 world, who] 1847; world who 1841

The comma changes the subordinate clause to a nonrestrictive and clarifies Emerson's meaning.

170.9 prophesying, half[-]insane] 1847; prophesying half-insane 1841

The comma changes the emphasis and clarifies the sense of the passage. For the hyphenation of "half-insane" see the Rejected Substantives entry.

170.16 miracle. I believe] 1847; miracle. That includes the miracle. My soul believes 1841

170.27 own; their] 1847; own: their 1841

The two prior clauses in the sentence are punctuated by semicolons; since this clause is parallel in structure, the colon seems a probable error.

171.5 which through their] RWE, 1847; which, though their 1841

Emerson corrected this printer's error by inserting the "r" in the Abel Adams copy. The source passages (*EL*, III, 17, 218, and "Thoughts on Modern Literature," *The Dial*, Oct. 1840, in *W*, XII, 321) also print "through."

171.6 beholds . . . blesses] 1847; beholdeth . . . blesseth 1841

171.9 His best communication] 1847; His greatest communication 1841

171.24 apprized] 1847; apprised 1841, 1865

Emerson varies his spelling of "apprize," although he slightly favors the "z" spelling (see *CW*, I, 30.36 and 38.6; *JMN*, VII, 315, 350; *L*, II, 194 and 198, for "apprize" and *JMN*, VII, 102, 995; VIII, 368; *L*, II, 156, for "apprise"). Worcester lists only the "z" spelling and, since Emerson tends to spell other such words with a "z," we accept the 1847 spelling as more characteristic than copy-text spelling.

171.33 circumstance,—the . . . Rome, the . . . saw, the] 1847; circumstance; the . . . Rome; the . . . saw; the 1841

Here and at 172.1, the changes clarify the catalogues. The dash after "circumstance" balances the one after "yesterday" at the end of the parenthetical remark (171.36).

171.37 ascends] 1847; ascendeth 1841

172.1 rose-color, no . . . friends, no . . . chivalry, no] 1847; rose color; no . . . friends; no . . . chivalry; no 1841

172.4 moment and] 1847; moment, and 1841

The comma makes the sentence meaningless, and the change is almost certainly Emerson's effort to clarify the passage.

172.12 ours. Nothing] 1847; ours. The mere author, in such society, is like a pickpocket among gentlemen, who has come in to steal a gold button or a pin. Nothing 1841

172.18 virtue even,—say] 1847; virtue, even, say 1841

173.3 unsearchable. It] 1847; unsearchable. Ever it 1841

173.30 byword] 1847; by-word 1841

173.36 anywhere] 1847; any where 1841

174.9 devotion. Even their prayers are] 1847; devotion. Their prayers even are 1841

174.10 own. Our] 1847; own. The soul makes no appeal from itself. Our 1841

174.25 It believes] 1847; It always believes 1841

174.27 that heaven] 1847; that holy heaven 1841

175.9 be the] 1847; be but the 1841

175.21 his life] 1847; his own life 1841

175.21 and with any] 1847; and any 1841

Rejected Substantives

159.7 forever] for ever 1847

159.22 baulk] balk 1847

161.29 subtle] subtile 1847

162.25 Shakspeare] Shakespeare 1865; Shakspeare 1876

163.35 better: so] better; so 1847

The 1841 colon sets off the final result clause from the earlier series of three balanced statements separated by semicolons.

164.9 enamored] enamoured 1847; enamored 1865

164.25 thence comes] thence come 1876

The singular verb is probably Emerson's, since it also appears in the source passage (*EL*, III, 42).

165.22 neighbors] neighbours 1847; neighbors 1865

165.27 Sheikhs] sheiks 1847

Copy-text spelling appears in both source passages (*JMN*, VII, 141, and *EL*, III, 19).

166.4 skeptic] sceptic 1865; skeptic R; sceptic C

167.9 extasy] ecstasy 1847

Emerson uses the 1847 spelling in the manuscript of *Representative Men*; in his journals he spells the word either "extacy" (*JMN*, VII, 338, 417) or "extasy" (*JMN*, VII, 351, 412). Since his practice is so variable and since either spelling could have been his, we retain copy-text spelling. See also 195.21.

170.9 half-insane] half insane 1847

Emerson also hyphenates "half-crazed" (in a passage deleted in 1847 [see the Emendations note for 190.12] and in *JMN*, VII, 387), although his practice with "half" compounds is variable (for example, "half human" at 18.22 and *JMN*, VII, 385; "half-artful, half-artless" at 101.16 and *JMN*, VII, 139).

171.1   Shakspeare] Shakespeare 1865; Shakspeare 1876
171.10   Shakspeare] Shakespeare 1865; Shakspeare 1876
171.17   forever] for ever 1847
172.24   Charles II.] Charles the Second 1847
172.24   James I.] James the First 1847
173.2   forever] for ever 1847

X. CIRCLES

Emendations in Copy-Text

177.1   CIRCLES / Nature centres into balls, / And her proud ephemerals, / Fast to surface and outside, / Scan the profile of the sphere; / Knew they what that signified, / A new genesis were here.] 1847; CIRCLES. [not in 1841] 1841
179.23   it this] 1847; it all this 1841
180.19   women a] 1847; women and children, a 1841
180.22   citizen; but] 1847; citizen, but 1841
         The semicolon emphasizes the contrast between "citizen" and "farmer," and parallels the balanced contrasts of the preceding sentence ("to women . . . ; to a merchant").
181.1   circumstance,—as . . . rite,—to] 1847; circumstance, as . . . rite, to 1841
181.14   Lo! . . . side rises] 1847; Lo, . . . side, rises 1841
         Both the lecture (*EL*, II, 255) and journal (*JMN*, V, 372) source passages omit the second copy-text comma, and the journal source carries the 1847 exclamation point.
182.32   thou] 1847; thee 1841
183.25   outgeneralled] ed.; out-/-/generaled 1841; out-generalled 1847
         The source passage (*JMN*, VII, 524) gives "outgeneralled." The 1847 spelling accords with Emerson's practice, except for a hyphen probably added by a printer reading the 1841 line-end division as a hyphenation. The word is also unhyphenated in *Essays II* (1844 edition, p. 135).
183.36   God IS; that] ed.; God is; that 1841
         Because small capital letters (as in copy-text and all later editions) are almost indistinguishable from lower case, large capitals are substituted here, as in "I AM" (92.36). In the source passage (*JMN*, VII, 216), only the first letter of "Is" is a large capital.
184.33   shakes and] 1847; shakes now and 1841
185.37   prized:—"Then] 1847; prized, "Then 1841

186.12 only,—are] 1847; only, are 1841

187.10 folly; as] 1847; folly, as 1841

The 1847 revision accords with the punctuation for the other two oppositions in the sentence and clarifies the application of the last clause to the sentence as a whole.

187.11 point. One] 1847; point of view. One 1841

187.25 injustice? Does he owe no] 1847; injustice? Owes he no 1841

188.17 pure, nor] 1847; pure; nor 1841

188.31 itself, suggesting to our thought a certain development, as if that] 1876; itself; but in vain; for that 1841; itself, but in vain, for that R

Though all other texts except the Little Classics edition of 1876 follow copy-text wording, the 1876 variation seems too extensive to be merely a printer's rather than Emerson's change.

189.1 names,—fever] 1847; names, fever 1841

189.8 seventy assume] 1847; seventy, assume 1841

Although Emerson often places a comma between subject and verb, the 1847 version is probably his rather than a printer's, since it agrees with the reading of the source passage (*JMN*, VII, 380), as do the similar punctuation changes in the rest of the sentence (see next entry).

189.8 all, they have outlived their hope, they renounce aspiration, accept . . . necessary, and] 1847; all; throw up their hope; renounce aspiration; accept . . . necessary; and 1841

189.24 sense,—we] 1847; sense, we 1841

The single dash of copy-text after "states" leaves the meaning of the sentence unclear; the 1847 change clarifies the parenthetical remark.

189.25 somewhat; but] 1847; somewhat, but 1841

189.25 growths and] 1847; growths, and 1841

The 1847 excision of the comma removes a false break between parallel nouns ("growths" and "movements").

190.8 tormentable; events] 1847; tormentable. He is so much, that events 1841

190.12 event. True] 1847; event,—they have not yet conquered. Is it conquest to be a gay and decorated sepulchre, or a half-crazed widow hysterically laughing? True 1841

190.12 the calamity to] 1847; the black event to 1841

The revision eliminates the awkward triple repetition of "black event[s]" within the paragraph.

190.19 wonderful: it] 1847; wonderful. It 1841

Rejected Substantives

181.12 enclosing] inclosing 1847; enclosing 1870; inclosing R

The source passage (*EL*, II, 254) also carries the etymologically correct copy-text form. Worcester lists both forms; the *OED* favors "enclose" for reasons of usage and etymology, but states that the "majority of recent Dictionaries give *inclose* as the typical form."

181.33 skepticism] scepticism 1865

183.1 enterprises] enterprise 1847

The original sources (*JMN*, VII, 166, and *EL*, III, 497) use the plural, indicating that Emerson meant "undertakings" rather than "daring" or "initiative." Apparently he balanced "enterprises" against "talents" within the sentence. The 1847 variant seems probably a printer's change.

184.16 packsaddles] pack/-/saddles 1847; pack-saddles 1865

Emerson writes the word solid in the source passage (*JMN*, VII, 360).

184.35 swift circumscription. Good] swift circumspection! Good 1847; swift circumscription! Good R

Since the paragraph is really discussing conversation as a "game of circles," the termini which limit the game are best described by "circumscription." Although Emerson could have meant the 1847 variant in the literal sense of "looking around," the change also carries the connotation of prudence, and seems probably a printer's change.

185.17 encyclopedia] encyclopædia 1847

In the source passage (*JMN*, VII, 523) Emerson spells the word "Encyclopædia." He also uses the "æ" spelling in the manuscript of *Representative Men* (267.21). His most common spelling, however, and the title of his journal of 1824–1836 (see *JMN*, VI, 115-234) is "Encyclopedia."

185.27 practice] practise 1876; practice R

The 1876 change to the verb form seems a probable printer's error, corrected in the next edition.

186.8 apprize] apprise 1865

186.27 behoves] behooves 1847

188.22 anything] any thing 1847

"Any" compounds are almost always printed as two words in copy-text and in the 1847 edition, although Emerson tends to write them solid in his manuscripts (see the Emendations note for 70.30). Here and at 197.35, the 1841 reading is possibly a printer's failure to "correct" his copy; the 1847 reading is probably a printer's change, in accord with that edition's consistent printing of "any thing" as two words.

188.30 Forever] For ever 1847

189.19 tomorrow] to-morrow 1847

Emendations in Copy-Text

191.1   INTELLECT / Go, speed the stars of Thought / On to their shining, goals;— / The sower scatters broad his seed,— / The wheat thou strew'st be souls.] 1865; INTELLECT. [not in 1841] 1841; INTELLECT. / Go, . . . seed, / The . . . souls 1847

Though the 1847 version establishes the form of the poem, it contains a misprint, the omission of the final period; hence the first complete version and that used here is the 1865.

193.3   wood, and iron, and] 1847; wood and stone, and 1841

193.19   The considerations of] 1847; The consideration of 1841

The disagreement of singular subject and plural verb occurs in the source passage (*EL*, II, 249-250) as well as in copy-text; the 1847 edition clarifies the syntax and the reading.

194.25   every expansion. The] 1847; every step. The 1841

194.30   to-day. In] 1847; to-day. Over it always reigned a firm law. In 1841

194.32   saith is . . . law; and this] 1847; saith, is . . . law. It has no random act or word. And this 1841

195.2   by secret currents of might and mind, and] 1847; by might and mind sublime, and 1841

195.9   night. Our] 1847; night. Always our 1841

195.18   By and by] 1847; By-and-by 1841

195.27   first contains] 1847; first always contains 1841

197.9   showeth. [¶] The] 1847; showeth. [¶] Our intellections are mainly prospective. The 1841

The third sentence in the original paragraph almost exactly repeats the first, and Emerson's 1847 revision avoids the awkward tautology.

197.12   least. Inspect] 1847; least. It is a little seed. Inspect 1841

197.14   he turns] 1847; he instantly turns 1841

198.13   tame: we] 1847; tame. We 1841

198.16   by and by] 1847; by-and-by 1841

199.4   then it is a] 1847; then is it a 1841

199.15   portrait] RWE, C; portraits 1841

Emerson's handwritten corrections in the Abel Adams copy of the 1841 edition show the deletion of the "s" on "portraits," which is plural in the source passage (*JMN*, VII, 247). The correction is also noted inside the back cover; it is one of the few changes in that copy that Emerson did not incorporate in the 1847 text.

199.15   [portrait]; they] 1847; portraits, they 1841

The 1847 semicolon balances the oppositions in the sentence. The bracketed word is an emendation accepted first in the Centenary edition (see the preceding note).

200.7 canvas] 1847; canvass 1841

The source passage (*EL*, III, 74) also reads "canvas." See the Emendations note for 213.17, an entry for which Emerson left instructions about the spelling of "canvas."

200.22 always much in] 1847; always greatly in 1841

200.23 that there] 1847; that always there 1841

202.11 oscillates. He] 1847; oscillates ever. He 1841

202.17 recognize] 1847; recognise 1841

203.11 has Hegel or his interpreter Cousin, seemed] 1847; has Cousin seemed 1841

204.3 Anyhow] 1847; Any how 1841

204.9 skies;—"The] 1847; skies; "The 1841

204.12 class who] RWE, 1865; class of men who 1841

Emerson wrote in his *Index Major 1847* (Houghton 106, pp. 94-95) the instruction to delete "of men" found on page 313 of the second American edition of "Essays I Series" (the 1847 edition). Emerson had promised Fields a "short list of errata" (*L*, V, 377) for the 1865 edition; this is one of three such corrections noted in his Index.

Rejected Substantives

194.34 self-tormentor's] self-tormenter's 1847; self-tormentor's 1865

The source passage (*JMN*, VII, 16) also spells the word with an "or."

195.9 our thinking is] our thing is 1870; our thinking is 1876

195.21 extasies] ecstasies 1847

196.7 surprizes] surprises 1847

Although the source passage (*EL*, II, 25) carries "surprises," copy-text spelling is retained here since Emerson spells the word almost equally with either a "z" or an "s" (see *JMN*, IV, 58, 116, 142; *EL*, I, 260; *L*, II, 9, 276, for "surprize" and *JMN*, VII, 60, 96, 444; *L*, II, 22, for "surprise").

197.13 Shakspeare] Shakespeare 1865; Shakspeare 1876

197.31 Shakspeare] Shakespeare 1865; Shakspeare 1876

197.35 anything] any thing 1847

200.17 enclosures] inclosures 1847; inclosures 1870; inclosures R

201.11 encyclopedia] encyclopædia 1847

In the source passage (*JMN*, VII, 302), Emerson spells the word "Cyclopædia" and "Encyclopædia"; but see Rejected Substantives note for 185.17.

204.13 high priesthood] high-priesthood 1847

In his journals Emerson writes other compounds with "high" without hyphens ("high breeding," *JMN*, VIII, 94, for example).

205.3 enamored] enamoured 1847; enamored 1865

Emendations in Copy-Text

207.1 ART / Give to barrows, trays, and pans / Grace and glimmer of romance; / Bring the moonlight into noon / Hid in gleaming piles of stone; / On the city's paved street / Plant gardens lined with lilac sweet; / Let spouting fountains cool the air, / Singing in the sunbaked square; / Let statue, picture, park, and hall, / Ballad, flag, and festival, / The past restore, the day adorn, / And make each morrow a new morn. / So shall the drudge in dusty frock / Spy behind the city clock / Retines of airy kings, / Skirts of angels, starry wings, / His fathers shining in bright fables, / His children fed at heavenly tables. / 'T is the privilege of Art / Thus to play its cheerful part, / Man in Earth to acclimate, / And bend the exile to his fate, / And, moulded of one element / With the days and firmament, / Teach him on these as stairs to climb, / And live on even terms with Time; / Whilst upper life the slender rill / Of human sense doth overfill.] 1847; ART. / [not in 1841] 1841

209.23 figures,—nature's] 1847; figures; nature's 1841

210.6 Hour sets] 1847; Hour always sets 1841

210.9 will retain] 1847; will always retain 1841

211.15 object,—so] 1847; object, so 1841

211.33 lion,—is] 1847; lion, is 1841

212.1 objects, we learn at] 1847; objects, learn we at 1841

213.1 the masteries of] 1847; the witchcraft of 1841

213.4 art,—that] 1847; art, that 1841

213.7 light, it] 1847; light; it 1841

The use in copy-text of a semicolon after a subordinate clause is uncharacteristic of Emerson and confuses the reading of the sentence.

213.11 influences overpower] RWE, 1847; influences, overpowers 1841

In the Abel Adams copy, the deletion of the "s" on "overpowers" and of the comma is marked in Emerson's hand in the text and margin, and the page number is noted in his list of corrections inside the back cover.

213.16 art of] 1847; art, of 1841

The excision of the comma corrects a false parallelism between "of art" and "of human character" and helps to clarify that the second phrase refers back to "radiation" rather than "work" as its position and punctuation in copy-text would suggest.

213.17 canvas] RWE, 1847; canvass 1841

In the Abel Adams copy, Emerson marked the second "s" for excision in the text and with a delete sign in the margin. His directed revision for 1847 is also adopted at 200.7 and 217.27.

214.8   proportion. He need not cumber himself with a conventional nature and culture, nor] 1847; proportion. Not a conventional nature and culture need he cumber himself with, nor 1841

214.15   poverty, will] 1847; poverty,—will 1841

214.17   through all. [¶] 1] 1847; through all [¶] I 1841

       The period did not print clearly in most copies of the 1841 edition. It does, however, appear in the Abel Adams copy.

214.28   forms,—unto] 1847; forms; unto 1841

       Since Emerson uses a semicolon to separate noun clauses introduced by "that" on three occasions within the sentence, the intrusion of the semicolon here creates a confusion of syntax.

214.30   I had had the] 1876; I had the 1841, R; I had had the C

       The inclusion of "already" within the sentence makes the past perfect almost essential. In the original source passage (*JMN*, VII, 222-223) the syntax was clearer, with the past perfect in a subordinate clause describing the first Naples experience ("that which had impressed me . . . in the . . . chapel in Naples"). This is one of the few substantive changes made in the 1876 edition. We accept it as an emendation because it both improves the sentence and is the type of change Emerson often made, although it could possibly have been made by Emerson's daughter Ellen or his biographer Cabot, who helped prepare the 1876 edition.

214.37   What, old] 1847; What old 1841

       Although Emerson's quotation from *Hamlet* is not quite accurate otherwise ("What" instead of "Well said"), the comma does appear in the source passage (*JMN*, VII, 222) and in 1847 to clarify the address.

215.25   the stream] 1847; the great stream 1841

216.9   originally a useful] 1847; originally an useful 1841

216.23   the paths of] 1847; the path of 1841

217.15   extravagances] 1847; extravagancies 1841

       Emerson often uses the slightly archaic form for nouns ending in "ces" / "cies" (for example, "emergences" and "excellences"), and the copy-text version may well have been a printer's misreading, corrected by Emerson in 1847. The printer of *Representative Men* made a similar error, changing the manuscript's "excellen*ces*" to "excellen*cies*" (60.11).

217.18   imaginations] 1847; imagination 1841

217.27   canvas] 1847; canvass 1841

218.26   works,—to . . . machinery,—the] 1847; works, to . . . machinery, the 1841

218.30   planet, is] 1847; planet,—is 1841

210.32 beatitude. [¶] Thus] beatitude? [¶] Thus 1847

Although Emerson frequently uses the question mark in rhetorical questions, his practice is sufficiently varied that a period may often be found after an apparent rhetorical question or even an exclamation. In the journal for 1839, for example, fifty-six rhetorical questions have end punctuation of a period (see *JMN*, VII, 3-262). Here, since Emerson's practice is so varied, we simply retain the copy-text reading.

211.26 well laid] well-laid 1847

211.37 frescoes] frescos 1876; frescoes R

214.13 log hut] log-hut 1847

215.6 common sense] common-sense 1847; common sense 1870; common-sense 1876

Emerson writes the phrase "common sense" in the source passage (*JMN*, VII, 227).

216.8 sculpture is long] sculpture has long 1876; sculpture is long R

216.14 oak tree] oak-tree 1847

217.32 farther] further 1870; farther R

Emerson also prefers "farther" at *CW*, I, 12.17, and there too the 1870 and 1876 editions change the word to "further."

218.18 miracles] mirales 1870; miracles 1876

218.20 roadside] road-side 1847; roadside 1870; road-side R

See the Rejected Substantives note for 18.30.

218.22 joint stock] joint-stock 1847

PARALLEL PASSAGES

It was recognized even by Emerson's earliest editors that he deliberately used his journals and notebooks as a "savings bank" (to use his own term, *JMN*, IV, 250) in which to deposit thoughts, outlines, quotations, and so forth, for future use in lectures, essays, or other forms of literary production. Thus a given passage or reference could appear several times in the journals of subsequent years, in the manuscripts of lectures prepared for oral delivery, and in the more formal addresses and essays. Sometimes the used passage would appear in the new context almost verbatim, but more frequently it would be altered in varying degrees for thought-content or for style; and frequently only the general idea was carried over. A prose work by Emerson must therefore be regarded as a composition—in the sense that one speaks of a musical composition or the composition of a painting—rather than as a piece of exposition or argument developed logically at a single sitting. The process of assembling the components of a composition and then organizing and revising them to produce the effect that he desired was an art which he developed slowly. In the 1820s, when he began to keep notebooks and journals, they served mainly as a place to record thoughts and impressions which he did not wish to forget; but in the 1830s and 1840s, when he was slowly developing as a professional lecturer, orator, and essayist, they became more nearly the instruments of the art of composition itself. He early formed the habit of drawing, either diagonally or vertically, a line through any sentence or paragraph when he carried it over in whole or in part into either oral lecture or written prose, but this reminder did not necessarily prevent him from using it again if a new context required it. By the 1840s he had also developed the habit of indexing the volumes of his journals and notebooks, and he even prepared an "Index major," an

"Index minor," and special topical indexes covering several journals in order to have his accumulated resources more easily available for his current work.

Emerson's indexes are part of the Houghton Library's collection of Emerson material. The collection includes, listed here by Houghton catalogue numbers, the following volumes: (104) "Index Minor 1843"; (104a) "Index Summary"; (106) "Index Major 1847"; (107) "Index II"; (107a) "Index Platonia"; (110) "Index Psi"; (131) "Index Minor [A]"; and (194f) "Index Swedenborg."

Most of Emerson's earlier editors were content to accept each finished work as Emerson released it for print without inquiring consistently into the process of its composition, even though the sources for such an inquiry had been carefully preserved by Emerson himself, by his first editor James E. Cabot, and by his son Edward. The last-named was probably the first editor to become aware of the importance of identifying earlier versions of the more finished work, and he marked on the manuscripts of the journals, notebooks, and lectures such later uses of any given passage as he could recall from his well-stocked memory of his father's thought and writing. The full significance of Emerson's method was not appreciated, however, until recent years, when a restudy of all his surviving manuscripts has been undertaken by professionally trained editors and has resulted in new editions of the journals and miscellaneous notebooks, the letters, and the lectures. As yet the sermons have not been so studied, but they are so early as to be little involved in this process of composition.

In the following list of used or parallel passages, the findings of recent scholarship have been brought together and collated. Even though it is obvious that many more parallel passages will be subsequently identified, we now have enough material for deeper and fuller examinations of Emerson's art and thought than were formerly possible.

2.1	I am owner . . . Shakspeare's strain. *JMN*, XII, 144.
3.1	There is one mind common to all individual men. *JMN*, V, 222; XII, 136.
3.2	He that is once admitted . . . he can understand. *EL*, II, 12.
3.6	Who hath access . . . sovereign agent. *EL*, II, 99.
3.8	Of the works . . . but one at a time. *EL*, II, 13.
3.9	Man is explicable . . . mind as laws. *JMN*, XII, 78.
3.16	A man is the whole encyclopædia of facts. *EL*, II, 14.
3.17	The creation of a thousand . . . manifold world. *EL*, II, 14.
3.22	This human mind . . . meaning for you. *EL*, II, 14–15.

4.14 We as we . . . learn nothing rightly. *JMN*, V, 252.
4.20 Stand before . . . hide itself.' *JMN*, V, 262; *EL*, II, 15.
4.22 This throws our . . . and Catiline. *JMN*, V, 256, 259; *EL*, II, 16.
4.27 the universal nature . . . of the firmament. *EL*, III, 20–22.
4.28 Human life as . . . complex combinations. *JMN*, VII, 139.
5.1 Universal history, . . . true of himself. *JMN*, VII, 130, 142.
5.13 We honor the rich . . . attainable self. *JMN*, VII, 142–143; XII, 316.
5.18 All literature . . . allusions. *JMN*, V, 361–362; XII, 285.
5.22 A true aspirant . . . firmament. *JMN*, VII, 62; XII, 317.
5.31 The student is to . . . doing to-day. *EL*, II, 181–182.
6.4 he can live . . . own person. *JMN*, XII, 140.
6.13 The instinct of the mind, . . . immortal sign? *JMN*, VII, 33.
6.23 "What is History," . . . agreed upon?" *JMN*, V, 508; XII, 327.
6.24 This life of ours . . . of them. *JMN*, VII, 138–139.
6.27 I believe in . . . own mind. *JMN*, VII, 186; XII, 477.
6.30 We are always . . . verifying them here. *JMN*, XII, 138.
6.31 All history becomes subjective; *JMN*, VII, 211; XII, 140.
6.32 there is properly . . . for itself— *JMN*, VII, 202, 216; XII, 139.
6.33 Every mind . . . better for him. *JMN*, V, 384; XII, 141, 244.
7.8 So stand before . . . proxy has done. *JMN*, V, 403.
7.17 All inquiry into . . . are *now*. *JMN*, VII, 111; XII, 136, 319; *EL*, III, 30.
7.30 A Gothic cathedral . . . reason. *JMN*, V, 402; *EL*, II, 268.
8.3 we have, . . . made the minster; *JMN*, XII, 141, 229.
8.33 Through the bruteness . . . before it, *JMN*, V, 217; *EL*, II, 29–30.
8.36 Nothing is so . . . her brows. *JMN*, V, 400; XII, 228.
9.2 as Io, . . . her brows. *L*, II, 337.
9.8 There is at the surface . . . of the understanding. *EL*, III, 72–73.
9.20 the "tongue on the balance of expression," *JMN*, V, 18, 108; VI, 200; VII, 63; XII, 88; *EL*, I, 348; III, 72.
10.3 I have seen . . . strata of the rock. *JMN*, VII, 171–172; XII, 322, 423.
10.6 There are men . . . the Parthenon, *JMN*, V, 363; XII, 140; *EL*, III, 93.
10.6 There are men . . . of all ages. *JMN*, VII, 139.
10.10 What is Guido's . . . morning cloud. *JMN*, VII, 209, 314–315.
10.15 A painter told . . . explained to him. *JMN*, VII, 214.
10.20 I knew a draughtsman . . . explained to him. *JMN*, V, 424; XII, 387.
10.23 It is the spirit . . . pictures, addresses. *EL*, III, 73.
11.1 Strasburg Cathedral is a . . . organs of the fish. *JMN*, V, 206–207.
11.6 The whole of . . . could ever add. *JMN*, V, 13; XII, 100, 166.
11.12 A lady, with whom . . . passed onward: *JMN*, VII, 61, 63.
11.17 The man who . . . of the world. *JMN*, VII, 10.
11.21 a broad cloud, . . . tower. *JMN*, V, 504; XII, 322.
11.33 we invent anew the orders . . . forefathers. *EL*, II, 52.

12.2 "The custom of making . . . interior?" *JMN*, VII, 49.
12.13 The Gothic church . . . vegetable beauty. *JMN*, XII, 131; *EL*, II, 52.
12.26 its ferns, . . . vegetable beauty. *JMN*, V, 215.
12.35 As the Persian . . . lotus and palm, *JMN*, VII, 46.
12.37 the Persian Court . . . for the winter. *JMN*, III, 319; IV, 304.
12.37 the Persian Court . . . nomadic life. *JMN*, VII, 48.
13.7 Agriculture . . . nomadism. *JMN*, VII, 48.
13.11 The nomads of Africa . . . Boston Bay. *JMN*, VII, 91; XII, 318, 328.
13.25 lives in his wagon, . . . Calmuc. *JMN*, VII, 79; XII, 318, 328.
13.26 At sea, or in the forest, . . . chimneys. *JMN*, VII, 78.
14.4 The primeval world, . . . ruined villas. *JMN*, VII, 186; XII, 139, 477.
14.8 What is the foundation . . . surpassed all. *EL*, II, 132–134.
14.19 whose eye-sockets . . . on that, *JMN*, IV, 322; XII, 88, 101; *W*, V, 104.
14.33 began to split wood; . . . good as he gets. *JMN*, V, 246.
15.4 The costly charm . . . speak simply, *JMN*, V, 244.
15.8 Our admiration . . . of the natural. *JMN*, XII, 89.
15.8 Our admiration . . . surpassed all. *JMN*, V, 198–199.
15.16 They combine . . . muse of Hellas. *JMN*, XII, 88; *EL*, II, 135.
15.22 the love of nature . . . run into one, *JMN*, V, 244.
15.23 In reading . . . Egyptian years? *EL*, II, 187.
15.29 When a thought . . . is no more. *JMN*, XII, 80.
15.35 The student interprets the age . . . confusion of tradition *EL*, II, 177.
16.6 Rare, extravagant spirits . . . divine afflatus. *JMN*, VII, 147.
16.11 Jesus astonishes . . . every word. *JMN*, VII, 148; XII, 139.
16.15 How easily these . . . mind. *JMN*, V, 465.
16.20 of labor and such . . . Capuchins. *JMN*, VII, 211.
16.24 The priestcraft of the East . . . very seldom?" *EL*, II, 177–178.
17.5 A great licentiousness . . . very seldom?" *JMN*, V, 191, 228; XII, 79, 112; *EL*, II, 178.
17.21 The beautiful fables of the Greeks, . . . of the Fancy, *EL*, I, 257.
17.23 What a range of . . . mechanic arts, *JMN*, VII, 506–507.
17.28 Prometheus is the Jesus . . . account. *JMN*, VII, 508.
17.35 a discontent with . . . independent of him. *JMN*, V, 7.
18.4 Apollo kept the flocks . . . Shakspeare were not. *JMN*, V, 12.
18.4 Apollo kept the flocks of Admetus, *JMN*, V, 209; *EL*, II, 105; *W*, VII, 176.
18.6 Antæus was suffocated . . . with nature. *EL*, I, 11.
18.11 clap wings to solid nature, *JMN*, VII, 524; *CW*, II, 185.
18.13 Proteus. What else am . . . agent or patient. *JMN*, VII, 385–386.
18.18 Tantalus is but . . . and me. *JMN*, VII, 385; XII, 47.
18.19 Tantalus means the impossibility . . . sight of the soul. *JMN*, VII, 297.
18.21 The transmigration of souls . . . many years slid. *JMN*, VII, 385.
18.29 that old fable of the Sphinx, . . . glorifies him. *EL*, III, 48–49.
19.7 See in Goethe's . . . own imagination. *JMN*, V, 315.

19.7   the same desire . . . be a thing. *W*, IV, 276.
19.27   Magic, and all that . . . in this world. *JMN*, XII, 53; *EL*, I, 260–261.
19.33   "to bend the shows . . . mind." *JMN*, III, 247; V, 190, 221; VI, 41, 173; *EL*, I, 162, 168, 260; *W*, V, 241.
19.35   In Perceforest . . . Boy and the Mantle, *JMN*, V, 89.
19.37   In the story of the Boy . . . gentle Genelas; *JMN*, V, 35.
20.3   that the Fairies . . . must not speak; *JMN*, XII, 53.
20.7   Bride of Lammermoor . . . in this world. *JMN*, III, 247; *EL*, I, 260–261.
20.18   His power consists in . . . civil society? *EL*, II, 17–18.
20.26   A man is a bundle of relations, *JMN*, V, 266.
20.30   He cannot live . . . civil society? *JMN*, V, 235–236.
21.20   Here also we are reminded . . . first time. *EL*, II, 18–19.
21.30   in the light of these two facts, . . . and written. *EL*, II, 19.
22.10   the calling of Abraham; . . . the Revival of Letters; *JMN*, VII, 396.
22.17   Is there somewhat overweening . . . antiquary. *JMN*, VII, 544–545.
25.2   "Ne te quæsiveris extra." *JMN*, IV, 318; V, 30, 211; VI, 19, 164; VII, 181.
27.1   I read the other . . . in such lines, *JMN*, V, 377; XII, 145.
27.5   To believe your . . . genius. *JMN*, V, 163; XII, 146, 161; *EL*, II, 152; III, 77.
27.7   Speak your latent . . . Last Judgment. *EL*, II, 151.
27.10   Familiar as the voice . . . they thought. *EL*, II, 152.
27.13   A man should learn . . . it is his. *JMN*, IV, 50.
27.16   In every work . . . thoughts: *JMN*, VI, 196.
27.16   In every work . . . majesty. *JMN*, V, 92; *EL*, III, 77.
27.19   abide by our . . . from another. *JMN*, V, 344; XII, 145, 148.
27.26   that he must take . . . him to till. *EL*, III, 101.
28.10   We but half express . . . cowards. *JMN*, IV, 108.
28.17   In the attempt . . . deserts him; *JMN*, XII, 148.
28.19   Trust thyself: every . . . string. *JMN*, VII, 297.
28.19   Accept the place the . . . the Dark. *JMN*, XII, 145; *EL*, III, 139.
28.23   absolutely trustworthy . . . and the Dark. *JMN*, VII, 12; XII, 278.
28.37   Infancy conforms . . . stand by itself. *JMN*, V, 349; XII, 148.
29.4   Do not think . . . unnecessary. *JMN*, VII, 81; XII, 318, 433; *EL*, III, 295.
29.9   The nonchalance of boys . . . human nature. *JMN*, V, 349; XII, 145, 193, 215.
29.11   A boy is in the parlour . . . be formidable. *JMN*, VII, 66; XII, 317.
29.25   He would utter . . . in fear. *JMN*, VII, 50; XII, 145, 148.
29.37   He who would gather . . . your own mind. *JMN*, XII, 144; *EL*, III, 308–309.
30.1   Nothing is at last sacred . . . of the world. *JMN*, XII, 146; *EL*, II, 151.
30.6   What have I to . . . of my nature. *JMN*, V, 48–49; XII, 144, 145.

30.18 affects and sways . . . such greeting, *JMN*, V, 470; XII, 288.

30.29 The doctrine of hatred . . . withhold. *JMN*, VII, 224; XII, 429, 509.

31.10 Virtues are in the popular . . . actually am, *JMN*, VII, 405–406.

31.28 What I must do, . . . people think. *JMN*, V, 479; XII, 146.

31.29 This rule, equally . . . of solitude. *EL*, II, 152.

31.31 you will always find . . . you know it. *JMN*, XII, 160–161.

31.33 It is easy . . . of solitude. *JMN*, IV, 367; XII, 162.

31.37 The objection to conforming . . . know you. *JMN*, VII, 225; XII, 429, 462.

31.37 The objection to conforming . . . emptiest affectation. *EL*, III, 309.

32.6 But do your work, . . . reinforce yourself. *JMN*, XII, 149, 252, 291; *EL*, III, 102.

32.7 A man must consider . . . emptiest affectation. *JMN*, VII, 179; XII, 137, 424, 508.

32.20 This conformity makes . . . chagrins us, *JMN*, VII, 179; *EL*, III, 309.

32.22 Their two is not the real two, *JMN*, XII, 147.

32.28 There is a mortifying . . . disagreeable sensation. *JMN*, V, 374; *EL*, III, 309–310.

32.30 "the foolish face of praise," *JMN*, II, 239, 365; XII, 139, 145, 193, 223; *EL*, III, 309.

32.36 For nonconformity . . . disappoint them. *EL*, III, 310.

32.37 a man must know . . . newspaper directs. *JMN*, VII, 69–70; XII, 145, 320.

33.7 It is easy enough . . . no concernment. *JMN*, VII, 69; XII, 433.

33.21 lest you contradict . . . public place? *JMN*, VII, 25.

33.23 It seems to be a rule . . . and live *JMN*, VII, 79; XII, 462.

33.26 In your metaphysics . . . shape and color. *JMN*, VII, 25–26.

33.29 Leave your theory . . . and flee. *JMN*, VII, 161.

33.31 A foolish consistency . . . his nature. *EL*, III, 310–311.

33.34 Speak what you . . . said to-day. *JMN*, VII, 223; XII, 147.

34.5 I suppose no man . . . curve of the sphere. *EL*, II, 171; III, 311.

34.5 I suppose no man . . . the same thing. *JMN*, V, 184; XII, 84, 320.

34.9 an acrostic . . . forward, backward, or across, *JMN*, VII, 40; XII, 93.

34.10 In this pleasing . . . hum of insects. *JMN*, V, 183–184.

34.11 let me record . . . see it not. *EL*, III, 311.

34.15 The swallow . . . web also. *JMN*, VII, 364.

34.17 Character teaches above our wills. *EL*, III, 282.

34.21 in whatever variety . . . Adams's eye. *EL*, III, 311.

34.25 The voyage of the best . . . tendency. *JMN*, V, 200; VII, 216–217; XII, 64, 428.

34.29 Act singly, and what . . . you always may. *JMN*, VII, 182; XII, 137, 147, 424, 461.

34.34 The force of character is cumulative. *JMN*, IV, 21; XII, 111, 146, 202.

34.36 What makes . . . Adams's eye. *JMN*, IV, 21; XII, 66–67.

35.5   Honor is venerable . . . young person. *JMN*, V, 257; XII, 99; *EL*, II, 140.

35.15   I do not wish . . . please me. *JMN*, VII, 389.

35.16   I will stand here for humanity, *JMN*, XII, 139.

35.18   Let us affront . . . of the times, *JMN*, VII, 517–518.

35.20   that there is a great responsible Thinker . . . a man works; *JMN*, XII, 139; *EL*, III, 7, 188, 242.

35.22   a true man belongs . . . all events. *JMN*, V, 376–377; XII, 139, 145, 148, 244.

35.22   that a true man belongs . . . of Clarkson. *EL*, III, 242–243.

35.24   every body in society . . . whole creation. *JMN*, VII, 146.

35.27   The man must be . . . circumstances indifferent. *JMN*, XII, 139.

35.28   Every true man is a cause, *JMN*, IV, 360.

35.28   Every true man . . . possible of man. *JMN*, VII, 100; XII, 145, 149, 318.

35.37   Scipio, Milton called "the height of Rome;" *JMN*, VII, 100, 183; *EL*, III, 12–13, 243.

36.1   all history . . . earnest persons. *EL*, III, 10–11.

36.5   a charity-boy . . . exists for him. *JMN*, V, 404; XII, 146; *EL*, II, 223.

36.8   To him a palace, . . . a true prince. *JMN*, V, 404; *EL*, II, 223.

36.22   In history, . . . us false. *JMN*, V, 397.

36.23   Kingdom and lordship . . . the same. *JMN*, V, 394.

36.26   Why all this deference . . . renowned steps. *JMN*, V, 397–398; XII, 141.

36.30   When private men . . . of gentlemen. *JMN*, V, 394–395; XII, 145.

36.33   The world has been . . . represent the Law *JMN*, XII, 151.

36.35   The joyful loyalty . . . his own scale *JMN*, VII, 177; XII, 146.

37.7   the reason of self-trust . . . Spontaneity or Instinct. *JMN*, XII, 150.

37.7   the reason of self-trust . . . appearances in nature, *JMN*, XII, 473.

37.14   We denote this . . . are tuitions. *EL*, III, 35.

37.17   For the sense of being . . . being also proceed. *EL*, III, 35.

37.24   inspiration which . . . is at fault. *EL*, III, 36.

37.31   Every man discriminates . . . to be disputed. *EL*, III, 36.

38.3   they do not distinguish . . . the sun. *JMN*, VII, 230; XII, 429.

38.4   But perception . . . the sun. *JMN*, VII, 223.

38.9   The relations of the soul . . . believe him not. *EL*, III, 141–142.

38.10   It must be . . . believe him not. *JMN*, VII, 149.

38.26   The centuries are conspirators against the sanity and authority of the soul. *JMN*, VII, 280.

38.32   Man is timid . . . saint or sage. *EL*, III, 282.

38.32   he dares not . . . God to-day. *JMN*, VII, 221; XII, 150, 428.

38.34   These roses under . . . above time. *JMN*, XII, 160, 446; *EL*, III, 283–284.

38.37   There is no time . . . above time. *JMN*, VII, 225–226; XII, 150.

39.9   This should be plain . . . called death. *EL*, III, 142–143.

39.9   This should be plain . . . rustle of the corn. *JMN*, VII, 149–150.

39.25   And now at last . . . not to man. *JMN*, VII, 150–151.

39.35   There is somewhat low even in hope. *JMN*, VII, 136; XII, 319.

39.36   In the hour of . . . what is called death. *JMN*, V, 467; XII, 278.

40.8   Life only avails, not . . . darting to an aim. *JMN*, VII, 518.

40.18   Who has more obedience . . . of spirits. *JMN*, VII, 368.

40.21   We do not yet see . . . who are not. *JMN*, VII, 407.

41.3   Thus all concentrates; let us not rove; *JMN*, VII, 177.

41.3   let us sit at home with the cause. *JMN*, VII, 404.

41.10   But now we are . . . goes abroad *JMN*, VII, 174; XII, 146.

41.13   I like the . . . ashamed of it. *JMN*, VII, 175; XII, 424.

41.21   But your isolation must not . . . keep thy state; *JMN*, VII, 189; XII, 146, 424.

41.27   No man can come . . . of the love." *JMN*, VII, 214; XII, 445.

42.6   I must be myself. I cannot . . . appoints. *JMN*, VII, 214.

42.28   There are two confessionals, . . . popular code. *JMN*, VII, 210; XII, 138, 147, 428.

43.1   it demands something . . . is to others. *JMN*, IV, 283.

43.7   If any man consider . . . afraid of each other. *EL*, III, 264.

43.18   We are parlor . . . revere him,— *EL*, III, 264–265.

43.21   If our young men . . . revere him,— *JMN*, VII, 201–202; XII, 139, 426.

43.38   shed healing to the nations, *JMN*, III, 64.

44.22   The prayer of the farmer . . . best gods." *JMN*, VII, 211–212; XII, 150.

44.25   Caratach, in Fletcher's . . . best gods." *JMN*, VII, 188; XII, 425.

44.30   Regret calamities, if . . . to be repaired. *JMN*, V, 335; XII, 146, 149, 208, 291.

45.8   "To the persevering . . . are swift." *JMN*, VII, 113.

45.16   Every new mind . . . on the first morning. *EL*, III, 140–141.

45.16   Every new mind is a new classification. *JMN*, VII, 28.

45.21   But chiefly is this . . . on the first morning. *JMN*, VII, 28.

46.7   It is for want of . . . axis of the earth. *JMN*, VII, 113; XII, 395.

46.11   In manly hours, we feel that duty is our place. *JMN*, VII, 118.

46.12   the wise man . . . at home still, *JMN*, IV, 17; V, 260; XII, 424.

46.18   I have no churlish . . . ruins to ruins. *EL*, II, 388.

46.24   his will and mind . . . ruins to ruins. *JMN*, VII, 118.

46.26   Travelling is a fool's . . . wherever I go. *JMN*, VII, 124, 204; XII, 138, 147, 395, 461.

46.30   and there beside me . . . wherever I go. *JMN*, XII, 427; *EL*, III, 314.

47.16   Insist on yourself; . . . half possession. *JMN*, IV, 324; XII, 69, 146, 460; *EL*, II, 151.

47.19   That which each . . . could not borrow. *JMN*, IV, 50; XII, 147.

47.25   Shakspeare . . . Shakspeare. *JMN*, V, 357; XII, 146.

47.27   There is at this moment . . . Foreworld again. *JMN*, VII, 186.

48.3   Society never . . . undecked boat. *JMN*, XII, 79, 173; *EL*, II, 174–175.

48.28   whether machinery does not encumber; *JMN*, V, 50.

48.34   A singular equality . . . twenty centuries ago. *JMN*, IV, 373.

49.1   Not in time . . . invigorate men. *JMN*, V, 185.

49.7   Hudson and Behring . . . undecked boat. *JMN*, III, 325.

49.17   Napoleon conquered . . . Bivouac, *JMN*, XII, 16, 147.

49.19   The Emperor held . . . bread himself." *JMN*, V, 487.

49.24   Society is a wave. . . . experience with them. *JMN*, XII, 461; *EL*, II, 175.

49.24   The wave moves . . . phenomenal. *JMN*, IV, 287.

49.36   But a cultivated man . . . takes it away. *JMN*, VII, 242; XII, 431, 461.

50.8   "Thy lot or . . . after it." *JMN*, VI, 388; VII, 400.

50.11   The political parties meet . . . than a town? *JMN*, VII, 403.

50.22   Ask nothing of men, and . . . surrounds thee. *JMN*, VII, 192; XII, 146.

50.27   rights himself, . . . on his head. *JMN*, V, 362; XII, 241, 290.

50.35   A political victory, . . . principles. *JMN*, VII, 145; *EL*, III, 150.

55.23   that judgment is . . . next life. *JMN*, VII, 182; XII, 425, 451.

56.4   What did the preacher . . . revenge tomorrow.' *JMN*, VII, 182–183.

56.27   our popular theology . . . has displaced. *JMN*, XII, 108.

56.33   For men are wiser than they know. *JMN*, VII, 123.

57.7   Polarity, or . . . condense there. *JMN*, V, 304; XII, 230.

57.7   action and reaction, we . . . flow of waters; *JMN*, XII, 95; *EL*, II, 153.

57.27   in the animal kingdom, . . . cut short. *EL*, II, 153.

58.4   Every excess causes . . . of folly. *JMN*, XII, 96.

58.5   Every faculty . . . its life. *JMN*, V, 246; XII, 162; *EL*, II, 153.

58.8   For every thing . . . lose something. *JMN*, V, 171; XII, 64, 93, 96, 161; *EL*, II, 145–146.

58.10   If riches increase, . . . kills the owner. *EL*, III, 147.

58.18   Is a man . . . balance true. *JMN*, VII, 95; XII, 293; *EL*, III, 147.

58.33   He who by force . . . hissing. *JMN*, VII, 125; XII, 293; *EL*, III, 146–147.

59.6   Things refuse . . . *administrari*. *JMN*, V, 280, 284; VI, 65; *W*, III, 205.

59.24   Every thing is made . . . of every other. *JMN*, XII, 108–109.

60.8   That soul which . . . by it." *EL*, III, 145.

60.13   The dice of God are always loaded. *JMN*, V, 124; VI, 178, 215; XII, 106; *CW*, I, 25; *W*, VI, 221.

60.14   The world looks . . . returns to you. *JMN*, XII, 90; *EL*, III, 252.

60.17   Every secret is told, . . . and certainty. *EL*, III, 145.

60.18   What we call retribution . . . is there behind. *JMN*, XII, 131.

60.23   Every act rewards itself, *JMN*, XII, 89.

60.30   The specific stripes . . . they accompany it. *JMN*, XII, 131–132.

60.32   Punishment is a fruit . . . in the seed. *JMN*, V, 352; XII, 290, 293; *EL*, III, 145–146.

61.19 Men seek to be great; . . . the bitter. *JMN*, VII, 125; XII, 95; *EL*, III, 146.

61.30 "Drive out nature . . . running back." *JMN*, VII, 45; VIII, 252; XII, 90.

61.32 Life invests itself . . . so much death. *JMN*, VII, 124–125; *EL*, III, 148.

62.16 Thus the Greeks . . . of its moral aim. *JMN*, V, 401; XII, 283.

63.1 There is a crack . . . God has made. *JMN*, IV, 362; V, 304; VI, 198.

63.6 all things are sold. *JMN*, XII, 82.

63.8 This is that ancient doctrine . . . beneath its fall. *EL*, II, 154.

63.9 The Furies, they . . . punish him. *JMN*, VI, 218.

63.13 the belt which . . . Ajax fell. *JMN*, VI, 218; *EL*, II, 154.

63.17 the Thasians erected . . . fall. *JMN*, VI, 169.

63.22 That is the best . . . moment wrought. *JMN*, VII, 185; XII, 425.

64.9 All things are double, . . . another. *JMN*, XII, 96; *EL*, II, 153.

64.9 Tit for tat; . . . confounds the adviser.— *JMN*, XII, 92.

64.9 an eye for an eye; . . . shall not eat. *EL*, II, 152–153.

64.10 measure for measure; *JMN*, VI, 216.

64.11 Give and it . . . you. *JMN*, VI, 215.

64.11 He that watereth . . . himself. *JMN*, VI, 217.

64.12 What will . . . take it. *JMN*, VI, 197.

64.13 Nothing venture, nothing have. *JMN*, IV, 322; V, 387.

64.14 Thou shalt be . . . no less. *JMN*, VI, 215.

64.15 Who doth not . . . eat. *JMN*, VI, 216.

64.15 Harm watch, harm catch. *EL*, II, 153.

64.17 If you put . . . around your own. *JMN*, IV, 92; VI, 215.

64.18 Bad counsel confounds the adviser. *JMN*, V, 368; XII, 290, 293.

64.19 The devil is an ass. *JMN*, V, 47; XII, 106.

64.27 Every opinion reacts . . . sink the boat. *EL*, III, 146.

64.27 It is a thread-ball . . . sink the boat. *JMN*, V, 302.

64.33 "No man had . . . Burke. *JMN*, VI, 157; *EL*, II, 153.

64.35 The exclusive . . . The exclusionist *JMN*, XII, 93, 106.

65.1 Treat men as pawns . . . lose your own. *JMN*, V, 199; XII, 59, 93, 105; *EL*, II, 107.

65.3 The senses would . . . the poor. *JMN*, VII, 43; XII, 104.

65.19 Fear is an instructer . . . must be revised. *JMN*, VII, 198; XII, 426, 481.

65.33 Experienced men of the world . . . small frugality. *EL*, III, 149.

65.35 The borrower runs . . . ask for it." *JMN*, XII, 142.

66.2 There arises on the deed . . . inferiority. *JMN*, XII, 107.

66.8 "the highest . . . for it." *JMN*, VI, 217; XII, 106, 293, 407.

66.10 A wise man will . . . some sort. *JMN*, XII, 125; *EL*, III, 149–150.

66.12 Always pay; for, first . . . with more. *JMN*, V, 476; VII, 144–145; XII, 290, 293.

66.17 Benefit is the end . . . to somebody. *JMN*, VII, 59; XII, 291, 293.

66.24   Beware of . . . in your hand. *JMN*, XII, 93.

66.26   Labor is watched . . . your estate. *EL*, II, 126–127.

66.26   Cheapest, say the . . . multiply your presence, *JMN*, V, 177; XII, 107, 135.

67.13   the doctrine that . . . without its price,— *JMN*, XII, 106.

67.16   is not less . . . and darkness, *JMN*, V, 240, 346; XII, 251.

67.18   I cannot doubt . . . imagination. *JMN*, XII, 254; *EL*, II, 243–244.

67.33   you cannot wipe . . . to the thief. *JMN*, VII, 197; XII, 426, 480.

68.1   All love is mathematically just, *JMN*, V, 208; XII, 93, 105; *EL*, II, 103.

68.8   "Winds blow . . . are nothing." *JMN*, XII, 106.

68.11   The good are befriended . . . blamed his feet, *JMN*, IV, 66, 270.

68.11   As no man had ever . . . want of the same. *EL*, II, 153.

68.11   no man had . . . to him, *CW*, II, 64. *JMN*, VI, 157.

68.17   As no man thoroughly . . . want of the same. *JMN*, IV, 66, 329.

68.27   A great man is . . . and real skill. *JMN*, V, 386; *EL*, II, 258–259.

68.32   The wise man . . . passed on invulnerable. *JMN*, V, 436; *EL*, II, 259–260.

69.2   I hate to be defended . . . enemies. *JMN*, VII, 95; XII, 104, 317.

69.6   As the Sandwich Islander . . . we resist. *JMN*, III, 283.

69.19   If you serve . . . him the more. *JMN*, IV, 15; XII, 68, 143–144.

69.24   endeavors to cheat nature, *JMN*, XII, 82.

69.25   to twist a rope of sand. *JMN*, V, 186; VII, 362; *EL*, II, 156; *W*, III, 200; VI, 173; VIII, 149.

69.27   A mob is . . . from side to side. *JMN*, V, 100–101; XII, 84; *EL*, II, 109.

70.28   We feel defrauded . . . and angels. *JMN*, V, 493; XII, 291, 293.

71.4   In a virtuous action, . . . horizon. *JMN*, V, 493.

71.21   I no longer wish . . . dig up treasure. *JMN*, VII, 178.

71.28   I learn the wisdom . . . own fault. *JMN*, III, 339; IV, 86; VI, 93–94; XII, 106.

71.33   The radical tragedy . . . grandeur he loves. *JMN*, VII, 36; XII, 385; *EL*, III, 107.

72.17   Every soul is . . . of yesterday. *JMN*, VII, 203; XII, 427, 471.

72.36   We are idolaters . . . look backwards. *JMN*, VII, 202–203.

73.10   And yet the compensations . . . of men. *JMN*, VII, 200–201.

73.10   compensations of calamity *JMN*, XII, 82, 426.

75.1   The living Heaven . . . Innocence. *JMN*, IX, 437–438, 442–443.

77.1   When the act of reflection . . . of memory. *EL*, II, 144.

77.3   Behind us, . . . do far off. *JMN*, V, 101; XII, 158.

77.8   Even the corpse . . . the house. *JMN*, V, 101; *EL*, II, 144.

77.11   If in the hours of . . . rare gifts. *EL*, II, 144–145.

77.22   No man need be . . . suffice us. *JMN*, V, 254–255.

78.10   "A few strong instincts . . . suffice us. *EL*, II, 145.

78.12   My will never . . . comparative value. *JMN*, V, 94, 226; *CW*, II, 152.

78.12   My will never . . . belongs to it. *EL*, III, 37.

78.26   Either God is there, or he is not there. *JMN*, VII, 442.

78.26   We love characters . . . native devils.' *JMN*, VII, 66–67; XII, 292.

78.29   Timoleon's victories . . . Plutarch said. *JMN*, V, 151; VI, 29; VII, 67; *EL*, I, 154; *W*, XII, 263.

78.35   the preponderance of nature . . . not in them. *EL*, III, 37.

78.35   the preponderance of nature . . . Napoleon; *JMN*, V, 226; XII, 406–407.

78.36   There is less intention . . . Napoleon; *JMN*, V, 94.

79.18   The lesson is forcibly . . . execute themselves. *JMN*, XII, 122–123; *EL*, III, 312–313.

79.25   we are begirt with laws *JMN*, V, 345; XII, 95.

79.25   laws which execute themselves. *JMN*, XII, 92.

79.27   Nature will not . . . my little Sir.' *JMN*, VII, 204; XII, 427, 448; *EL*, III, 299.

79.34   We are full of . . . they are asked. *JMN*, XII, 123.

79.34   We must needs intermeddle, . . . are odious. *JMN*, XII, 93.

80.16   Our society is encumbered . . . just as well. *JMN*, XII, 129.

80.24   nature, which always . . . forever and ever. *JMN*, VII, 167; XII, 129, 423.

80.31   The simplicity of the universe . . . to the soul. *EL*, III, 292.

81.15   A little consideration . . . and the sun. *EL*, III, 280–281.

81.29   Why need you choose . . . of beauty. *JMN*, VII, 91; XII, 291; *EL*, III, 139–140.

81.29   Why need you choose . . . wilful election. *EL*, III, 281.

82.13   We must hold . . . character. *JMN*, VII, 204; XII, 137, 427.

82.18   Each man has his own vocation . . . persons therein. *EL*, II, 147–148.

82.18   The talent is the call. *JMN*, III, 223; XII, 89.

82.29   His ambition is exactly . . . of the base. *JMN*, IV, 38; XII, 63, 160.

82.32   The pretence . . . persons therein. *JMN*, V, 169.

83.4   Somewhere, not only . . . honor him aright. *JMN*, V, 469; XII, 322.

83.5   let out all the length of all the reins; *JMN*, IV, 428; V, 459; VI, 134; VII, 284; VIII, 107; *W*, V, 303.

83.17   Foolish, whenever you . . . and aims. *JMN*, V, 470.

83.21   We like . . . is elevation. *EL*, III, 138–139.

83.23   We think greatness . . . hidden. *JMN*, V, 488.

83.32   The parts of hospitality, . . . elevation. *JMN*, V, 483; XII, 14.

83.36   What a man . . . as he exists. *JMN*, V, 204; *EL*, II, 95.

84.5   He may have his own. *JMN*, XII, 92.

84.5   A man's genius, . . . splinters of steel. *EL*, III, 36–37.

84.8   A man is a method, . . . he goes. *JMN*, V, 114; XII, 58; *CW*, I, 24.

84.9   a selecting principle, . . . drift-wood, *JMN*, VII, 50; XII, 319.

84.15   Those facts, words, . . . no regard. *JMN*, V, 442.

84.15   Those facts, words, . . . always right. *EL*, III, 37–38.

84.23 A few anecdotes, . . . in literature. *JMN*, VII, 158.
84.36 That mood into . . . can compel. *EL*, II, 150.
84.36 That mood into . . . dominion over us. *JMN*, XII, 69.
85.5 de Narbonne . . . Imperial Cabinet. *JMN*, V, 486; XII, 90.
85.11 Nothing seems so easy . . . of bonds. *JMN*, VII, 89.
85.15 If a teacher . . . the unseen. *JMN*, III, 283–284; XII, 62.
85.15 If a teacher . . . of Kant? *EL*, II, 148–149.
85.24 A man cannot . . . find them. *JMN*, V, 184; XII, 62.
85.26 Plato had . . . Kant? *JMN*, V, 31; XII, 62.
85.28 Therefore, Aristotle . . . not published." *JMN*, IV, 337; V, 245.
85.30 No man can learn . . . like a dream. *EL*, II, 149.
85.31 A chemist may . . . the wiser,— *JMN*, IV, 51.
85.34 Our eyes are . . . cannot see *JMN*, IV, 377; V, 95, 245; *EL*, III, 162, 211.
86.1 Not in nature . . . rocks and sky. *JMN*, V, 279; XII, 104.
86.7 People are not the . . . men than others. *JMN*, V, 418; XII, 104, 193, 229.
86.10 There are graces . . . reached us. *JMN*, V, 348; XII, 105.
86.14 Our dreams are . . . of the day. *EL*, III, 155.
86.14 Our dreams are . . . waking knowledge. *JMN*, V, 371.
86.15 The visions of the night . . . day. *JMN*, V, 398.
86.16 Hideous dreams are . . . than yourselves." *EL*, III, 155–156.
86.16 Hideous dreams are . . . is terrific. *JMN*, III, 317–318.
86.20 "My children," said . . . than yourselves." *JMN*, IV, 212.
86.22 As in dreams, so . . . his circumstances. *JMN*, III, 318; *EL*, III, 156–157.
86.27 He is like a quincunx . . . terminal acrostic. *JMN*, V, 184, 236; XII, 90, 93, 248.
86.35 What can we see . . . in the room. *JMN*, III, 327; XII, 90; *EL*, II, 149.
87.5 It is with a good book . . . not their fellow. *JMN*, XII, 74.
87.10 What avails it . . . lord? *JMN*, VII, 171; XII, 423, 443, 482.
88.2 The scholar . . . follow him. *JMN*, VII, 193; XII, 425, 480.
88.8 the affinities by . . . be formed, *JMN*, XII, 89.
88.11 He may set his own rate. *JMN*, VII, 164.
88.11 It is a maxim . . . acquiesce. *JMN*, VII, 60; XII, 90.
88.11 It is a maxim . . . of the stars. *EL*, III, 101–102.
88.16 It will certainly accept . . . revolution of the stars. *JMN*, VII, 164.
88.20 The same reality pervades . . . the other. *EL*, II, 423–424.
88.20 The same reality pervades all teaching. *JMN*, XII, 283.
88.22 He teaches who . . . receives. *JMN*, V, 408; VI, 142; XII, 89; *EL*, III, 502.
88.23 There is no teaching . . . at the other. *JMN*, V, 504.
88.28 We see it advertised . . . not a man. *JMN*, VII, 166; XII, 104, 137, 423; *EL*, III, 244.

88.34   The sick would be carried in litters. *JMN*, VII, 518.

88.37   A like Nemesis presides over all intellectual works. *EL*, III, 146.

88.37   We have yet to learn . . . being spoken. *JMN*, V, 42; *EL*, II, 163.

89.1   the thing uttered . . . affirmed. *JMN*, XII, 105.

89.5   The effect of any writing . . . hour. *JMN*, VII, 98; XII, 90, 318; *EL*, III, 146.

89.6   depth of thought. How . . . if it lift *JMN*, VIII, 62.

89.10   The way to . . . write sincerely. *JMN*, V, 342; XII, 195.

89.12   The argument which . . . reach yours. *JMN*, IV, 197; XII, 116, 203.

89.13   But take Sidney's . . . write." *JMN*, IV, 434; V, 112.

89.15   That statement only . . . own curiosity. *JMN*, IV, 52; XII, 115; *EL*, II, 151.

89.17   The writer who . . . ourselves valuable. *JMN*, V, 46; XII, 98–99; *EL*, I, 381–382.

89.22   Life alone can . . . ourselves valuable. *JMN*, IV, 17; *EL*, III, 206.

89.23   There is no luck . . . mind of man. *EL*, I, 212; II, 65–66; III, 205–206.

89.37   "No book," said . . . itself." *JMN*, VI, 217; XII, 115; *EL*, II, 65.

90.6   "the light of the public square will test its value." *JMN*, IV, 369; V, 140; XII, 115; *EL*, II, 66.

90.8   the effect of every . . . it proceeds. *JMN*, XII, 90.

90.9   The great man knew . . . institution. *JMN*, VII, 177; XII, 104, 424.

90.20   The laws of disease, . . . as the laws of health. *JMN*, V, 503; *EL*, III, 130.

90.22   as every shadow points to the sun. *JMN*, III, 244.

90.25   Human character . . . show it. *JMN*, V, 170–171; XII, 89, 102; *EL*, II, 129–130.

90.25   The most fugitive . . . you sleep, *JMN*, V, 260; XII, 195.

90.28   You think because . . . her voice? *JMN*, V, 333–334.

91.1   Truth tyrannizes . . . of the body. *JMN*, XII, 89.

91.1   Faces never lie, it is said. *JMN*, V, 170; XII, 100, 164.

91.3   When a man . . . sometimes asquint. *JMN*, V, 101–102, 217.

91.7   I have heard . . . indignation. *JMN*, V, 396–397; *EL*, II, 300.

91.11   This is that law . . . he made it. *JMN*, XII, 128, 202; *EL*, II, 270.

91.15   Swedenborg expressed, . . . to indignation. *JMN*, IV, 342–343; V, 7, 115.

91.20   A man passes for that he is worth. *JMN*, XII, 90; *CW*, II, 92.

91.20   Very idle is all . . . by all persons. *JMN*, V, 419.

91.20   Very idle is all . . . out tomorrow.' *EL*, II, 301–302.

91.25   into every assembly . . . gauged and stamped. *JMN*, V, 426; XII, 105, 194.

91.26   In every troop of . . . tomorrow.' *JMN*, V, 396.

91.33   'What has he . . . abolished slavery. *JMN*, IV, 369; XII, 165; *EL*, II, 151.

92.5   As much virtue . . . accept it unexpectedly. *EL*, II, 94–95.

92.5   As much virtue . . . appears; *JMN*, XII, 89.
92.5   As much virtue . . . command mankind. *JMN*, V, 282.
92.6   All the devils . . . command mankind. *JMN*, XII, 111.
92.6   All the devils respect virtue. *JMN*, V, 21, 150, 203.
92.8   Never was a sincere word utterly lost. *JMN*, VI, 61, 157; *EL*, II, 95.
92.9   Never a magnanimity . . . unexpectedly. *JMN*, V, 267; XII, 66; *EL*, II, 294.
92.10   A man passes for that . . . of a king. *EL*, II, 95; *CW*, II, 91.
92.13   There is confession . . . the grasp of hands. *EL*, III,18.
92.15   His sin bedaubs . . . of a king. *JMN*, V, 204–205.
92.20   If you would not . . . be mistaken for *JMN*, IV, 21–22.
92.20   If you would not . . . be concealed!" *JMN*, XII, 67; *EL*, II, 150.
92.26   "How can a man . . . be concealed!" *JMN*, V, 120; VI, 391; XII, 104, 164.
92.28   On the other hand, . . . incident. *JMN*, V, 205.
92.28   On the other hand, . . . I AM. *EL*, II, 95.
92.32   Virtue is the adherence in action to the nature of things, *JMN*, V, 204.
92.34   It consists in . . . I AM. *JMN*, V, 282; XII, 111.
92.37   The lesson . . . Be, and not seem. *JMN*, XII, 89.
93.3   Let us lie low in the Lord's power, *JMN*, V, 427, 482; VII, 532; *EL*, II, 293, 351.
93.5   If you visit your . . . substance is not. *JMN*, VII, 192–193; XII, 425.
93.15   We are full of these superstitions . . . our lifetime. *EL*, III, 266–267.
93.15   the worship of . . . yet at one. *JMN*, VII, 195; XII, 137, 426.
93.36   Why should we make . . . is to act. *EL*, III, 267–268.
94.1   A good man is . . . another shape. *JMN*, VII, 179–180; XII, 136.
94.1   I do not wish to be Epaminondas. *JMN*, XII, 424.
94.6   Epaminondas, if he was . . . joy and peace, *JMN*, XII, 483.
94.24   Besides, why should . . . name of Action? *JMN*, XII, 480.
94.26   The poor mind . . . and is Nature. *JMN*, VII, 200; XII, 426, 483.
94.31   To think is to act. *JMN*, III, 298; V, 4.
94.33   Let us, if we must . . . with the best. *EL*, III, 230–231.
94.36   Let us seek *one* peace by fidelity. *JMN*, VII, 175.
95.2   How dare I read . . . correspondents? *JMN*, VII, 176.
95.5   It is peeping. *JMN*, VII, 178; XII, 424.
95.5   Byron says . . . with the best. *JMN*, VII, 173–174.
95.7   "He knew not . . . he swore." *JMN*, II, 386; *EL*, III, 231.
95.10   It is a very extravagant . . . Washington. *JMN*, XII, 423.
95.17   This over-estimate . . . living nature. *EL*, III, 231–232.
95.19   Bonaparte knew . . . the good player. *JMN*, V, 507.
95.21   The poet uses the names . . . disguises. *JMN*, VII, 188–189.
95.21   The poet uses the names . . . player of Cæsar; *JMN*, XII, 425, 472.
99.6   the enchantment . . . to human society. *JMN*, XII, 385; *EL*, III, 52.
99.14   The natural association . . . to-day and yesterday. *EL*, III, 54–55.

100.18   Each man sees over . . . fair and ideal. *JMN*, VII, 12.

100.19   Let any man go back . . . beloved name. *JMN*, V, 456; XII, 385.

100.24   Every thing is beautiful . . . seemly and noble. *JMN*, XII, 385.

100.27   In the actual . . . to-day and yesterday. *JMN*, VII, 67; XII, 311.

100.32   The strong bent of nature . . . winning pictures. *EL*, III, 55.

100.36   How we glow over these novels *JMN*, V, 503; XII, 385.

101.5   All mankind love a lover. *JMN*, VII, 369.

101.8   The rude village . . . other's personality. *JMN*, VII, 171; XII, 423, 443.

101.16   engaging, half-artful, half-artless . . . great men. *JMN*, VII, 159; XII, 385; *EL*, III, 55–56.

101.32   in some public discourses . . . other circumstances. *EL*, III, 56–58.

102.8   they have no fairer . . . embalmed them. *JMN*, V, 8–9.

103.2   of love,—"All other . . . pains:" *JMN*, III, 249; VI, 180; XII, 384.

103.22   Moonlight walks, . . . and owls, *JMN*, XI, 373.

103.26   He is a palace . . . his veins; *JMN*, VII, 9.

104.1   The like force . . . with themselves, *EL*, III, 59.

104.12   welcome as the sun . . . with themselves, *JMN*, V, 414.

104.14   The lover cannot . . . steps. *JMN*, VII, 168; XII, 307, 423.

104.20   she indemnifies him . . . things and virtues. *JMN*, XII, 307.

104.23   For that reason the lover . . . or to others. *JMN*, XII, 443.

104.24   His friends find in her . . . song of birds. *JMN*, VII, 129.

104.28   The ancients called . . . and evanescent. *JMN*, V, 302–303.

104.28   The ancients called . . . of a sunset. *EL*, III, 59–60.

104.28   beauty the flowering of virtue. *JMN*, III, 147; *EL*, II, 264; *CW*, I, 15.

105.1   doves'-neck lustres, *JMN*, VIII, 86.

105.4   Jean Paul Richter . . . not find." *JMN*, V, 346; VI, 227; VII, 137–138.

105.17   Landor . . . existence." *JMN*, V, 43.

105.27   "If I love you, what is that to you?" *JMN*, VI, 181; XII, 307, 426, 481; *CEC*, 97–98.

105.27   "If I love . . . never know. *JMN*, VII, 199.

105.31   This agrees well with . . . other aim. *EL*, III, 60–62.

106.37   words that take hold . . . no other aim. *JMN*, IV, 351; XII, 385.

107.8   In the procession of the . . . impersonal every day. *JMN*, VII, 86.

107.8   In the procession of the soul . . . to the epithalamium. *EL*, III, 63–66.

107.21   Little think the youth . . . marriage. *JMN*, V, 297.

107.31   "Her pure and . . . body thought." *JMN*, V, 340.

107.34   Romeo, if dead, should . . . universal aims. *JMN*, VII, 86–87.

108.23   detects incongruities . . . of the other. *JMN*, V, 297–298.

109.1   "The person love does . . . all in it." *JMN*, V, 340.

109.3   The angels . . . are united. *JMN*, V, 298; *EL*, II, 283.

109.7   Their once flaming regard . . . designs. *JMN*, VII, 87.

109.14   At last they discover . . . consciousness. *JMN*, V, 298.

109.28   Thus are we put . . . and so on for ever. *EL*, III, 67.

109.30   We are by nature . . . blend with God, *JMN*, VII, 80.

113.1 We have a great . . . knoweth. *JMN*, V, 384; XII, 221.

113.1 We have a great . . . sweetness of life. *EL*, II, 282.

113.17 The scholar sits . . . chosen words. *JMN*, V, 34; VII, 405.

113.22 A commended stranger . . . no more. *JMN*, VII, 76; XII, 433, 480, 509.

114.21 What is so pleasant . . . feeling? *JMN*, VII, 333.

114.25 The moment we indulge . . . persons. *JMN*, IV, 359–360.

114.25 The moment we indulge . . . thousand years. *EL*, II, 290.

114.32 I awoke this morning . . . the new. *JMN*, VII, 324; XII, 482.

114.33 Shall I not call . . . traditionary globe. *JMN*, VII, 212; XII, 442, 482.

115.6 My friends have . . . to me. *JMN*, VII, 324; XII, 428, 481.

115.7 By oldest right, . . . chanting still. *JMN*, VII, 212.

115.16 Will these too . . . may be. *JMN*, VII, 324.

115.22 It is almost . . . little modified. *JMN*, VII, 325.

115.24 A new person is to me a great event, *JMN*, VII, 259; XII, 482.

115.24 A new person . . . from sleep. *CEC*, 255.

115.26 but the joy . . . yields no fruit. *JMN*, XII, 443.

115.28 I must feel pride . . . maiden. *JMN*, VII, 327–328.

115.28 I must feel pride . . . in his virtues. *JMN*, XII, 443, 482.

115.31 We overestimate . . . from his mouth. *JMN*, V, 162; *EL*, II, 100–101.

115.32 His goodness seems . . . his mouth. *EL*, II, 287.

116.26 I see well . . . like me. *JMN*, VII, 337; XII, 226.

116.34 Is it not that the soul . . . or society. *JMN*, V, 363; VII, 372; *EL*, II, 279.

116.34 Is it not that the soul . . . forth leaves, *JMN*, XII, 226.

117.6 Thus every man passes . . . or never. *JMN*, VII, 337.

117.29 We are armed . . . gifted! *JMN*, VII, 106–107.

117.31 Almost all people descend to meet. *L*, II, 168; *JMN*, VII, 106, 141; *EL*, III, 19, 96; *CW*, II, 165.

117.31 All association must be a compromise, *JMN*, XII, 325.

118.1 we must be tormented . . . us true, *JMN*, VII, 333.

118.6 I ought to be equal . . . toiled." *JMN*, VII, 339–340.

118.16 Bashfulness and apathy . . . rainbows. *JMN*, VII, 81; XII, 318.

118.34 I do not wish . . . we know. *JMN*, VII, 244.

119.1 the solidest thing . . . husk and shell. *JMN*, VII, 326; *EL*, III, 253–254.

119.11 He who offers . . . of all these. *JMN*, VII, 244.

119.17 but all the speed . . . trifles. *JMN*, VII, 244.

119.30 Every man alone . . . hypocrisy begins. *JMN*, IV, 314.

120.3 the advantage of bringing . . . is it not? *JMN*, VII, 491–492.

120.28 Can another be . . . tenderness? *JMN*, VII, 370; XII, 226.

120.33 "I offer myself . . . devoted." *JMN*, VII, 378.

121.1 We chide the citizen . . . fidelity and pity. *JMN*, VII, 378.

121.25 Friendship may be said . . . than two. *EL*, II, 288.

121.37 Do not mix waters . . . into one. *JMN*, XII, 224; *EL*, II, 288–289.

122.7   In good company, the individuals . . . limited to his own. *JMN*, V, 374–375.

122.22   Conversation is . . . his tongue. *JMN*, VII, 232; XII, 444, 462, 481, 509.

122.31   Let me be alone . . . his echo. *JMN*, IV, 374; *EL*, II, 289.

122.35   I hate, . . . a mush of concession. *JMN*, XII, 224.

123.3   There must be very . . . unites them. *JMN*, VII, 332–333; XII, 224.

123.8   who is sure that . . . eternal. *JMN*, VII, 286.

123.10   Let him not intermeddle . . . ages to grow, *JMN*, XII, 482.

123.13   We talk of choosing . . . self-elected. *JMN*, VII, 231; XII, 430, 443, 481.

123.14   Reverence is a great . . . a spectacle. *JMN*, XII, 482.

123.25   Why should we desecrate . . . yet made good. *JMN*, VII, 370.

124.2   Worship his superiorities; . . . them all. *JMN*, VII, 371.

124.15   Respect so far . . . the whole world. *EL*, III, 254.

124.17   There is at least . . . the whole world. *JMN*, VII, 317.

124.19   *Crimen quos inquinat, æquat. JMN*, VI, 55.

124.21   Yet the least defect . . . the entire relation. *JMN*, XII, 482.

124.27   Who set you . . . lips. *JMN*, VII, 286.

124.37   We see the noble . . . already they. *JMN*, VII, 269.

125.8   love is only . . . other men. *JMN*, VII, 327, 329; XII, 443.

125.9   Men have sometimes exchanged . . . his own soul. *JMN*, VII, 112; XII, 136, 443.

125.13   We walk alone . . . shadows merely. *EL*, III, 254–255.

125.24   By persisting in your . . . shadows merely. *JMN*, VII, 286.

125.35   We are sure . . . more our own? *JMN*, VII, 493–494.

126.8   he looks to the past . . . greater friend. *JMN*, VII, 220; XII, 428, 442.

126.11   I do then with . . . parted not. *JMN*, VII, 215.

126.11   I would have them . . . seldom use them. *JMN*, XII, 428, 442, 481.

126.14   I cannot afford . . . my friend. *JMN*, XII, 197.

127.1   It has seemed to me . . . deify both. *JMN*, VII, 325–326; XII, 482.

127.11   But the great . . . cannot be unrequited. *JMN*, XII, 443.

129.1   Theme . . . cohere. *JMN*, IX, 444.

131.1   What right have I . . . praise. *JMN*, VII, 420–421.

131.6   whoever sees my garden, . . . other garden. *JMN*, VII, 379.

131.10   We paint those qualities . . . praise. *JMN*, VII, 371–372.

131.18   Prudence is the virtue . . . where it works. *EL*, II, 311.

132.5   There are all degrees . . . out of these books. *EL*, II, 311–313.

132.5   There are all . . . chink and cranny. *JMN*, V, 326.

132.37   The spurious prudence, . . . comedy. *JMN*, XII, 209.

133.13   the laws of the world . . . young inhabitant. *EL*, III, 40.

133.17   the sun and moon, the great formalists *JMN*, VII, 45.

133.23   We eat of the bread . . . never dream of. *EL*, II, 313–314.

133.31   Do what we can, . . . wet coat. *JMN*, V, 49.

134.19   The domestic man, . . . as they burn on the hearth, *JMN*, IV, 366.

134.28   gets his tool-box . . . pleasant anecdotes. *EL*, II, 314.

134.28   gets his tool-box . . . long housekeeping. *JMN*, V, 367; XII, 146.

135.1   On the other hand, nature . . . prudence. *EL*, II, 314.

135.4   It is vinegar . . . whip him."*EL*, II, 314.

135.7   Our American character . . . mistake." *JMN*, VII, 280.

135.10   But the discomfort . . . of to-morrow, *EL*, II, 314.

135.15   A gay and pleasant . . . make hay? *JMN*, VII, 496.

135.19   "afternoon men" *JMN*, V, 185, 375; *EL*, II, 229, 315.

135.23   The last Grand . . . of all the figures." *JMN*, V, 300–301; XII, 227;
         EL, II, 315.

136.3   This perpendicularity . . . find them. *EL*, II, 315.

137.2   The man of talent . . . to his art. *EL*, II, 315.

137.8   On him who scorned . . . on an empire, *EL*, II, 315–317.

137.9   He that despiseth . . . little and little. *JMN*, V, 227; VI, 43; *EL*, II,
         315.

137.10   Goethe's Tasso is very . . . and to others. *JMN*, V, 415.

137.29   He resembles . . . glorified seers. *JMN*, V, 173.

138.7   Let him make . . . day, day. *JMN*, IV, 17; VI, 154, 163; *EL*, II, 316–317.

138.12   There is nothing he will . . . whilst he sleeps; *EL*, II, 317.

138.14   buying by the acre, to sell by the foot; *JMN*, IV, 257; VI, 214; XII,
         133, 199; *EL*, II, 317.

138.15   the thrift of the . . . he sleeps; *JMN*, III, 314; *EL*, II, 317.

138.16   the prudence which consists . . . in our speed. *EL*, II, 243.

138.19   Iron, if kept at . . . in our speed. *JMN*, V, 412; XII, 109.

138.25   keep the rake, . . . the rake. *JMN*, V, 348; XII, 251.

138.32   In skating over . . . in our speed. *JMN*, V, 402.

138.34   Let him learn a prudence . . . distant climates. *EL*, II, 317.

139.5   When he sees . . . distant climates. *JMN*, V, 41.

139.14   We must not try . . . symmetrical. *EL*, II, 318.

139.16   The prudence which secures . . . politic man. *EL*, II, 318.

139.25   Every violation . . . destructive tax; *EL*, II, 318.

139.28   frankness invites . . . will be true *EL*, II, 319.

139.29   Trust men, and they will be true to you; *EL*, III, 246.

139.33   So, in regard to disagreeable . . . feeble folk. *EL*, II, 319–320.

140.1   The Latin proverb . . . June. *JMN*, V, 439; XII, 228.

140.1   "in battles, the eye is first overcome." *JMN*, VI, 82.

140.12   Every man is actually . . . feeble folk. *JMN*, V, 400; XII, 223.

140.21   It is a proverb, . . . melted into air. *EL*, II, 320–321.

140.22   Love is fabled . . . into air. *JMN*, V, 294; XII, 206; *EL*, II, 320–321.

140.29   If they set out . . . hope. *JMN*, VII, 25.

140.35   So neither should you . . . infirmity of a doubt. *JMN*, V, 504; XII, 291.

141.4   The natural motions . . . half witness. *JMN*, V, 467; XII, 291.

141.10   really, and underneath . . . heart and mind. *JMN*, V, 505; XII, 291.

141.13   We refuse sympathy . . . easy to the feet. *JMN*, V, 322.

141.13   We refuse sympathy . . . in garden beds. *EL*, II, 321.
141.21   These old shoes are easy to the feet. *JMN*, IV, 19; VI, 161.
141.24   life would be dearer . . . in garden beds. *JMN*, V, 346.
143.1   "Paradise is under the shadow of swords." *JMN*, VI, 388; VII, 401.
145.8   there is in their plays . . . into poetry. *JMN*, VII, 380.
147.6   I do not readily . . . fife. *JMN*, VII, 380.
147.11   Scott will . . . Burley. *JMN*, V, 155; VI, 272.
147.16   In the Harleian . . . read. *JMN*, VII, 291.
147.23   Plutarch, who is . . . ancient writers. *JMN*, V, 351.
147.31   Life is a festival only to the wise. *JMN*, V, 119.
148.1   A lockjaw . . . wife and babes, *JMN*, IV, 349.
148.13   take both reputation . . . his speech, *JMN*, XII, 214.
148.19   To this military attitude . . . dissoluteness. *JMN*, XII, 217.
149.25   Heroism, like Plotinus, . . . its body. *JMN*, III, 251; *EL*, I, 299.
149.28   What joys has . . . creatures! *JMN*, V, 136.
149.37   "Indeed, these humble considerations . . . other for use." *EL*, I, 298.
150.12   "When I was . . . other country." *JMN*, VI, 322.
150.35   It seems not worth . . . poetic. *JMN*, VII, 38.
151.2   John Eliot . . . before it." *JMN*, V, 155.
151.5   Better still, . . . lives. *JMN*, VII, 160.
151.9   It is told . . . shade." *JMN*, V, 355; *W*, XI, 226.
151.15   Poverty is its ornament. *JMN*, V, 299.
151.31   Why, slaves, . . . scorn ye." *JMN*, VII, 160.
152.11   the forbidden book under his bench at school, *JMN*, V, 89–90, 94, 226; *EL*, III, 37; *CW*, II, 78.
152.25   and art and nature, . . . delicate spirits. *JMN*, V, 377–378; XII, 216.
152.34   The pictures . . . splendor, *JMN*, V, 395.
153.4   We have seen or heard . . . furrow. *JMN*, V, 293–294.
153.18   Or why should . . . recesses of space. *JMN*, V, 410.
153.28   The fair girl . . . vision. *JMN*, V, 445.
154.1   The heroic cannot . . . decorous age. *JMN*, V, 414.
154.11   A simple manly . . . from the battle. *JMN*, IV, 351.
154.15   There is no weakness . . . fellow creature. *JMN*, IV, 255.
154.21   We tell our charities, . . . his charities. *JMN*, V, 44; XII, 215.
154.37   The circumstances of man, . . . better not to live. *JMN*, V, 437.
155.28   "Let them rave: . . . subjugated in him? *JMN*, IV, 325–326; XII, 214.
159.1   There is a difference . . . was mean? *JMN*, VII, 505–506.
159.8   We give up the past to the objector, *EL*, III, 14.
159.10   What is the ground . . . discontent? *EL*, III, 14.
159.11   What is the universal . . . claim? *JMN*, VII, 19.
159.13   Why do men feel that the natural . . . worthless? *JMN*, VII, 163.
159.19   Man is a stream . . . visions come. *EL*, II, 343.
160.5   The Supreme Critic . . . eternal ONE. *EL*, III, 280.
160.16   succession, in division, . . . eternal ONE. *JMN*, VII, 105–106.

160.19   And this deep power . . . object, are one. *EL*, III, 284.
160.21   the act of seeing . . . are one. *JMN*, VII, 252.
160.23   We see the world . . . is the soul. *JMN*, VII, 318; *EL*, III, 284.
160.25   Only by the . . . of this deity, *EL*, III, 280.
161.1   If we consider what happens . . . to obey. *EL*, III, 15–16.
161.28   Of this pure nature . . . to wound them. *EL*, II, 85.
161.31   We know that all spiritual . . . Freedom, Power. *JMN*, V, 229–230.
161.32   "God comes . . . without bell:" *JMN*, IV, 16; V, 229; VI, 179.
162.14   "Can crowd eternity . . . eternity." *JMN*, VII, 140; *W*, VII, 317.
162.18   Some thoughts always . . . to mortal life. *JMN*, IV, 260; *W*, IX, 89.
162.26   See how the deep, . . . is clothed. *EL*, III, 38–39.
162.26   See how the deep, . . . to do with time. *JMN*, VII, 124.
162.33   we refer all things . . . is clothed. *JMN*, VII, 119.
163.20   The growths of genius . . . populations of men. *JMN*, V, 472; XII, 434; *EL*, III, 312.
163.25   With each divine impulse . . . visible and finite, *L*, II, 229.
163.33   The soul requires . . . virtuous. *JMN*, IV, 383; *EL*, II, 84.
164.4   Those who are capable . . . and powers. *EL*, III, 300.
164.18   One mode of the divine . . . and war. *EL*, III, 41–42.
164.26   Persons are supplementary . . . higher self-possession. *EL*, III, 43.
164.31   In all conversation . . . God. *JMN*, VII, 67; XII, 136.
164.33   And so in groups . . . higher self-possession. *JMN*, VII, 102.
165.4   It shines for all . . . and obstruct. *EL*, III, 16.
165.13   We owe many valuable . . . vain. *JMN*, VII, 130.
165.13   We owe many valuable . . . each other. *EL*, III, 16.
165.19   We know better than . . . retirements. *JMN*, VII, 141; *EL*, III, 19.
165.25   Men descend to meet. *JMN*, VII, 106, 141; *EL*, III, 19, 96; *CW*, II, 117; *L*, II, 168.
165.32   In my dealing . . . loves with me. *JMN*, VII, 164–165; XII, 423, 445; *EL*, III, 282.
166.3   The soul is the perceiver . . . over things. *EL*, III, 16–17.
166.5   Foolish people ask . . . intelligence." *JMN*, VII, 115–116.
166.13   In the book I read, . . . over things. *JMN*, VII, 123.
166.32   For this communication is an influx . . . heart of nature. *EL*, II, 87–88.
167.4   Every moment . . . makes society possible. *EL*, II, 89–90.
167.18   What was in the case . . . universal soul. *EL*, II, 92.
167.29   solutions of the soul's . . . by words, *EL*, III, 277.
167.31   The soul answers never by words, *JMN*, VII, 259.
167.33   The popular notion of . . . and places. *EL*, III, 276–277.
168.1   But we must pick . . . *patois*. *JMN*, VII, 259; XII, 432.
168.10   To truth, justice, . . . evidences. *JMN*, V, 306–307.
168.10   To truth, justice, . . . be finite. *EL*, III, 277.
168.25   These questions which . . . are one. *EL*, III, 277.
168.32   The only mode of obtaining . . . are one. *JMN*, VII, 259–260.

169.1   By the same fire, . . . own character. *EL*, III, 18.

169.9   We know each other . . . their own verdict. *EL*, III, 18–19.

169.13   We are all discerners . . . unconscious power. *JMN*, VII, 152.

169.17   men offer themselves . . . judge themselves, *JMN*, VII, 152.

169.24   By virtue of this . . . over our head. *EL*, III, 282.

169.26   That which we are, . . . Character teaches *JMN*, VII, 217; XII, 428.

169.27   Thoughts come into . . . left open, *JMN*, V, 79–80.

169.30   The infallible index . . . is another. *JMN*, VII, 155; *EL*, III, 20.

170.4   The great distinction . . . confess it. *JMN*, VII, 157.

170.34   There is in all great poets, . . . from the tongue? *EL*, III, 17–18.

170.34   There is in all great poets, . . . they exercise. *EL*, III, 218; *W*, XII, 321.

171.4   For, they are poets . . . its works. *EL*, III, 218; *W*, XII, 321.

171.10   Shakspeare carries us . . . rock. *JMN*, VII, 73.

171.20   This energy does not . . . sea of light. *EL*, III, 284–285.

171.28   The vain traveller . . . sea of light. *JMN*, VII, 29.

172.7   Converse with a mind . . . superior men. *JMN*, VII, 120.

172.16   Souls, such as these, . . . flatter not. *EL*, III, 285.

172.31   Souls like these . . . of praising." *EL*, III, 285.

172.31   sincerity is more excellent . . . of praising." *JMN*, VII, 124.

173.4   How dear, how soothing . . . his presence. *JMN*, IV, 342.

173.14   He is sure that . . . of being. *EL*, III, 281.

173.18   The things that are really . . . from going? *EL*, III, 281.

173.19   You are running to seek . . . for the best. *JMN*, VII, 134.

173.26   Has it not occurred . . . from going? *JMN*, VII, 43.

173.28   O believe, as thou . . . tide is one. *JMN*, VII, 268; *EL*, III, 329–330.

174.2   Let man then learn . . . made his own. *EL*, II, 355.

174.10   Our religion vulgarly . . . his company. *EL*, III, 282; *JMN*, VII, 133–134.

174.15   When I rest . . . Swedenborg say? *EL*, II, 346.

174.25   It believes in itself. *JMN*, VII, 254.

174.29   We not only affirm . . . fatigue and invade. *JMN*, VII, 296.

174.36   The soul gives itself . . . light its own, *JMN*, VII, 254.

175.6   I am born into the great, . . . of the heart. *EL*, II, 355–356.

175.14   "its beauty is immense," *JMN*, V, 385.

175.23   the whole future in the bottom of the heart. *JMN*, IV, 52, 58, 87; VI, 197.

177.1   Nature centres . . . genesis were here. *JMN*, IX, 439–440.

179.4   whose centre was . . . nowhere. *JMN*, V, 57.

179.10   around every circle another can be drawn; *JMN*, VII, 283; *EL*, III, 235.

179.12   another dawn risen on mid-noon, *JMN*, IV, 361; V, 38.

179.19   The universe is fluid and volatile. *JMN*, V, 182; *CW*, I, 44.

179.20   Permanence is but a word of degrees. *JMN*, VII, 364.

193.8　　Gladly would I unfold . . . transparent essence? *EL*, II, 246–247.

193.18　Intellect and intellection . . . a few principles. *JMN*, V, 446–447; *EL*, II, 249–250.

194.8　　The making a fact the subject of thought, raises it. *JMN*, V, 212.

194.8　　The making a fact the subject . . . intellectual beings. *EL*, II, 58.

194.16　We behold it as a god upraised above care and fear. *JMN*, V, 212.

194.19　It is the past . . . intellectual beings. *JMN*, V, 206.

194.25　The growth of the intellect . . . conscious thought. *EL*, II, 250.

194.34　In the most worn, . . . degree. *JMN*, VII, 16–17; *EL*, III, 10.

195.5　　Our spontaneous action . . . bring you, *JMN*, V, 375.

195.5　　Our spontaneous action . . . from the fact, *EL*, II, 250.

195.14　We have little control . . . we have seen, *JMN*, V, 79.

195.21　we carry away . . . not truth. *EL*, II, 250.

195.28　We want, in every . . . spoken. *JMN*, VII, 382.

195.36　All our progress . . . you believe. *EL*, II, 250–251.

195.37　You have first an . . . believe. *JMN*, V, 186; XII, 65.

196.5　　A true man . . . other's secret. *EL*, II, 251.

196.10　Do you think . . . class of facts. *EL*, II, 251.

196.26　What is the hardest . . . live. *JMN*, VII, 151.

196.33　Yet thoughts are flitting . . . as at first. *JMN*, V, 351–352.

196.33　Yet thoughts are flitting . . . Soul showeth. *EL*, II, 251–252.

197.10　The immortality of man . . . attics withal. *JMN*, V, 389–390.

197.11　Every intellection is . . . attics withal. *EL*, II, 253–254.

197.23　The difference between . . . lacked. *JMN*, VII, 490; VIII, 448.

198.1　　If you gather apples . . . thought. *JMN*, V, 361.

198.12　It is long ere we . . . Universal History. *JMN*, V, 428; *EL*, II, 254.

198.36　We must learn the language of facts. *JMN*, VII, 121.

199.1　　The ray of light . . . to me. *JMN*, VII, 121; *EL*, III, 458.

199.5　　The rich, inventive genius . . . adequate rhyme. *JMN*, VII, 228.

199.14　In common hours, . . . web. *JMN*, VII, 247.

199.24　Not by any conscious . . . with grief. *EL*, III, 74.

199.27　Without instruction . . . on the subject, *JMN*, V, 443–444.

199.36　We may owe . . . of woods, *JMN*, VII, 143.

200.12　a good sentence or verse . . . twenty years. *JMN*, VII, 299; *EL*, III, 209–210.

200.29　Truth is our element of life, . . . even death. *JMN*, V, 445–446.

201.1　　Every thought . . . horizon. *JMN*, VII, 231.

201.8　　When we are young, . . . never meet. *JMN*, VII, 302.

201.19　Although no diligence . . . smallest fact. *JMN*, VII, 302–303.

201.24　an index or mercury . . . strangers in nature. *JMN*, VII, 181.

201.26　strangers in nature. *JMN*, VII, 74.

201.28　the poet, . . . feels a strict consanguinity, *JMN*, VII, 181.

201.31　We are stung . . . really enriched. *JMN*, VII, 160.

202.3　　Exactly parallel is . . . of his being. *EL*, II, 256.

INDEX

Index

Sunday schools, 79–80
Supreme Being, 152
Supreme Critic, 160
Supreme Mind, 62, 164
Susa, 13
Swedenborg, Emanuel, 45, 166, 167, 174, 203; *The Apocalypse Revealed*, 91; *Concerning Heaven and Hell*, 254–255 (n188.17); *The Doctrine of the New Jerusalem*, 252 (n166.10); *The Economy of the Animal Kingdom*, 233 (n57.10)
Symbol, 36, 84, 132, 184, 209, 214
Syrian, 152
Synesius, 204

Tacitus, *Germania*, 248 (n140.1)
Talent, 136, 137, 189
Tamerlane, 95
Tantalus, 18
Tartar, 11, 80
Taylor, Jeremy, *Holy Dying*, 247 (n137.9)
Teaching, 56, 88, 164, 170, 203
Tempe, 86
Temperance, 79, 150
Tenderness, 120
Tennyson, Alfred, Lord, "A Dirge," 251 (n155.28)
Thasians, 63
Thebes (Thebans), 7, 16, 46
Theism, 17
Themis, 153
Theogenes, 63
Theology, 55, 56
Thetis, 62
Thinking, 35, 94, 183, 195, 196
Thor, 41
Thoreau, Henry David, xxii
Thought, 3, 10, 27, 34, 79, 89, 93, 141, 159, 162, 164, 166, 169, 172, 180, 191, 195, 198, 199, 201, 204
Thucydides, 9
Ticknor and Fields, xliii, xlv, xlvi
Time, 6, 38, 39, 40, 53, 100, 119, 133, 134, 135, 162, 188, 207
Timoleon, 78
Tithonus, 62

Titian, 214
Tivoli, 86
Town-meetings, 80
Transcendental club, 79
Transcendentalism, 187
Traveling, 46, 215
Trismegisti, 204
Troy, 6
Truth, 30, 40, 41, 42, 68, 91, 100, 116, 119, 139, 154, 165, 166, 184, 189, 193, 194, 195, 196, 197, 199, 200, 201, 202, 204
Turkey (Turks), 4, 59
Tuscan masters, 213
Tyre, 6

Unattainable, the, 179
Undulation, 197
Unity, 49, 160, 175
Universe, 59–60, 63, 77, 80, 164, 175, 179
Unknown, the, 210
Useful, the, 217

Valor, 183
Vatican, 46, 213, 215
Venetian masters, 213
Venus, 217
Vermont, 43
Verses, 201
Very, Jones, 246 (n110.34)
Vice, 34, 67, 92, 159, 187
Vienna, 85
Vinci, Leonardo da, 214
Virgil, 86
Virtue, 31, 34, 35, 36, 37, 40, 61, 66, 67, 71, 78, 80, 92, 121, 124, 139, 141, 151, 163, 187
Vision, 39, 193

Walpole, Horace, 89; *Royal and Noble Authors*, 240 (n89.31)
Warburton, William, Bishop, *History of the Rebellion and Civil Wars in England*, 255 (n190.22)
Ward, Samuel, xviii, xix, xx
Washington, George, 35, 47, 91, 95, 152, 155